The
Akedah
or Sacrifice of Isaac

A HISTORY OF INTERPRETATION

Stephen Vicchio, Ph.D.

Wisdom
Editions
Minneapolis

Minneapolis
SECOND EDITION DECEMBER 2022

10 9 8 7 6 5 4 3 2

Cover and interior design: Gary Lindberg
ISBN: 978-1-960250-72-8

This book is dedicated to my son, Reed Cahill Vicchio, who has learned a great deal about the meaning of sacrifice.

Contents

The **Akedah**
or Sacrifice of Isaac

A HISTORY OF INTERPRETATION

Chapter One:
Human Sacrifice in the Ancient World

There stands in the midst a bronze statue to Kronos. Its hands are extended over a bronze brazier, the flames of which engulf the child. When the flames fall upon the body, the limbs contract and the open mouth seems almost as if it were laughing.

—Plato, *Republic*

Whether it is a sacrifice or not, this is a sacrificial altar, so it is not a place where you would bury a person. It's not a cemetery.

—David Gilman Romano, Archaeologist, University of Arizona

So the question arises, were sons and daughters—as opposed to infants—sacrificed in ancient times? Is there any archaeological evidence?

—Hershel Shanks, "First Person: Human Sacrifice to an Ammonite God?"

Introduction

Beginning in the late nineteenth century, we now know from archaeological evidence that many prominent ancient societies practiced ritual human sacrifice. The ancient Greeks, Vikings, Mayans, Egyptians and the ancient Chinese, all have been shown to have partaken in some form of human sacrifice. The methods used for these sacrifices were as varied as the cultures themselves.

Steeped in religion and the myths, symbols and rituals in these varied cultures, many of these human sacrifices were thought to be necessary and, at least in some cases, they appear to have been done voluntarily. Even the most prominent and, dare we say, civilized of these ancient cultures practiced some form of human sacrifice—from the burying of virgins to the burning of babies—there was very little that ancient people were not willing to do to appease their gods.

The primary purpose of this first chapter is to describe and discuss the practice of human sacrifice in the ancient world. We will begin with an analysis of the evidence of the earliest examples of human sacrifice in places such as Egypt, Babylonia, Assyria, Ammon, Greece, China, among the Canaanites, at Stonehenge, and at other ancient sites. This material will be followed by a discussion of the practice of human sacrifice among the Phoenicians, as well as in their colonies in Tunisia, Sicily and Sardinia, and in their off-shoot, the city of Carthage, where, in 1921, archaeologists P. Gielly and F. Icard conducted extensive excavations of the city.

In the third section of this chapter, we will describe and discuss the practice of human sacrifice in other cultures before the modern era in Europe, particularly among the Vikings, the German and the ancient Celts.

Observations on Early Egyptian Beliefs on the Afterlife

Among the earliest evidence for the practice of human sacrifice in the ancient world are sites found in ancient Egypt around 3000 BCE, the Mesopotamian Royal Cemetery at Ur around 2600 BCE, a Bronze Age cemetery at Basur Hoyuk in present-day Turkey from 3,000 to 2500 BCE, and during the Shang Dynasty in China beginning around 1600 BCE. Before we move to an analysis of these cultures, we first will make some very general comments about the ancient Egyptian beliefs about the afterlife.

The ancient Egyptians had a complex view of the afterlife. In philosophical terms, it appears that they believed in the transmigration of the soul, or reincarnation, as well as the immortality of the soul. Like ancient Greek philosophers such as Plato and Aristotle, the ancient Egyptians believed that the soul had three parts. These parts are called the *ka*, the *ba* and the *akh*. The first of these, the *ka*, was the life force of the person. At death, the *ka* separated from the body, which among the Egyptians went through an elaborate procedure to preserve the body.

The *ba*, or the second element of the Egyptian soul, was symbolized by a human-headed bird that hovered over the deceased. The *ba* was the part of the soul that could travel between the worlds of the living and the dead. During the Age of the Pyramids, it was believed that only the king possessed a *ba*. Much later in Egyptian history, it was a common belief that all humans have a *ba*.

Pictures of the *ba* often appeared in early Egyptian literature and funerary art. Ramesside's *Book of the Dead*, for example, show the *ba* as perching on the arm of the deceased, or hugged to its body, like a pet parrot.[1] The small pyramids built over tomb chapels at Deir el-Medina, had a small niche near the top of the tomb, where the *ba* could perch, to watch the rising sun, or to observe the goings-on of the village where the *ba* lived when in the body.[2]

The third element of the Egyptian soul was called the *akh*; the part of the soul that is capable of mingling with the gods. This appears to have only been true of morally good people on Earth, perhaps even in more than one life. Condemned criminals in ancient Egypt did not have proper burials, so their *akhs* did not survive in the afterlife.[3] The process of the judgment of the soul was known as the *Maat Kheru*. The goddess *Maat* was the ruler of Truth and Balance. She is symbolized by an ostrich feather. In the afterlife, the person's heart was placed on a scale, and the feather was placed on the other side. If the heart balance the feather, the soul was allowed into the afterlife. But if the weight of the heart did not balance the feather, a monster named the "Devourer" consumed the heart.[4]

The ancient Egyptians, like the ancient Hebrews, believed that the heart was identified as the "seat of intelligence and moral judgment," as well as the locus of the emotions. The god Osiris was responsible for conducting the *Maat Kheru* and the designation of where the soul will go after death.[5] Indeed, some ancient Egyptian sources held that at death the *ka* might have been given to a person who has just been born. In fact, this process was conducted by *Hekat* or *Meskhenet*, who breathed into the new baby the energy of the *ka*.[6]

Hekat was the goddess of fertility. She is identified with the frog, an ancient symbol of fertility. *Meskhenet* was the Egyptian goddess of childbirth and the god who transferred the *ka* of a dead person to the body of a newborn. *Meskhenet* was also associated with fate among the ancient Egyptians. Thus, in later history, she was paired with the god *Shai*, who was called the "god of destiny."[7]

From this analysis, it should be clear that the ancient Egyptians believed in two separate forms of survival after death—immortality of the soul and transmigration of the soul, or reincarnation. The former view, for the most part, applied to the *ba*, while the latter view was associated with the *ka*. This brings us to the earliest evidence of human sacrifice as practiced by the ancient Egyptians, the topic of the next section of this first chapter.

Human Sacrifice in Early Egypt

As Jacques Kinnaer points out, it is important to distinguish between two different kinds of human sacrifice in Egypt. In his book, *Human Sacrifice*, he tells us this about the two types: The ritual killing of human beings as part of an offering presented to the gods on a regular basis or on special occasions. And retainer sacrifice, or the killing of domestic servants to bury them along with their master.[8]

One form of Kinnaer's first type may have been the slaying of criminals and prisoners of war. Some early dynastic depictions of sacrifice show a man holding a bowl, perhaps using it to catch the blood shed during the sacrifice of a man seated before him.[9] There is some evidence suggesting that human sacrifice was practiced during the predynastic period in ancient Egypt, as well as during the First Dynasty.

The earliest known example of human sacrifice in Egypt may be found in predynastic burials in the south of Egypt dated to the Naqada II period beginning around 3500 BCE. One of the bodies discovered during this period showed marks on the throat, indicating it had been cut before decapitation.[10] Human graves of early pharaohs were also discovered at Abydos, the center of the cult of Osiris, the god of the underworld. It appears that human sacrifice went on there and gradually was phased out by the time of the Pyramids of Giza, around 2500 BCE.

A fragmentary label from the reign of Horus Aha was found at Abydos, as well as another label from the time of Aha's successor, Djer, found at Saqqara, may bear witness to a ritual involving the killing of a human being. In both of these cases, a kneeling figure sticks a long weapon into the chest of a bound victim sitting before him. A bowl between the assailant and the victim may have been employed to capture the blood of the victim.[11]

Also present in both cases is some sort of fence-like sign or barrier drawn above the sacrificial scene. In the label fragment of Aha's, an obvious figure of authority, identified by his long stick, observes the killing. Behind the victim is a fetish that, in later times, was associated with the god Anubis, who was the god of mummification, as well as the patron god of lost souls and the helpless. It is not known, however, if the fetish was related to the practice of human sacrifice.[12] The context of representation on King Djer's label shows a number of ritual objects being presented in the name of the king. The killing of a human being also appears to be part of the ritual, which would probably exclude the possibility that the victim was a prisoner. At any rate, the purpose of the ritual and its connection with human sacrifice are not entirely clear.

At the royal cemetery of Umm El-Qa'ab, the tombs of the First Dynasty kings, from Aha to Qa'a, are accompanied by subsidiary burials. These burials are arranged in blocks or rows, extending from the royal tomb, in the case of Aha, or surrounding it. Several of these subsidiary tombs contained skeletal remains. Research done on these remains associated with Aha's tomb suggests that none of the people were older than twenty-five years of age. This suggests that these individuals may have been chosen to be buried along with the king.[13]

From the time of King Djet, the owners of the subsidiary tombs would be identified. Their names, painted in red ink, appear on the south wall of their graves. Their names are also on small stelae that were placed in the tombs. This identification often included the individual's title. Thus, for example, we learn that a "Royal Seal-Bearer" was buried adjacent to King Qa'a's tomb.[14] The most elaborate stela in the subsidiary graves related to King Qa'a belonged to a man named Sabef.

On his stela, he is standing and holding a long stick, the normal position of a nobleman. From the written material associated with Sabef, we learn that he also was the "Keeper of the Tomb" and was a priest and "Keeper of the Secrets and Decrees" of King Qa'a.[15]

Some of the subsidiary graves around the tombs of the kings involved a large number of graves. King Djer, for example, was accompanied by 317 subsidiary graves, King Djet by 174, and Aha by thirty-five tombs generating from his. Altogether, eight different kings of the First Dynasty can be related to human sacrifice in their reigns. In King Aha, we see the first "sacrificial" burials," as well as a label dating from his reign depicting sacrificial scenes.

During the reign of Djer, we see the largest number of subsidiary burial, 317 in all. Both royal and subsidiary tombs were discovered during the rule of Kings Djer, Anedjib, Semerkhet, and Qa'a.[16] By the close of the First Dynasty, the issue of human sacrifice had come to an end. Some speculate that after the First Dynasty, noblemen related to the king were not convinced of the immediate need to die for their pharaohs.

Another possible reason for the decline of human sacrifice and the use of subsidiary tombs in Egypt is the rise of the phenomenon called *Shabti* figures. These crudely fashioned figures were to take the place of the sacrificial victims. These Shabti figures were believed to carry out a wide variety of tasks and roles, including everything from the cultivation of crops and the establishment of water sources, to replacing the sacrificial victims of the First Dynasty and the serving of the dead.[17] Many of these Shabti figures were engraved with magical texts that sought to ensure they would carry out their assignments. These Shabti figures represented the kings, their noblemen and servants, as well as sacrificial victims. King Qa'a was the final pharaoh suspected of having included sacrifice enclosures, bringing an end to the practice at the close of the First Dynasty.[18]

Among contemporary scholars, there has been some disagreement over the cause of death of many of the Egyptian victims. Nancy Lovell, a physical anthropologist, believes they were strangled.[19] Others suggest the cause of death was poisoning, particularly with substances such as cyanide, which was available in the ancient world.[20] Indeed, there is evidence that as early as 2500 BCE, the Sumerians used cyanide and may have introduced it into Egypt. Finally, at the Deir el-Bahri site of mortuary temples on the West Bank of the Nile opposite the city of Luxor, the remains of a man known as "Unknown Man E" was found among the remains of royal mummies. He was interred with a horror-filled look on his face, not unlike the work of Edvard Munch called *The Scream*. Many scholars believe the man was buried along with the pharaohs.[21] The Unknown Man E was in his early twenties. His face seems to silently scream. His coffin was white and undecorated but was made from cedar, an expensive wood in ancient Egypt. He was unwrapped by Drs. Daniel Fouquet and S. Mathey in 1886, when they discovered that the body showed some unusual burial practices. For one, he was wrapped in sheepskin. Under the sheepskin was a layer of bandages, and then another layer of natron-soaked bandages. The bandages were of a high quality, yet they had been knotted and wrapped around his wrists.[22]

Under the layers of bandages, the man's skin was coated with a thick layer of natron, crushed resin and quicklime. His body still contained its internal organs. Most scholars date the mummified remains to the late Eighteenth or early Nineteenth Dynasties, somewhere between 1300 and 1189 BCE. The layer of quicklime on the body indicates that when it was applied, there was no struggle from the young man. The quicklime layer also indicates that the body had been dehydrated, suggesting again that he was already dead.[23]

At around the same time of the First Dynasty of Egypt, around 3,000 BCE or shortly after, several other societies in the world also practice human sacrifice. In present-day Turkey, there is a Bronze Age cemetery at a site called Basur Hoyuk. Eleven graves have been found at the site, both male and female. They range in age from eleven years old to early adulthood.[24]

The skeletal remains of a man discovered at Stonehenge showed that he was five foot ten and of a robust build. He died when he was repeatedly shot with arrows. The excavation was dated sometime between 3000 and 2500 BCE. Most scholars believe the man's death was the product of a sacrificial ritual.[25] There are also archaeological discoveries made of a Mesopotamian Royal Cemetery in the city of

Ur in modern-day Iraq. The site, which is dated around 2600 BCE, contained the bodies of sixty-eight women and six men.[26]

Excavation has also taken place at the ancient Babylonian city of Uruk. The site dates to a period around 2200 BCE. It appears that human sacrifice occurred there until the time of Alexander the Great in the fourth century BCE.[27] Sufficient archaeological evidence reveals that human sacrifice was often practiced in ancient China, particularly during the Shang Dynasty.[28] During this dynasty, oracle bones were used in order to find the expected outcomes of perilous situations. Sometimes the answers were found on oracle bones, and at times those answers appear to have been human sacrifice.[29]

Generally, the sacrificial victims in China were both male and female servants of the king. This form of human sacrifice lasted for many centuries in China from around 1600 to 1050 BCE.[30] The use of oracle bones was most likely the earliest form of writing in China. They could only be read by specified religious functionaries. There is also evidence that servants were buried with their masters.

Another kind of human sacrifice in ancient China was called the *Renji Ceremony*. It usually involved males, most often prisoners of war. These sacrifices were made to the god *Shang-Di*. The *Renji* sacrifices most often involved decapitation. Afterward, the victims were buried in a large pit.[31] The Ammonites, a Semitic people who established a kingdom north of Moab in the thirteenth century BCE, also practiced child sacrifice to the god Molech. In 1955, Australian archaeologist John Basil Hennessy excavated a late Bronze Age building he identified as a temple near the Amman, Jordan, airport. In the center of the building, Dr. Hennessy found two flat stones, one on top of the other. Hennessy identified the site as an altar where there was a large number of burnt offerings.[32] The site included pottery, gold jewelry, small bronze pins, scarabs and cylinder seals. In the words of one of the excavators:

> The most surprising feature of all in the final analysis of the material is that the several thousands of the small, bone fragments are almost exclusively [over ninety percent] human. There can be little doubt that a major concern of the ritual at the Amman airport temple was the burning of human bodies.[33]

In an essay for the *Biblical Archaeological Review*, Scholar Hershel Shanks adds this commentary about the Amman site, "Hennessy's general impression was that the bones represented an 'immature group.' One was a youth between fourteen and eighteen years of age."[34]

In 1976, Larry G. Herr, who is now Professor of Religious Studies at the Canadian University College, continued the excavation near the Amman airport. He also found numerous bone fragments at the site. Dr. Herr also reconstructed what he believed to be a square altar about twenty feet from the temple. The stone pile had functioned as a pyre. As he put the matter, "Many small fragments of burned human bones were strewn all about the building, but the thickest concentration was near the stone pile."[35] Not all subsequent scholars have agreed with the theory that the Jordan site is a place of human sacrifice. Noted Polish scholar, Father Jakub Waszkowiak, for example, has questioned Dr. Hennessy's theory. Dr. Herr rejected the view that the building is a temple and argues instead that it was a crematorium where the bones of the dead were buried. Another scholar, Ami Mazar, an Israeli archaeologist, observes the following about Dr. Herr's view, "This conclusion is difficult to accept...since there are no parallels for the existence of special cremation buildings in the Ancient Near East."[36]

Professor Herr responded to Dr. Mazar that, if it is a crematorium, it is "the first such site ever found in this part of the world." On the other hand, if the site were a place of human sacrifice, this would be the first and only such site discovered in the Ancient Near East. If the site was a temple where humans were sacrificed, it could have served the ancient Ammonite capital of Rabat Ammon, two miles west of the site.

Dr. Shanks adds another interesting observation about the site when he writes, "The site mystifyingly also contained Hittite, Mycenaean and Egyptian artifacts."[37] At the close of his essay, after mentioning Biblical references about human sacrifice, Dr. Shanks asks this question, "Is the Temple at the Amman airport a shrine to the Ammonite god Milkom, like those referred to in the Bible, where human beings were sacrificed? Certainly an intriguing possibility."[38]

There also is evidence that the Assyrians in the eighth century BCE most likely practiced some forms of human sacrifice. One intriguing bit of evidence is a treaty between Assyrian King Assur-nerari V and King

Mati'ilu of Arpad. The treaty suggests that if either party breaks the agreed provisions, then the kings' heads, or those of their sons, should be cut off.[39] Evidence also exists that indicates that the Canaanites, the possessors of the land of Israel before the Hebrews arrived, also at times practiced child sacrifice to their god Baal, apparently the first-born son.

The Bible, at places such as Deuteronomy 12:31 and 18:9–10, called this practice "detestable." In fact, the Bible's repeated condemnation of child sacrifice shows that Yahweh, the God of the Jews, hated the practice, especially among his own Chosen People. Nevertheless, under the reign of King Ahab, with his wife's encouragement, the king built a temple to Baal at his capital in Samaria.

Meanwhile, prophets like Elijah, Hosea, Isaiah and Jeremiah thundered against the worship of Canaanite gods, arguing that Yahweh alone deserves the allegiance of the people of Israel. It took the Assyrian destruction of Israel and the Babylonian captivity of Judah to convince the Israelites that only one omnipotent God, Yahweh, was to be worshipped.

In the Book of Judges, we see the on-going struggle of the Israelite attraction to, and abhorrence of, child sacrifice, as practiced by the Canaanites to the gods Baal and Molech, another Canaanite deity that demanded the sacrifice of the first-born son. Thus, a variety of Ancient Near East cultures appear to have practiced human sacrifice to their gods.

There is also sufficient evidence that human sacrifice was practiced on the island of Crete in the Minoan civilization beginning around 3000 BCE. Evidence pertaining to human sacrifice has been found there in three separate locations. The first site is a temple at Anemospilia that was destroyed by an earthquake. This site is near Mount Juktas in north-central Crete.[40] The second site is a sanctuary complex at Fournou Korifi in south-central Crete, and the third at the ancient city of Knossos, where a mass grave of sacrifices has been excavated and remains found. One of the most interesting features of the Knossos site is that many of the remains were those of young children.[41]

In the temple ruins at Anemospilia, four skeletons were found. One, that of a young man, was found in an unusual contracted position and placed on a raised platform, suggesting he may have been trussed up for sacrifice. A fifteen-inch long dagger also was found with an image of a boar on either side of the hilt. The bones were on a raised platform at the center of the middle of the three rooms of the building next to a large pillar.[42]

The positions of the other three skeletons suggest that they were caught in an earthquake. The body of a twenty-eight-year-old woman was found spread-eagle on the ground in the same room as the sacrificed male. Next to the raised platform was the body of a man in his late thirties with two broken legs. His arms were raised as if protecting himself from falling debris. A fourth skeleton was in the front hall of the building. It was too badly damaged to determine its age or gender.[43]

At the sanctuary complex of Fournou Korifi, several fragments of a human skull were discovered in a room near a small hearth used for cooking purposes. This skull has been interpreted by archaeologists as the remains of a human sacrifice. The excavations at Knossos, as well, uncovered additional mass burials, also suggesting the practice of child sacrifice. Dr. Peter Warren has done some of the excavations at the site. He suggests that the victims may have been sacrificed, as well as the victims of cannibalism.[44]

Dr. Warren reveals this about the skeletons at Knossos:

There is clear evidence that the flesh was carefully cut away, much in the way of sacrificed animals. In fact, the bones of slaughtered sheep were found among those of the children... Moreover, as far as the bones are concerned, the children appear to have been in good health. Startling as it may seem, the available evidence so far points to an argument that the children were slaughtered and their flesh cooked and possibly eaten in a sacrificial ritual made to a fertility god.[45]

In the "North House" at Knossos, the bones of at least four children, who also had been in good health, were butchered in the same way that the Minoans sacrificed their sheep and goats. This suggests that the four sets of bones had been sacrificed and then eaten. Nicholas Platon, one of the archaeologists, was so horrified by Dr. Warren's suggestion, that he insisted that the bones must be those of apes and not humans.[46]

The bones found by Dr. Warren date to the Late Minoan period between 1580 and 1490 BCE, before the Mycenean period, beginning around 1320 BCE. But other archaeologists, like Dennis Hughes and Rodney Castleden, believe that the bones found by Warren were deposited as part of a second burial. Indeed, they argue that it was not uncommon to bury a person at death, and then again after the flesh is gone from the skeleton. The major weakness of this view is that it does not explain the type of cuts and marks that appear on some of the bones.[47]

There is also some evidence of a 1000 BCE skeleton in Greece found at a site near Mount Lykion, where animal sacrifices to Zeus were made in earlier ages. In fact, Zeus was said to have been born on the same mountain. The skeleton was discovered by a Greek-American team of archaeologists. It was the remains of a teenage boy lying on his side. Given the place of the find, Dr. Jan Bremmer at the University of Groningen observes, "It is almost too good to be true."[48]

There is another Greek parallel to the Akedah in the Greek legend of the sacrifice of Iphigenia by her father, Agamemnon. Like in the case of Isaac, Iphigenia substituted herself obediently to be sacrificed. She was willing to die for the honor of her Motherland, and she said that the fall of Troy should be her marriage feast and her monument. In the final moment, however, when Agamemnon turned his head away, Iphigenia miraculously was saved and carried away by the goddess Artemis who sent a hind for a vicarious sacrifice.

Another tale similar to the Akedah is an Indian legend of Cunacepha, the son of a Brahman who intended to sacrifice him to the god Varuna. Ultimately, however, other gods intervened, and Cunacepha was saved and then adopted by a Hindu priest.[49]

Perhaps the most significant materials related to ancient human sacrifice are the activities of the Phoenicians, who descended from the Canaanites and Ammonites. The Phoenicians had several colonies in Tunisia, Sicily and Sardinia, where archaeological finds suggest that human sacrifice may have gone on. The most important of these are excavations from the early 1920s of the ancient city of Carthage. These findings are the subject matter of the next section of this first chapter.

Phoenician and Carthaginian Human Sacrifice

The Phoenicians were an ancient Semitic people of the Mediterranean that originated in Lebanon and parts of Syria in the western portion of the Fertile Crescent. The territory of Phoenicia included modern-day Lebanon, parts of what is now northern Israel and southern Syria. The Greeks used the name "Phoenicia" to designate a people who exported a cloth dyed Tyrian purple.

Like the Greeks, Phoenicia was organized in city-states. The most notable of these were Tyre, Sidon, Arwad, Berytus, Byblos and Carthage. Each city-state was an independent entity, for the Phoenicians did not see themselves as having a national identity. In terms of archaeology, language, history and lifestyle, there was little that set them apart from others in the area.

For the most part, Phoenicia was an enterprising maritime trading culture that spread across the Mediterranean in the first millennium BCE. The boundaries of the city-states fluctuated, but the southern-most border was the city of Tyre. The city-state of Sarepta, between Sidon and Tyre, has been the most thoroughly excavated city-state of the Phoenician empire.

The religion of the Phoenician was a variety of ancient Canaanite polytheism. The supreme divine couple was that of Tanit and Baal Hammon. For our purposes, it is now clear that child sacrifices took place in most of the Phoenician city-states, particularly in the North African city-state of Carthage.

One of the earliest indications of child sacrifice in a Phoenician territory was at a place called Tell Sukas on the Syrian coast. These finds date from the thirteenth and the twelfth centuries BCE. The site was initially excavated from 1958 to 1963 by Danish archaeologists. They uncovered an Iron Age cemetery south of the tell that was dated between the thirteenth and tenth centuries BCE.[50]

In addition to the evidence at Tell Sukas, there also were *tophets* at several sites on the coast of Sicily, as well as several sites on Sardinia, including Sulcis, Bithia, Tharros and Nora. The most important Phoenician colonial *tophet* was found in the city of Carthage. It was first used for that purpose in the eighth century

BCE and continued until the fall of Carthage in the Punic Wars beginning in 264 BCE.

In addition to the archaeological evidence for child sacrifice at Carthage, there is also a body of literary sources that speaks of the phenomenon. Plutarch, in the first and second centuries CE, as well as fourth century BCE, Greek historian Cleitarchus, Tertullian, Orosius, Diodorus and Philo, all comment on child sacrifice at Carthage. Cleitarchus said of the Carthaginian practice:

> There stands in the midst of Carthage a bronze statue to Kronos, its hands extended over a bronze brazier, the flames of which engulf the child. When the flames fall upon the body, the limbs contract and the open mouth seems almost to be laughing until the engulfed body slips entirely into the brazier. Thus, the grin is known as "sardonic laughter," since they die laughing.[51]

Kronos was a regional name for the Canaanite god Baal Hammon. The Greek historian Plutarch also wrote about the sacrifice of children at Carthage. He tells us:

> With full knowledge and understanding, they themselves [the Carthaginians] offered up their own children, and those who had no children would buy little ones from poor people and slit their throats as if they were so many lambs or sheep. Meanwhile, the mother stood by without a tear or moan, but they had to forfeit money, and the child was sacrificed nevertheless. And the whole area before the statue was filled with the loud noise of flutes, and drums, and the cries of wailing drowned out by the music.[52]

Interestingly enough, however, Livy and Polybius, two usually accurate ancient scholars, say nothing of child sacrifice in Carthage. Nevertheless, in the first century BCE, Diodorus gives a typical comment about the child sacrifices at Carthage. He informs us:

> In former times they, the Carthaginians, had been accustomed to sacrifice to the gods the noblest of their sons, but more recently, secretly they buy and nurture children they then sent to the sacrifices.[53]

In his *Republic*, even philosopher Plato refers to the Phoenician sacrifices, and his comment is used as an epigram for this chapter. Plato repeats the observation of Cleitarchus mentioned earlier in this chapter:

> There stands in the midst of Carthage a bronze statue of Kronos, its hands extended over a bronze brazier, the flames of which engulf the child. When the flames fall upon the body, the limbs contract and the open mouth seems almost to be laughing until the contracted body slips entirely into the brazier.[54]

Archaeologists Lawrence Stager and Samuel Wolff, who completed archaeological digs at Carthage in the 1970s, suggest that initially, children at Carthage were sacrificed by their parents, but later, children were stolen from the streets and nurtured in families, eventually to be employed for a similar purpose.[55]

The term *tophet*, derived from the Old Testament at Jeremiah 7:21, for example, refers to a place near Jerusalem where the Canaanites, and perhaps the Israelites, practiced child sacrifice. The word *tophet* is now employed as a term used for any child sacrifice. In the Old Testament, *tophet* is called a "place of burning."[56] Several apparent *tophets* have been identified in Phoenician lands and colonies. The largest of these is at Carthage and was known as the "Tophet of Salammbo" after the neighborhood where it was unearthed beginning in 1921.

The ancient city-state of Carthage was founded in the ninth century BCE when Queen Dido fled Phoenicia along the Eastern Mediterranean shore for what is now Tunis in Tunisia. The empire became a powerful one in the ancient world and fought several wars against the Romans and other people. The *tophet* today is located in a suburb of Tunis.

French archaeologists P. Gielly and F. Icard conducted extensive excavations in 1921 of the ancient city of Carthage. These excavations yielded the following material:

1. Many burial urns containing ashes and bones of young infants, along with animal remains.

2. The excavation of several stelae. One speaks of a valuable coin that the parents had to pay to affect the sacrifice.

3. In another stela, the parents take great pride in having their child sacrificed. This stela reads, "It was to the Lady Tanit Face of Baal and to Baal Hammon that Bolmicar, grandson of Milkiathon, vowed the son of his own flesh, bless him you."[57]

The analysis of the remains within this *tophet* also reveals that internment was regular and individual, not *en masse*. From the seventh to the sixth century BCE, the deceased, for the most part, were newborn babies, while those dating from the fourth century BCE were children up to the age of three years. From the very beginning of the finds at Carthage, the bones of animals could also be found. In fact, these account for thirty percent of the bones from the early period and only ten percent in the fourth century.[58]

In both the early and later periods, there are examples of urns with a mix of human and animal bones. Analysis of these urns reveals that when the bones are mixed, eighty percent of them are those of newborn babies or fetuses. This is very different from the findings at Tharros, where ninety-eight percent of the remains were from babies younger than three months old.[59]

Altogether, the *tophet* at Carthage contained thousands of graves, sometimes as many as six to eight urns under the same stela. The burial ground dedicated to the goddess Tanit had nine different levels and took up an area of several acres. The soil in the *tophet* is rich with oil wood charcoal, indicating that the fires continued to burn at the site for long periods of time.

Over the last several decades, the *tophet* at Carthage has also been the subject of controversy. Some say the largest of the nine terraces at the *tophet* that contains many thousands of skeletal remains is actually a cemetery for stillbirths, fetuses and neonates. An opposing camp believes that the skeletons are the remains of live-born infants. Perhaps as important as the bones are, the many inscriptions on the stelae often begin:

To the Lord Baal Hammon, I now say a vow...[60]

Similar pleas appear in many of the 20,000 stelae at the Carthage *tophet*. As suggested earlier, however, some individuals believe in the human sacrifice there, while others think it is simply a cemetery for fetuses and neonates. Thus, at this point in the scholarship, there is a difference of opinion about the site. This brings us to the final section of this opening chapter, where we discuss pre-modern human sacrifice in other European cultures.

Human Sacrifice in Pre-Modern Europe

In this first chapter, we have already described and discussed the possible use of human sacrifice in pre-modern Europe in Greece and at Stonehenge in southern England. There is also sufficient evidence to indicate that human sacrifice occurred in several other pre-modern European cultures, including evidence in Germany, in Viking culture, and among the Celts.

Before moving to the site in Germany, we must point out that in addition to Stonehenge, there is another site near Stonehenge called Woodhenge, a Neolithic period site most likely built around 2300 BCE. Initially, it was believed to be the remains of a large burial mound surrounded by a bank and a ditch. When excavated between 1926 and 1929, however, it turned out to be three concentric circles, much like Stonehenge.

The most important aspect of Woodhenge for our purposes, is that at the center of the innermost circle, archaeologists found the burial site of a three-year-old child whose skull had been split open with an ax. Apparently, the child was a sacrificial victim, much like the man's skeleton remains found at Stonehenge. There are traces of two other structures like Woodhenge found within a large enclosure known as Durrington that lies two hundred and thirty feet north of Woodhenge.

The exact function and purpose of Woodhenge are not clear, but Native Americans built a similar structure in the Cahokia Mounds in Illinois. The placement of posts indicates that the site most likely celebrated the solstices indicating that the American Woodhenge may be little more than a calendar.

In excavations by Melville Fowler in the 1960s and 70s at "Mound 72," as it is called at Cahokia near Saint Louis, skeletal remains were unearthed of two hundred and seventy-two people, many of whom appear to be sacrificial victims. Dr. Fowler discovered the site of the ten-foot mound in 1967. Carbon dating of the wood at the site revealed that it dated from around the year 1000 CE. Thus, it appears that Native Americans living near Saint Louis on the Mississippi River around 1000 CE also conducted rituals involving human sacrifices.

In Germany, aerial photography in the early 1990s identified what was called the "German Stonehenge" southwest of Berlin. Reports in *Smithsonian* revealed a new study of the German site at a place called Pommelte that suggests it shares a number of similarities to its "famed cousin in Great Britain."[61] The study was originally published in the journal *Antiquity*, in which researchers looked at items collected from twenty-nine shafts. They found that the site was in continuous use for about three hundred years.

The oldest layers at Pommelte were dated between 2321 and 2211 BCE. At this level, they discovered pottery, stone axes and animal bones, all smashed to pieces, suggesting they were used for cultic purposes. The site in Germany also yielded the dismembered bodies of ten children, teenagers and women in positions that suggested they were thrown into the shafts. Four of the women revealed skull and rib fractures before death.[62]

The director of the study, Andre Spatzier, revealed that one of the skeletons of a teenage girl had her hands tied behind her back before she was tossed into a pit. Spatzier comments, however, that:

> It remains unclear whether these individuals were ritually killed or if their deaths resulted from inter-group conflict, such as raiding.[63]

The site at Pommelte also had concentric rings like the ones at Stonehenge. The remains of thirteen men were found to the east of the rings with no signs of trauma to the skeletons. They were buried in a dignified manner, and the orientation of the remains suggest a cult that associated death with the sunset. Spatzier's team, however, is not clear whether the association indicates a belief in reincarnation or that the spirit survives death.[64]

The site at Pommelte appears to have gone out of use around 2050 BCE. Spatzier says at that time they "extracted the posts, put offerings into the postholes and most likely burned all the wood and back-shoveled it into a ditch...So they closed it completely, though it was still visible above ground, but only as a shovel depression."[65]

The fact that the site was employed for cultic purposes connects it to Stonehenge and other Neolithic circles in Great Britain, like the one called Woodhenge. This raises the possibility that the building of circular henges was not limited to Britain but may have spread across Europe. One archaeologist, Daniela Hofman of the University of Hamburg, comments in the *Smithsonian* article, "I would say it is certainly appropriate to reconsider the idea that Britain at this time was entirely a special case."[66]

There is, however, one important difference between Stonehenge and Pommelte. At the British site, there is evidence that people traveled long distances to visit Stonehenge. Researchers of Stonehenge have found that people from all over Britain, including northern Scotland, came to the site, as well as people from the Alps. Goods from France, central Europe, and even Turkey, were found at Stonehenge. Nothing comparable has been found in the site in Germany.[67]

There is also sufficient archaeological evidence that the Vikings sacrificed slaves to be buried with their masters. An archaeological excavation near Flakstad, Norway, uncovered multiple graves and ten bodies, some of which were decapitated. Upon further analysis, scholars of the site concluded that the skeletons were those of slaves, and that the diets of the decapitated were markedly different from those of the complete skeletons. This evidence prompted the scholars to conclude that the victims were slaves, beheaded as gifts to their dead masters.[68]

To establish the relationship between the skeletons in Norway, Elise Naumann of the University of Oslo, analyzed mitochondrial DNA inherited from the mother, as well as carbon and nitrogen isotopes from various parts of the skeletons, including their teeth. The results suggest that individuals in multiple burials did not share maternal ancestry. They also found that the diet of the decapitated individuals (four of the ten) ate more fish than the full skeletons. Whereas the whole skeletons' diet (the other six of the ten) had more land-based protein, such as meat and dairy products.[69]

The Vikings had a reputation as fierce, seafaring raiders who plundered and raided vast territories beginning in the eighth century and capturing slaves along the way. Slaves were used for hard labor on farms and large agricultural properties, while women were employed as domestic and sex slaves, often bearing children who would grow up in servitude.

Experts from the University of Bristol in England uncovered human remains in a large pit of bones excavated in the 1970s and 80s. Early research on the site suggested that the graves spanned several centuries. However, new radiocarbon dating revealed that the skeletons were those of Viking soldiers and seamen that drove Burgred, king of Mercia, into exile in the late ninth century CE.[70]

At the British site, researchers found the skeletal remains of four young people between the ages of eight and eighteen together in a single grave with a sheep jaw at their feet. Two of the four showed evidence of traumatic injuries suggesting they may have been sacrificial victims in a ritual to accompany the dead. Bristol archaeologist Cat Jarman said this about the find:

> This grave is very unusual. I don't know of any examples
> of four young people buried in a single grave like this from
> anywhere else in England in this same period...They are also
> placed in unusual positions—two of them back to back—and
> they have a sheep jaw placed at their feet.[71]

Throughout the Viking Empire from the late eighth century on, there are historical accounts from elsewhere suggesting that human sacrifice often was part of Viking funerals. Perhaps the most interesting narrative of this phenomenon comes from a tenth-century Arab Muslim writer named Ahmad Ibn Fadlan. He describes the funeral of a Swedish chieftain where a female servant volunteered to join the chief in the afterlife. The young woman was administered intoxicants before being stabbed to death and then laid with her master.[72]

The Great Viking Army/Navy was known to the Anglo-Saxons as the "Great Heathen Army." A coalition of warriors and sailors from Denmark, Norway and Sweden came together to invade the four kingdoms of the Angles, or English, in 865 CE. Their ships landed in East Anglia, whereupon they made peace with Edmund the Martyr in return for horses before they marched north to York in the following year.[73]

Later, over the next decade or so, the Viking Army spread to Wessex, where Alfred the Great paid them to leave. Then, they marched instead on London and Northumbria. By the year 873, the Vikings reached the kingdom of Mercia, where they overwintered at Repton. At Mercia, they drove King Burgred into exile and installed Cleowulf as his replacement.[74]

In the excavation at Saint Wystan's Church in Repton, archaeologists Martin Biddle and his wife Birthe Kjolbye-Biddle found a pit containing three hundred people underneath a shallow mound in the village garden. Among the bones were Viking weapons—axes and knives—and five silver pennies dating between 872 and 875. Eighty percent of the remains were male, mostly ages eighteen to forty-five.[75]

A separate grave nearby contained the remains of two men. The elder was buried with a Thor's hammer pendant and a Viking boar's tusk between his legs. He had a gaping wound to his left femur. Some scholars suggest that the injury may have severed his penis or testicles, and the tusk was positioned to act as a replacement in the afterlife.[76]

Subsequent radiocarbon dating of the site revealed that the bones spanned several centuries and could not have been the remains of the Viking Army. This was different from earlier results, which apparently were misleading. It turns out that the Vikings' high fish diet was responsible for the mistake. Dr. Jarman, an archaeologist of the site, explains:

> The previous radiocarbon dates from this site were all affected by something called marine reservoir effect, which made them seem too old. When we eat fish or other marine foods, we incorporate carbon into our bones that is much older than in terrestrial foods. This confuses radiocarbon dates from archaeological bone material and we need to correct for it by estimating how much seafood each individual ate.[77]

At any rate, it is quite possible that a number of the skeletons at the Repton site were the victims of human sacrifice, being perfectly consistent with other Viking archaeological findings elsewhere in the kingdom. One final pre-modern European society that also appears to have practiced human sacrifice is the Celts, who we will examine next in this opening chapter.

The Celts were a diverse and disjointed people who began to come to Britain around 700 BCE. The Briton Celts, however, were not a single people. The word "Celt" began to be employed in Britain in the eighteenth century to link together a variety of peoples with similar customs, languages and religions. One of those cultural practices appears to be the use of human sacrifice.

Many bodies preserved in European bogs appear to have been murder victims. One of the most famous of these victims is a man now called Fissured Fred discovered in an archaeological dig conducted at Fiskerton, Lindisfarne, in 1981.[78] Carbon dating suggested that Fissured Fred was executed around 500 BCE. We cannot be certain that this was a human sacrifice, but it seems probable. Many bodies preserved in other European bogs clearly were murder victims—many of them most likely Celts.[79]

Many contemporary scholars have dismissed the idea of Celts in ancient Britain. There are some findings that they flourished in Turkey. In 278 BCE, King Nicomedes the First of Bithynia welcomed some 20,000 European Celts as allies, mostly veterans who had invaded Macedonia two years earlier. These warriors called themselves the Galatai. These warriors marched into northwestern Anatolia with two thousand wagons and ten thousand non-combatants, along with their wives and families.[80]

In excavations at Gordion, Turkey, revealed evidence of cultural practices indicating that they were Celts. They found "chilling evidence of strangulation, decapitation, as well as bizarre arrangements of both human and animal bones." Such practices, as we have shown, are well known from Celtic sites in Europe, and are now documented for Anatolian Celts, as well.[81] The Holy Qur'an, at surah 6:137, also suggests that pre-Islamic Arabs may have practiced child sacrifice. An English translation of the *ayat*, or verse, tells us:

> In the same way have the Companions shown many unbe-
> lievers the killing of their children as desire in order to ruin
> them and to falsify their faith. If Allah had willed it they never
> would have done so. Leave them to their falsehoods.[82]

Finally, in the Greco-Roman world, among Italian peoples such as the Sabines and their off-shoot, the Samnites, they practiced a ritual they called the *Ver Sacrum*, in which a Greco-Roman city would make a *votum*, or vow, to the god Mars that everything to be sacrificed the following spring, whether animal or human, to a god, must be sacrificed to relieve some calamity in the city. Often the *votum* was made in the context of battle.[83]

Conclusions to Chapter One

We began this first chapter with an analysis of ancient Egyptian beliefs about the afterlife. In that analysis, we pointed out that the ancient Egyptians thought the soul was made of three parts—the *ka*, the *ba* and the *akh*. After discussing the particular functions of these parts, we moved on to the second section of this opening chapter, where we outlined the practices of human sacrifice in ancient Egypt.

Indeed, we have shown in this chapter that it is important to distinguish between the sacrifice of servants in royal tombs from those in subsidiary graves, where nobles were sacrificed to honor the kings. We also have shown that examples of human sacrifice in ancient Egypt were only found in the First Dynasty. In subsequent material in this first chapter, we introduced the use of human sacrifice in other ancient cultures, including Mesopotamia, Babylonia and ancient China during the Shang Dynasty.

Additionally, we indicated that several cultures in the Ancient Near East also practiced human sacrifice, including the Canaanites, the Ammonites, the Assyrians, the Mycenaeans and possibly the ancient Hebrews. In another section, we explored the phenomenon of human sacrifice among the Phoenicians and their many colonies, particularly on Crete, Sardinia and at the most important *tophet* of the Phoenicians at their colony in Tunisia, in the city of Carthage.

Indeed, we dedicated a section to an examination of the *tophet* at Carthage, principally by using written sources, as well as archaeological findings of the site beginning in 1921, where excavations began there by the French. We have shown that the material found at ancient Carthage revealed that human sacrifices appear to have been conducted from the seventh century BCE until the time of the Punic Wars beginning in the third century BCE.

Along the way, we showed that, in the last three or four decades, the theory of human sacrifice in ancient Carthage was questioned. Some contemporary scholars maintain that the *tophet* at Carthage is, in fact, a cemetery for fetuses and neonates and not a place of human sacrifice at all. This counterview has been held by several scholars, including a group at the University of Pittsburgh.[84]

In the final section of Chapter One, we analyzed and discussed many places in pre-modern Europe, where it appears that human sacrifice took place. Chief among these locations we have analyzed were those at a German site called Pommelte, at various locations in the Viking empire from the eighth to the twelfth centuries, as well as among the European Celts.

The major conclusion we have made about this material is that beginning very early on in Europe, a number of cultures appear regularly to have conducted human sacrifices in their religious myth, ritual and symbols, going back to 500 BCE and even earlier. Thus, later in this study, when we speak about the use of human sacrifice among the ancient Jews and the Akedah, we first must realize that if it did occur, human sacrifice was not isolated to the ancient Hebrews.

To that end, we shall turn our attention to the phenomenon of human sacrifice in Biblical literature, other than that found at the twenty-second chapter of the Book of Genesis.

Chapter Two:
Child Sacrifice Elsewhere in the Old Testament

Whereas under the Priestly legislation the people were required to visit the sanctuary, or sanctuaries, for the slaughter of any or all animals, the Deuteronomic Code requires the sanctuary visit only for the annual slaughter of the firstlings.

—Bergsma and Hahn, *Bible Basics for Catholics*

But they mixed with the nations and learned to do as they did. They served their idols, which became a snare to them. They sacrificed their sons and daughters to the demons; they poured out innocent blood, the blood of their sons and daughters, whom they sacrificed to the idols of Canaan, and the land was polluted with blood.

—Psalm 106:35–38 (Author's translation)

Consecrate to me all the firstborn, whatever is the first to open the womb, among the Israelites, of human beings and animals, is mine.

—Exodus 13:1–2 (Author's translation)

Introduction

In this second chapter, our main goal is to explore the phenomenon of child sacrifice in the Old Testament in places and passages other than the twenty-second chapter of the Book of Genesis, verses one to nineteen. We will begin with an analysis of some background material, which will help us understand the idea of child sacrifice among the ancient Jews.

This first section will be followed by an attempt to answer the question, "Does the Old Testament condone or prohibit the practice of child sacrifice?" This will then be followed by an introduction and discussion of the Book of Judges, chapter eleven, where Jephthah makes a vow after he petitions God for victory in battle, only to show that the vow backfires on him. The narrative of Jephthah and his daughter is the only other narrative besides the Akedah, where child sacrifice comes into play in the Old Testament. This brings us to an analysis of some background material for this chapter.

Background Material on Old Testament Child Sacrifice

In Chapter One, we introduced materials suggesting that many of the people and cultures surrounding the ancient Jews, such as the Canaanites, the Ammonites, the Moabites, the Phoenicians, the Carthaginians, and many other Ancient Near Eastern societies, practiced the phenomenon of child sacrifice. In the second section of Chapter Two, we will say more about a number of these practices, beginning with the Canaanites, the people who occupied Palestine/Israel before the ancient Jews.

North Mesopotamian texts between the tenth and seventh centuries BCE, suggests burnt offerings of male children to honor the god Hadad.[85] A Syrian inscription indicates that those adults burnt their children to the gods Adrammelech and Anammelech.[86] In Chapter One, we suggested that the Canaanites practiced child sacrifice to honor the gods Baal and Molech.[87] Among the Moabites, the god Chemosh was an object of adoration and to whom the Moabites made child sacrifices.[88]

Among the Canaanites, the god Molech is sometimes identified with the deity Baal-Hadad, who was considered the king of the gods by the ancient Canaanites. Evidence that Molech was seen this way comes from the fact that the pagan altars in the Valley of Ben-Hinnom, where children were sacrificed, are also described as altars to Baal by the Prophet Jeremiah. Furthermore, Assyrian texts suggest that child sacrifices were made to a god named "Adad," the Assyrian equivalent of Hadad. This makes it reasonable to conclude that child sacrifices were made to Hadad and that a cult of child sacrifice was most likely related to him.

We have seen in Chapter One that the Ammonites also practiced child sacrifice to the god Molech. And in Carthage, where the best evidence can be found for child sacrifice in the Ancient Near East. Children in jars and accompanying stelae reveal that child sacrifice was practiced regularly. Other Phoenician archaeological sites across the Mediterranean also suggest that child sacrifice went on at these locations.[89] When the Old Testament mentions the sacrifices of the Ammonites, it is usually in the context of children being "passed through the fire," as indicated by First Kings 11:7, which mentions "Molech and the abomination of the children of Ammon."

Before the excavation of the Canaanite Ras Shamra and the discovery of Bronze Age artifacts, including cuneiform clay tablets, very little was known of the Canaanites and Ammonites except for the accounts of those peoples in the Old Testament. The preferred method for recording material for these two people was writing on papyrus, but over the centuries, most of these have turned to dust.

There are, however, a few secondary or tertiary Greek sources, including Lucian of Samosata's *De Syria Dea*, or the "Syrian Goddess," and fragments from the *Phoenician History of Philo* found at Byblos. More recently, the Ugaritic materials from Ras Shamra—together with inscriptions from the Elba archive at Tell Mardikh, as well as various other archaeological sites—have shed more light on the Canaanite and the Ammonite religions.

Since the 1920s, we learned that both the Canaanites and the Ammonites practiced a form of polytheism. In Canaan, their pantheon included Anat, the goddess of war; Ashereth, an early Mother Goddess; Astarte, the goddess of Love; Baal, the chief deity at Byblos; Baal Hammon, the god of fertility; Yam, the god of the Sea; Resheph, the god of Plague and Healing, and many others. And there is much evidence that the Canaanites practiced child sacrifice to honor the god Baal.

The gods El, Milcom (or Melcom), and Baal were also the principal deities of the Ammonites. King Solomon erected an altar to honor Milcom. At First Kings 2:4–5, Milcom is called an "abomination of the Ammonites," And a variety of other Old Testament passages mention the god Milcom, usually in terms of child sacrifice. Among these passages are Second Samuel 12:30, First Kings 11:33, Second Kings 21:3 and First Chronicles 20:2.

The chief god among the Moabites—at least in terms of child sacrifice—is the god Chemosh. King Solomon built an altar to Chemosh at First Kings 11:7, but it was destroyed by King Josiah, according to Second Kings 23:10. Many other Old Testament passages make references to the god Chemosh, including Numbers 21:29 and Jeremiah 43:7, 13 and 46. Like the Canaanites and the Ammonites, the chief god of the Moabites, Chemosh, demanded child sacrifice.

In addition to these materials, the burnt offerings of children in Canaan and Israel have been discovered going back to the second millennium BCE. The charred skeletons of children were found at Gezer, Ta'anach, and ancient Megiddo. The archaeological dig and remains at Megiddo date to the first half of the fifteenth century BCE.[90] The archaeological remains of Gezer found skeletal remains dating from the fourteenth century BCE.[91] The ancient city Ta'anach was first excavated between 1902 and 1904 by Austrian Ernst Sellin.[92]

Another aspect of the background for this chapter is the many places in the Hebrew Bible that attest to the conclusion that the burnt offerings of children also was current in early Palestine/Israel. Consider Leviticus 20:2 and Deuteronomy 12:31–32, for example. The former text relates:

> Any Israelite or any foreigner residing in Israel who sacrificed his children to Molech, shall be put to death.[93]

This verse, if nothing else, is a condemnation of the child sacrifice practices of the Canaanites and the Ammonites—both of whom made offerings to the god Molech. The passage from Deuteronomy mentioned above, 12:31–32, tells us this:

> You shall not worship the Lord your God in their way, because in worshipping their Gods, they do all kinds of detestable things that the Lord hates.[94]

Again, these verses appear to be referring to the sacrificial practices of the Canaanites or the Ammonites. Consider II Kings 16:3 and 17:31, the former verse relates:

He followed the ways of the kings of Israel and even sacrificed his son in the fire, engaging in the detestable practices of the nations of the Lord.[95]

At Second Kings 17:31, we find the following:

The Avvites made Nibhar and Tartek have the Sepharvim who burn their children In the fire to Abemmelech and Anam-melek, the gods of the Sepharavim.[96]

Second Kings 23:10 also mentions child sacrifice. This text relates:

He destroyed Topheth, which was in the valley of Ben Hinnom where they used to sacrifice their sons and daughters in the fire of Molech.[97]

Once again, we see the mention of the child sacrifice practices of the Canaanites or the Ammonites, both of whom sacrificed to the god Molech. This third passage from Second Kings also appears to take a negative view of the practice. This brings us to three passages in the major prophets that also refer to child sacrifice in Palestine/Israel. These three come at Jeremiah 7:30–32 and 19:3–5, and Ezekiel 16:20–21. The last of these tells us this:

And you took your sons and daughters, whom you bore to me, and then used as food for the idols. You slaughtered my children, sacrificed them to the idols.[98]

In many places where the Prophet Jeremiah mentions child sacrifice, he speaks of having built a high place to the god Baal, where the sons of Israelites were burned in fire as offerings to the Canaanite god. Both Jeremiah 7:30–32 and 19:3–5 speak of that phenomenon. This also suggests that the Israelites sometimes practiced human sacrifice in relation to some of the gods of the Canaanites, the Ammonites and the Moabites.

Perhaps the most famous child sacrifice in the Hebrew Bible, except for Genesis 22:1–19 the Akedah, is the figure of Jephthah and his only daughter at Judges 11:29–40, who asks to go into the hills to weep for two months before being sacrificed in fire by her own father. Jephthah had made a vow that if he were victorious in battle, he would sacrifice whatever came out of his house when he returned home, and unfortunately, it turned out to be his daughter.[99]

The evidence for the burnt offering of children in Palestine/Israel is plentiful and ambiguous. Indeed, there is ample evidence that ancient Israel supported child sacrifice, as well as many examples that they did not. This leads us to the second section of Chapter Two, where we will examine some of that evidence.

One final aspect of background materials for this chapter is the realization that the idea of God testing human beings in one way or another is something that frequently occurs in the Torah. For example, at Exodus 15:25 and 16:4, the text tells us that God put the Jews "to the test." At Deuteronomy 8:2 and 16, to cite other examples, speaks of "testing to see what is in the heart."

At the Book of Judges 2:22, we see, "In order to test Israel, whether or not they would take care to walk in the ways of the Lord." And certainly, one way to understand the prologue of the Book of Job is to say that Yahweh was testing the heart and character of the patriarch from the Land of Uz, Job. It is not unusual, then, in the Hebrew Bible to see the idea of God testing His people or even particular individuals like Job and Abraham.

One way to see both the Akedah narrative and the prologue of the Book of Job is to say that Yahweh only tests Abraham and Job in order to reveal their loyalty to Him, in both good times and in bad times, as well.

The most evidence for human sacrifice by the Canaanites comes from Old Testament references to the god Molech, the fire-god tutelary deity of the children on Ammon. The god Molech is mentioned dozens of times in the Hebrew Bible, including at Jeremiah 49:1–3, Amos 1:15, Second Kings 23:5, Hosea 10:5, Zephaniah 1:4, First Kings 11:7, and Second Samuel 12:30–31.

The god Molech is also known as "Milcom," at First Kings 11:5–7, and sometimes as "Malcam," such as at Second Samuel 12:30–31. The adjective *bosheth* or "shame" is often associated with the god Molech. The Levitical ordinances against Molech worship, however, are perfectly clear at places such as Leviticus 18:21 and 20:2–5.

The god Molech was worshipped in high places by the Canaanites and Ammonites. For a while, these high places were also used by the

Jews. But by the rule of King Josiah, the destruction of these sites or "high places" were destroyed as part of Josiah's religious reforms in the seventh century BCE.

At first, the provisions against Molech worship did not work, and it revived continually in ancient Israel all the way up to the time of the destruction of the temple. The major prophets, however, maintained a consistent attack on the high places reserved for the god Molech, such as at Isaiah 30:33 and 57:5 and Ezekiel 16:20, 26 and 31.

One remarkable fact about the worship of Molech in the Old Testament is how scant of facts the texts about it give information regarding the practices in the cult of Molech. At any rate, we move next to evidence both for and against the idea of child sacrifice in ancient Palestine/Israel.

Evidence For and Against Child Sacrifice in Ancient Palestine/Israel

The most convincing evidence that the ancient Jews engaged in child sacrifice are Genesis 22:1–19 the Akedah narrative, and the narrative of Jephthah and the sacrifice of his daughter at Judges 11:30–39. There are, however, a variety of other Old Testament passages that also seem to imply the practice. At Exodus 22:29, for example, tells us:

> Do not hold back offerings from your granaries, or your vats. You must give me the firstborn of your sons.[100]

At Leviticus 27:28–29, we learn that the Israelites have been commanded that every "devoted thing," of both man and beast, shall surely be put to death. These two verses from Leviticus reveal:

> But no devoted thing that a man devotes to the Lord, of anything that he has, whether of man or beast, or of his inherited fields, shall be sold or redeemed. Every devoted thing is most holy to the Lord. No one devoted, who is to be utterly destroyed from among men, shall be ransomed. He shall be put to death.[101]

Moses commanded his officers to kill every Midianite male and female who were not virgins, but to keep the virgins for themselves, with the exception of one in a thousand that was to be given to God. At Numbers 31:25–40, after examining the females, the Hebrew soldiers found 32,000 virgins, thirty-two of which became offerings to God. Moreover, sixteen of the thirty-two were sacrificed to God as "heave offerings."[102] The heave offering, or *terumah* in classical Hebrew, is an offering made by priests that often involved first fruits rituals.

At Second Samuel 21:1 and 8–14, God sent a famine to David's kingdom that lasted for three years. When David asks God about it, God told him, "It is for Saul and his bloody house because he slew the Gibeonites." To appease God and to end the famine that was caused by his predecessor Saul, David agreed to have two of Saul's sons and five of his grandsons killed and offered up to the Lord. Then God ended the famine.[103]

At First Kings 13:1–2, King Josiah ordered the killing of "all the priests in high places," referring to the sacrificial altars of the Canaanites. After this was done, the bones of the priests were burned upon their own altars. The text in question tells us:

> And behold there came a man of God out of Judah by the
> word of the Lord... And he cried against the altar in the word
> of the Lord, and said, "Oh altar, oh altar, says the Lord. Behold
> a child shall be born unto the house of David, Josiah by name;
> and upon thee shall he offer the priests of the high places,
> that burn incense upon thee, and men's bones shall be burnt
> upon thee."[104]

This same act is also described at Second Kings 23:20 and tells us, "And Josiah…slew all the priests of the high places that were there upon the altars, and burned men's bones upon them."[105] At Second Chronicles 34:1–5, the topic of Josiah and the Baal priests again can be found. It tells us that, "Josiah…did that which was right in the eyes of the Lord…and he burned the bones of the priests upon their own altars."[106]

Many of the Old Testament passages that mention child sacrifice are given in similar circumstances. When the Hebrews first arrived in Canaan, the Lord tells them the following at Deuteronomy 18:9–12:

When you enter the land of the Lord your God is giving you, do not learn to imitate the detestable ways of the nations there. Let no one be found among you who sacrifices his son or daughter in the fire...Anyone who does these things is detestable to the Lord, and because of these detestable practices, the Lord your God will drive out those nations before you.[107]

At Deuteronomy 12:31, we find another prohibition against following the Canaanite practice of child sacrifice. This text tells us,

"You must not worship the Lord your God in their way, because in worshipping their gods, they do all kinds of detestable things that the Lord hates. They even burn their sons and daughters in the fire as a sacrifice to their gods."

The Prophet Jeremiah at 19:4–5 also speaks of the Canaanite sacrifices to Baal "on high places." Jeremiah remarks:

For they have forsaken me and made this a place of foreign gods; they have burned sacrifices in it to gods that neither they nor their fathers nor the kings of Judah ever knew, and they have filled this place with the blood of the innocent. They have built up the high places of Baal to burn their sons in the fire as offerings to Baal—something that I did not command, nor mention, nor did it enter my mind.[108]

The Psalmist, at 106:38, also mentions the prohibition against following the practices of the Canaanites. The verse relates:

They shed innocent blood, the blood of their sons and daughters, whom they sacrificed to the idol of Canaan, and the land was desecrated by their blood.[109]

Other Old Testament passages that answer the question of this section of Chapter Two in the affirmative are Exodus 13:1–2 and 22:29–30. In the former, the Lord tells Moses:

Consecrate to me all of the firstborn, whatever is the first to open the womb among the people of Israel, both of man and of beast is mine.[110]

At Exodus 22:29–30, the Torah again informs us that:

You shall not delay to offer from the fullness of your harvest
and from the over-flow of your presses. The firstborn of your
sons shall give to me. You shall do likewise with your oxen and
with your sheep. Seven days it shall be with its mother, and
on the eighth day you shall give it to me.[111]

Another passage that seems to endorse a positive answer to the
question of sacrifice in the Torah and the historical books is Exodus
34:19–20. This Hebraic couplet tells us:

All that opens the womb is mine, all your male cattle, the
firstlings of cow and sheep. The firstling of an ass you shall redeem with a lamb, or if you will not redeem it, you shall break
its neck. All the firstborn of your sons you shall redeem. And
none shall appear before me empty.[112]

The beginning of Second Kings 21 also seems to endorse the idea
of child sacrifice in early Judaism, where it says of King Manasseh
that:

And he built altars for all the host of heaven in the two courts
of the house of the Lord. And he burned his son as an offering
and practiced soothsaying and augury, and dealt with medi-
ums and with wizards.[113]

Similar claims in the same chapter are made of King Ahab of Israel,
as well. Ahab built "altars on high places" to perform sacrifices.[114] This
material, of course, supplements the narratives of Abraham and Isaac
and Jephthah and his daughter to conclude that human sacrifice was
practiced in early Judaism.

Other passages from the Torah and from the historical books,
however, clearly come down on the side of answering the question
of this section of this chapter in the negative. Consider Deuteronomy
18:10, where we are told:

There shall not be found among you anyone who burns his
sons or his daughters as an offering. Anyone who practices
divination, a soothsayer, or an augur, or a sorcerer.[115]

A few chapters earlier, in the same book at Deuteronomy 12:29–30, when the Hebrews were about to dispossess the lands of the Canaanites, again the Torah relates:

> When the Lord your God cuts off before you the nations whom you go to dispossess, and you dispossess them and take their land, take heed that you not be ensnared to follow them, after they have been destroyed before you, and that you do not inquire about their gods, saying, "How did these nations serve their gods, that I also may do likewise." You shall not do so to the Lord your God, for every abominable thing that the Lord hates they have done for their gods. For they even burn their sons and daughters in the fire to their gods.[116]

At Leviticus 18:21, we also see a prohibition in the Torah against the practice of child sacrifice. This verse tells us:

> You shall not give any of your children to devote them by fire to Molech, and so profane the name of your God: I am the Lord.[117]

Another passage of relevance to our discussion of Psalm 89:34 is when God says, "I will not violate my covenant, nor to alter the words that went forth from my lips." Many Jewish interpreters over the years have suggested that this refers to the condemnation of child sacrifice practiced by the societies around the ancient Jews.

From the material in this section of Chapter Two, we may make the following conclusions about child sacrifice in the Torah and historical books. First, that the Canaanites and the Ammonites practiced human sacrifice prior to the Hebrews entering the land of Canaan. Secondly, the evidence for a judgment about whether in the earliest periods of the Jews in Israel appears to be mixed. And thirdly, even early on in their history, the writers of the Torah and the historical books often give negative assessments of the practice of child sacrifice in the cultures around them—particularly the Canaanites, the Moabites and Ammonites. This brings us to an examination of what can be found in the period of the *Nabiim*, or Prophets, with respect to child sacrifice, the topic of the next section of this second chapter.

Child Sacrifice Among the Hebrew Prophets

If the evidence about child sacrifice in the Torah and the historical books is ambivalent about child sacrifice, it is not ambivalent at all among the major and minor prophets. For the most part, the prophets are against the idea, and comments about the phenomenon most often arise in the context of speaking of other cultures in the Ancient Near East, such as the Canaanites, the Ammonites and the Moabites.

For example, in the writings of the Prophet Jeremiah he regularly speaks about the idea of child sacrifice. At chapter 7:31–32, for example, he refers to *topheth*, where the Canaanites performed their sacrifices. Jeremiah relates:

> And they have built their high place of Topheth, which is in the valley of the son of Hinnom, to burn their sons and daughters in the fire, which I did not command, nor did it come into my mind. Therefore, behold the days are coming, says the Lord, when it no longer will be called Topheth, or the valley of the son of Hinnom, but the valley of Slaughter; for they will bury in Topheth because there is no room elsewhere.[118]

At chapter 19:4–6, Jeremiah again speaks of *topheth* and the valley of the son of Hinnom. He tells us:

> Because the people have forsaken me, and have profaned this place of Baal to burn their sons in the fire as burnt offerings to Baal, which I did not command or decree, nor did it come into my mind. Therefore, behold the days are coming, says the Lord when this place shall not be called Topheth, or the valley of Ben-Hinnom, but the Valley of Slaughter.[119]

At Jeremiah 32:34–35, the prophet speaks of both sacrifices to Baal, as well as to Molech. Jeremiah relates:

> They set up their abominations in the house which is called by my name to defile it. They built the high places of Baal in the valley of the son of Hinnom, to offer up their sons and daughters to Molech, though I did not command them, nor did it enter into my mind, that they should do this abomination to cause Judah to sin.[120]

What is true of Jeremiah's condemnation of the sacrifices to Baal and Molech is also true of the other major prophets, Ezekiel and Isaiah. At Ezekiel 20:31, the prophet takes a negative view of child sacrifice when he writes:

> When you present your gifts and offer up your children in fire, you defile yourselves with all of your idols to this day. And shall I be inquired of by you, oh house of Israel, as I live, declares the Lord God, I will not be inquired of by you.[121]

Ezekiel takes a similar attitude toward the Canaanites and their child sacrifices at chapter 20:25–26. There he tells us about the worshippers of Baal and Molech:

> Moreover, I gave them statutes that were not good and rules by which they could not have life; and I defiled them through their very gifts in their offering up of all of their first-born, that I might devastate them. I did it so that they will know that I am the Lord.[122]

Ezekiel also speaks of the moral character of the Canaanites at chapter 23:37, when he tells us:

> "For they have committed adultery and blood is on their hands. With their idols they have committed adultery and they have even offered up to them for food the children of whom they had borne to me."[123]

The attitudes toward human sacrifice of Jeremiah and Ezekiel are similar to what the Prophet Isaiah has to say about the issue at hand. The Prophet Isaiah speaks of human sacrifice and to the Canaanites in the very first chapter of his book when he says at 1:15:

> When you spread out your hands, I will hide my eyes from you, even though you make many prayers, I will not listen, for your hands are full of blood.[124]

At chapter 57:4–6, the Prophet Isaiah again speaks of his moral attitude toward the sacrificial practices of the Canaanites. At those verses, Isaiah reveals:

Are you not children of transgression, the offspring of deceit?
You who burn with lust among the oaks, under every green
tree. You who slay your children in the valleys under the clefts
of the rocks?[125]

This negative response to child sacrifice can be seen among a
number of the minor prophets, as well. The Prophet Hosea, for example,
at chapter 13:1–2, also takes a negative view of sacrifices to Baal. The
prophet tells us:

When Ephraim spoke, men trembled, he was exalted in Israel.
But he incurred guilt through Baal and died. And now they
sin more and more, and make for themselves molten images,
idols skillfully made of silver, all of them the work of crafts-
men. "Sacrifice to these!" they say. Men kiss calves.[126]

Another minor Prophet, this time Amos, speaks about the practice
of the Ammonites conducting child sacrifice when he writes:

For three transgressions of the Ammonites and for four, I
will not revoke the punishment because they have ripped up
women with children in Gilead.[127]

There can be little doubt that the "transgressions" Amos has in mind
here is the child sacrifices to Molech that regularly occurred among the
Ammonites. And like the other prophets, Amos has a negative view of
that practice. The same can be said of Jonah, who, in his book at 2:8–9,
also speaks negatively of those who worship idols, like the Canaanites,
the Ammonites and the Moabites. The prophet Jonah relates:

Those who pay in regard to vain idols, forsake their true
loyalty; but I with the voice of thanksgiving will sacrifice to
thee, what I have vowed I will pay. Deliverance belongs to the
Lord.[128]

Two conclusions may be made about this couplet from Jonah.
First, he is starkly against those who sacrifice to idols. And secondly,
Jonah is in favor of sacrificing to Yahweh, but it is not clear in this
passage whether he is referring to a grain sacrifice, an animal sacrifice
or a human one.

Finally, the Prophet Micah at 6:7 also raises the question of human sacrifice. He relates:

Will the Lord be pleased with thousands of rams, with ten thousand rivers of oil? Shall I give my firstborn for my transgression, the fruit of my body for the sin of my soul?[129]

The meaning of this passage from the Prophet Micah is not entirely clear. Some have suggested it is a commentary on Second Kings 3:27. Others say that the import of these verses is to be found in Micah's willingness to sacrifice his son if it was required. Thus, some liken it to Abraham in the Akedah narrative. At any rate, this brings us to what the third part of Hebrew scriptures, the *Kethuvim*, or the "Writings," have to say about the phenomenon of child sacrifice, the topic of the next section of this second chapter.

Child Sacrifice in the Writings

Among the books of the Writings, many passages also can be found where the issue of child sacrifice is a topic of discussion. Among the *Kethuvim*, passages from the Psalms, Proverbs, and the Book of Daniel, all make explicit references to the phenomenon of child sacrifice. Consider, for example, Psalm 5:3–6 that tells us:

Oh Lord, in the morning you hear my voice, and in the morning I prepare a sacrifice for you, and then watch, for you are not a God who delights in wickedness. Evil cannot sojourn with You. The boastful may nor stand before your eyes. You hate all evil-doers. You destroy those who speak lies, but the Lord abhors the bloodthirsty and deceitful men.[130]

The beginning of this passage speaks of the Psalmist making sacrifices, followed by a pronouncement that the Lord despises wickedness, and finally indicates that the Lord is not fond of the "bloodthirsty," perhaps a reference to the child sacrifices of the people near the Hebrews—those in Canaan, Moab and Ammon.

At Psalm 105:34–35 and 36, the Psalmist again takes up the question of sacrifice. In the former passage, he speaks of the "Locusts who came and the young locusts without number, that devoured all the

vegetation in the land and ate up the fruit from the ground."[131] This is
followed by, "He smote all the firstborn in their land, the first issue of
all their strength."[132] It is not clear whether the Lord is referring to the
Canaanites or the tribes of Israel.

These verses are followed by Psalm 105:37–38 that informs us:

> Then He led forth Israel with silver and gold, and there was
> none among his tribes who stumbled. Egypt was glad when
> they departed, for dread of them had fallen upon it.[133]

At Psalm 106:36–38, the Psalmist speaks of the Canaanites when
he relates:

> They served their idols, which became a snare for them.
> They sacrificed their sons and their daughters to the demons.
> They poured out innocent blood, the blood of their sons and
> daughters whom they sacrificed to the idols of Canaan, and
> the land was polluted with blood. Thus, they became unclean
> by their acts, and they played the harlot in their doings.[134]

It should be clear that in this passage, the Psalmist makes the same
judgment about Canaanite child sacrifice that we have seen in the Torah,
the historical books, and both the major and the minor prophets. We
find a similar moral judgment in the Proverbs at 6:16–17 and 21:3. The
former of these begins by speaking of those things that the Lord hates,
and one of those is "hands that shed innocent blood," again perhaps
another reference to the sacrifices of the Canaanites.[135]

In a few chapters later at 21:3, the writer again returns to the issue
at hand when he relates:

> To do righteousness and justice is more acceptable to the
> Lord than is sacrifice.[136]

It is not clear whether the writer is referring to the Jews or to the
Canaanites. Nor is it clear whether the Lord refers to human sacrifice
or some other kind. It may be a reference to child sacrifice, or it may
mean grain or even animal sacrifice. What is clear is that righteousness
to God and justice is far more valuable than the sacrifice mentioned in
the passage.

Another set of passages in the writings that may speak of child sacrifice is Daniel 9:27, 11:31 and 12:11, all of which speaks of "abomination of desolation."[137] It is clear that the writers of the Gospels, at least Mark, Luke and Matthew, all understood the expression as the practice of child sacrifice, as is indicated at Mark 13:14, Luke 21:20–21 and Matthew 1:15–16.[138]

The Hebrew expression in question is *ha Shukuts menshomam*, or the "abomination of desolation." The expression comes from the classical Hebrew verb *siqqus* that means "to soil" or "to defile." Some say it refers to the destruction of the Temple in Jerusalem, like John Wesley and Joseph Smith, for example. Others maintain that the expression refers to the practice of human, child sacrifice in places like Canaan, Ammon and Moab.

Whether or not this is the proper interpretation of the Hebrew expression "abomination of desolation" is not clear. But after the time of the New Testament, many interpreters in the Christian tradition understand the expression the same way that the writers of the Gospels did, as a reference to child sacrifice, or they believe it refers to the destruction of the Temple in Jerusalem.[139]

At any rate, this brings us to the next section of Chapter Two, where the subject matter is the phenomenon of child sacrifice in non-canonical literature.

Child Sacrifice in Non-Canonical Literature

By the term "non-canonical" we primarily mean the Apocrypha and the Pseudepigrapha of the Hebrew Bible, or Old Testament. The former term is applied to works, usually written, of unknown authors and provenance, that supplemented traditional Hebrew and Greek scriptures. The Roman Catholic Church considers some of these works to be canonical, while the Protestant churches do not. The term "apocrypha" comes from the classical Greek word, *apocryphos*, meaning "obscure."

The Pseudepigrapha are falsely attributed works whose claimed authors are not the true writers of these texts, or they are works where the true authors have falsely attributed them to people from the past. The word "pseudepigrapha," comes from two classical Greek terms, *pseudes*, or "false," and *epigraphe*, or "writing." Thus, the expression means "false writing."

Several texts among the Apocrypha mention the idea of child sacrifice or directly refer to the sacrifice of Isaac in Genesis 22. Among these texts are the books of the Maccabees. Indeed, First Maccabees 9:45; Second Maccabees 2:23–28, chapters 6 and 7, and 12:39–45, all refer to the issues at hand. This is also true of Fourth Maccabees 5:4ff and 8:3ff.

A Jewish author wrote the first book of Maccabees after the restoration of the independent Jewish kingdom of the Hasmoneans in the late second century BCE. At chapter 9:45, and throughout the book, it points out that Antiochus IV forbade the practice of Jewish religious activities in general, and sacrifice, in particular. The Jews refused this edict, and they also refused to worship the Greek gods, as well.

At Second Maccabees 2:23–28, these verses begin with this:

> When the king had finished speaking these words, a Jewish man came forth to offer sacrifice on the altar of Modein.[140]

The town of Modein was in the northwest lowlands of Judea, just south of the road from Jerusalem to Joppa. This is another example of the Jews offering sacrifice against the prohibitions of Antiochus IV. First Maccabees 6:7 speaks of "pulling down the abomination that Antiochus had built there in Jerusalem." This appears to be a reference that Antiochus established a place for sacrifice to the Greek gods in Jerusalem, and the Jews destroyed that place.

Chapter seven verse seventeen of First Maccabees speaks of, "The flesh of your faithful and their blood that was spread around Jerusalem and no one was left to bury them."[141] Again, this appears to be a reference to the ancient Jews winning a battle during the Maccabean Revolt, and, being victorious, slaughtered the forces of Antiochus.

At Second Maccabees 12:39–45, we see another battle where Jews were slaughtered during the Maccabean Revolt, and "Money was sent to Jerusalem for sacrifices that were to be offered for the sins of the dead."[142] Fourth Maccabees 5:4ff and 8:3ff, also refers to the practice of sacrifice. In both of these narratives, Antiochus IV attempts to induce a group of Jews to eat pork. The first narrative involves the Jewish priest,

Eleazar, who refuses. And those in the second narratives, the one from chapter eight, also follow suit.[143]

Other texts from the Apocrypha also say something about sacrifice or the Akedah itself. The 17th and 18th chapters of the Book of Jubilees are other good examples. In the former chapter, verses 1–14, Hagar and Ishmael are sent out from Abraham's home. In verses 15–18, Mastema, a demonic figure, proposes that Abraham should sacrifice Isaac to "test his love and obedience."[144]

At Jubilees 17:15–15, the text informs us:

> Words came in heaven concerning Abraham that he was faithful in everything that was to him, and he loved the Lord and was faithful to him in all afflictions. And Prince Mastema came in and said before God, "Behold Abraham loves Isaac his son, and he is more pleased with him than anything. Tell him to offer him as a burnt offering upon the altar. And you will see if he would do this thing. And you will know whether he is faithful in everything in which you test him."

Here the author[s] of Jubilees combines two theories concerning the meaning of Abraham's suffering. First, a demonic force of some kind may influence the patriarch, and secondly, God is testing Abraham to see if he is as good as God believes he is.

Another theory that arises in non-canonical literature about the cause of Abraham's suffering can be seen in Chapter 32:1–2 of *The Biblical Antiquities of Pseudo-Philo*. This text relates:

> God gave Abraham a son in his late old age, and took him out of a sterile womb, and all of the angels were jealous of him, and the worshipping hosts envied him. And since they were jealous of him, God said to him, "Kill the fruit of your body for me, and offer for me as a sacrifice what has been given to you by me."[145]

Another non-canonical theory about the origins of Abraham's suffering is put forth in a legend from the Targum Pseudo-Jonathan, dated in the seventh century CE, where the word *debarim*, or "words," is understood as the brothers Ishmael and Isaac "having words with each other" over who is the proper heir—a kind of Sibling Rivalry Theory.[146]

In chapter eighteen, Abraham is willing to go through with the sacrifice until the final moment when an angel appears, and Mastema is put to shame in verses one to thirteen. In verses fourteen to nineteen of chapter eighteen of Jubilees, Abraham is blessed by God, and he returns to Beersheba.[147]

Other passages in the Apocrypha that deal in general with sacrifice, or particularly with the Akedah, can be found at Judith 11:16–19, the *Wisdom of Solomon* 3:5–7 and 14:2–3, in the Book of Tobit, and in Enoch.[148] In the Judith verses at 11:16, the text tells us:

> For every sacrifice is a first fruit offering and a small thing; and
> the fat of the burnt offering to you is a very little thing, but
> whatever pleases the Lord is a great thing forever."

Verse eighteen also speaks of "burnt offerings, free will offerings, and gifts," and these appear to be related to the normal Jewish sacrifices of grain and animals.

The Wisdom of Solomon is a Jewish work, written in Greek and most likely produced in the city of Alexandria in the mid-first century BCE. It has three separate parts. The first part deals with eschatological issues, mostly related to resurrection and the End Times. Part two is dedicated to the idea of *hokmah* or *Sophia*, "Wisdom" in classical Greek. The third part of the *Wisdom of Solomon* is devoted to the history of the Jews, particularly from the time of Antiochus to the end of the second century BCE.

In the passage from chapter three, the text reveals:

> Having been disciplined a little, they will reclaim a great good
> because God tested them and found them worthy of Himself.
> Like gold in a furnace he tried them, and like a sacrificial offer-
> ing, he accepted them in the time of his restitution, they will
> come forth, and they will be like sparks among the stubble.[149]

The passage at chapter 14:2–3 and later in the chapter speaks of idolatry. The text informs us:

> But the idol made with hands is cursed, and so is the one who
> made it. He for making it, and it for believing it is God...But
> there will be a visitation upon the idol.[150]

Regarding the Pseudepigrapha, the most relevant texts for our purposes are the books of Enoch. First Enoch chapter fourteen and Second Enoch chapters 59 and 69:11–16 are two of the most important sections. In the former, Methuselah constructed a sacrificial altar at Achuzan, where his father Enoch ascended to Heaven. This place was considered holy ground, much like the place of Mount Moriah.[151]

In a variety of passages in First Enoch, such as chapters 8:1–3, 10:1–8 and 54:3–6, the subject of the Azazel, or the scapegoat lamb, can be found. In the first two of these, the text likens the scapegoat to the survival of the Nation of Israel and the sacrificial parallels of the goat to the Jews.[152] At Second Enoch 59 and 69:11–16, Enoch ascended to Heaven. After a short stay there, he returns to Earth to teach his son and grandson what he learned in Heaven. As a result, a priestly sacrificial cult is formed, and Enoch's son Metusalem and his grandson Nir ate the first two leaders of the cult. Among the things that Enoch revealed to his two descendants is that they should not allow any sacrifices to be made honoring demons. Among the idols that Enoch has in mind are those associated with Baal, Chemosh, and what in olden times "went on at the *tophet* on high places."[153]

It is likely that Second Enoch, also called Slavonic Enoch, was originally written in Greek sometime in the first century CE. The text survives in approximately twenty Bulgarian manuscripts that, most likely, worked from the now-lost Greek original. Second Enoch is important because it contains an outline for provisions in the conducting of sacrifices in Judaism.[154]

Another first century CE work, the "Apocalypse of Moses," at chapter five, verses one to fifteen, sketches out some provisions for firstling sacrifices (v. 5) and animal sacrifices in general in verses six to eight. The Apocalypse of Moses was written in Greek. The provisions for animal sacrifice are similar to others of the time in Palestine.

The "Testament of Job," another Pseudepigraphic work, completed sometime in the first century BCE to the first century CE, also centers on the patriarch from Uz conducting sacrifices for his sons, "in case they may have sinned in their hearts." At chapters 1:9, 2:1–3, and chapter 4:1–6, the testament deals with the issue at hand. It appears that the work was originally written in Greek.[155]

Another work from the Pseudepigrapha, the "Testament of Levi" completed in Aramaic sometime before 100 BCE, was found in the Cairo Genizah. It was part of the larger work called "The Testaments of the Twelve Patriarchs."[156] The most relevant passage in the Testament of Levi is chapter nine, verses eleven to fourteen.[157] Verse eleven tells the sacrificer to bathe beforehand, then bathe again just before the slaughter, and then to wash afterward. Chapter 9:13 suggests the sacrifices should only be "clean" beasts and birds, and verse 14 indicates that these sacrifices should be of the First Fruit variety.[158]

The provisions for sacrifices sketched out in the Testament of Levi look very much like those found in the Torah in passages such as Genesis 7:2 and 8:20, Leviticus 1:14, Deuteronomy 12:23–25, and in portions of the Prophets, like Ezekiel 39:17–20.[159] This brings us to the major conclusions we have made in this second chapter.

A final work from the Pseudepigrapha that discusses child sacrifice in general and the Akedah, in particular, is the Targum Pseudo-Jonathan, a West Semitic targum on the Torah. Geza Vermes and others date this text to the ancient world, but other contemporary scholars believe it was completed sometime between the eighth and the fourteenth centuries.[160]

The first printed edition of the Targum Pseudo-Jonathan was produced in Venice in 1591. The British Museum owns a manuscript of the text that was published by Ginsburger in 1903. This manuscript has become the standard text.[161] The Pseudo-Jonathan is important for our purposes because it offers many alternative understandings of narratives like the Akedah. For example, the writer(s) suggest that the reference to Abraham's only son Isaac, in 22:1–2, may have been the result of sibling rivalry between Hagar's son Ishmael and Sarah's son Isaac.

Several other differences between the Masoretic text of Genesis 22 and the version in Pseudo-Jonathan also provide some theological explanations of portions of the Akedah narrative that are radically different between the two texts. In Pseudo-Jonathan, for example, Isaac is thirty-six years old with nothing similar to that in the Masoretic text. The two texts disagree about what Abraham says to the servants before traveling to the altar of sacrifice.[162] Pseudo-Jonathan suggests that

Sarah's maid, Hagar, is a daughter of the Pharaoh and that Nimrod is a personal enemy of Abraham. Indeed, he wishes to burn him alive.[163] Isaac in Pseudo-Jonathan is presented as a proto-martyr, a version of the Jobus Christi Model.

The Targum Pseudo-Jonathan has Isaac say in 22:1, "If the Holy One, blessed be He, were to ask for all of my limbs, I would not hold back."[164] The text also indicates that God "heard these words, and then He immediately tested Abraham."[165] At 22:8, the Targum suggests that God "chose for Himself the lamb for the offering," and nothing comparable appears in the Masoretic text.[166]

In the Targum's version of 22:10, when Abraham stretched forth his hand with the knife, Isaac exclaims, "Father, bind me well unless I struggle in mortal agony and be thrown into the pit of destruction, and therefore to be found a blemish in your sacrifice."[167] Nothing comparable can be found in the Masoretic text.

At Genesis 22:20, the Targum Pseudo-Jonathan tells us this:

> After Abraham had bound Isaac, Satan came and told Sarah that Abraham had killed Isaac. And Sarah rose up and cried out and choked and died because of the anguish she had been brought.[168]

The Targum at 22:18 also has a view radically different from the Masoretic text. Pseudo-Jonathan puts the verse in question this way:

> And all the nations of the Earth shall be blessed because of "the merit of your son, and because you have accepted My words."[169]

The Masoretic text says nothing of why the nations of the Earth shall be blessed, and what the relationship is between those nations and the sacrifice of Isaac. The Hebrew text tells us the reason is, "because you have obeyed my voice."[170] At 22:14, the Masoretic text says that Abraham called the name of that place "God will provide." The Targum ends v. 14 will these words:

> And Abraham bound Isaac, his son, and it was there that the *Shekinah* was revealed to him.[171]

The Targum uses the word, *Shekinah*, a word that implies that God is present, which is not used in the Masoretic text narrative. And after the scene on Mount Moriah, Isaac was brought by angels to the school of Shem the Great, where he was a student for three years studying the Torah and the Talmud.

Thus, it should be perfectly clear that, at times, the writer(s) of the Targum Pseudo-Jonathan takes a radically different approach to the sacrifice of Isaac than does the traditional Hebrew, Masoretic text. Of all the works of the Pseudepigrapha, this one comments more on the Akedah than any of the other sources outlined in this chapter.

The subject matter of Chapter Three of this study on the sacrifice of Issac is a close reading of Genesis 22:1–19. As we shall see in this analysis, there are a variety of styles or theories about the meaning of the Akedah from the standpoints of history, philosophy and theological exegesis.

Conclusions to Chapter Two

We began this second chapter by sketching out some background materials on the history of sacrifice in the Ancient Near East. More specifically, we examined the practice of human and animal sacrifice among the Canaanites, the Ammonites, the Moabites and the Phoenicians.

In the second section of Chapter Two, we conducted an inquiry into whether the ancient Jews did, or did not, practice child sacrifice. In this inquiry, we have seen several passages supporting the claim that they did engage in the practice. Among these was Jephthah, who was willing to sacrifice his daughter, and Abraham, who was willing to sacrifice his son.

We also enumerated several other passages in the Torah and the historical books of the Old Testament, where it appears that God/ Yahweh desired human sacrifice. Leviticus 27:28 and 29, for example, as well as numbers 31:25–40, and Second Samuel 21:1–14 would seem to answer our question in the affirmative.

Over and against this judgment, however, we enumerated a host of Old Testament passages indicating that the ancient Jews should not have practiced child sacrifice. These passages include Deuteronomy

12:29–31, Leviticus 18:21 and 27:28–29, among many other Torah and historical texts.[172] In the third section of this chapter, we discussed the idea of child sacrifice among the major and minor prophets of the ancient Jews, including passages from Jeremiah, Ezekiel, Isaiah, Amos, Micah and Hosea. The conclusion to this third section is that the evidence is mixed about whether the *Nabiim*, or Prophets, supported the idea of child sacrifice in ancient Israel. This was followed by an analysis of what the *Kethuvim*, or the "Writings," indicated regarding the practice of child sacrifice in ancient Israel.

In section four of this chapter, we analyzed and discussed several passages from the Psalms, as well as the references in the Book of Daniel to the Abomination of Desolation that some critics interpret as a prohibition against child sacrifice, however, others believe, as we have indicated, that the expression is a reference to the destruction of the Temple in Jerusalem.

In the fifth and final section of this chapter, we explored the many places in non-canonical literature that have commented upon the issues of human and animal sacrifices. In this section, we chiefly concentrated on texts found in the Apocrypha and Pseudepigrapha literature.

In the final section, we discussed passages on sacrifice in the Books of Maccabees, the Book of Jubilees, the Book of Judith, the Book of Tobit, and the Wisdom of Solomon. And in this material, we have seen some parallels to Old Testament references to both child and animal sacrifices, while we have also seen some differences.

In the same section of Chapter Two, we explored many places in the Pseudepigrapha where sacrifice was at the center of our discussion. Among the texts where we introduced passages related to or discussing child and animal sacrifices, were materials from First and Second Enoch, the Apocalypse of Moses, the Testament of Levi, the Testaments of the Twelve Patriarchs, the Testament of Job, and the Targum Pseudo-Jonathan on the Torah in general, and the Akedah in particular.

From these sources from the Pseudepigrapha, again, we have seen parallels to the Biblical materials in Deuteronomy, Leviticus, as well as passages in other books in the Torah and the historical books. We also saw among these passages from the Pseudepigrapha a concerted effort against the worshipping of and sacrificing to idols, and to foreign gods.

As we have seen, many of the dissimilarities between works of the Pseudepigrapha and the Masoretic text, such as in Pseudo-Jonathan, the views of Hagar, Isaac, and Ishmael, are often radically different from the traditional Hebrew text.

In Chapter Three to follow, we will do a close reading of the sacrifice of Isaac passage in the twenty-second chapter of the Book of Genesis. We will also catalog several theories to understand the meaning of Abraham's willingness to sacrifice his son Isaac in the pericope known as the Akedah. It is to Akedah, then, that we turn next.

Chapter Three:
Models for Interpreting the Akedah

The story of the binding of Isaac, the Akedah, is a
multi-layered, sharply paradoxical story with many meanings and symbols. On one level, we might adduce that the
meaning of the story is about the development of ethical
and religious thought.

—Jenny Chambers, "The Binding of Isaac: The Akedah"

The nineteen verses of the Akedah comprise one of the
most poignant and enigmatic narratives of the Bible. No
single explanation satisfies, and each of its many exposi-
tors seems to be able to untangle only single strands.

—Jo Milgrom, *The Akedah: The Binding of Isaac*

Behold My servant, whom I uphold
My chosen in whom my soul delights.

—Book of Isaiah 42:1 (Author's translation)

Introduction

We will begin this third chapter by offering a model of interpretation
regarding the Akedah passage. In that model, we will suggest fourteen
different theories or interpretations of the meaning of Genesis 22:1–19.
Throughout the remainder of this history, the model will be employed
in the creating comparisons of many of the sources in this study.

The other goal of this chapter is to give a close and comprehensive reading of the Akedah narrative, according to the Masoretic text from the *Ashar* and *Naphtali* families in the High Middle Ages, around 1000 CE.[173] We move first, then, to our heuristic model for interpretations of the Akedah.

A Heuristic Model for Interpreting the Akedah

Over the many centuries in the Judeo-Christian-Islamic tradition, fourteen separate theories of interpretation have arisen about Genesis 22:1–19. We list these interpretations here and will speak about them one at a time. These fourteen theories look like this:

1. The Test Perspective
2. The Divine Plan Theory
3. The Jobus Christi Model
4. The Ban Sacrifice Perspective
5. The Divine Command Theory
6. The Deontological Explanation
7. The Suspension of Ethics Model
8. The Moral Qualities Approach: Trust and Fortitude
9. The Atonement Model
10. The Sanctity of Human Life Model
11. The Influences of Demonic Forces Theory
12. The Sibling Rivalry Perspective
13. The Isaac as Remnant Theory
14. Message was Garbled or Miscommunicated in Some Way

The first of these fourteen theories suggest as verse 1 does that God uses the Akedah narrative to "test" the moral character of the patriarch Abraham.[174] The second theory, which we have called the Divine Plan Theory, says that Abraham and Isaac may have suffered in the Akedah narrative, but everything works out for the good in the end. And this theory says that God planned it that way.[175]

The Jobus Christi Model posits that the most relevant element of the Akedah narrative is that Abraham and Isaac act as Christ figures in their suffering. Needless to say, this is primarily a Christian explanation for Genesis 22, and it was employed mainly by the early church fathers.[176] The Ban Sacrifice Perspective argues that the most important element of the Akedah story is that the ancient Jews banned the practice of child sacrifice when many of the cultures around them were regularly practicing it, like the Canaanites, the Ammonites and the Moabites, for example.

Our fifth explanation of the Akedah, the Divine Command Theory, says that the most relevant feature of the Akedah narrative is that if God commanded Abraham to sacrifice Isaac, then that alone makes the action morally good, even if an angel stops the sacrifice in the middle of the act.[177]

The Deontological Explanation argues that the most important element of the Akedah narrative is that it is morally wrong to take human life. This theory is connected to the fifth commandment that clearly says, "Thou shalt not kill."[178] The proponents of theory number seven, like nineteenth-century Danish philosopher, Soren Kierkegaard, suggest that the best way to understand the Akedah narrative is the realization that it involves a "teleological suspension of the ethical."[179] The Talmud (the *Sanhedrin* 89b) takes a similar position about Abraham's actions. The Talmud relates in that tractate that a prophet has the right to suspend a moral rule if he believes it to be appropriate.[180]

The *Mishnah*'s Genesis Rabbah at 58:8 also implies a version of the Kierkegaard theory. But Ibn Ezra, in his commentary of Genesis, rejects the notion that a prophet may suspend the ethical norms. The same section of the Genesis Rabbah concludes that Isaac was thirty-seven years old at the time of the Akedah. This raises the question of why a grown man (Isaac) was unable to overcome an elderly man (Abraham) in the sacrifice of Isaac narrative.

In our eighth model, the Moral Qualities Approach, believers say that the most relevant feature of the Akedah narrative is that God sometimes uses evil and suffering to improve the moral characters of his followers. More specifically, in the case of Abraham in the Akedah story, the development of moral features such as trust and fortitude.[181] Elsewhere, we have outlined a number of these approaches to evil and suffering in the Judeo-Christian-Islamic tradition. Indeed, we will use this heuristic model and these eight approaches throughout the remainder of this history of interpreting the Akedah narrative.

In our ninth theory for interpreting the Akedah narrative, the adherents to the Atonement Theory believe that the most crucial view about the Akedah story is importance for the idea of atonement, both to explain the sacrifice of Isaac and other Jewish, Christian and Islamic figures in later history. Needless to say, like the Jobus Christi Model, the Atonement Theory has been quite popular in the Early Christian Church, from the New Testament to around the year 1000 CE.

The tenth theory mentioned above for understanding the meaning of the Akedah is the view that the sanctity of human life is the major reason that God, or His angel halted the sacrifice. And in the eleventh model for explaining the Akedah has to do with the demonic figures of Mastema and/or Satan. In this model, the overall theory that lies behind the Akedah is the view that the demonic works against Abraham and his son, Isaac.

Our twelfth theory for explaining the Akedah narrative is mostly to be found in the Midrash, as well as later Islamic views of Ibrahim's sacrifice. This view says that the most fundamental issue at the heart of the sacrifice of Isaac narrative is the idea of sibling rivalry between Ishmael and Isaac.

Our thirteenth theory for explaining the meaning of the Akedah narrative is the understanding that after the Akedah narrative, Isaac stands as a "Remnant" of the Nation of Israel, a reaffirmation, if you will, of the everlasting *Berith*, or Covenant, between Abraham and the Yahweh, the God of Israel.

Finally, in the fourteenth theory, some exegetes of the Akedah narrative suggest that the command to Abraham to sacrifice his son was garbled, or in some way, miscommunicated. This point of view is seen, for example, in several Midrashim on the sacrifice of Isaac in early Rabbinic Judaism.

There are many other theories about the central meaning of the Akedah narrative. Recently, some commentators suggest that, like the Nazi figures, Abraham was just following orders. Another important question that arises relating to the Akedah narrative is how does Abraham know for sure that it is God who is talking to him, particularly since the Canaanite god Molech demanded the sacrifice of the firstborn son. Over the course of this study, we will point to a number of other philosophical and theological theories about the central meaning of the sacrifice of Isaac story.

This brings us to an analysis, or a close commentary, on Genesis 22:1–19, the other goal of this chapter. We will begin by dividing the narrative into the following parts:

1. The Command to Abraham (vv. 1–3)

2. Father and Son (vv. 4–8)

3. The Sacrificial Altar (vv. 9–10)

4. Abraham's Reward (vv. 11–18)

5. Father and Son Return (v. 19)

In our analysis in this chapter, we shall devote a separate section to each of these five parts, beginning with the command to Abraham in the initial two verses of Genesis 22. Before moving to our close reading, however, we first will make some brief observations about Abraham and Sarah up to the Akedah narrative.

Abraham and Sarah Before the Akedah Narrative

We first hear about Abram and Sarah in Genesis at the end of chapter eleven, where we learn that Abram is the son of Terah and that Sarah, Abram's wife, is barren. The two are called by Yahweh to leave Haran, where these nomadic people had settled. Abram was seventy-five, and he and Sarah, along with Abram's nephew Lot, went to the land of Canaan. They begin their journey at the oak of Moreh in Shechem, where, because Yahweh had promised that land to their offspring (12:7), they build an altar before moving on into the Negev.

A severe famine causes Abram and Sarah to go to Egypt, where Sarah, disguised as Abram's sister, becomes part of the harem of

Pharaoh. After their deception is discovered, they leave Egypt with much livestock and pieces of gold and silver (13:2). At this point, Abram and Sarah return to the oak of Moreh. What follows next is that Lot, who is as wealthy as Abram, takes his herd and travels to Sodom on the plain of the Jordan River, while Abram and Sarah settle at the oaks of Mamre in Heron.

What follows next is that Yahweh makes a *berith*, or covenant, with Abram and Sarah. The Lord tells them that they will have heirs even though Sarah is barren. Abram asks Yahweh if the heir will be a "slave born in my house" (15:3). The Lord replied, "Look toward the heavens and count the stars, if you are able to count them…so shall your descendants be" (15:5). And Abram appears to believe the Lord.

Sarah, on the other hand, is not so sure of the arrangement. She convinces her husband that her slave Hagar should bear their children. After Hagar conceives her son, Ishmael, she becomes contemptuous of Sarah, who in turn, treats Hagar harshly, as well. This causes Hagar to run away. While Hagar is sitting by a spring on the way to Shur, an angel appears to her and says that her offspring will be so multiplied that they will not be able to be counted (16:10). At this point, Hagar gives birth to her son, Ishmael, when Abram is eighty-six years old (16:15).[182]

When Abram was ninety-nine years old, and his son Ishmael was thirteen, they and all the men of their household were circumcised (17:27). As Abram rests in his tent by the oaks of Mamre, three strangers approach who are on their way to Sodom. Sarah prepares a meal for them. The men ask about Sarah's welfare, and they tell her that "in due season" (18:10), she will bear a son, an observation that makes Sarah laugh because she is an old woman. After more discussion with Abraham, the three strangers depart for Sodom.

Following the destruction of Sodom, the death of Lot's wife, and the impregnation of his daughters, Abraham moves again towards the Negev Desert, settling as an alien in a place called Gerar. In a narrative that parallels the Egyptian pharaoh narrative, Sarah again poses as Abraham's sister. The story now, however, centers on the ethical nature of the deception. In due time, Sarah conceived and gave birth to Isaac, who was circumcised when he was eight days old.

The two sons, Ishmael and Isaac, play with each other, but Sarah becomes concerned that Ishmael would inherit what is rightfully the inheritance of Isaac. Thus, Sarah convinces Abraham to send Hagar and her son away. Yahweh sends Hagar into the desert, where she is rescued from certain death. After another move, this time to Beer-Sheba, Abraham has a dispute over a well with a man named Abimelech. This dispute is settled when Abraham swears an oath of loyalty to Abimelech (21:22–31).

In addition to the rehearsing of this short history of Abraham and Sarah up to the time of Genesis twenty-two, several facts serve as background for the interpretation of verses one to nineteen. It is to some of these facts to which we next turn.

Background Facts of the Akedah Narrative

Among the many facts that lie beneath the Akedah narrative are the following. First, we know from Chapters One and Two that the willingness of a parent to offer a child as a sacrifice was not a rare phenomenon in the Ancient Near East. The Masoretic text mentions that King Mesha of the Moabites did so. So did Jephthah, the least admirable leader in the Book of Judges. Two of the Hebrews' most wicked kings, Ahaz and Manasseh, introduced the practice of child sacrifice into Judah, after which they were loudly condemned.

As we have seen in the first two chapters of this history, there is copious archaeological evidence that child sacrifice regularly was practiced throughout the Ancient Near East. We have also shown that child sacrifice was widespread in places controlled by Phoenicia in Carthage and on Sardinia, Corsica, Sicily, and at Malta.

A second background fact with respect to the Akedah narrative is the fact that the evidence for child sacrifice occurring during the age of the patriarchs is mixed, at best. As we have shown, there is a good bit of evidence that it went on among the ancient Jews, as well as voluminous passages in the Old Testament that indicate child sacrifice was forbidden among the Jews.

The Prophet Micah rhetorically asks, "Shall I give my firstborn, the fruit of my body as expiation for my sin?" Micah answers his own question by saying:

> He has shown you, oh man, what is morally good, so what
> does the Lord require of you? To act justly and to love mercy
> and to walk humbly with your God.[183]

How could Abraham serve as a role model if what he was prepared to do if it is what his descendants were commanded not to do? More specifically, Abraham was chosen to be a role model as a father. Yahweh says of him:

> For I have chosen him so that he will instruct his children and his
> household and after him to keep the way of the Lord, by doing
> what is right and just. How could he serve as a model father if he
> was willing to sacrifice his own child? To the contrary, he should
> have said to God, "If you want me to prove to you how much I
> love you, then take me as a sacrifice and not my child."[184]

A fourth background fact has to do with the clear imperative to reject Soren Kierkegaard's idea of the teleological suspension of the ethical. This is an idea that gives free rein to the religious fanatic to commit crimes in the name of God. We must reject the law of the suicide bomber and the Spanish Inquisition. It is not the logic of Judaism, at least rightly understood. God does not ask us to be unethical. We may not always understand ethics from God's point of view, but we must believe that, "He is our Rock. His works are perfect, and His ways are Just" (Deut. 32:4).

A fifth, and background fact, has been pointed out by anthropologist, Mary Douglas. One of the most striking facts about the history of the age of the patriarchs is that the Torah includes no references to the worshipping of, or the veneration of, or sacrifices towards, dead ancestors. In Judaism, seeking the aid of the spirits of the dead is explicitly forbidden in ancient Judaism.[185]

Another piece of background material pointed out by the ancient rabbis is that, like the three-day journey to Mount Moriah, the Old Testament offers a series of miraculous events, all of which occur on the third day. These include:

1. The day of resurrection at Hosea 6:2.

2. The words of Joseph to his brothers at Genesis 42:18.

3. The day of the giving of the Torah (Exodus 19:18).

4. The hiding of the spies (Joshua 2:19).

5. Esther putting on her dress before meeting Ahasuerus at Esther 5:1.

6. Ezra and the exiles from Babylon, who remained in Jerusalem for three days (Ezra 8:32).

The background point, of course, will be far more important when we get to the reliance of the Jobus Christi Model in the early church fathers that will be examined in a later chapter of this history. It is enough now to point out that Jesus remained in the tomb for three days after his crucifixion.

Regarding Julius Wellhausen's "Documentary Hypothesis," most scholars identify three literary traditions in the Book of Genesis and the Akedah narrative. These are usually identified as the Yahwist, the Elohist, and the Priestly strains, or the J, E, and P Sources. The Akedah narrative is usually attributed to the E source because it employs the name Eholim for God, with a number of glosses by a redactor. Hence the tetragrammaton, YHWH is used as well in the narrative.

Unlike other cultures around the ancient Jews where succession passed to the firstborn son, in the Abraham narrative inheritance passes to the second son, Isaac, or, shall we say, the first Jewish son. We might also add, and not to Esau, but to Jacob, and not to the tribe of Reuben, but rather to the tribe of Levi (for priesthood), and Judah (for kingship), and, of course, not to Aaron, but to his brother Moses.

Perhaps the most important piece of background materials for the Akedah narrative is the fact that Abraham went through nine other "tests" before he arrived for the Akedah on Mount Moriah. These nine trials or tests may be summarized this way:

1. Abraham's rejecting of his father's idolatry (Joshua 24:2).

2. Leaving his homeland for an unknown land (Genesis 12:1).

3. Being tested with famine when he entered the Promised Land (Genesis 12:10).

4. Responding to the abduction of Sarah (Genesis 12:14–15 and 20:2).

5. Interceding for Lot and fighting against the four kings (Genesis 14:12–16).

6. Experiencing the dreadful vision of future captivity (Genesis 15:1–21).

7. Undergoing painful circumcision at the age of ninety-nine (Genesis 17:10).

8. Coping with the barrenness of Sarah, despite the promise of progeny (Genesis 11:30 and 15:3).

9. Evicting Hagar and his firstborn son Ishmael (Genesis 21:9–14).

10. Sacrificing his beloved son Isaac.

We must understand, then, that by the time we get to Genesis 22, the patriarch Abraham had already gone through a series of nine other tests or trials, and he comes out well in each of those.

This brings us to a close reading of the Akedah narrative, beginning with the first of the five parts of the story outlined earlier—that is, vv. 1–3, the command of Yahweh to Abraham. This will be followed by the other four parts of the narrative: vv. 4–8, vv. 9–10, vv. 11–18, and v. 19.

The Command to Abraham: Genesis 22:1–3

The Akedah narrative begins with these words:

> After these things, God tested Abraham, and said to him, "Abraham!" And he said, "Here I am." Then He said, "Take your son, your only son Isaac, whom you love, and go to the land of Moriah, and offer him there as a burnt offering." And he arose and went to the place that God had commanded him.[186]

Needless to say, many features in these three verses require explanation. After "these things" in v. 1, what does the word *nissah*, or "tested," mean in the first verse? Where is the "land of Moriah"? Didn't

Abraham already have another son, Ishmael, by Hagar? So in what sense is Isaac his "only son"? And, what did God mean by a "burnt offering"? Some of these questions are easier to answer than others. We will begin with the land of Moriah.

The expression, "After these things," or "After these words," is only used four times in the Old Testament. These come at Genesis 15:1, 22:20 and 48:1, in addition to the opening verse of Genesis 22.

The word *debarim* in v. 1 is a plural word that generally designates "words," such as at Genesis 39:17 and 19, and 44:4–7; Deuteronomy 1:1 and 4:12, for example; or it means "acts" or "things," such as at Genesis 18:15 and Second Chronicles 32:1, for example. Thus, the reference to *debarim* either means "after these words" or "after these things, or acts."

At Genesis 22:2, we see the first use of the words *ahab* and *ahabab* in the Hebrew Bible/Old Testament. These were are also found at Genesis 27:4 (*ahab*) and 29:20 (*ahabah*). Although there are a variety of other classical Hebrew words to express love, such as *racham* at Psalm 18:1, *chasaq* at Deuteronomy 7:7, and *ray'ah* used in the Song of Songs 1:15 and 2:2.

Clearly, it is no accident that the first time Yahweh uses the word "love" in the Hebrew Bible/Old Testament, is in connection with the figure of Abraham, the father of three faiths—Judaism, Christianity and Islam.

There are many disagreements about why an All-Good God would require a man to sacrifice his son. Some of the ancient rabbis believed it was because of Abraham's treaty with Abimelech at Genesis 21:27. God was angry about the patriarch making this covenant since He had promised to give all the land of Canaan to his descendants. Now Abraham's children would be unable to conquer the land until Abimelech's grandson dies.

In short, Abraham's decision to make a *berith*, or covenant, with the Philistine king, resulted in the exile to Egypt. The test of the Akedah, then, was meant to refine Abraham's faith and obedience, perhaps a version of the Moral Qualities Approach. Others say that the test of Abraham was meant to call to mind God's test of the patriarch Job. Many other theories also have arisen in the Judeo-Christian-Islamic traditions about the answer as to why God would require such a test of Abraham. Many of these theories will be discussed throughout this work.

The location of the land of Moriah has been debated over the centuries. The only other reference to that place in the Old Testament is at Second Chronicles 3:1, where we learn:

> Then Solomon began to build the house of the Lord in Jeru-
> salem, on Mount Moriah, where the Lord had appeared to
> David his father, at the place where David had appointed, on
> the threshing floor of Ornan, the Jeb'usite.

In this passage, the land of Moriah is a mountain upon which King Solomon built his temple, "which appeared to David," a phrase that is clarified in the Septuagint version where "God appeared to David."[187] That Moriah is the place where the temple was built is confirmed by Josephus.[188] The Samaritans, however, identify the place of the Akedah to be Mount Gerizim.[189] This latter view cannot be the proper one simply because the journey from Beersheba to Mount Gerizim is more than the three-day journey suggested by the Hebrew text. In the Syriac of the Peshitta, we find that the land of Moriah is referred to as the "land of the Amorites."[190]

The Targum Pseudo-Jonathan interprets the land of Moriah as "The Land of Worship."[191] Some rabbinic sources identify it with Mount Sinai, as does the Babylonian Talmud at *Ta'anit*.[192] In Islam, the land of Moriah is identified with Mount Marwah, a small hill outside of the city of Mecca. It is spoken of at Al-Qur'an's surah 2:158 that tells us:

> Truly Safa and Marwa are the symbols of Allah. Whoever goes
> on a pilgrimage to the House of Allah, or on a holy visit, is not
> guilty of wrong if he walks around them. And he who does
> good by his own accord will find appreciation with Allah who
> knows all things.[193]

Thus, there are a variety of interpretations for the land of Moriah. There is no reason for not accepting the traditional Jewish view that it is the mountain on which Solomon built his temple. We move now to the idea of Abraham being "tested."

The classical Hebrew word *nissah*, or "tempt," "try," "test" or "prove," is used thirty-eight times in the Old Testament. In many of these, such as at the Book of Job 4:2 where Job is being "tested," Daniel at 1:12, and the Queen of Sheba when she tries out her riddles on King Solomon at Second Chronicles 9:1. In most of the uses of *nissah*, God tries men, either singly or collectively, and a few where men "try" God.

These examples of where men try God usually occur in the desert between slavery and the arriving in the Promised Land. Exodus 17:2–7 and Psalm 78:18 are two good examples. The former asks, "Give us water...why do you quarrel and try [*nissah*] with the Lord?" At Psalm 78:18, we learn, "They tried God in their hearts, asking for more food."[194] Two other examples where *nissah* is employed are at Numbers 14:22 and Psalm 78:56. In the former passage, God observes, "They see my glory...and they have tried me ten times."[195] At Psalm 78:56, the narrator of the passage tells us:

> Yet they tested and rebelled against the Most High God, and they did not keep His testimonies.[196]

The classical Hebrew verb *nissah* is also found at Exodus 15:25 and 16:4, and Deuteronomy 8:2ff and 13:2ff. All of these are about God testing humans with a lack of rain. At Exodus 15:25, the narrator relates, "There He made for them a fixed rule, and there He put them to a test."[197] Exodus 16:4 speaks of manna in the desert. The text relates, "I will rain down bread for you from the sky...that I may test them."[198]

At Deuteronomy 8:2ff, again in the desert, God proclaims, "Remember the long way...that I might test you by hardships."[199] The passage at Deuteronomy 13:2ff, again the desert, the Jews say, "Let us follow another God...do not heed the words of that prophet, for the Lord is testing you."[200]

It should be clear from these many passages that the word *nissah* has been employed in examples where humans test God, and others where God tests humans, like the use of the verb at Genesis 22:1. This brings us to a discussion of Isaac being Abraham's "only son," at Genesis 22:2. Perhaps when the text calls Isaac Abraham's only son, it means his only Jewish son, and if that is the meaning, then the text is correct. Since Ishmael's mother, Hagar, was not a Jew, it follows that her son was not a Jew, as well.

Many exegetes of Genesis 22 make the same point. If the unfolding of the history of Yahweh's "Chosen People" is to continue, it clearly should proceed in an unbroken line from Abraham to Isaac, then to Jacob, and beyond. And this interpretation of the "only son" appears to be the one made by the writer(s) of the Akedah narrative. This brings us to the idea of an *olah*, or "burnt offering," in the sacrifice of Isaac narrative.

The classical Hebrew noun *olah* is employed 262 times in the Old Testament, beginning with Noah's sacrifice at Genesis 8:20. The word *olah* is used six times in the Akedah narrative. These come at verses 2, 3, 6, 7, 8 and 13. The same word is sometimes used to refer to the "ascent of a stairway." *Olah* is employed seven times in Genesis, six of those in the story of Abraham's sacrifice of Isaac. *Olah* is also seen sixteen times in Exodus, 58 in Leviticus, 53 in Numbers, and six in Deuteronomy.[201]

The word *olah*, however, is not the only classical Hebrew noun to designate a "sacrifice." The word *hereg* is also used for that purpose at Genesis 31:54, and Exodus 12:27 and 29:28, for example.[202] Another classical Hebrew word, *saraph*, is sometimes used to designate a burnt offering in the Old Testament, such as at Leviticus 10:16. However, the word *saraph* is most commonly employed as the adjective "burnt" or "burned."

The two "lads" or "servants" mentioned in verses 3 and 19 are identified as Ishmael and Eliezer, respectively. Abraham cut the wood for the offering beforehand, but this is left unexplained in the account in the Torah. The Septuagint refers to the two as "servants," the Hebrew as "lads." We will say more about this issue later in this close reading of the text. This brings us to the second part of our analysis of Genesis 22, the relation of father and son in the narrative, verses 4 to 8.

The Relation of Father and Son: Genesis 22:4–8

In these verses, Abraham arose early in the morning, saddled his ass with his own hands and prepared the wood for the fire and the sacrifice. He took along two servants, and his son Isaac, who by now is a full-grown man. They begin on their journey to Mount Moriah. He soon realizes what was the purpose of his being taken on this trip.

Both father and son are firm in their decision to fulfill Yahweh's command. Many obstacles are put in their way to make the journey difficult to go through with the test. With firm hearts and solemn determination, however, Abraham and Isaac continued on their way until they arrive at Mount Moriah on the third day of their travels. There Yahweh shows Abraham the place where he wishes him to build an altar and to bind Isaac on it. Then Abraham and Isaac ascend to the place that God had designated.

Verses four to eight are full of repetition. "My father" and "My son" are used four times, in two verses. The word "son" appears ten times between v. 2 and v. 16, perhaps a literary technique to emphasize the horror and wonder that Yahweh would require a father to sacrifice his son. We will say more about this process of repetition below, as well as throughout this study. That the son is willing to go along with the plan is made clear with the use of the phrase, "and the two of them went together," employed twice as the frame of the dialogue.

Verses four to eight seem to imply that Isaac learns something of substance in the short dialogue with his father. At v. 5, there is a wordplay connected back to chapter 15:5 that has God saying to Abraham:

Go out and look at the Heavens. If you can count the stars, *koh*, that many will your seed be.[203]

The expression *lekh lekha*, or "go forth," was also employed at Genesis 12:1, when God tells Abraham to, "Go from your country and kindred and your father's house to the land that I will show you."[204]

At 22:5, we see the parallel, this time with Abraham speaking to his servants. He tells them:

Stay here with the ass. The boy and I will go [*koh*] that far. We will worship and then we shall return to you.[205]

In verse 5, Isaac is called a *na'ar*, usually translated as "lad" or "boy." The same word is repeated throughout the Abraham narrative at 14:24; 18:7; 19:4; 21:12, 17, 18, 19 and 20. The word *shachah*, or "worshipped," literally means "to bow down." It is also repeated at 18:2; 19:1; 23:7 and 12, as well as 24:26 and 48. The same verb is repeated at 22:3, 12 and 19. Another significant element in v. 5 is what Abraham says to his servants,

> You stay here with the ass. The boy and I will go up there,
> then we will worship and return to you.[206]

By using "we" rather than "I," it seems clear that Abraham expected that both he and his son would return.

Thus, v. 5 raises the question of whether Abraham really believed that Isaac was about to be sacrificed. If he thought that way, then how can we explain what he says to the servants in verse five? Another question raised by verse five is why the two lads/servants are not permitted to be present for the Akedah scene.

Another repetition in v. 7 in the Akedah narrative employs the expression *hineni*, or "Here I am." In the opening verse of chapter 22, Abraham uses the same expression when God calls him. *Hineni* is used again at v. 11, when the patriarch responds to the angel when after being called, he says, "Here I am." When Moses is called by Yahweh at Exodus 3:4, God says, "Moses, Moses!" and Moses' response is *hineni*, "Here I am." Thus, this passage in Exodus and the one at Genesis 22:7 links the patriarchs Moses and Abraham together with their God Yahweh.

Besides each of the patriarchs answering Yahweh with *Hineni*, Moses and Abraham also have a number of other parallels. Both answer their God on a solitary, holy mountain, Moriah for Abraham and the burning bush for Moses at Exodus 3:4 and 12. Both patriarchs were designated as officiating priests, when it came to the Cult of Yahweh. Both Moses and Abraham revealed their own, personal feelings in the context, in the process of their moral growth. Abraham in the self-serving manipulation of his wife, at Genesis 12:20; and Moses at Numbers 20:10, when he displayed hubris in trying to act like God.

Both Moses and Abraham experienced theophanies at a sacred spot in the world—Abraham at Mount Moriah in Jerusalem and Moses at Mount Sinai. Indeed, in the Midrashim, Mount Sinai is identified with Mount Moriah.[207] From all of this, we certainly may assume that both Moses and Abraham had a fidelity to their God Yahweh that was unsurpassed in the ancient world.

Perhaps the two biggest parallels between Abraham and Moses can be seen at Genesis 22:1 and 12 and Exodus 20:20. In the case of Abraham, the Hebrew root NSH is found in 22:1, where it tells us that "God tested Abraham." At verse 13, God says to Abraham:

Do not lay your hand on the boy or do anything to him, for now I know that you fear God, for you have not withheld your son, your only son, from me.[208]

These two verses tie the testing of Abraham with the fact that the patriarch, Abraham, fears the Lord. At Exodus 20:20, God tells Moses:

Do not be afraid for God only has come to test [nassoth] you, and to put the fear of him upon you so that you do not sin.[209]

Like the figure of Abraham, where testing is tied to the fear of God, in the case of Moses, the narrator employs another word from the same NSH root, the word *nassoth*, which also implies a "test." Moses is also told not to be afraid and that the Almighty has put the fear of the Lord in him.

Verses 8 and 15 of Genesis provide another repetition in the Akedah narrative. At 22:7, Isaac asks, "Father, here is the fire and the wood, but where is the lamb for sacrifice?" At verse 8, Abraham responds to his son by saying, "God Himself will provide a lamb for the sacrifice." A few verses later, at 22:14, the narrator tells us that the name of the place of the sacrifice is, "The Lord will provide." The Hebrew expression in both places is *Yahweh Yireh*—the "Lord will provide." This brings us to an analysis of vv. nine and ten, the next section of the Akedah narrative, the sacrificial altar.[210]

The Sacrificial Altar: Genesis 22:9–10

Having prepared the altar upon which he bound his beloved son, Abraham lifted the knife to sacrifice his son Isaac. At that moment, an angel called out to him to halt and to not do anything to harm his son, for this was only a test, and Abraham had proved his loyalty to Yahweh. Full of gratitude and holy inspiration, Abraham looked around and saw a ram that had been caught in a thicket. And Abraham took the ram and offered it, instead of his son, Isaac.

Verses nine and ten of the Akedah narrative have a number of important features in understanding the narrative as a whole. Verse nine uses the expression *va ya-kod*, from which the word Akedah is derived. The noun *mizbe'ach*, or "altar," in classical Hebrew is used twice at Genesis 8:20, and also in the Abraham narrative at 12:7 and 8, 13:14 and 18, and twice at verse 9.[211]

The word Akedah is derived from the Hebrew verb *akod*, often translated as "bound" or "to tie," translated in v. 9. It is an unusual word that often means "ringed" or "striped." Rashi explains it as the rope marks left on the ankles and wrists of a person who has been bound. So it is from this particular verb, *akod*, that we derive the word Akedah. Thus, we might say that the entire narrative is named after the marks on Isaac's body.[212]

Verse nine also employs the verb *shachats*, a word that means "to slay." This verb is only used ten times in the Old Testament, all of them in the Torah, except Ezekiel 40:39 and 44:11. The other uses of *shachats* occur at Exodus 29:16, Leviticus 4:29 and 33, Leviticus 14:13, and the Book of Numbers 19:3, in addition to Genesis 22:9.

Makeleth is the Hebrew term for "knife" found in Genesis 22:10. It is used throughout the Torah and at verse 6 of chapter 22. It appears to have been a large knife, big enough for Abraham to slit his son's neck. The normal classical Hebrew word for "knife" is *hereb*. This is the knife used for circumcision (see Joshua 5:2). A butcher knife was called a *mahalaph*, and smaller knives were called *ta'ar*, very sharp instruments like a razor.[213]

The two final elements of vv. 9 and 10 are the "wood" and the "fire." The common word for the former in the Torah is *ets*. Before vv. 9–10, this noun had been employed at Genesis 6:4, as well as 22:3, 6, 7, and now twice in v. 9. The word *ets* comes from the verb *atsah* that most often is employed "to fasten" something. Another word in classical Hebrew, the term *ya'ar*, is also used throughout the Torah. It comes from a verb that means "to thicken." *Ya'ar* is found at Joshua 17:15 and 18, for two good examples.[214]

Although Genesis does not tell us why Abraham cut the wood for the sacrifice beforehand, several of Midrashim takes up the question, including the view that it was to ensure that the wood was kosher—that is, it was free of worms. Others say that the particular wood or tree was considered sacred to Abraham, perhaps cut from the terebinth tree he had planted earlier, at Genesis 14:6.0.

The word for "fire" used in Genesis 22 is *esh*. Before vv. 9–10, it had been used at 22:6 and 7. *Esh* is the general term used for "fire" throughout the Torah. Although another word, *be'erah*, that more implies "burning" is employed a few times in Exodus, such as at Exodus 22:6.[215]

It is probable that the "fire" in Genesis 22 does not refer to a flame. Rather, it most likely means traveling with "coals" or "embers" from which a fire may be started for the purposes of conducting the sacrifices. Fire had many uses for the ancient Jews: for heat to cook, to make metals softer (Exodus 32:24), and as a weapon in war (Numbers 31:10 and Joshua 8:8). It was in the midst of fire that Yahweh concluded his covenant with Abraham (Genesis 15:7), and He called Moses to be the leader of His people in fire at Exodus 3:2.[216]

Yahweh frequently makes his presence known by the phenomenon of fire. In the wilderness, he appears as a "pillar of fire" at Numbers 14:14. Yahweh often shows Himself as a devouring fire, such as at Deuteronomy 4:33 and 5:42. After being asked to establish that He was more powerful than the Great Baal, Yahweh responded by consuming the Canaanite sacrifices with a Great Fire. Thus, the idea of fire has many symbolic meanings in the earliest parts of the Old Testament.

The landscape in Palestine was much more plentiful with forests than it is now. Wood was used in ancient Israel for the construction of dwellings (Leviticus 14:45), as well as in the building of vessels (Exodus 7:19). The primary need for wood, of course, was for fuel, for both heat and for cooking (Deuteronomy 29:11). And like fire, wood sometimes appears in the early Old Testament in a figurative sense, sometimes to represent the people of Yahweh.[217]

Thus, both *ets* and *esh*, or "fire" and "wood," are often used in symbolic ways throughout the Old Testament. This brings us to an analysis of the fourth part of the Akedah narrative, the phenomenon of Abraham's reward, at verses 11 to 18—the subject matter of the next section of this third chapter.

The Reward of Abraham: Genesis 22:11–18

Many important features may be pointed out in these verses. For one, vv. 11–18 contain a number of parallels to the Ishmael narrative of chapters 16 to 21. There is, for example, a divine summons at 16:7 and 8, as well as 22:11. The human response to those summons come at 16:8b and 22:11b. We find a divine imperative to save the child at 16:9 and 22:12a. Both 16:10–12 and 22:12b provide a reason for the salvation. A reference to a kind of miraculous sight occurs at 21:19 and 22:14. And both narratives end with a concluding response at 16:13–14, 21:20–21, and at 22:14 and 15–18.

When Ishmael is rescued, however, at 21:18, it is because "I shall make him a great nation." When Isaac is saved, the only indication about why, is that it was because God knew the extent of Abraham's faith. Verses 11 to 18 also continue to use verbs related to sight, appear, vision, and to the opening of eyes. This practice began at 21:1 when Yahweh "showed" something to Abraham and at 12:7 where the narrator uses the verb "appeared" twice. It continued in chapter 15:1, where a "vision" is mentioned and 15:5 where the verb "to look" is employed.[218]

These terms continue in 16:3, where "saw" is employed, and 17:1 where the verb "appeared" is used. At 21:19, there is a reference to "opening eyes." And these reference to sight, appear, vision and the opening of eyes is not found very often in Genesis 22 in general and vv. 11–18 in particular. "See" is used in 22:12, "saw" in v. 13, and "will see" and "will be seen" in v. 14.

Many of these references use the verb *ra'ah*, which generally means "to see" or "to look." This verb appears in Genesis 6:12, 8:13, 16:13, 18:2 and 16; 19:26 and 28, as well as in 22:13. The past tense of *ra'ah*, sometimes rendered as "appeared," also is employed at Genesis 12:7, twice; 17:1; 18:1; and at Genesis 26:2. Additionally, at Genesis 15:1, the narrator uses the noun *machezeh* that generally stands for a "vision."[219]

These references do not include the several in the Abraham narrative where someone is asked to "look up and see" or "raise up your eyes and see," such as at Genesis 13:14, 22:4, and 22:13 that uses "looked up and saw."[220]

There is also an extensive vocabulary and plays on words in verses 11 to 18 that are connected to the fear of God and the fear of the Lord, not to mention the two appearances of the Angel of the Lord in Genesis 22:11–18. These come at verses 11 and 15. This material says nothing of the odd claim in these verses that the ancient Jews will "occupy the gates of their enemies," in verse 17. We will begin with this question next in this chapter.

Among the ancient Jews, the gates of the city was a place where elders gathered (Deuteronomy 21:12–19). It was also a meeting place where decisions might be made (Proverbs 31:23 and 33). If one occupied the gates of a city, it meant they could disrupt the administration of the city. At Psalm 107:15–16 and Isaiah 45:2, there are references to "shattering the gates" of the enemies. At Genesis 24:60, as well as 22:17, it also refers to the occupation or possession of the gates of one's enemies. This brings us to a discussion of the Angel of the Lord in Genesis 22:11–18.

The classical Hebrew names *Malak Yahweh* and *Malak Elohim*, or the "Angel of the Lord," and the "Angel of God," appear many times in the Old Testament and the Abraham narratives. At Genesis 16:7–14, for example, an angel appears to Hagar, and in that passage, the Angel speaks of God in the first person. Curiously enough, at Genesis 22:11–14, the Angel of the Lord also refers to God in the first person.

Verse twelve gives us a reason why God is happy that Abraham did not lay a hand on Isaac. It is "because you have feared God, and have not withheld your son from me." In verse 13, the passages in sight continue when Abraham "saw" a ram caught in the thicket by his horns. Verse 13 also employs the word *olah*, the noun for "burnt offering" again. The Hebrew for the new place name for the sacrifice is *Yahweh Yireh*, that is, "God will provide." This verse harkens back to Isaac's question about where the animal for sacrifice is to be found. At that verse, Abraham said, "God will provide the lamb for the burnt offering."

The expression *Yahweh Yireh* is similar to the reason given for why Abraham will be blessed. It is because you "feared the Lord," or *yirat Elohim*. The word *yirat* comes from the verb *ra'ra*, which generally means "to fear." Usually, this verb is employed when the fear of the Lord or the fear of God is implied. Another verb, *pahad*, is also used in classical Hebrew to express fear. The notion of the fear of God was used at Genesis 20:11 in the Hagar and Ishmael narrative. It is employed again at verse 12 of Genesis 22.

The fear of God or the fear of the Lord is also associated with many other Old Testament worthies. Jacob swears by the fear of God at Genesis 31:53. At Genesis 35:5, God sends a terror of Himself to the people. Jacob again mentions the fear of God at Genesis 46:1–7, and Joseph, at Genesis 42:18, also speaks of the fear of the Lord. It is not unusual, then, for an ancient Hebrew patriarch to be associated with the fear of the Lord or the fear of God, *Yahweh Yireh*, or *Elohim yireh*.[221]

The normal word for "ram" in v. 17 is *ayil*. It is connected to a root that means "strong." It is employed at Genesis 15:9; Genesis 22:13, two times; as well as at places like Exodus 29:15, twice and 29:17–18. Above all, of course, the ram on Mount Moriah was symbolic of Yahweh's "choosing life," in the same way the shofar at Mount Sinai also confronted Israel with the opportunity to save life.[222]

The *ayil* of Genesis 22:13 and 17 is a surrogate for Isaac's life and for the Nation of Israel. Abraham could have said no to the sacrifice, but not to choose life would have been the death of Isaac and, by extension, the death of the Nation of Israel, as well. In parallel, the death of Ishmael would have been the death of what was to be Islam.

The expression, "by myself I have sworn," is perhaps the most solemn oath that God makes in the Hebrew Bible/Old Testament. It should be regarded as an inviolable vow similar to what may be found at Isaiah 45:23, Jeremiah 22:5, 49:13, and 51:14, and at the Prophet Amos 6:8.

At any rate, because of Abraham's great faith and obedience to Yahweh, "because you have obeyed my voice," God personally vowed to establish his covenant with Abraham, as well as with his descendants—forever. The promise given to Adam and Eve in the Garden of Eden was preserved through the Godly line of Seth to Noah. And then again, after the flood, from Shem to the promised seed of Abraham.

One final feature of verses 11 to 18 involves another parallel to chapter 12 of Genesis. There at 12:2, "I will bless you now" becomes "I will greatly bless you" by the time we get to 22:17. This kind of progressive intensification is another element of the Abraham narratives. This brings us to our analysis on the fifth and final section of the Akedah narrative, verse 19, the father and son return.

The Father and Son Return: Genesis 22:19

At verse 19, we see the end of the Akedah narrative. The first consists of three parts:

1. Abraham's return to the young men, the servants.

2. They rose and went together to Beersheba.

3. Abraham lived in Beersheba.

The first of these three parts raises the obvious question, "What happened to Isaac?" There is no mention of the son in verse 19. This has led some critics to argue that the sacrifice actually did take place. Other interpreters relate that Isaac was sent to a Yeshiva, or a Talmudic academy, a great place for a young, unmarried Jewish man.[223]

Beersheba was the largest city in the Negev Desert. It is the place where Abraham made a covenant with Philistine leader Abimelech in Genesis 21. Both Isaac and Jacob later lived there, as indicated by Genesis 26, 28 and 46. The name "Beersheba" appears to be a play on words—*beer*, meaning "well," and *sheva*, meaning "oath" or "seven." If it is the latter, it may be referring back to the seven lambs in Genesis 21. It also recalls, perhaps, the seven wells dug by Isaac at Genesis 17:19.

At any rate, Beersheba, at one time or another, was the home of Abraham, Isaac and Jacob. Abraham quarreled with Abimelech over a well (*beer*) at Genesis 21:22–34. Later, Isaac argued over a well as well at Genesis 26:26–33. One aspect of the end of the Akedah narrative that is often overlooked is the importance of water in a place like the Negev. It is an extraordinary scarce commodity. The narrative ends by telling us that Abraham settled in the desert in a place where there is water, or life. This is exactly what Yahweh affirmed by saving Isaac.

Several Midrashim exists, as we shall see in the next chapter, about the ram, his two horns, and their places in the history of Judaism.

Indeed, we learn that there is a great deal to know about the mysterious ram caught by his two horns. Many of the Midrash suggest that the two horns of the ram became the two trumpets that are the *Shofarot* of God. One of the same horns blown at Mount Sinai when the Torah was given to Moses. Some traditions suggest the other horn will be blown at the End of Time to announce the arrival of the *Moshiac*, or the Messiah.[224]

There is an interesting textual problem concerning the description of the ram of the Akedah narrative. There is an unusual grammatical form employed at verse thirteen that has caused many a rabbi to scratch his head. The verse in question literally reads:

> And Abraham lifted up his eyes, and looked, and behold a ram
> **after** caught in the thicket.

The Hebrew preposition *achar* is most often rendered as "after." The word's appearance here seems somewhat clumsy and/or misplaced. To explain the meaning of this preposition at Genesis 22:13, many interpretations have been offered over the years. The most widely accepted view, however, is the one found in the King James Version of the verse that renders the sentence, "…and behold, behind him, a ram caught in a thicket."

But some of the ancient rabbis suggest that the ram only became caught in the thicket "after Abraham had seen it." There are a number of other interpretations as well, including the view that when he saw the ram, he saw the future sacrifice too. There is also some disagreement among the ancient interpreters about when Abraham saw the ram, as well as the origins of this particular ram. The *Mishnah Avot* at 5:6, for example, tells us that this particular ram "was created on the first day of creation."

The question about where Isaac is in verse 19 is not the only question that the Akedah narrative calls to mind about Abraham and his son. Consider these questions as well:

1. Why is Isaac silent and offers no resistance on Mount Moriah?

2. Why did Abraham not question God?

3. Where is Sarah, and what are her feelings and beliefs about the matter?

4. Why is the Akedah not mentioned again in the Hebrew Bible/Old Testament?

5. Why would an All-Good God prescribe such an action?

6. Why does God appear to be absurd, unethical, cruel, inconsistent, and unreliable in Genesis 22?

7. How old is Isaac when the Akedah narrative occurred?

8. Why is Genesis 22:2 the first mention of the word "love" in the Hebrew Bible/Old Testament?

9. Why does God never speak to Abraham again in the Hebrew Bible/Old Testament?

If we add our question about why there is no mention of Isaac in verse 19 of Genesis 22, that will bring the number of our questions about the narrative to ten. Throughout the remainder of this work, we will often refer back to these ten questions, so that we may more easily, at times, compare the various thinkers in this study.

This brings us to one final section of this third chapter—a return to the heuristic model with which we opened the chapter, a collection of explanations or interpretations of the meaning of the Akedah narrative.

Return to the Heuristic Model for Explaining the Akedah

At the beginning of Chapter Three, we cataloged a variety of ways that the history of Judaism, Christianity and Islam have understood the Akedah narrative. In this section, we will point out that the writers of the sacrifice of Isaac story may be employing several of these interpretations. For example, it is clear that in verse one, the narrator refers to the story as a "test" of Abraham. Earlier in this chapter, we argued that Moses went through a test as well in Exodus. Thus, the Akedah narrative calls to mind what we have called the Test View—Yahweh used suffering as a way of testing the character of Abraham.

Related to this first perspective, perhaps, is the realization that Yahweh never really wanted Abraham to go through with the sacrifice. In this sense, he may have had a Divine Plan by which everything will work out for the good in the Akedah narrative and in the history of early Judaism, as well.

It should be just as clear that what we have called the Divine Command Theory was also at work in the Akedah narrative. Abraham appears blindly to follow the command of Yahweh for no other reason than that command was not to be disobeyed. In this sense, the Deontological Theory of Ethics may have been at play in the Akedah narrative, as well. The Ten Commandments explicitly forbids murder. They do not say, "Thou shalt not kill, except under the following conditions." The prescription against murder appears to be universal and without exceptions. Thus, Deontological Theory may have been at work in the Akedah narrative, as well. It should also be clear that another way the writers may have understood the narrative, is that God used the anxiety and mental suffering caused by the command to allow Him to develop certain and important moral characteristics in Abraham's personality, perhaps in Isaac, as well.

More specifically, we have in mind here moral terms related to trust, fidelity and, dare we say, faith. Another way the writers of the Akedah narrative may have wished it to be understood is what we labeled the Moral Qualities Approach back at the beginning of Chapter Three.

In this sense, the writers also may have had in mind that Abraham and Isaac were to be moral exemplars regarding how to respond in the face of anguish and suffering. This idea of a moral exemplar, of course, is what we have called the Jobus Christi Motif, where the sacrifice of Isaac and the anguish of Abraham were used as a model for future suffering in Judaism, Christianity and Islam.[225]

Earlier, in Chapters One and Two, we have suggested that the purpose of many passages in the Old Testament, like the Akedah narrative, may have been an indication of what the ancient Jews refused to do, namely the practice of child sacrifice that went on in many of the other cultures of the Ancient Near East. In this sense, the most fundamental explanation for the Akedah narrative is what the ancient

Jews refused to do, and thus the ban on human sacrifices. Needless to say, the Jobus Christi Motif will become the underlying theme and explanation for early Christian understandings of the Akedah, where Abraham was seen as a Christ figure in the first five centuries of the Church, both East and West.

Finally, Abraham's consciousness at the time of the Akedah narrative raises the issue of whether he believed that under certain conditions the proscription against killing could be violated in what Soren Kierkegaard called a "Teleological suspension of the ethical." In this view, the rule about murder may have been broken simply because the consequences of the killing outweigh the broken universal rule.[226]

In short, from our analysis in this final section of Chapter Three, it appears as though at least all of the eight models for interpreting the Akedah narrative may very well have been at work in the sacrifice of Isaac tale. It is conceivable that any of the eight may be the most fundamental understanding of the narrative in question. We will see all eight of these models appear throughout the remainder of this history.

The subject matter of this chapter is what thinkers in the earliest periods of Judaism believed about the Akedah. Our discussion will move to that material, then, after the conclusions to this third chapter.

Conclusions to Chapter Three

The two major goals of Chapter Three have been to first, introduce a heuristic model for understanding the most fundamental meaning of the Akedah narrative of Genesis 22:1–19; and secondly, to give a close reading of the five parts of that same narrative: The Command, the Relation of Father to Son, the Sacrificial Altar, the Reward of Abraham, and the Return of Father and Son.

In the first section of Chapter Three, we introduced and discussed eight principal theories for understanding the primary meaning of the Akedah narrative. We called these the Test Perspective, Divine Plan Theory, the Jobus Christi Model, the Ban Human Sacrifice View, Divine Command Theory, the Deontological Approach, the Teleological Suspension of the Ethical Theory, and the Moral Qualities Approach.

In the second section of this chapter, we provided a short history of the figures of Abraham and Sarah, and Hagar and Ishmael, from chapter

11 of Genesis until chapter 22, the Akedah narrative. In that history, we have established certain historical facts about these Biblical characters that may relate to how best to understand the Akedah narrative.

Similarly, in the third section of this chapter, we introduced a collection of seven "background facts" that also must be remembered in the context of understanding the Akedah narrative. These facts were: child sacrifice was not unusual in the Ancient Near East, that there is evidence both for and against the practice of human sacrifice in ancient Israel, Abraham could not be the father of a great nation if he had no progeny, Kierkegaard's view is out of bounds for early Judaism, that the ancient Jews did not practice ancestor worship, and finally, the rejection of traditional inheritance views of the Ancient Near East.

These background materials were followed in this third chapter by an analysis of the five separate parts of the Akedah narrative. These parts were the following:

1. The Command to Abraham (vv. 1–3)

2. Father and Son (vv. 4–8)

3. The Sacrificial Altar (vv. 9–10)

4. The Reward of Abraham (vv. 11–18)

5. The Father and Son Return (v. 19)[227]

In each of these five sections, we have made linguistic, ethical and theological observations about the Akedah text. Along the way, we also raised some fundamental questions about the Akedah narrative, such as "Where is Isaac in verse 19?" And, what are the parallels to other patriarchs like Moses, Isaac and Jacob, not to mention Hagar and Ishmael?

Indeed, in Chapter Three, we introduced the classical Hebrew vocabulary found in Genesis 22:1–19, including verbs related to testing and the fear of God, as well as nouns related to sacrifice and burnt offering, such as *olah* and *hereq*; and words that designate wood, fire, altar and ram. We have also spoken of the extensive Hebrew vocabulary of words related to sight, appearance and associated words.[228]

Finally, in this third chapter, we returned to the heuristic model introduced in the beginning of the chapter, and have shown that the Akedah narrative, at its most fundamental level, may be understood as using all of the fourteen theories introduced there. As indicated earlier, we will turn our attention to the Akedah narrative in the earliest portions of the Jewish faith—the Talmud and the *Mishnah*.

Chapter Four:
The Akedah in Early Judaism

The meaning of the Akedah is that the divine command
itself is all one needs to determine morality.

—Kalonymus Shapira, Rabbi of Piaseczna

It was a merit of Abraham to be willing to sacrifice his
only son to his God. It was God's nature and merit that He
would not accept an immoral tribute.

—Milton Steinberg, *The Anatomy of Faith* (1960)

Even the ancients, long ago, were surprised that immediately after the Akedah—after Isaac was bound on the altar
to be sacrificed by his father at God's command, and then
just as categorically ordered to be released and not to even
so much as bruised—that immediately after that, all traces
of Isaac, son of father Abraham, disappear.

—Shalom Spiegel, *The Last Trial: The Akedah*

Introduction

The purpose of this chapter is to make some observations regarding
what the earliest sources, after the Bible, have related about the Akedah
narrative, Genesis 22:1–19, in the history of Judaism. Among these
sources, we will examine places in the Talmud, the *Mishnah*, and
other early remarks about the sacrifice of Isaac narrative in the Jewish
tradition. We will take a similar approach in Chapter Five of this study,

where we will examine the Akedah as understood by the earliest of Christian sources. We begin this chapter with what the Babylonian Talmud and the Jerusalem Talmud have had to say about the Akedah narrative at Genesis 22:1–19.

The Akedah in the Talmud

Several issues raised about the Akedah text in Chapter Three of this work also appear in the rabbis of the Talmud. For example, at tractate 89b of the *Sanhedrin*, we find the discussion of whether a genuine prophet of Judaism can call for the temporary suspension of a Torah law. The rabbis of the *Sanhedrin* say that ordinary people are required to obey the prophet, and it specifically speaks of the case of the Akedah.[229] Clearly, however, the rabbis of this section of the *Sanhedrin* refer here to the Suspension of Ethics Theory introduced in Chapter Three.

Speaking of the same issue, the Minhat Hinnukh indicates that if a believing Jew sees another disregarding the prophet's command, he may force that person to obey the command (or suspension), even at the cost of his own life.[230] The Makkot 13b applies this notion of suspending the rules by a prophet in relationship to the Akedah. The Makkot tells us that if the two lads/servants were allowed to witness the Akedah, they too would have been morally required to force Isaac to acquiesce, for his father was a prophet.[231] In fact, Rabbi Hizumi, in quoting from the Bekhor Shor, gives a reason why the two servants were kept away from the sacrifice. It was because, Rabbi Hizumi says, that Abraham worried they might have kept him from carrying out the sacrifice. Rabbi Hizumi, then, believed that Isaac was legally and morally mandated to obey the orders of his father, Abraham.[232] At the *Sanhedrin* 89b, we see the rabbis accuse the angels of condemning Abraham for making a covenant with Abimelech at Genesis 21:27–31.[233]

Another place in the Talmud, the rabbis make the claim that the test of Abraham came as the result of the patriarch failing to offer a thanksgiving sacrifice after Isaac's birth.[234] Another interpretation from the same tractate says that God tested Abraham because he questioned out loud, God's Goodness and Justice. Connected to this view is the speculation that Abraham wonders if God will fulfill His promise.[235] Here in this section of the Talmud, then, we see references to the Test

View, as well as the Isaac as Remnant Theory, as introduced in Chapter Three.

This tendency of the sages of the Talmud to find fault with Abraham, and thus, in one way or another, to say that he deserved the test, stands in marked contrast to the early church fathers, who never attach any moral blame to the patriarch. At the Babylonian Talmud's 89b, the rabbis also suggest the superiority of Isaac to Ishmael, to explain why the former was chosen, rather than Ishmael, as the designated heir.[236]

The rabbis need to have explained how the selection of Abraham could be reconciled with Deuteronomy 21:15–21, which argues for the inheritance of the firstborn son, in this case, Ishmael.[237]

Both forms of the Talmud are full of interpretations of why Abraham was so blithely willing to follow and obey the command to Abraham in the Jerusalem Talmud. At *Ta'an* 65d, for example, the rabbis say about the issue:

> May it be Your will, oh Lord, our God, that whenever Isaac's children enter into distress, and there is no one to speak in their defense, You shall speak in their defense.[238]

The Talmud seems here to be assenting to a form of the Remnant Theory. In the same text of the Jerusalem Talmud, again at 65d, tells us that, "Since Isaac was redeemed, it follows that Israel is redeemed."[239] Saadiah Gaon, in referring to this passage, relates:

> You are the Lord who chose Abram and brought him out of Ur of the Chaldeans and then named him Abraham. You made a covenant with Isaac and swore to him on Mount Moriah.[240]

The Babylonian Talmud, at *Avodah Zarah* 55a, contains a lengthy discussion of idols and idolatry, the business of Abraham's father, Terah. The final word of that debate, however, comes from Rabbi Akiba who observes:

> You know in your heart, as I know in mine, that there is nothing of worth to be found in idolatry.[241]

The Babylonian Talmud's *Baba Mezia* 87a relates a dialogue between the angels and Abraham concerning the meaning of Genesis

18:1, which suggests that the purpose of the Akedah was to make Sarah more beloved in the eyes of Abraham.[242] Gregory the Great held a similar view, as we shall see in Chapter Five, to follow.

At *Semahot* 8:11, Rabbi Akiba marvels at the love of God and is also critical of Abraham's silence. Akiba tells us:

> There are four kinds of men (the King has four sons). One is whipped and is silent; One is whipped and pleads his case; one is whipped and then says, "Hit me again;" And one is whipped and protests. Abraham is the only one who is whipped and remained silent. When God said, "Take your son..." He should have said, "But yesterday you said that through Isaac there will be integrity of the seed for me."[243]

Again, this seems like an assenting to the Isaac as Remnant Theory. The Babylonian Talmud at Sotah 6:5 ties a famous passage in the Psalms to the Akedah. The Talmud relates:

> The same angels who said, "What is man that you pay attention to him" (Ps. 8:5), also said, "Come and see the song. And when they saw Israel, they began to sing (Ps. 8:10), O Lord, our Lord, how majestic is your name in all the Earth." But Rabbi Simon ben Eleazar said, "This was only said on account of the Akedah."[244]

Another passage of the Babylonian Talmud's *Sanhedrin*, this time at 38b, suggests that the angels were jealous of humanity's special status and relationship with God. This is because, when the Divine consulted the angels about making mankind, they complained of the harm humans would bring in events like the Akedah.[245] Indeed, throughout the Babylonian Talmud, it is argued that the angels were resentful of Abraham and made a number of specific accusations against him, which they brought to God's attention.

Another Midrash from the *Sanhedrin* 89b points out the similarities between the sacrifice of Isaac and the testing in the prologue of the Book of Job. It tells us, "One day the angels came to minister to the Lord and Satan was among them. And the Lord said to Satan, "From where have you come?" Then the Talmud switches to Abraham. Then

Satan asked God, "Does Abraham fear God for nothing? He had no sons for a long time and he built altars to please you. But after his request for a child, he has forgotten you." The author of the *Sanhedrin* points out the similarity of this language to that of the first two chapters of the Book of Job.

The same tractate, *Sanhedrin* 89b, gives the following dialogue between God and Abraham:

> Sacrifice your son.
> But I have two sons.
> Thine only son.
> Each is the only son of his mother.
> Whom you love.
> I love them both.
> Isaac!

The same tractate goes on to say that Satan approached and said, "If we assay to commune with Thee, will you be aggrieved." Then, the writer employs the Midrash of Satan, pretending to be Isaac and whispering to Sarah. But Sarah does not heed the Evil One.[246]

The Babylonian Talmud, at Gittin 65b, speaks of the woman and her seven sons in Deuteronomy 26 and Second Maccabees, who suffered by death rather than bow down to idols, and says this about her sons at Gittin 65b:

> Go tell Father Abraham, "Let not your heart swell with pride.
> You built one altar, but I have built seven altars and on them
> have offered up my seven sons. What is more, yours was a
> trial, mine was an accomplished fact.[247]

In the same tractate, the mother of the seven sons also relates this about her suffering compared to that of Abraham:

> She said to him, "My son, go and say to your father Abraham,
> you did blind one son on the altar, but I have bound seven
> altars." Then she also went up onto the roof and threw her-
> self down and was killed. A voice thereupon came forth from
> Heaven saying, "A joyful mother of children."[248]

Another tractate at Mas. K'rithoth 28b, speaking of Abraham's progeny, Rabbi Eleazar said in the name of Rabbi Hinina:

All of thy children will be taught of the Lord, and great shall be the place of your children.[249]

The rabbis speak here both of the progeny of Ishmael and that of Isaac, but primarily they have in mind the descendants of Isaac. The Jerusalem Talmud, at *Shabbot* 15c, tells us that, "Those who write down blessings are like those who burn the Torah."[250] This remark was made in the context of a discussion of whether one is morally required to kill one's son if commanded by God to do so.

The Meggillah, at tractate 31a of the Jerusalem Talmud, gives a lengthy account of the relationship of Abraham and Sarah, ending the proclamation, "And God remembers Sarah."[251] Indeed, many tractates in the Jerusalem Talmud give accounts of the importance of the figure of Sarah in the development of early Judaism, such as at Mikkot 13b, for example. At this tractate, the rabbis discusses for what crimes an observant Jew "may be cut off from the community, including the moral implications for the Akedah narrative, as well as Sarah's response and death in Genesis 23.[252]

The discussion in question occurs between Rabbi Tarfon and Rabbi Akiba and the debate centers on the admission of circumstantial evidence, or only on the evidence of reliable witnesses. During the discussion, the issue of murder arises, and, consequently, the morality of the Akedah narrative. The same passage also discusses various views on sexual crimes.[253] This may be seen as a version of the Divine Plan View that God knew beforehand that it would all work out for the good.

At tractate 4a of *Ta'anit*, the rabbis, amid a discussion of the Akedah, quote directly from Jeremiah's exhortation against child sacrifice. They say it never crossed the mind of God that He would ever allow Abraham to go through with the sacrifice of Isaac.[254] This may be an application of the Sanctity of Life Theory, as described in Chapter Three.

Shabbot 88a, among many other things, suggests that the ram on Mount Moriah was a symbol of God's ability to "save life." It adds, "If you are willing to accept the Torah, that is great, but if not, here is your grave."[255] Another portion of the *Ta'anit*, at II:4 and 65d, also speaks of the Shofar in regard to the binding of Isaac. It reveals:

> May he who answered Abraham, our father on Mount Moriah, answer to you and listen to your crying voice on this day.[256]

This passage appears to be consenting to what we have called the Isaac as Remnant Theory. The rabbis in this passage are referring to the times when the ancient Jews found themselves in the midst of suffering and hardship. They seem to suggest that God will respond in precisely the same way that he responded to "our Father Abraham, on Mount Moriah."[257]

Two other tractates of the Talmud are important for our purposes. These come at *Berakoth* 62b and *Talkot* sections 99 to 102. Both of these are in the Babylonian Talmud. *Berakoth* 62b mentions the "ashes of the ram of Isaac," and "God will see for Himself a lamb," perhaps quoting Genesis 22:8.

At the Jerusalem Talmud's *Berakoth* 12d to 13a, the rabbis are engaged in a conversation about the relationship of Sarah and Abraham. In that conversation the text relates:

> It is impossible for there to be a man independent of a woman, not that it is impossible for there to be a woman without a man. Neither is it possible for both of them to be independent of the *Shekinah*.[258]

The word *Shekinah* usually translates as "dwelling" in English. The word does not appear in the Old Testament/Hebrew Bible, but it can be found throughout the Talmud. The word comes from the Semitic root SHKHN that is often employed to designate that God is present. In the case of Abraham and Sarah, the word is a sign of the great bond that dwells between them.[259]

Many places in the Babylonian Talmud tell us that, "There can be no atonement where there is no blood." This claim is made at places like Yoma 5a, Zebahim 6a, and Manahot 93b. These pronouncements, of course, were made in the context of Old Testament/Hebrew Bible sacrifice, connected to Levitical laws about those practices.[260]

At Shabbat 89b, after the rabbis praise Isaac for his refusal to protest the Akedah, the son of Abraham and Sarah observes:

Instead of acclaiming me, acclaim the Holy One, blessed be He. And with his own gaze, Isaac shows them the Holy One, blessed be He. Immediately, they lifted up their eyes upward and say, "Thou, oh Lord, are our Father, our Redeemer, from everlasting is Thy name."[261]

At the Babylonian Talmud's 57b, the rabbis discuss the remembrance of Isaac's ashes in the context of a public fast. Among these rabbis are Benaiah, Judah the Prince, Johanan and Hoshaya Rabba, who is considered the father of the *Mishnah*. All of these sages praise the faithfulness of Isaac. In fact, God says to Isaac in that same tractate, "You are an unblemished, whole burnt offering."[262] Perhaps this is another application of what we have labeled the Isaac as Remnant Theory introduced in Chapter Three of this history.

In several places in both the Babylonian and the Jerusalem Talmuds, the role of Satan is spoken of in the context of the Akedah, applications of the Influences of Demonic Forces Theory in Chapter Three. Usually, in these passages, Satan is given the responsibility of inducing Abraham to sacrifice Isaac. At *Sanhedrin* 89b, for example, Satan entices the patriarch to take his son to Mount Moriah for the purpose of sacrificing him. In the context of Genesis 22:1, "and it came to pass after these words," Rabbi Johanan tells us:

Thereupon Satan said to the Almighty, "Sovereign of the Universe, to this old man you graciously gave to the womb of a hundred-year-old woman, yet he did not sacrifice even one turtle dove or pigeon before You." God responds to Satan by saying, "And yet if I were to say to him, 'Sacrifice your son before Me,' he would do it without hesitation."[263]

Again, this appears to be a version of the Influences of Demonic Forces Theory. Later in the same work, indeed in the same tractate, Satan is allowed to tempt, or "test" Abraham to see if he would acquiesce to the entreaties of Satan. The text tells us:

On the way, Satan came towards him and said to Abraham, If
we assay to commune with you, will you be grieved? Behold,
you have instructed many and you have brought strength to
weak hands. Your words have upheld people from falling, and
you have strengthened feeble knees. But now, it has come
upon you, and you soon faint.[264]

To this, Abraham answered:

I will walk in my integrity.[265]

To which, Satan responds:

Should not your fear of God be your confidence? Who has
ever perished that has been innocent?[266]

But Abraham would not listen to Satan, and he said to him,
"Now a thing was secretly brought to me and thus have I heard from
behind a curtain, the lamb for a burnt offering, but not Isaac for a burnt
offering."[267] Then Satan replied:

It is the penalty of a liar, that should he even tell the truth, he
would not be listened to.[268]

Thus, in this Talmudic narrative, as well as many others like it,
Abraham refuses to follow the entreaty of Satan, even though Yahweh
will require the same of Abraham later in the Akedah narrative.
Nevertheless, again we have here an application of the Influences of
Demonic Forces Theory, as outlined in the third chapter of this history.

Finally, the Babylonian Talmud's *Talkot* sections 99 to 102 in
the context of crimes for which execution is morally required, the
Akedah is called into question and whether the perpetrator should be
punished capitally. After a long discussion, the sages conclude that it is
sometimes permissible for a prophet, in this case Abraham, to suspend
the normal moral dicta of traditional Judaism. Thus, the rabbis in this
passage seem to be assenting to Kierkegaard's Teleological Suspension
of the Ethical View.[269]

This brings us to a discussion of the figures of Abraham, Sarah
and Isaac, as portrayed in a text called the Genesis Rabbah, a Midrash
comprising the early views of many rabbis in the early portions of

Judaism, the topic of the next section of this fourth chapter. It is to the Genesis Rabbah, then, to which we turn next.

Abraham and Isaac in the Genesis Rabbah

The Genesis Rabbah was a Hebrew text most likely completed between 300 and 500 CE. It is a Midrash consisting of a collection of ancient, Rabbinic interpretations of *Bereshith*, or Genesis. The work is attributed to Rabbi Hoshaiah, a Palestinian Jew who lived around 200 CE. The Genesis Rabbah is an exegetical Midrash that gives consecutive expositions of the Book of Genesis, chapter by chapter and verse by verse, or even at times, word for word.

The Genesis Rabbah is divided into 101 sections. Except for seven of them, they are introduced by one or many *proems*—sometimes as many as nine. *Proem* is a Latin word that means "preface." The entire Genesis Rabbah contains 246 proems. The language of the Genesis Rabbah most resembles that of the Jerusalem Talmud. It is chiefly in Mishnaic Hebrew, with some Galilean Aramaic. The Aramaic is usually employed for the most important of the Genesis narratives.

The most relevant passages of the Genesis Rabbah for our purposes come at tractates 55 and 56. Jo Milgrom, in her excellent work, *The Binding of Isaac*, divides these two tractates into four parts. These look like this:

Part I (Sections 55:1–6b)
Part II (Sections 55:7–9)
Part III (Sections 56:1–6)
Part IV (Sections 56:7–11)[270]

Milgrom divides the two tractates into thirty paragraphs, corresponding to the edition of the Midrash Rabbah, edited by Freedman and Simon, published in London by Soncino in 1951. Tractates 55 and 56 of the *Bereshith* Rabbah make a wide range of comments about Abraham, Isaac and Sarah that we will explore. In commenting on Genesis 1:27, the Genesis Rabbah observes:

And God said let us make man...with whom is He taking counsel?

Rabbi Joshua ben Levi said,

> He took counsel with the works of Heaven and Earth, like a
> King who had two advisors without whose knowledge he did
> nothing whatsoever....

Rabbi Ammi said,

> He took counsel with his own heart. It may be compared to a
> King who had a palace built by an architect... [Genesis Rab-
> bah, 8:3.][271]

At the Genesis Rabbah's 55:4, the rabbis pay keen attention to what comes before the Akedah, a subject of interest that the early church fathers appear to have little interest. In the Genesis Rabbah 55:4, the rabbis are mostly concerned with how these events that preceded it contributed to the understanding of God's test of Abraham.[272] Here we see both reference to the Test Theory and the Sibling Rivalry Theory introduced in Chapter Three.

In the same section of tractate 55, the rabbis explain that "After these words" refers to a disagreement between Isaac and Ishmael about whom Abraham loves more. Ishmael appears to have won the argument because he was circumcised before Isaac.[273]

At Genesis Rabbah 39:9 and 55:7, the ancient sages provide a dialogue between God and Abraham that goes like this:

> God said to Abraham, "Please take your son."
> Abraham says, "But I have two sons."
> Then God says, "Your only son."
> Abraham replies, "The one is the only son of his mother, and
> so is the other."
> Then God replies, "The one you love."
> And Abraham says, "I love them both."
> God responds, "Isaac!"[274]

The rabbis then go on to disagree, of course, about why the circumlocution in this dialogue, with at least ten different responses as to the meaning of the going about the bush, as they say.[275] In 56:10 of the Genesis Rabbah, the rabbis provide a catalog of descriptions of Abraham's response to God's command in verse one. Many of these speak of a psychological turmoil that they believed went on in the soul or heart of the patriarch. Indeed, one rabbis related, "Abraham needed to 'suppress his compassion for Isaac' before he was able to follow God's command."[276]

At Genesis Rabbah 55:7, the rabbis engage in a discussion of priesthood and whether Abraham was a priest. God explains to Abraham in the passage that he had already been appointed a priest, citing Psalm 110:4, as clarification of that fact. This text tells us:

> The Lord has sworn and will not change His mind. You are a
> Priest forever, according to the order of Melchizedek.[277]

Genesis Rabbah 56:8 has a lengthy discussion of the age of Isaac at the time of the Akedah. The consensus regarding that question is that he was thirty-seven "when he was offered upon the altar."[278] Other rabbis in the Talmud, as we have seen earlier in this chapter, suggest both twenty-six and thirty-six years of age.[279] It is significant that all the rabbis in the Genesis Rabbah on this issue point out that Isaac was a mature man, strong enough to carry the wood.

At the Genesis Rabbah's 56:7, we learn that Sarah is warned by Abraham not to weep; otherwise, she might "put a blemish on the sacrifice."[280] At 56:1, in connection to the three-day journey to Mount Moriah, the rabbis provide a catalog of miraculous events that all happened on the third day.[281] And a few paragraphs later, at 56:9, in connection to sacrificing the ram rather than his son, Abraham is portrayed by the rabbis as asking God, "Shall we regard the blood of this ram as the blood of my son, Isaac?"[282] This is, perhaps, another application of the sacrifice of Isaac as Remnant Theory, which we introduced earlier in Chapter Three.

Needless to say, God's response is in the affirmative. In his response to Abraham, God uses the word *emurim* to refer to the same identity of whatever is provided as a sacrifice. Thus, in Hebrew, the ram's sacrifice is identified with the sacrifice of Isaac. Indeed, at 56:9, Abraham asks God to accept the sacrifice of the ram "as if it were Isaac." A version, perhaps, of the Atonement Theory.[283]

At 56:10 of the Genesis Rabbah, the rabbis again speak of Abraham's suppression of his emotions to question God about the sacrifice, and this overcame his love for his son, Isaac. Some say,

"Abraham suppressed his feelings in order to do the Will of God."[284] At the Genesis Rabbah's 65:10, the rabbis discuss various views of what they call the "trembling of Isaac." One explanation says this:

> When our Father Abraham bound his son on the altar, he [Isaac] looked up, and gazed at the *Shekinah*, said the Holy One, blessed be He, "If I slay him now I will make my friend Abraham suffer. Therefore, I decree that his eyes shall be dimmed."[285]

At Genesis Rabbah 56:2, the rabbis discuss the destruction of the Temple in 70 CE, and whether that signaled the end of the covenant between Yahweh and the Nation of Israel. The rabbis answer that question in the negative, citing the Lord's pronouncement, "This is My resting place forever," at Psalm 134:14.[286] The rabbis of the Genesis Rabbah, at 55:7, point out that Abraham's love of Isaac made the test of Abraham much more severe. "The purpose," they say, "is to make Isaac more beloved in the eyes of God and Abraham."[287]

Perhaps the most surprising passage in the Genesis Rabbah comes at 56:3. In the context of Isaac carrying the wood, the Genesis Rabbah says, "like a man who carries his cross on his shoulder."[288] It is interesting that after the comment is made, there is no more elucidation of what it means. Certainly, in early Judaism, it may have been a way of identifying Isaac carrying the wood with Jesus carrying his cross. More will be said of this possible interpretation in Chapter Five of this history.

This brings us to the third section of Chapter Four, where we will discuss the phenomenon of the Akedah in the Jewish *Mishnah,* what is known as the "Oral Law" in early Judaism. There are six "orders," or *sedarim*, in the *Mishnah*. Each of these consists of between seven and twelve tractates each.

The Akedah in the Mishnah

The six orders of the *Mishnah* are the following:

> The *Zeraim* (or "Seeds")
> The *Moed* (Festivals)

The *Nishim* (Women)
The *Nelekin* (Damages)
The *Kodeshim* (Holy Things)
The *Tohorot* (Purities)[289]

There are many references to the Akedah in the *Mishnah*. As Edward Kessler, in his work *Bound by the Bible*, has pointed out:

> The earliest liturgical references to the Akedah in the *Mishnah* relate to prayer on any fast day. "May He who answered Abraham our Father on Mount Moriah answer you and harken to the hearing of your voice on this day."[290]

Kessler tells us that in the earliest prayer books of Judaism, we find, "May He who answered Isaac his son, when he was bound on the altar, answer us." This prayer is called, May He Who Answered Us.[291] Indeed, many of the earliest references to the Akedah in the *Mishnah* are in relation to the establishment of *Rosh Hashanah*. In fact, it is universally accepted that the Akedah is to be identified with the *Tishrei* 2, the second day of *Rosh Hashanah*.

This connection can be found very early on in Rabbinic literature, and the mention in the Babylonian Talmud supports it at *Megillah* 31a quoted earlier in this chapter. By the third century CE, the Akedah was explicitly being connected to *Yom Ha Truah*, or the Feast of Trumpets, as *Rosh Hashanah* 16a establishes.[292] The original place in the Jewish calendar associated with the Akedah is the 14th of Nisan, and this date is later to be designated as a day for sacrifice on the *Pesach*, or "Passover."[293]

Discussed in an earlier chapter, according to the Book of Jubilees 17:15–18:19, also maintains that the Akedah took place in the month of Nisan. Prince Mastema, the fallen angel, challenges to test Abraham, which he does on the "twelfth day of the first month," and thus on the 14th or the 15th of Nisan, depending on how one counts the days. At any rate, this is an application of the Influences of Demonic Forces Theory.

In the first century CE, the entire story of Abraham and his son of promise, from birth to death, is intertwined with the Passover story. In fact, at the *Mishnah*'s *Rosh Hashanah* 10b to 11a indicates that Isaac was born on Passover. In this same section of the *Mishnah*, the near-sacrifice of Isaac is compared with the sparing of the Israelite's firstborn sons in the tenth plague. And both occur on the 14th of Nisan.

But this raises the question, of course, of why the Akedah is not now associated with Passover. Some ancient sages and contemporary interpreters, like Rabbi Kaunfer, for example, suggest that the connection between the Akedah and Passover was severed after the destruction of the Temple in 70 CE. As Rabbi Kaunfer puts the matter:

> The selection of Genesis 22 as the reading for the second day of *Rosh Hashanah* reflected a conscious decision by certain of the rabbis to move the Akedah away from its original calen-drical home: Passover. This transfer was completed in order to distance the story of the Akedah with a time of the year that was increasingly associated with another martyr/sacri-fice narrative, that of Jesus. The transfer of the Torah reading to Tishrei represented one strategy on the part of the rabbis to combat the Christological associations with the Akedah narrative.[294]

This liturgical development, which must have occurred as early as the early *Mishnah* around 200 CE, gave the rabbis a weapon that could be used by the Jews to reject early Christian understandings of the Akedah. In fact, according to Rabbi Kaunfer, the Rabbinic teaching of Isaac as an atoning sacrifice for the Jews, and for early Christians, was copied from the Messianic Community.[295]

Thus, the first associations of the Akedah with early Judaism came in relationship with the liturgical calendar. Other mentions of the Akedah in the *Mishnah* also can be seen in the *Ta'anit*, particularly in tractate 2. At *Ta'anit* 2:4, for example, we are told:

> May He who answered Abraham our Father on Mount Mori-ah, answer you and listen to your crying voice this day.[296]

The day in question, again, is *Rosh Hashanah*. At *Ta'anit* 2:4, we are again told that the salvation of Isaac is equivalent to the salvation of Israel.[297] At *Ta'anit* 3:8, the text quotes Numbers 21:8 in relationship to Exodus 17:11. And the same passage ties these other two to the Akedah.[298] Similarly, at *Ta'anit* 2:2, the *Mishnah* observes:

> You are the Lord Who chose Abram and brought him from Ur of the Chaldeans, and named him Abraham, and you made a covenant with Isaac and swore to him on Mount Moriah.[299]

The *Mishnah*'s *Ta'anit* 4:1 describes the daily "binding of the lamb offering in the Temple, with the forelegs being bound to the hind legs." The Dead Sea Scrolls text 4Q225 also employs the same verb to describe the "binding."[300] The *Mishnah*'s 2:1 and 4 also mention the Akedah. The latter speaks of the sacrifice in the context of prayers said on fast days.[301] The former tells us that, on fast days, ashes were placed on the Ark and on the heads of believers.[302] And in the same tractate at 16a we are told that this was a reminder of the ashes of Isaac.[303]

At the *Mishnah*'s *Ta'anit* 4a, as well as in passages of the *Yalkot*, implies that the injunction against child sacrifices at Jeremiah 19:5 and Micah 6:7 are explained and are referring explicitly to the sacrifice of Isaac.

At the *Mishnah*'s *Rosh Hashanah* 16a the text asked the question:

> Why is the ram's horn used? So that I might remember in your behalf the Akedah of Isaac, the Son of Abraham.[304]

The *Mishnah* at *Megillah* 31a indicates what day the reading of the Akedah is to take place during the Jewish holidays. But it also appears that the date for the Akedah has changed in the Jewish liturgical calendar, but no real reason is given in that tractate for the change.[305]

The *Mishnah*'s *Avodah Zarah* at 5:6 tells us that the ram of the Akedah was created "on the sixth day of creation, and he has been waiting since that day to fulfill his destiny."[306] In other words, this particular ram was created for this purpose since the beginning of time. Indeed, other accounts even say it was created on the first day of creation since the creation of the world. This view is similar to one found in the New Testament's First Peter 1:19–20. This text tells us,

> With the precious blood of Christ, like the perishable things like gold or silver, but with the precious blood of Christ, or that of a lamb without blemish. He was destined before the

foundation of the world, but was revealed at the end of the ages for your sake.[307]

The *Mishnah's Zakanot*, or "Remembrance," speaks of the prayer on *Rosh Hoshanah* that calls to mind the Akedah, particularly the Macedonian version published in Skopje and published in 1998.[308] And the *Parashat Vayera*, another *Mishnaic* text, gives an account of the life of Isaac from his birth until the Akedah (chapter 18:1 to 22:19).[309]

At the *Mishnah's Pirkei Avot* 5:6, we find a discussion of whether the ram was caught in a thicket or tethered, and the *Mishnah* in this passage argues for the latter view.[310] Many other references in the *Mishnah* may be found in relation to the Akedah, but we will move to the fourth section of this chapter, where we will explore the views of Philo, what is called *Pseudo-Philo*, and the historian Josephus on the meaning of the Akedah narrative.

The Akedah in Philo, Pseudo-Philo, and Josephus

Josephus Flavius, who lived from around 30 CE until the year 100, was a Romanized Jewish historian, who wrote about Israel during the time of Jesus and the New Testament period. Indeed, among other things, Josephus apparently believed that Jesus was the Messiah. In the course of his work, *The History of the Jews*, Josephus made a number of observations about Abraham, Isaac and the Akedah.

One of those observations is that Josephus believed Isaac was twenty-five years old at the time of the Akedah. The Roman historian says of Isaac, "He was old enough and strong enough to carry the load of wood sufficient to consume the intended sacrifice." Edward Kessler tells us this about Josephus' understanding of the Akedah that implies that Josephus believed in Determinism: Josephus viewed Abraham's willingness to sacrifice Isaac as a great example of faith in God. Abraham believed that nothing would "justify disobedience to God since all things have been ordained by God."[311]

Indeed, in many places in his history, Josephus suggests that "Abraham was determined to reform mankind's ideas about God." One of the ways he did that was by speaking of the "irregular patterns of the heavenly bodies," suggesting that the Jewish historian may also have been a believer in astrology.

Josephus also indicates that the place of the Akedah was "The Mount where David was to erect his Temple."[312] Josephus says nothing, however, about the sibling rivalry between Ishmael and Isaac, nor does he blame the sacrifice on Mastema or Satan. There is also nothing in Josephus' account of the Akedah about Eleazar and Ishmael's participation, nor regarding Satan's later revenge on Sarah. Here we have the employment of both the Influences of Demonic Forces Theory and perhaps the Sibling Rivalry explanation, as well.

What is central in Josephus' account of the Akedah is that the act was a form of martyrdom and that Abraham and his son were nobility. This is made clear in the following confrontation between father and son, as described by Jo Milgrom:

> When all was ready, he said to his son, "My son, myriad were the prayers in which I besought God for your birth, and when you came into the world, no pains were there that I did not lavish upon your upbringing. No thought had I of higher happiness than to see you grown to man's estate and to leave you at my death to my dominion.[313]

Milgrom seems to believe here that Josephus assents to a version of the Divine Plan Theory and that Josephus not only expressed what he saw as Abraham's love for his promised son, but he also speaks glowingly of the son's love and obedience of the father. In fact, Kessler argues that Josephus "intended to contrast his own portrayal of Isaac with that of Euripides portrayal of Iphigenia, who both approached their sacrifices with enthusiasm."

On the other hand, Josephus, like Philo, makes two major changes in the story of the sacrifice of Isaac. First, it appears that Josephus was concerned with any possible negative connotations of the binding, so he omitted the act of binding altogether. Secondly, rather than an angel halting the sacrifice, for Josephus, it is God, rather than the angel, who ordered the father to halt. Josephus implies that the reason is clear—God could not possibly order the killing of innocent human life.[314] Josephus seems to believe that Yahweh was not interested in the sacrifice per se, as much as he was the piety of Abraham. Perhaps this is because Josephus assents to the Sanctity of Human Life Theory.

Indeed, at the end of Josephus' account of the Akedah, he offers an extended description of the patriarch's piety and obedience, and a promise that Isaac will be given a "great dominion."[315] At the very end of Josephus' account, a ram "appears from obscurity," and is sacrificed, and expression comparable to "out of nowhere," in contemporary times.[316]

It is also significant that in Josephus' account of the Akedah, there is absolutely no discussion of moral merit to be found in the *Antiquities*. As the historian relates:

> It was for no craving of human blood that He had given the command; nor had he made him a father only to rob him in such an impious fashion of his offering. No, he wished but to test his soul, and to see whether even such orders as these would find the son obedient.[317]

First, it is clear that Josephus applies the Test View here. One final observation about the views of Josephus on the Akedah is that he considers Abraham's son, Isaac, to be "passionately loved." This is a requirement, Josephus says, "of a priest with a son as the sacrificial victim." However, the historian also points out that "whoever carries the wood for the burnt offering must also be tied to the priesthood."[318]

Philo Judaeus, also known as Philo of Alexandria, lived from approximately 15 BCE to 50 CE. Among other things, Philo offered the clearest views of the development of Judaism in the Diaspora. He was from a noble family of Alexandrian Jews, and he wrote extensively on the Torah, as well as many other philosophical topics. Other than Josephus, no other ancient Jewish source mentions the work of Philo. But there are, perhaps, traces of Philo's views to be found in several of the Midrash on Abraham and Isaac.

Above all, like other Jewish and Christian Alexandrians, Philo concentrates on the allegorical understandings of the biblical text. Philo wrote in Greek, and his views were preserved by the Church in the original language. Philo constructed a lengthy work on the Akedah, but it is no longer extant. Above all, Philo defends and vindicates Abraham from many hostile critics in the Greco-Roman world.

Philo gives a lengthy analysis of reasons given by others as the reason or purpose of the sacrifice. For example, he is negative of those who say they sacrifice their children "because it is custom." About this view, Philo says, these people are "among those who have very little constructive thoughts."[319] He says these people hide behind the slogan, "Everyone does it."[320] Philo is equally critical of those who say that Abraham acted out of fear, but he says, "Those people deserve no praise because praise should only be made on those who do the good."[321]

Next, Philo discusses those who perform the will of God simply for the honor of it. Philo gives four reasons why this view does not apply to the figure of Abraham. First, it was not the custom in Ur of the Chaldeans to practice human sacrifice. Secondly, he had nothing to fear from others because they did not know about his command. Thirdly, no honor should come for one who is in isolation. And finally, there was no public pressure that might have called for the sacrifice of Isaac.[322]

In an overall criticism of whom he calls "quarrelsome critics," they do not consider Abraham's actions as wonderful, and he is clearly critical of the detractors, for many of them use "vitriolic language in their diatribes."[323]

After dealing with Abraham's detractors, he turns his attention to the positive assessments that he had of Abraham and his son Isaac. He states, for example, that the name Isaac means "laughter," but it is not the laughter of amusement, but rather "the emotion that is known as joy." Philo says in the relationship of father to son, "Joy is mixed with grief, in the same way that light is not free from darkness."[324] Interestingly enough, Philo suggests that Sarah is without joy because she is "afraid to usurp something that belongs only to God."[325]

More than any two other thinkers in the ancient world, both Josephus and Philo concentrate on the obedience of both Abraham to the call and Isaac to his father. Both interpreters also put a premium on the idea of faith. Philo says of Abraham, "His love for God overcame his affection for his son." But for Philo, Abraham's response to the command was "entirely unique, a totally new and unusual series of events." In fact, Philo calls the Akedah, "Abraham's greatest event."[326] This brings us to a discussion of a text called *Pseudo-Philo*, one of the oldest Midrashic works in early Judaism.

The work known as *Pseudo-Philo* is extant in eighteen complete and three fragmentary Latin manuscripts dated from the eleventh to the fifteenth centuries. Most scholars date the original material and writing of these texts sometime between the mid-fifth and mid-seventh centuries. One of the most interesting aspects of *Pseudo-Philo*'s analysis of the Akedah is that the author relates the events of Genesis 22 to the figure of Balaam in Genesis 18. In that chapter, Balaam seeks permission to curse Israel, and that curse ultimately brings about the Akedah.

The author of *Pseudo-Philo* also ties the Akedah to two other events in the Old Testament, or Hebrew Bible. The second is Deborah's victory in Genesis 32, and the third is Jephthah's sacrifice of his daughter in Judges 11. About the latter event, God asks, "What if a dog comes out of the house first?"[327]

The writer of *Pseudo-Philo* concentrates on the willingness of both Jephthah's daughter and Isaac in their respective narratives. *Pseudo-Philo* quotes Deuteronomy 6:5 that tells us:

You shall love the Lord your God with your whole heart, with your whole soul, and all your might.

For *Pseudo-Philo*, the "with all your heart" refers to Abraham and Jephthah. The "with all your soul" refers to Isaac and Jephthah's daughter.[328] Like Philo and Josephus, the writer of *Pseudo-Philo* believed that the Akedah was a source for controversy and attacks for "those who malign God." Finally, the writer of *Pseudo-Philo* explains that the test of the Akedah took place as an example to other believers, for it "made you [Abraham] known to those who do not know you."[329]

The final section and source of early ancient Jewish views of Abraham and Isaac, as well as the Akedah narrative, is a number of texts found among the Dead Sea Scrolls that speak of the subject matter at hand. It is to the Dead Sea Scrolls, then, to which we now turn.

Abraham and Isaac Among the Dead Sea Scrolls

A variety of texts found among the Dead Sea Scrolls are related to the figures of Abraham and Isaac and the Akedah. Among these texts is a manuscript known as the Genesis Apocryphon, another called The

Book of Isaac, as well as several references in finds at Cave 4 of the Dead Sea Scrolls. The Jewish Apocryphon is a first-person narrative by Abraham, written in Aramaic. In Cave 4, at least three mentions of Abraham and the Akedah are relevant for our purposes.

A fourth text of some relevance, discovered in Cave 1, consists of several fragments of Genesis, including Genesis 22:13–15. There are also fragments related to Genesis 23:17–19 and 24:22–24, as well as Genesis 21:13. In regard to this manuscript from Cave 1, the Aramaic gives us this for the beginning of Genesis 22:13–15:

> So Abraham lifted up his eyes and looked, and saw that be-
> hind him a ram caught in a thicket by his horns.[330]

This text from Cave 1 continues with a fairly accurate Aramaic rendering of Genesis 22:14–15. The fragment called The Book of Isaac consists of several chapters on the life of Isaac corresponding to Genesis 15 to 22. The fragment also found in Cave 1 is not related to any known Hebrew work in the ancient world.[331]

Of the Dead Sea Scroll texts that are most important for our purposes are three fragments that come from a text that is designated as 4Q225. The first of these fragments suggest that God tested Abraham because of the accusations of Mastema. The fragment says that after Abraham named his son, the Prince of Mastema came to God and accused Abraham of bad behavior in regard to Isaac. Like some other Midrashim, this text from Cave 4 blames the tempting of Abraham on Mastema. Again, we see here applications of the Test Theory, as well as the Influences of Demonic Forces Approach.

In the second fragment on Abraham and Isaac in 4Q225, it is mentioned that Abraham and Isaac saw a "cloud" that "enveloped the mountain." Neither of the lads, or servants, however, appear to perceive the cloud. Abraham identifies the cloud as the *Shekinah*, that is, with the "Presence of God." Later, Midrashim, like the Pirkei de-Rabbi Eliezar, speaks of a "pillar of fire that extends from the Earth to the Heavens."[332]

In the third fragment on Abraham and Isaac designated as 4Q225, we find the longest narrative among the Dead Sea Scrolls. In this fragment, Isaac asks his father about the lamb for sacrifice. This is what comes next in the fragment in question:

Isaac said to his father Abraham, "Here are the fire and the
wood, but where is the lamb for the whole burnt offering?"
And Abraham said to his son Isaac, "God will provide the lamb
for Himself." Then Isaac said to his father, "It is well." The Angels of holiness were standing weeping above the altar...And
the Angel Mastema was happy and said of Isaac, "Now he
will perish." And in all this the Prince of Mastema was testing
whether he would be found weak, and whether Abraham
would be found faithful entirely to God.[333]

Needless to say, this passage diverges in several ways from the
traditional Masoretic text, which says nothing of Mastema, nor the
idea that a host of angels could be seen weeping over the altar. 4Q225,
however, as we have seen is not the only text in the Jewish ancient world
where some figure of the Demonic, either Mastema, a fallen angel or
Satan, are attributed, or are connected, to the cause of the Akedah.

One final comment about the Akedah, as it appears in the Dead
Sea Scroll texts, is that Cave 4 has the best examples and fragments on
the Akedah and is the same cave that has the most relevant fragments
of the Book of Job in the Dead Sea Scrolls, as well.[334] This brings us
to the major conclusions we have made in this chapter of the study of
Jewish, Christian and Islamic on the sacrifice of Isaac. The principal
subject matter of Chapter Five to follow is the views of the Akedah in
the earliest centuries in the Christian tradition up to around the year
1000 CE.

Major Conclusions of Chapter Four

In the first section of Chapter Four, we have analyzed and discussed
many places in the Babylonian Talmud and the Jerusalem Talmud,
where the sacrifice of Isaac is presented and/or discussed. Selections
from the *Avot Zara*, the *Sotah*, the *Gittin*, as well as the *Talkot*, the
Megillah, the *Berakoth*, and many comments in the Talmud from other
tractates, have been analyzed and discussed in the beginning of Chapter
Four.

This initial section of Chapter Four was followed by a description
of several passages in the Genesis Rabbah, where the test of Abraham

is in center stage. In our analysis, we have seen many passages that reflect the views of the writers of the Masoretic text. We have also seen a number of positions on Abraham and Isaac that diverge in whole or in part with the traditional Hebrew version of the Akedah narrative. These divergent issues include the age of Isaac at the time of the sacrifice, the roles of Sarah and the two servants in the narrative, and the possibility that the Demonic may have served a role in the drama.

In the third section of this chapter, we analyzed and discussed many places in the *Mishnah*, where discussions of Abraham and Isaac can be found. Among the *Mishnah* we have dealt with have been tractates of the *Ta'anit,* the *Mishnah*'s *Rosh Hashanah* text, and the *Pirkei Avot*. For the most part, these passages are best seen as a companion piece to the insights from the Talmud.

Following the section on the *Mishnah* in Chapter Four, we introduced the ideas of three other ancient Jewish thinkers who have commented at some length on the Akedah narrative. These views were those by Josephus, Philo of Alexandria, and what has come to be known as *Pseudo-Philo*. In this material, we have seen observations about the place of the sacrifice, about the motives and the moral character of the command, as well as original observations about the ram and the binding.

In a fifth and final section of Chapter Four, we enumerated and discussed several places in the Dead Sea Scrolls where Abraham, Isaac, and/or the Akedah were a subject for discussion. Indeed, we introduced and then discussed a text called The Book of Isaac, the Jewish Apocryphon, a first-person narrative told from the perspective of Abraham, and, most importantly, three fragments about the Akedah from the text usually designated as 4Q225.

Again, in this material, we have seen both parallels to the Masoretic text and some profound differences, such as the reliance on the figure of Mastema in the fragments from 4Q225, as well as the angels weeping over the sacrificial altar during the events of the Akedah.

We also stated in Chapter Four that a tractate of the Babylonian Talmud at *Sanhedrin* 89a points to the similarity of the language about the testing of Job to that of the testing of Abraham in Genesis 22. In fact, the Hebrew word *nasah*, or "to test," is employed at Genesis 22:1, as well as the Book of Job 4:2. At the Babylonian Talmud's *Ta'anit* 4a, the rabbis also pick up on this notion of "testing." But they also take another step—that God never intended Isaac to be sacrificed.

Another Midrash also holds a similar view on the Prophet Jeremiah's 7:31 that God never wanted the sacrifice of Isaac by his father, Abraham. This Midrash quotes the Lord, "And that never entered my mind."

Finally, we also pointed out that the principal findings on the Akedah, found in Cave 4 of the Dead Sea Scrolls, is precisely the same cave where the most important fragments on the Book of Job also may be found. Perhaps this is not surprising given that these two narratives of Abraham and Job are the most important texts in the Hebrew Bible Old Testament about the Problem of Evil and Theodicy, as well as moral dilemmas that arise in the context of discussions of the nature, and the extent, of the Moral Good.

We shall now turn our attention to perspectives of Christin thinkers on the Akedah in the first one thousand years of Christianity, from the New Testament Period and the early church fathers, up to the beginning of the High Middle Ages, around the year 1000 CE.

As we have seen in this fourth chapter, the Akedah narrative of Genesis 22:1–19 has had an important place in the history of the Jews from the earliest portions of the history of the Jews. The Talmud, the *Mishnah*, Midrashim, and historians like Josephus, and theologians like Philo, all have made extensive commentaries on the sacrifice of Isaac narrative.

Along the way in this chapter, we also identified a host of themes that will be returned to throughout the remainder of this history of interpreting the Akedah in Judaism, Christianity and Islam. Among these themes and questions we have seen, include the following:

- Why does Abraham not complain?
- Why did Isaac disappear from the text at verse 19?
- What is Sarah's attitude toward the Akedah?
- How is Sarah's death in chapter 23 related to the events in chapter 22?

- What role did the Demonic (Mastema and/or Satan) play in the Akedah story?

- How is the Akedah narrative related to other biblical texts like Jephthah and his daughter?

- What role does fear play in the Akedah narrative?

- What role does faith play?

- What is the relationship between the saving of Isaac in Genesis 22 and the survival of the Nation of Israel?

- How is the Akedah narrative related to the earliest of Jewish liturgies?

- What kind of criticisms existed in the ancient world regarding the Akedah?

- What role did sibling rivalry play in the tale?

- What role does the *Shekinah* have in the Akedah narrative?

- How old was Isaac during the Akedah?

- Why was the date for the reading of the Akedah changed in the *Mishnah*?

This brings us to Chapter Five and an examination of the earliest Christian sources on Genesis 22:1–19, the story of the sacrifice of Isaac.

Chapter Five:
The Akedah in Early Christianity

Isaac, the passive victim of Genesis 22, who emerged in the Targumic tradition as a prototype whose ordeal has a saving effect in Israel.

—Jo Milgrom, *The Akedah*

Was it not by his action, in offering his son Isaac upon the altar that our Father Abraham was to be justified?

——The Epistle of James 2:21

By faith Abraham offered up Isaac…For he reckoned that God had power even to raise people from the dead—and from the dead He did, in a sense, receive him back.

—Hebrews 11:17–18

Introduction

The principal purpose of this fifth chapter is to explore the views of the earliest Christian thinkers on the phenomenon of the Akedah. We will begin by carefully looking at the places in the New Testament, where the figures of Abraham and Isaac are discussed. Followed by the second section of Chapter Five on the earliest of the church fathers on the sacrifice of Isaac, including a figure known as Melito of Sardis in the second century CE, as well as other early church fathers, like Origen, Cyril of Alexandria, Clement of Alexandria, Justin Martyr, John Chrysostom, and many other Christian thinkers before the High Middle Ages, around the year 1000 CE.

This brings us to an analysis of the many places in the New Testament where Abraham, Isaac, and/or the Akedah are mentioned or discussed. As we shall see, there is a plethora of New Testament sections that speak of these phenomena.

Abraham, Isaac and the Akedah in the New Testament

The very opening line of the New Testament speaks to the connection between the patriarch Abraham and the Christian faith. Matthew 1:1 informs us:

> An account of the genealogy of the Messiah, Jesus, the son of David, the son of Abraham.[335]

A few Chapters later, at 5:17, Jesus again asserts this connection to the patriarchs of the Old Testament when he observes:

> Do not think that I have come to abolish the Law or the prophets. I have come not to abolish but to fulfill.[336]

Another important New Testament passage where the Akedah narrative is mentioned can be found at Hebrews 11:17–19, where the text informs us:

> By faith, Abraham...offered up Isaac...for he reckoned that God had power even to raise people from the dead—and from the dead, He did, in a sense, receive him back.[337]

The Epistle of James also refers to Genesis 22 when it says, "Was it not by his action, in offering his son Isaac upon the altar that our Father Abraham was justified."[338] As Jo Milgrom observes about this passage: "Although Isaac is not specified here as a type of Jesus, an unmistakable resemblance suggests itself."[339]

In the Book of Romans 8:32, Saint Paul speaks of God, "giving His only son." The same phrase appears in the Gospel of John 3:16, which echoes Genesis 22:12, and tells us, "You did not withhold your son, your only one."[340] The Epistle of Barnabus, a noncanonical work, was completed sometime between 70 CE and 132 CE. The text of Barnabus is preserved in a fourth-century codex called Codex Sinaiticus. The text speaks of Isaac in connection to a discussion of fasting:

The Lord gave such a commandment to fast, since He was
destined to offer the vessel of the Spirit as a sacrifice of our
sins, so that the "type" which is based on Isaac's having been
offered up on the altar, also might be fulfilled.[341]

The Acts of the Apostles 20:28 also appears to tie the sacrifice of
Isaac to God sacrificing His son. This New Testament text reveals:

Keep watch over yourselves and over all the flocks of which
the Holy Spirit has made you overseers to shepherd the
Church of God that He obtained with the blood of His son.[342]

At the close of Second Corinthians 6:16–18 in the New Testament
relates:

What agreement has the Temple of God with idols? For we
are the Temple of the Living God, as God has told us: I will live
with them and walk among them, and I will be their God, and
they shall be my people. Therefore, come out from them, and
be separated from them, says the Lord, and touch nothing un-
clean. Then I will welcome you and I will be your Father, and
you shall be my sons and daughters, says the Lord Almighty.[343]

Some scholars point to the Gospel of Luke 1:31 as another
parallel to the Akedah narrative. The verse tells us, "And now you will
conceive in your womb and bear a son and you will name him Jesus.
He will be great and he shall be called the Son of the Most High. And
the Lord will give him the throne of his ancestor David. He will reign
over the house of Jacob forever."[344] This is perhaps a use of the Isaac
as Remnant Theory.

Philippians 2:7 observes that Jesus Christ "though he was in the
form of a God, did not identify himself with God, but he emptied himself
taking the form of a slave, being born in the human likeness."[345] Again,
some scholars like Edward Kessler, for example, identify this New
Testament passage with the Akedah narrative.[346] Similarly, it has been
suggested by some New Testament scholars that the Akedah story may
have influenced Paul in several passages in his Letter to the Galatians,
such as 1:4–5 and 2:20, for example.

In the first of these, Paul speaks of Jesus Christ, "who gave himself for our sin to set us free from the present evil age, according to the will of our God and Father, to whom be the glory forever and ever, amen." At Galatians 2:20, Paul tells us the following, "And it is no longer I who live, but it is Christ who lives within me. And the life I now lead is in the flesh by faith in the Son of God who loved me and gave himself to me." In these two passages from Galatians, Paul is clearly endorsing what we have called the Atonement Model back in Chapter Three of this history.

In a third passage from Galatians 6:14, as Kessler has pointed out, other New Testament scholars, like Chilton and Davies, have made the identification of this passage with the Akedah story. Similarly, at Romans 11:25, Paul speaks of "all of Israel being saved," perhaps a comment that ties the Akedah narrative to the death and resurrection of Jesus Christ. If so, then Paul is assenting to the Jobus Christi Model we have introduced back in Chapter Three of this history.

For the most part, Paul places Golgatha as the central place of the new faith. If, in Isaac's sacrifice, there was something of merit for the Nation of Israel, at Golgatha, there was something to affect the whole world, and to redeem it from its sin, and to deliver it from death. Paul points out that from these two calamities that came to the world through the Serpent's plotting, an indication of the Influences of Demonic Forces Theory, "from these calamities, there could neither be escape nor liberations, had it not been for the Father offering His only son."[347]

Paul points out that what is different from Abraham is that he did not finish what he began, whereas, with Jesus, the son actually was crucified. The sin of Adam's rebellion, Paul says, brought guilt to all of humanity. By the resurrection, however, he was brought back from the dead so that he might be the first of all those who sleep in the dust to awake to life.[348]

Perhaps the most relevant Pauline passage, in reference to the sacrifice of Isaac, comes at Romans 8:32–33, where Paul tells us, "He who did not withhold his own Son, but gave him up for all of us, will he not with him also give up everything else? Who will bring any charge against God's elect? It is God who does the justifying."

Paul seems to imply that this was all part of a Divine Plan from the beginning of time, whereby the firstborn of Creation should also be the firstborn of Resurrection. All who are baptized in Christ cleave to him, to his death, and to his rising again. With Christ, so that the evil impulse may be slain within them and the old Adam comes to death. But with the New Adam, one of Paul's names for Jesus, humans are washed clean of sin and freed from the obligations of the Old Law.[349]

Even as early as the Epistle of Barnabus, which was written in Greek sometime between 70 CE and 132, makes it one of the earliest Christian writings outside the New Testament.[350] The epistle survives in a fourth-century manuscript in which it comes after the books of the New Testament and before the Shepherd of Hermas, another early Christian work usually dated to the first half of the second century CE.

The Epistle of Barnabus is important for our purposes because, in that text, Isaac is referred to as the prototype for the suffering and the trials of Jesus. Irenaeus, Bishop of Lyons, exhorts Christians that in their faith, they too must be on the alert to take up the cross just as Isaac bore the wood for the woodpile of the burnt offering. This image of every Christian bearing his own cross became a ubiquitous one in the early centuries of Christianity and continues even to this day.

It is in the New Testament, then, that we find the first uses of the Jobus Christi Model, as well as the foundations for subsequent employments of the same model in the Christian tradition.

Indeed, by the fifth century, Isaac was called, "The sheep for the burnt offering," for he "threw himself down before his father like a sheep to be sacrificed." From the fifth century on, Isaac and Jesus were often referred to as "the lambs of God." In that regard, the Gospels set the date for the death of Jesus to be on the Passover holiday, and early Christians also saw this as the period of the sacrifice of Isaac.

Perhaps the New Testament work that tells us the most about the sacrifice of Isaac is the Letter to the Hebrews. One reason this is true is that Hebrews points out a number of features about Abraham's faith. For example, at 4:17–21, the text mentions the patriarch's faith in the promise he had been given that he would have great progeny. At 11:8–9, Hebrews speaks of Abraham's faith that he could leave his homeland and travel to a promised foreign land.

At Hebrews 11:17–19, we see an examination of the relationship of faith in the presence of suffering. The text puts Abraham in the presence of like-minded Jewish patriarchs, such as Isaac, Jacob and Joseph, all of whom prevailed in situations of deep and extended suffering. And again, these acts of faith also threatened the continuation of the promised Kingdom of God for the ancient Jews.

In chapters 7 and 11 of Hebrews, we also learn that in Christianity, we find a capacity to raise people from the dead. And in Hebrews 7, we also learn that the priesthood of the New Covenant is to be seen as far superior to the Levitical priesthood of the Old Testament. A variety of other New Testament passages, including non-canonical, also speak of the Akedah and its relationship to the models we have called the Jobus Christi Theory, as well as the Atonement rubric discussed in Chapter Three of this history. In the next section of Chapter Five, we shall examine and discuss Christian attitudes toward the Akedah during the first five centuries of Christianity.

The Akedah in Early Christianity: First to Fifth Centuries

Of all the many commentaries on the Akedah in the first five centuries, by far the fullest treatment of Genesis 22 can be found in the work of Second Century Bishop of Sardis, Melito, who died around 180 CE. The city of Sardis was near Smyrna in Anatolia. In his treatment, Melito was coming from the point of view that Christianity was still considered a sect by the ancient Jews, and persecuted by the Roman Empire.

Melito's point of view, therefore, was coming from the fact that the New Testament was not yet considered to be authoritative sacred scripture. His polemical views showed that the old view of the Old Law was inadequate for discussing the sacrifice of Isaac. Most of what Bishop Melito says about the matter comes from three separate fragments of a work called the Paschal Homily.[351] The first fragment is quite instructive in understanding the earliest view of the importance of the Akedah for the beginning of Christianity. In that fragment, Melito tells us this:

> He was bound as a ram as is said about our Lord Jesus Christ...
> and he bore the wood on his shoulders, being led to be
> sacrificed as Isaac by his Father to the mountain for sacrifice,

whom when he had bound him, he placed on the wood for
the offering... Isaac, however, was silent bound, as a ram,
neither opening his mouth nor making a sound with his voice.
For neither fearing the knife, nor trembling at the fire, nor
grieving because he was about to suffer, he courageously bore
the type of the Lord. Isaac, then, was set forth in the midst
bound as a ram and Abraham stood alongside, holding the
bare knife, not ashamed to slay his son.[352]

Thus, for Bishop Melito, both Isaac and Jesus were bound and led to sacrifice. Jesus carried his cross, and Isaac carried the wood. Both traveled fearlessly and voluntarily. Both moved silently and without apparent grief. But Melito separates the two narratives when he observes, "Christ suffered, and Isaac did not."[353] Melito's conclusion about this difference is that "Israel's claim to God's mercy is based on an inadequate sacrificial offering." Only to be replaced, of course, by the suffering and death of Jesus Christ to die for our sins.[354]

The second fragment from Bishop Melito's Paschal Homily complements the first to a great degree. "When the lamb was sacrificed," says Melito, "It redeemed Isaac." This, of course, is another use of the Atonement Theory.[355] Consequently, the ram appears as a "type of Christ," and Isaac becomes a way of "redeeming Israel." Thus, the Church, the New Israel, is redeemed by the sacrifice of Jesus, superseding the old, unredeemed Israel.[356] Thus, it appears that Melito assents to the Jobus Christi Model and the Isaac as Remnant Theory, at the same time.

In the third fragment from Melito, we see a further expansion of the use of the Jobus Christi and the Atonement models from Chapter Three. The bush, by which the ram is entangled, now becomes the Cross, and the place of the Akedah ordeal, at least for Bishop Melito, now becomes Jerusalem.[357]

Thus, in the work of Bishop Melito of Sardis, we see the first Christian evidence in the direction of the combination of the Jobus Christi Model with the Atonement Point of View. Both Jesus dying for the sins of his followers and Isaac dying for the reinvigoration of Israel may find their roots in a passage found in Fourth Maccabbes 6:29.

All tolled, Bishop Melito finds eight parallels between Isaac and Jesus. These may be summarized this way:

1. Isaac carried the wood, and Jesus carried his cross.

2. Both remained silent, suggesting their acceptance of the sacrifice.

3. Isaac, like Jesus, carried with fortitude the model of the Lord.

4. Jesus, like Isaac, knew what will befall them.

5. Both Isaac and Jesus were bound.

6. Both were led to the sacrifice by their fathers, which caused great astonishment.

7. Neither was sorrowful at their impending sacrifice.

8. Both Isaac and Jesus are sacrificed on a mountain or hill.[358]

These comments by Bishop Melito remind us of a passage from the Genesis Rabbah, "And Abraham placed the wood of the burnt offering on Isaac, his son, like a man who carries his cross on his shoulder." This brings us to a variety of other Christian thinkers in the first five centuries on the sacrifice of Isaac. Another second-century Christian text, the Epistle of Diognetus, turns its attention to the Akedah. This text tells us:

But God was patient, He bore with us, and out of pity he took our sins upon Himself. He gave up His own son as a ransom for us, the Holy One for the Lawless, the innocent one for the wicked, the righteous for the unrighteous, the imperishable for the perishable, the immortal for the mortal...Of the sweet exchange.[359]

Hippolytus of Rome, who lived from around 170 to 235 CE, in his *Commentary of the Song of Songs*, relates that "The blessed Isaac became desirous of the anointing and he wished to sacrifice himself for the sake of the world."[360] Church Father, Irenaeus, in his work, *Against Heresies*, around the year 180 CE, at Book IV, Chapter 5, makes this observation about Abraham:

> Righteously, also the apostles, being of the race of Abraham, left the ship and their Father and followed the Word. Righteously also do we, possessing the same as Abraham, and taking up the cross as Isaac did the wood, follow Him. For in Abraham man had learned beforehand, and had been accustomed to follow the Word of God. For Abraham, according to his faith, followed the command of the Word of God, and with a readied mind delivered up as a Sacrifice to God His only begotten and beloved, in order that God might also be pleased to offer up for all his seed His own beloved and only-begotten Son, as a sacrifice for our redemption.[361]

Another Christian and Alexandrian scholar and ascetic who wrote about the Akedah narrative was Origen (184–253 CE). In his *Homilies on Genesis,* he makes a number of observations about the story of Abraham and Isaac in Genesis 22. For instance, Origen reminds us that Isaac was not only a victim of sacrifice but was also a priest, because "whoever carried the wood to a sacrifice must also have borne the office of priest."[362] This view was most likely borrowed from Philo, another Alexandrian who also indicated that Abraham began "the sacrificial rite as a priest." Origen's conclusion about this matter is clear: if Abraham was a priest, then Isaac was like a Christ-figure, even though Christ was a priest forever.[363]

Another observation of Origen regarding the Akedah narrative is the Alexandrian's quotation of Psalm 110:4 that parallels the Christ narrative by reference to the figure of Malchizedech for the purpose of claiming the superiority of Christ's priesthood over that of Levitical priesthood in the Old Testament.[364] Origen also quotes from Psalm 110 to point out the obsolete character of Temple worship. Christ was viewed by Origen as a High Priest, after the order of Malchizedech, and not after the order of Aaron.[365]

In Origen's *Homilies on Genesis,* he shows several affinities to rabbinic literature concerning the Akedah narrative. They use the same scripture passages to speak of the sacrifice. Both believe the narrative is principally about priesthood and authority. In Origen's view, Abraham is a priest forever, and in a similar way that Jesus is always to play the role of the priest.[366]

Finally, in his Genesis homilies, Origen writes a great deal about the three-day journey by Abraham and Isaac to Mount Moriah as a parallel to the three days that Jesus was in the tomb, as well as the parallel that afterward God can be seen as a sign of life in both of the narratives. For Isaac, his salvation from the sacrifice, for Jesus, of course, his resurrection from the dead.[367]

Clement of Alexandria (ca. 150–215) was another second- and third-century Christian thinker who wrote about the Akedah. Clement, who taught in the Catechetical School of Alexandria and knew a great deal about Greek philosophy and literature, also emphasized the three-day journey and its parallel to the Resurrection of Jesus.[368] Clement also makes the connection in his *Homilies of Isaac* carrying the wood to his sacrifice and Jesus carrying his cross to his death.[369]

In his *Homilies*, Clement of Alexandria also adopts the Jobus Christi and the Atonement models from Chapter Three. Clement puts the matter this way:

> He [Jesus] is Isaac...who is a type of the Lord, a child as a son; for he was the son of Abraham as Christ is the Son of God, and a sacrifice of the Lord, but he was not immolated as the Lord. Isaac only bore the wood of the sacrifice, as the Lord the wood of the Cross.[370]

Clement finishes his thought:

> Isaac did everything but suffer, as was right, yielding the precedence of suffering to the Word. Furthermore, there is an imitation to the divinity of the Lord in not being slain. For Jesus rose again after his burial having suffered no harm, like Isaac released from his sacrifice.[371]

It should be clear that Clement of Alexandria was a proponent of the Atonement Theory, as well as the Jobus Christi model. We find that Clement was also a proponent of the Isaac as Remnant Theory. We also may add the view of the Divine Plan Theory, in Clement's mention of an "imitation to divinity."

In places in *Homilies,* Clement suggests that Isaac was a type of Christ because he was returned to his father Abraham in the same way that Jesus was returned to His Father, God. For Clement, then, the Akedah should be viewed as a pale shadow of a sacrifice to come, one in which the sacrifice will atone for all the sins of humankind. This is another indication of a belief in the Atonement Model introduced in Chapter Three of this history.

Another early church Alexandrian thinker, Cyril of Alexandria, also wrote about Abraham and Isaac and their story of sacrifice. Cyril, who lived from 376 until 444, was the Patriarch of Alexandria. His time in office was characterized as full of controversies, including his famous dispute with Nestorius and his presiding over the execution of female philosopher Hypatia.[372]

Carol Delaney, in her book *Abraham on Trial,* sums up a number of the early church fathers on the Akedah narrative. She relates:

> Origen, writing in the early third century, devoted a large section of his Homilies on Genesis to the figure of Abraham. Ambrose, in the fifth century, wrote two books on him. Gregory of Nyssa, Chrysostom, and others preached about him regularly. Cyril of Alexandria in the early fifth century discusses him extensively in a book on Genesis and in his Easter Sermon. And Augustine devotes a dozen chapters to him in *The City of God*, and numerous other writers hold him up as a model and example for Christians.[373]

Delaney says of Cyril of Alexandria that the patriarch believed that Abraham preferred the love of God over the love of his own son, Isaac. He says, "Likewise, we must as Christians prefer the love of God over that of those closest to us, as well as the love for ourself."[374] For Cyril, as for most of the early church fathers, Isaac is to be seen "as a type of Christ"—the Jobus Christi Model. And like many of the Christian thinkers before him, like Origen and Irenaeus, for example,

Cyril of Alexandria employed the Atonement Model, as well as the Jobus Christi Theory introduced back in Chapter Three of this history of attitudes toward the Akedah.

More than any of the other early church fathers, Cyril of Alexandria (376–444), who was Patriarch of Alexandria from 412 until his death in 444, writes at great length about the significance of why Isaac was not sacrificed. Cyril maintains that no other Biblical figure, including Isaac, could approach the status of Jesus, who was the first and the only person to die and, at the same time, at least according to Cyril, to defeat death.[375]

Cyril of Alexandria was known to his contemporaries as the "Pillar of Faith." He also holds some distinct views on Abraham and Isaac, not held by the rabbis or other church fathers. For one, Cyril, unlike the rabbis, believed that Isaac was not a child. Secondly, only Christ suffered and died, only to live again, while Isaac suffered, did not die, and thus did not live again. To that end, Cyril believed that the Akedah was a pale comparison to the death and resurrection of Jesus.[376]

Thirdly, Cyril put more emphasis than the rabbis on the importance of the spilling of the blood of Isaac. Cyril maintains that it was irrelevant whether Isaac's blood was spilled or not, Cyril was apparently aware of the Midrash that the sacrifice actually did take place. Indeed, more than any other church father, much of what Cyril says about the Akedah appears to be little more than responses to earlier Rabbinic materials. Nevertheless, Cyril appears to be a proponent of the Isaac as Remnant Theory, as well.

In fact, earlier in Alexandria in the writings of Athanasius (296–373) whose episcopate lasted forty-five years, also put much emphasis on the fact that Isaac did not shed a drop of blood, while at the same time, in a Paschal letter, the Coptic bishop warned against any of his followers to practice Passover. Indeed, about the Akedah, Athanasius suggested that it was through the expectation and the vision of Christ that Abraham had experienced any festive joy in his later life.[377]

For Athanasius, it is clear that the subject of the Akedah was a subject of disagreement between Christians and Jews. However, the figure of Isaac was of particular importance for the early Christians because he is a model for Christ, but also offers a prophecy of "the one who is to come."[378] Like Cyril, after him, it is clear that Athanasius knew a great deal about Midrashic comments on the Akedah. But Athanasius puts far more theological emphasis on the figure of Abraham than did many of the other early church fathers, including Cyril.

Finally, another early church father who made many observations on the sacrifice of Isaac is Gregory of Nyssa (335–395). For example, Gregory observed that Abraham's love for Isaac "made the Test even more severe." The purpose "was to make Isaac more beloved" than he had been earlier in Abraham's life.[379] Here Gregory assents to the Test View of explaining the Akedah as introduced in Chapter Three.

Gregory of Nyssa also composed the following imaginary dialogue between Abraham and God:

> Why do you command these things, oh Lord, On account of this you made me a father, so that I now could become a child-killer? On account of this you made me taste the sweet gift so that I could become a story for the world. With my own hands will I slaughter my own child and pour an offering of the blood of my family to you. Do you call for such things and do you take delight in such a sacrifice? Do I kill my son by whom I was expected to be buried? Is this a marriage chamber I prepare for him? Is this the feast of marriage that I prepare for him? Will I not light a marriage torch for him, but rather a funeral pyre? Will I crown him in addition to these things? Is this how I will be a Father of the Nations, one who has not produced a child?[380]

In this passage, Gregory appears to combine the Sanctity of Human Life Theory with the Isaac as Remnant View, in regard to the "Father of many nations" comment "one who has not produced a child," in this case, Isaac.

Gregory of Nyssa also posits a reason why the two lads, or servants, were left behind. This was to ensure that they would not interrupt the sacrifice in any way.[381] Regarding Isaac's age during the Akedah narrative, Gregory observes, "He was old enough to be considered for marriage and to be able to carry the wood."[382]

In Gregory of Nyssa's commentary on Genesis, he also raises the issue of what is more astounding, the courage of the father or the obedience of the son? Gregory's answer to this question is this:

At which of the two should I be more amazed? The one who throws his hand upon his son for the love of God, or the one who obeys his father even unto death. They strive for honor with each other, one lifting himself above nature, the other reckoning that disobedience towards his father was more difficult than death itself.[383]

Gregory of Nyssa also associates the Akedah narrative with Isaiah 9:6, where he finds a parallel between the sacrifice of Isaac narrative where an angel interrupts the sacrifice and the appearance of a "wonderful counsel" in the Isaiah story.[384] Gregory of Nyssa says about Genesis 22:8, that the purpose "is to test the soul of Abraham." This, of course, is an assenting to the Test View in regard to explaining the Akedah narrative.[385] Finally, Gregory suggests that Abraham judged his wife Sarah too critically, something also found in the Rabbinic commentaries.[386]

Finally, another fourth-century church father, who wrote about the sacrifice of Isaac, is Ephrem the Greek, also known as Ephrem the Syrian (306–377). He was born into a Christian family near the city of Nisibis in present-day Turkey. Ephrem is important for our purposes because in his work "On Abraham," he relates a great deal about the nature and extent of early Christian views on the patriarch.

For example, Ephrem says in this work the following about Abraham:

Having become obedient in response to his Divine command, he kindled his love furiously than the fire and his desire sharper than the sword. And he cut the chains of nature, as if leaving some earthly mass of sympathetic disposition. Willingly, he had given over his whole self and was completely following the commandment to slaughter his son.[387]

A little later on in the same work, Ephrem suggests that the figure of Sarah was to become a model for Mary, the mother of Jesus. Ephrem says of Sarah:

It was not an act of nature for her almost dead womb to conceive and for her dried breasts to furnish milk for Isaac. And it was not an act of nature for the maiden Mary to conceive

without a man, and to bear the Savior of all free men from
mortality.[388]

Indeed, many early Christian commentators, like Melito, for example, draw several parallels between Sarah, the mother of Isaac, and Mary, the mother of Jesus, like the barren/virgin parallel, and the serving as saviors in both examples.

In another place in his "On Abraham," Ephrem the Greek turns his attention to the age of Isaac at the time of the sacrifice. Ephrem relates:

The child grew up, reached the age of blossoming adoles-
cence and was joyful. At this age, the virtues of his soul and
the beauty of his body increased and he was pleasing to his
parents.[389]

Thus, it appears that Ephrem was of the view that Isaac was a grown man at the time of the sacrifice, easily capable, as Ephrem says, to overcome his one-hundred-year-old father.[390] Ephrem also spoke of many parallels of Isaac to Jesus, which we cataloged earlier in this chapter. For example, Ephrem the Greek relates:

Isaac carried the wood and was taken up into the mountains to
be sacrificed as a blameless Lamb. And the Savior took up the
Cross, to be sacrificed on Calvary as a lamb on behalf of us.[391]

Like many exegetes before him, Ephrem makes a number of the analogs between Isaac and Jesus that we saw developed earlier in the three fragments from Melito of Sardis and other early church fathers.

In another portion of "On Abraham," Ephrem the Greek turns his attention to the angels at the sight of the Akedah. Ephrem says that the angel who halts the Abraham sacrifice is to be identified with Christ. "The heavens took notice, the sun and the moon, and the choruses of stars at the unexpected sight."[392] Kessler points out the amazing similarity to a passage in the Isaiah targum that speaks of the angels "quaking and shaking in their amusement."[393]

This brings us to an analysis of Christian views of the Akedah narrative from the final sack of Rome in 430 CE, until approximately the year 1000, the beginning of the High Middle Ages, the topic of the next section of this fifth chapter.

Christian Views on the Akedah: Fifth to Tenth Centuries

From the sack of Rome in 430—the beginning of the Dark Ages in the Christian tradition—until 1000 CE, thinkers in both the East and the West have commented on the Akedah in the Christian development of theology and philosophy. Augustine of Hippo, for example, in both his *The Confessions* and the *City of God*, makes references to the sacrifice of Isaac. In *The Confessions* at III, 9, most likely with the Akedah in mind, Augustine says, "Many things that appear to be disapproved by Ethics, may in fact have been commanded by God."[394] This, of course, is a reference to Divine Command Theory introduced in Chapter Three.

In his *City of God*, Augustine points out that the sacrifice of Isaac calls to mind "God's willingness to sacrifice His own son for the redemption of mankind."[395] In the same passage, the Bishop of Hippo goes on to make many of the parallels of the Akedah to the death and resurrection of Jesus, seen earlier in this history.

The teacher of Augustine of Hippo, Ambrose of Milan, also made some unusual observations about the sacrifice of Isaac. Ambrose (340–397) was Archbishop of Milan from 374 until his death in 397. He was one of the most influential Christian leaders of the fourth century.

In the context of a discussion of child sacrifice, and in the early Christian spirit of identifying Isaac with the suffering of Jesus, Ambrose connects the act of circumcision with the death of Jesus in his Crucifixion. Connected to this observation, Ambrose also discusses many of the parallels between the two figures, as put forth by Melito and other thinkers we have seen earlier in this chapter.

Sixth-century Byzantine hymnist, Romanos, wrote a great deal about the role of Sarah in the Akedah narrative. He suggests, for example, that Sarah pleaded with her husband to not take Isaac to Mount Moriah. Romanos has Sarah say, "I beg you that he [Isaac] not leave me and kill me with grief." Abraham responds to Sarah, "You should not cry and bring a blemish to the sacrifice."[396] A little later on, in the same work, he observes that Isaac's hands "were bound to his ankles," in a description that looks very much like the Mishnah.[397]

Isidore of Seville (560–636) was Archbishop of Seville, Spain, for nearly three decades and understood the story of Abraham as a sign of what will happen in the future, namely that God will offer His own son as a sacrifice.[398] This is a confirmation of the Jobus Christi Model, as well as the Atonement Point of View. Carol Delaney, in her book *Abraham on Trial*, points out that the Venerable Bede (672–735) stopped his *Commentary of Genesis* with the sacrifice of Isaac narrative. Delaney makes this comment about that phenomenon:

> The propriety of this stopping place is self-evident: the effect of the Fall have by then been fully displayed, and the Redemption has been fully foreshadowed.[399]

Saint John the Great (752–846) was born in Asia Minor, but a scholar in the Eastern Church, like Augustine, Romanos, the Venerable Bede and Isidore. Saint John employed both the Jobus Christi and the Atonement models for explaining the Akedah narrative. But he puts more emphasis on the meaning of the "Test" of Abraham, and thus he ascribes to the Test View, as well.[400]

Other Christian thinkers on the Akedah narrative in the Dark Ages include Alcuin of York (735–804); Syrian Bishop Ishodad of Merv (who flourished around 850 CE); and Aelfrich of Eynsham (955–1010), English Abbot and writer of homilies and Biblical commentaries. The remarks on the Akedah from Alcuin can mostly be found in the *Glossa Ordinaria*, a collection of Biblical opinions constructed by Gilbert of Auxerre (906–951).[401] In the *Glossa*, Alcuin observes:

> He [Abraham] was willing to sacrifice his son with an undoubting soul, and praise-worthy in the constancy of his offering and in his trust in resurrection.[402]

In his remarks on the Akedah in the *Glossa Ordinaria*, Alcuin suggests that God told Abraham, "to go to the Land of Vision, where it will be revealed to you what I will foretell with this sacrifice." Like many of the Rabbinic commentaries on the Akedah, Bishop Ishodad of Merv repeats a tradition that "Abraham saw a column of Light from Mount Moriah, stretched all the way to Heaven."[403] Ishodad also tells us that the altar Abraham built for the Akedah was in the same spot, "where King Solomon built the Temple," as well as "where Adam lay buried, and where the Lord was to be crucified."[404] A remarkable passage from the Targum Pseudo-Jonathan makes the same points. This text tells us that the Akedah altar was built on the same place that "Adam also built an altar, that was destroyed by the Flood."[405]

The *Glossa Ordinaria* is a collection of Biblical commentaries in the form of "glosses," mostly from the church fathers from the second to the eleventh centuries. The *Glossa* is organized by subject matter in the early twelfth century. Until the twentieth century, the *Glossa Ordinaria* had been attributed to Wilifred of Strabo (808–849), a Benedictine monk. But more recent scholarship indicates it was organized by a group of scholars by Gilbert of Auxerre, who was also the Duke of Burgundy for much of the twelfth century. He also wrote an extensive commentary on the Prophet Jeremiah.[406]

The *Glossa Ordinaria* was an important primary source for Christian philosophers and theologians in the High Middle Ages, including Peter Abelard, Anselm, Albertus Magnus, Thomas Aquinas, Nicholas of Lyra, among many others.

Aelfrich of Eynsham (955–1010), English Abbot and student of Aethelwold of Winchester, completed a commentary on the Book of Genesis, along with several other Old and New Testament books. In his remarks on the sacrifice of Isaac narrative, Aelfrich quotes many of the early church fathers on Chapter 22 of Genesis, including Melito, Irenaeus, Gregory of Nyssa, and others.[407]

Aelfrich also relates quite a bit on the nature of the knife in Abraham's sacrifice, and the English Abbot, like Melito and others, gives a catalog of the connections between the Akedah and the death and resurrection of Jesus Christ. Among these include the carrying of the wood/cross that both involved sacrifice, the three-day journey and three days in the tomb, and the animal for sacrifice and Jesus as the Lamb of God, among many other parallels.[408]

As we have indicated earlier, many of the Christian comments on the sacrifice of Isaac, like those from Alcuin and Isidore, can also be found in the *Glossa Ordinaria*, a kind of compendium of remarks on Holy Scripture from the time of Augustine until the twelfth century. One final figure from the period to say something about the sacrifice of Isaac is Saint Anselm (1033–1109), Archbishop of Canterbury and inventor of the Ontological Argument for the existence of God.

Anselm's comments on the Akedah come in his *Cur Deus Homo: Why the God-Man?* Anselm relates that because of original sin, human beings are faced either with punishment or reconciliation and forgiveness. In the person of Jesus, Anselm sees the vehicle by which the reconciliation and forgiveness can take place. At the same time, since it was humans who committed the first sin, it must be a human who brings about the reconciliation. Thus, in Anselm's view, the reason for why God became man.[409]

Anselm goes on to speak of the sacrifice of Isaac in the same work in connection to, or parallel to, Jesus' death and resurrection. In *Cur Deus Homo*, Anselm relies much on Isaac as the reconciliation of God to the Nation of Israel. Like many thinkers before him, Anselm provides a catalog of the many parallels of the Akedah to the death and resurrection of Jesus Christ, including the carrying of the wood and the three days for the journey/in the tomb. Paba De Andrado, in his book *The Akedah Servant Complex*, describes Anselm's view of what he calls "satisfaction." He writes:

> Anselm's *Cur Deus Homo* theory of satisfaction is based on the view that human sin has disrupted the order of the universe and offended God's honor. However, if God were to compensate for the disturbance out of sheer mercy, that would be contrary to justice. The principle must be either satisfaction or penalty. And since the offense is against an infinite God, an infinite satisfaction is necessary. Christ, the God-Man, being sinless and not subject to death, through his voluntary death as a man, makes satisfaction, paying human debt through his merit.[410]

In the same section of *Cur Deus Homo*, Anselm goes on to compare the sacrifice of Isaac to that of Jesus, suggesting that the former is to be a foreshadowing of the latter. A similar view was held by Peter Abelard (1079–1142). His comments on the Akedah being an analog to Jesus' death and resurrection may be found in Book III of his *Commentary on Romans*.[411] Finally, Thomas Aquinas (1225–1274), in the second part of his *Summa Theologica*, discusses at some length the phenomenon of sacrifice in general, as well as the sacrifice of Isaac in particular.[412]

In this section of his major work, Thomas raises a variety of questions about the issue of sacrifice: Are we required to offer sacrifices? Doesn't Exodus 22:20 and other Old Testament passages explicitly forbid human sacrifice? Should we not consider Abraham and other figures in the Old Testament to be products of their times?[413] Later, Thomas turns his attention to God's command that Abraham sacrifice Isaac.

In his analysis of the scene in Genesis 22:1–19, Thomas argues that what is most important about the narrative is that God has commanded that Abraham kill Isaac, but that does not mean Abraham would be a murderer. The reason Thomas arrives at this conclusion is, as he puts the matter, "He who follows Divine authority can be no murderer."[414] Thus, Thomas Aquinas appears to rely on what we have labeled the Divine Command Theory in Chapter Three of this history of views on the Akedah.

So far, in this section of Chapter Five, we have maintained that in the early medieval Christian period, the three explanations most commonly employed for the Akedah are what we have called the Test View, the Jobus Christi Model, and the Expiation, or Atonement Theory. This brings us to a number of places in medieval Christian art where the theological points we have made so far in this chapter are often verified by Christian art in the same period.

The Akedah in Christian Art: Fifth to Eleventh Centuries

Paba De Andrado begins his book, *The Akedah Servant Complex*, with these words:

> The mosaic representation of Genesis 22 in a vaulted apse at Calvary in the Holy Sepulchre Church in Jerusalem depicted the conventional figures of Abraham with upraised hands, his bound son Isaac, the intervening angel and a ram caught in a bush.[415]

De Andrado then goes on to give a commentary of the image in the Jerusalem Church. He observes:

> Although a modern work, the mosaic reflects an ancient tradition since the Fourth Century CE, which had localized

the Sacrifice of Isaac on Golgotha. By its juxtaposition to the
site of the Crucifixion of Jesus, the mosaic epitomizes the
meaning that the narrative acquired within the early Christian
tradition.[416]

Although this piece of Christian art is a modern one, it nevertheless
sets the stage for artistic representations of the sacrifice of Isaac in the
first twelve centuries of the Christian Church, as we shall see next.

Perhaps the earliest Christian image of the sacrifice of Isaac is a
Russian fresco owned by the Museum of Saint Sophia in Kiev, Ukraine.
The fresco is undated, but it likely came from the third or fourth century
CE. In the fresco, Isaac kneels, Abraham stands, his knife in his right
hand. His left hand holds back the head of his son so that the boy's
neck is exposed. Abraham's ass and his two servants are on the right.
An angel in the upper left corner restrains the right arm of Abraham,
halting the sacrifice. Both the angel and Abraham have haloes around
their heads, while Isaac does not. On the far right, the substitute ram is
caught in a thicket.[417]

Another of the earliest Christian depiction of the sacrifice of Isaac
is a mural in the ancient Christian catacombs on Via Latina in Rome.
This image by an anonymous Christian artist shows Abraham with a
sword-length knife in his right hand. To the left is the sacrificial altar
with a fire burning atop it. To the left of the altar is the substitute ram
for the sacrifice. In the image, Isaac kneels before his father, with his
hands bound behind his back.[418]

Another image of the sacrifice of Isaac in early Christianity can be
seen in a psalter owned by the Conde Museum in Chantilly, France. The
anonymous artist displays Isaac as a prefiguration of the Crucifixion.
Abraham stands to the right, sword in his right hand and a torch in his
left. Isaac is to the left of his father. He carries the wood for the sacrifice
on his back. The wood is shown as a cross. To the left of Isaac is the ass
on which they journeyed to Mount Moriah.[419] Behind the ass, again on
the left of the image, can be seen three figures, two men and a woman.
Presumably, these are Sarah and the two lads or servants.[420]

Two other of the earliest pieces of Christian art in the Dark Ages
that depict the sacrifice of Isaac are the "binding scenes" depicted in

the *Life of Saint Remy and King Clovis*, from around 535 CE, and the *Sacrifice of Isaac* in the Basilica of San Vitale in Ravenna, dated around 547 CE. The former works show depictions of three separate bindings. For our purposes, the first two are the most important for they depict the binding of Isaac, from Genesis 22, and the binding of Jesus before his Crucifixion.[421] Here we see an assent to the Jobus Christi Model, as well as the Atonement Theory for explaining the sacrifice of Isaac.

The artist for this piece is anonymous, but the construction of the depictions are such that the Isaac and Jesus figures have similar faces and are bound in similar ways. It is quite clear that the artist wishes us to identify one with the other, and thus a nod in the direction of the Jobus Christi Motif, as described in Chapter Three of this history.[422]

The scene depicted at the Church of Saint Vitale in Ravenna also depicts the sacrifice of Isaac. Abraham is on the right with a sword-like knife in his right hand. Isaac is on the sacrificial altar on the right. Sarah can be seen in the far right. An angel, or perhaps God, can be seen to halt the sacrifice, accompanied by the substitute ram.[423]

Another early Christian rendition of the sacrifice of Isaac can be seen in the fourth-century Necropolis at El Bagawat in Egypt. Abraham and Isaac stand in the center of the image. The father holds the knife in his right hand. With his left hand, he holds back the head of his son to expose Isaac's throat. To the right is the flaming altar of sacrifice, now empty. To the left is the ram caught in the thicket. In the upper-right corner of the image, the angel, or perhaps God, halts the sacrifice, with the figure's right had extending to Abraham.[424]

The site at El Bagawat is one of the oldest churches in Christianity. It was originally built around 350 BCE. In addition to the church, the site also contains two tombs with early Christian paintings, including one that depicts the Akedah narrative. The tombs at El Bagawat are modeled after ancient Egyptian tombs of the Pharaohs.[425]

Another early Christian image of the Akedah can be seen on a fifth-century ivory Pyxis owned by the Rheinisches Landesmuseum Trier. Abraham stands on the left with a sword in his right hand. Isaac to his left, bound on the altar. The Angel of the Lord is on the far-right, gesturing toward the pair. The angel is in human form and stands upright.[426]

A British Saint Edmunds cross, made between 1180 and 1190 and made of walrus ivory, contains an image of the sacrifice of Isaac. The image can be seen on the bottom of the cross. Abraham has the knife in his left hand, above the altar where Isaac can be seen.[427]

A sacrifice of Isaac scene can also be seen in a thirteenth-century French Bible. The sacrifice of Isaac is in a figure above. Isaac carries the wood on his back, while in a lower image, Jesus carries his cross. The artist who illustrated the Bible is unknown, but he clearly endorsed both the Jobus Christi and the Atonement Models. Abraham is accompanied by Sarah. She seems to be trying to dissuade her husband, while in the lower register, Mary accompanies her son on his journey to Calvary.[428] The Los Angeles Museum of Art owns an illustrated *Vita Christi* that comes from East Anglia. At folio eleven of this manuscript, the sacrifice of Isaac is depicted.[429]

A French limestone capital, dated from around 1150, also contains a scene of the Akedah. The knife is in Abraham's left hand. Isaac is prone on the altar. God can be seen on the right of the image, where He appears to be halting the sacrifice.[430] The Victoria and Albert Museum also owns a number of representations of the sacrifice of Isaac scene, including one image called *The Sacrifice of Isaac* dated between 1180 and 1190. The two servants are standing on the far left. Abraham's ass is to the right of them. Abraham stands with his knife in his right hand. The left hand holds back the son's head to expose his neck.[431]

The Fitzwilliam Museum of Cambridge University owns a life of Isaac cycle that includes a depiction of the Akedah scene. Isaac kneels in the scene, while Abraham stands erect. This scene is accompanied by a second that shows the Crucifixion.[432] This work was meant to call to mind the Jobus Christi and the Atonement theories, as introduced in Chapter Three.

A twelfth-century Abraham sacrificing Isaac can be seen on a relief of a portal of the Saint Petronius Basilica in Bologna, Italy. Isaac stands in the middle of the image, his hands bound behind him. Abraham holds a sword-size knife in his right hand. An angel holds back his right arm. The ram can be seen beneath the angel as if he or she has brought it along.[433]

Finally, another depiction of the sacrifice of Isaac in early

Christianity is named *The Angel of the Lord Prevents Abraham From Sacrificing Isaac on Rock Moriah*. The angel can be seen on the upper left. She holds back Abraham's right arm. Isaac kneels on the altar, beneath which there is a raging fire. The ram can be seen on the lower right, caught in a thicket. Another image of Isaac can be seen on the far left. He carries the wood on his back. The image appears to be making a connection between the wood with Isaac and Jesus with his Cross.[434] This is clearly another employment of the Jobus Christi Model.

From these twenty or so early Christian images of the sacrifice of Isaac, we may make the following conclusions. First, the three principal motifs for explaining the Genesis 22 narrative—the Test View, the Jobus Christi Theory, and the Atonement Model—are also present in the artistic renderings of the Akedah.

Secondly, in these early Christian images of the sacrifice, most of them show Abraham in the act of the sacrifice and an angel, or God Himself, bringing the scene to a halt. Third, the figures of Sarah, the two servants, and the ass often appear in these early Christian pieces of art, but the figures of Abraham and Isaac always predominate the scenes.

A fourth conclusion we can make about depictions of the sacrifice of Isaac in early Christian art is that in many of these artistic renderings, the sacrifice of Isaac is shown as a parallel to the sacrifice of Jesus Christ on his Cross. Indeed, in many of these artistic works, the sacrifice of Isaac is seen as pointing in the direction of another sacrifice many centuries later on Calvary. Often in these early Christian pieces of art, we have seen commitments to the Test View, to the Jobus Christi Model, and to the Isaac as Remnant Theory, as well.

This brings us to the major conclusions we have made in this fifth chapter. The subject matter of Chapter Six will concentrate on the perspectives of medieval Jewish scholars on the Akedah.

Conclusions to Chapter Five

The major goal of this fifth chapter has been to describe and discuss how the sacrifice of Isaac narrative, at Genesis 22:1–19, has been interpreted by thinkers from the earliest portions of Christianity from the first to the thirteenth centuries. To that end, we began the chapter with an analysis of many of the places in the New Testament, as well as some early noncanonical works such as the *Epistle of Barnabus* and the *Shepherd of Hermas*, where the Genesis narrative of Abraham and Isaac is called to mind.

In our analysis, we have seen several passages from the Gospels related to the sacrifice of Isaac, as well as many portions of the letters of Paul, where he appears to be discussing Abraham and Isaac, and often their relation to the life and death of Jesus Christ. More particularly, we have seen that the eleventh chapter of the letter to the Hebrews, as well as Romans and First Corinthians, were texts of relevance for our purposes.

In the second section of Chapter Five, we introduced and discussed the analyses of several early Christian thinkers, from the second to the fifth centuries, who have made important observations about the sacrifice of Isaac. Among these Christian thinkers explored in this section include Melito of Sardis; Hippolytus; Irenaeus, Bishop of Lyons; Origen; Clement of Alexandria; Cyril of Alexandria; and fourth-century theologian and exegete Gregory of Nyssa.

For the most part, what we have seen in these early Christian thinkers is a reliance on three of the explanatory models introduced in Chapter Three of this history. These were the Test View, the Jobus Christi Model, and the Atonement Theory. Like the New Testament period, we also saw a positing of the view that the Akedah narrative was to be understood as a forerunner to the death and resurrection of Jesus Christ.

Christian thinkers on the sacrifice of Isaac from the fifth to the thirteenth centuries were the focus of the third section of Chapter Five. Among the thinkers on the sacrifice of Isaac explored in this section were Augustine, the Venerable Bede, Romanos, Isidore of Seville, Saint John the Great, Alcuin, Ishodad of Merv, Anselm, Peter Abelard, and selections from the twelfth-century *Glossa Ordinaria*.

Again, for the most part, these thinkers from the Dark Ages tended to rely on both the New Testament and the early church fathers in formulating their views on the sacrifice of Isaac, often quoting directly from the New Testament, as well as figures like Melito, Origen, Irenaeus, Hippolytus, and others.

In the fourth and final section of Chapter Five, we introduced and discussed twenty pieces of Christian art from the catacombs in the earliest Church to images from the early High Middle Ages in the twelfth and thirteenth centuries. Generally speaking, what we have discovered in this artistic material is that the same four explanations or models for understanding the Akedah narrative were the same as those in the earliest period of the Church. That is, the Test View, what we have called the Jobus Christi Model, the Atonement Theory, and the Isaac as Remnant Point of View, as introduced in Chapter Three of this history.

Indeed, we have seen that many of the Christian artists who have created renderings of the sacrifice of Isaac narrative often have tied the suffering of Abraham and Isaac to be seen as a forerunner of the sacrifice and reconciliation of the life, death and resurrection of Jesus Christ, the Son of God.

As we shall see, the material in Chapter Six to follow should be seen as a companion to Chapter Five, in that, in Chapter Six we shall explore the thinking and writing of several medieval Jewish scholars on the Akedah narrative, including Saadiah Gaon, Rashi, Moses Maimonides, and many other Jewish philosophers and theologians from the period. It is to the medieval Jewish period, then, to which we turn in Chapter Six.

Chapter Six:
The Akedah in the Jewish Medieval Period

Just as he stretched out his hand to take the knife, a Heavenly voice came forth and said to him, "Do not stretch out your hand against the boy."

—Midrash *Tanhuma*

You are the Lord who chose Abraham and brough him from Ur of the Chaldeans and named him Abraham. You made a Covenant with Isaac, and you swore to him on Mount Moriah.

—Saadiah Gaon, quoted in Edward Kessler's *Bound by the Bible*, p. 147.

God said to Abraham, "You became proud of your son that I gave you and you made a covenant with the Philistines. Now go and make him a burnt offering [*olah '*] and let us see what will happen with the Covenant."

—Rabbi Samuel ben Meir, commentary on Genesis 22.

Introduction

As we have mentioned at the end of Chapter Five, this sixth chapter should be seen as a companion to Chapter Five, for it covers Jewish views on the Akedah from roughly 500 CE until the year 1500. We will begin the chapter with an analysis of the Midrash *Tanhuma*, a collection of Rabbinic opinion in the fifth to the seventh centuries of the common era. As we shall see, the Midrash *Tanhuma* is full of Rabbinic views on the Akedah.

This first section of Chapter Six will be followed by an introduction and discussion of about a dozen Jewish philosophers and theologians who have commented at some length on the twenty-second chapter of the Book of Genesis. Among the scholars we shall explore are Saadiah Gaon, Rashi, Moses Maimonides, Abraham Ibn Ezra, Ephraim ben Jacob of Bonn, and many other scholarly figures in medieval Judaism.

In the third section of this chapter, we will explore a dozen or so pieces of Jewish art depicting the Akedah from the earliest centuries of the Common Era until the year 1500. In this section, we will see that Jewish artistic works on the Akedah in the post-Talmudic period to the end of the High Middle Ages is rich, variegated and often theological in content.

The role of the Akedah in the Crusades, and more specifically in the First Crusade, shall be the subject matter of the fourth and final section of this sixth chapter. The reading of, as well as discussions of, the importance of the Akedah was a very common theme among Jews from 900 until 1500 CE. This brings us to a discussion of the Midrash *Tanhuma*, the first topic of this chapter.

The Akedah in the Midrash Tanhuma

The Hebrew text known as the Midrash *Tanhuma*, or the Midrash *Tanhuma Yelammedenu*, is the only complete Midrash that is extant on the Torah, or the Pentateuch. The first part of the title is named after Tanhuma bar Abba, an early rabbi who lived in the fourth century CE. He is considered the original author of the text of the *Tanhuma*.[435]

The second word of the title, *Yelannedenu*, is part of a dictum employed in the Rabbinic period that meant "May the Sages teach us." This dictum was frequently used from the fifth century CE on. The *Tanhuma* is important for our purposes because it contains one of the earliest medieval Jewish texts on the Akedah narrative, for its final form was completed sometime between 600 and 700 CE.[436]

One of the most interesting features of the *Tanhuma* is that, in the text, the rabbis are often reacting to Christian claims that they now owned the Scriptures and claimed to be the "New Israel." To illustrate this point, consider the following passage from the *Tanhuma*:

When the Holy One, Blessed be He, said to Moses, "write," at
Exodus 34:27, Moses wanted to write the *Mishnah*, as well.
However, the Holy One, Blessed be He, foresaw that ultimate-
ly the nations of the world would translate the Torah into
Greek and would claim, "We are Israel!"[437]

This piece of the *Tanhuma* appears to be an endorsement of the Divine Plan Point of View. This passage of the *Tanhuma* also suggests that the rabbis were familiar with the Christian claim to the ownership of Scripture, and the rabbis believed that this fact required a direct response. Kessler points out that the *Dialogue of Timothy and Aquila*, another rabbi speaks of, "You Christians, according to your will, wrestle away the Scriptures."[438] There are two versions of the *Tanhuma*, both of which had been written after Christianity had established itself as the dominant, and the dominating religion in Israel.

In a second passage from the *Tanhuma,* the rabbis asks a question about Isaac. The text in question asks, "To whom was Isaac comparable? To one who, after being condemned, was going to be burned with his wood on his shoulder."[439] Again, this seems primarily to be a reference against the notion that Jesus' Crucifixion was to be understood as an analog to the sacrifice of Isaac narrative, and that the sacrifice of Isaac is superior to the death of Jesus Christ.

Kessler points out that in the period between the writing of the Genesis Rabbah and the emergence of the *Tanhuma*, Emperor Justinian's famous "Code of Conduct" had been established to solidify Roman law, which included many restrictions regarding the Jews in the Empire.[440] Thus, both of our first two passages from the *Tanhuma* primarily were about responses to Christian claims to Scripture and to being the "New Israel."

A third important passage from the *Tanhuma* shows its familiarity with the idea that early Rabbinic views on the Akedah suggest that a quarter of Isaac's blood was shed at the sacrifice. This may indicate that the Midrash compilers were familiar with the Rabbinic idea that Abraham actually went through with the sacrifice. As Kessler has pointed out, however, many ancient and modern scholars have been dissuaded from this view primarily because "The Akedah was worthy of reward, but not because of the sacrifice."[441]

A fourth passage about the Akedah in the *Tanhuma* tells us that, when the Patriarch cut the wood, "Abraham deliberately chose the fig and palm trees," mostly because these were the woods that were acceptable for sacrifices conducted in the Temple at Jerusalem.[442]

This fourth passage from the *Tanhuma* employs the expressions, "the blood of the binding of Isaac" and the "ashes of Isaac," implying again that either Isaac's blood was shed or the son was actually sacrificed. Another passage from the Buber version of the *Tanhuma*, published in Vilna in 1885, shows the view that Satan, disguised as Isaac, fools Sarah. The *Tanhuma*, at this point, tells us that Satan "pushed Abraham's hand" to effect the sacrifice. Thus, the text employs the Demonic Forces explanation of the sacrifice of Isaac.[443] This is, perhaps, an assent to the Influences of Demonic Forces Theory, as outlined in Chapter Three of this history.

The *Tanhuma* also suggests that Isaac willingly engaged in the Akedah with full comprehension and full intention. The text tells us, "He went along, as if he was brought up and placed on the altar."[444] In section 23 of the Buber text, the *Tanhuma* also ties the sacrifice of Isaac to the death of Sarah in the opening of Genesis 23. The text sees the two as being connected in a cause and effect relation.

In another portion of the *Tanhuma*, Isaac asks his father Abraham to bound him, so that he would not inadvertently flinch as the knife came down and thereby preventing a clean-cut and making the ritual invalid.[445] In the same section of the Buber version, the text relates:

> Just as he stretched out his hand to take the knife, a Heavenly voice came forth and said to him, "Do not stretch out your hand against the boy."[446]

The *Tanhuma* suggests that the reason behind the pronouncement of the Heavenly voice is a respect for human life—or what we have called the Sanctity for Human Life Theory in our analysis in Chapter Three of this history. The text does use the noun *yeled*, or boy, however, suggesting an early age for Isaac. Another passage has Isaac saying to his father, "Do not tell my mother when she is by the well, or when she is standing on the roof, lest she fall and die."[447] Presumably, Isaac made this comment just before the proposed sacrifice. And Sarah does die in the opening of chapter 23.

The *Tanhuma* in the Buber edition also claims that "It would never occur to one that God requires or delights in the act of human sacrifice." This may be another endorsement of the Sanctity of Human Life Theory. The Midrash also weighs in on one of the controversies regarding the age of Isaac. The text tells us, "He was thirty-seven years old when he was bound on the altar."[448] It also points out that the father would have been unable to bind the son if the son was not entirely cooperative if Isaac was a full-grown man.[449]

Shalom Spiegel quotes section 46 of the Buber edition of the *Midrash Tanhuma*, in which Spiegel says, "When Isaac's children are sinning before Thee, remember for their sake the Akedah of their father, Isaac, and redeem them from their distress."[450] Spiegel points out that the Targum Pseudo-Jonathan, as well as the Genesis Rabbah at 56:10, make exactly the same claim.

Two final observations made by the rabbis of the *Tanhuma* are that Sarah is the real hero of the Akedah narrative and that, after the near sacrifice of Isaac, he was no longer his father's favored son.[451] This may also be the first attempt to point out the parallels in Judaism of the life of Sarah to that of Mary, the mother of Jesus.

A second avenue for explaining early Jewish medieval interpretations of the Akedah narrative are the many Middle Ages *piyyutim*, or poems written about the sacrifice of Isaac, the topic of the second section of this sixth chapter. To which we turn next.

The Akedah in *Piyyutim* in the Middle Ages

In addition to the insights on the Akedah in the medieval Midrash *Tanhuma*, another source for garnering Jewish Middle Ages views of the Akedah can be found in Aramaic and Hebrew *piyyutim*, or liturgical poems from the period. Indeed, poems about the Akedah became very popular in late medieval Judaism, particularly at the time of the First Crusade in 1096.

Additionally, scholars like Saadiah Gaon (882–942), also wrote a number of *piyyutim*, including one on the Akedah in Hebrew. This poem can be found in both the Brody edition, as well as that of A. Z.

Idelsohn.[452] These Akedah poems began to appear between the fourth and the seventh centuries and continued all the way to the High Middle Ages in Judaism.

There is some debate about the dating of *piyyutim* on the Akedah narrative. The earliest known poets were Yose ben Yose, Yannai and Eleazer ha-Kallir, all of whom were in Palestine. Yose ben Yose, who most likely lived in Palestine in the fourth or fifth century, completed a poem called the *Yozer*, of which only the first line is extant. This line uses the word *olah*, or "sacrifice," and it may have been about the Akedah.[453]

Rabbi Yannai, who most likely lived in Palestine in the third century CE, was, perhaps, the earliest of liturgical poets of the Amora. His name is mentioned 200 times in the Babylonian Talmud and another 250 times in the Jerusalem Talmud. Among his many *piyyutim* are two poems that sing the praises of both Abraham and Isaac.

Eleazer ha-Kallir was an Israeli Rabbi (570–640) and poet.[454] His many *piyyutim* have been preserved, two of which speak explicitly about the Akedah narrative. These two poems have often been quoted subsequently by other Hebrew and Aramaic poets who wrote about the Bible.[455] One of these poets is Saadiah Gaon. Among his many observations about the Akedah is his belief that the Shofar blown on Mount Sinai was one of the horns of the ram sacrificed on Mount Moriah.[456]

Concerning his poetry, the earliest prayer book of Saadiah, known as his *Siddur*, refers to the Akedah narrative this way:

> You are the Lord who chose Abram and brought him out of the Uz of the Chaldeans, and named him Abraham. You made a covenant with Isaac, and you swore to him on Mount Moriah.[457]

Kessler makes this statement about Saadiah's comment of the Akedah:

> It is worth emphasizing that Saadiah states that God's oath was sworn to Isaac, not to Abraham, as is recounted in the Biblical story.[458]

Saadiah's comment came as part of a tendency among Hebrew writers of *piyyutim*, in the fifth to tenth centuries, who referred to the

Berith, or Covenant, was made with Isaac and not with Abraham. Indeed, during the Jewish Middle Ages, it was often the case that the figure of Isaac was held in more regard than his father, Abraham. At any rate, Saadiah Gaon wrote many *piyyutim* in his scholarly career, including at least one poem on the Akedah narrative, and perhaps more, as well.[459] We will say more about Saadiah's views on the Akedah narrative in a later section of this chapter.

The *Selihot,* from the word *Selihah* meaning "forgiveness," is a poem read or played on fast days and on Holy Days in the Jewish Middle Ages. The prayer exalts the behavior of Isaac in the Akedah narrative and asks for forgiveness for the many sins of his progeny. The poem indicates that Abraham "passed the test, but he failed as a Father."[460] This text also points to the tendency in medieval Jewish interpreters of the ascendancy of the importance of Isaac and the lowering of Abraham.

In his classic book on the Akedah, Louis Berman suggests that the Jewish *piyyutim* on the Akedah from the fifth to the tenth centuries were mostly written with three themes in mind. Berman describes these this way:

> First, the redemptive power of the Akedah is an important theme in Jewish prayer, but it is not the only theme linked with the Akedah. The piyyutim composed during the Middle Ages linked two more ideas with the Akedah: the identification of martyrdom and a belief in Isaac's death and resurrection.[461]

Berman continues his analysis:

> These piyyutim are supported by Midrashic references to Isaac's "ashes heaped upon the altar." This Midrashic phrase had been interpreted to mean either that Isaac has died of fright on the altar and was quickly revived by a Heavenly voice, or that Isaac was actually sacrificed, rose to Heaven and was resurrected some time later.[462]

As we shall see later in this chapter, Berman's view is very much like that of Rabbi Ephraim ben Jacob of Bonn on the same point. Thus, in Louis Berman's view, the subject matter of these medieval Jewish poems on the Akedah was motivated by the redemptive power of suffering, or that Isaac died of fright, or was actually sacrificed. This brings us to the third, and central section of Chapter Six, the views on the Akedah of major philosophers and theologians in the High Middle Ages on the meaning and significance of the Akedah narrative.

The Akedah in Medieval Jewish Philosophy and Theology

In the late medieval period in the Jewish faith from the tenth to the fifteenth centuries, a dozen or so principal Jewish philosophers and theologians have written a great deal about the Biblical Akedah narrative of Genesis 22:1–19. Among those Jewish philosophers and theologians were the following figures:

1. Saadiah Gaon (882–942)

2. Rashi (Rabbi Shlomo Yitchaki) (1040–1105)

3. Joseph Kara (1065–1135)

4. Samuel ben Meir (1083–1174)

5. Abraham Ibn Daud (1110–1180)

6. Moses Maimonides (Rambam) (1135–1204)

7. Nahmanides (1194–1270)

8. David Kimchi (Radak) (1160–1235)

9. Abraham Ibn Ezra (1089–1164)

10. Gersonides (1288–1344)

11. Isaac Abravanel (1437–1508)

12. Obadiah ben Jacob Sforno (1475–1550)

13. Ephraim ben Jacob of Bonn (1132–1196)

We will examine the views on the Akedah of these nine thinkers by looking at them sequentially in three groups of threes, beginning with Saadiah, Rashi, and Samuel ben Meir. We already introduced

Saadiah Gaon in our discussion of *piyyutim* on the Akedah earlier in this chapter.

Regarding the question "Did God tell Abraham to kill Isaac?" Saadiah answers, "The text does not say that God only wanted Abraham to prepare him for the *olah* sacrifice." It says nothing about killing him. Saadiah thinks this is important because God was saying something about the intrinsic value of human life. In other words, Saadiah assents to the Sanctity of Human Life Theory.[463]

Saadiah points out in his commentary on *Bereshith*, or Genesis, "Abraham trusted that God, in any case, could resurrect Isaac in order to fulfill his promise to him. Indeed, some Jewish traditions even suggest that Isaac was actually killed and resurrected."[464] Saadiah does, however, argue against the Isaac-died view, if, for no other reason, the Nation of Israel continued after the incident on Mount Moriah. This appears to be an endorsement of the Isaac as Remnant Theory. It is clear, however, that Saadiah Gaon had the same views as Louis Berman's three themes mentioned earlier in this chapter.

Saadiah also points out that Abraham knew that if he actually did kill Isaac, he trusted that "God could resurrect the son in order to fulfill his promises to him." In several Midrashim, Saadiah also tells us that Isaac was killed only to be subsequently resurrected.[465]

Rabbi Shlomo Yitchaki, better known by his acronym Rashi, wrote an extensive commentary on Genesis, in which he makes many claims about the Akedah narrative. Among these are that Rashi believed that God never intended to let Abraham go through with the sacrifice. Rashi also thought that the provision at Jeremiah 7:31 forbidding human sacrifice was actually an allusion to the Akedah narrative.[466] Rashi adds, "Don't think for a moment that God never had any intention of Abraham killing Isaac."[467] Of course, one way to interpret this view of Rashi's is simply to say that he is endorsing the Divine Plan Theory, as introduced in Chapter Three of this history.

In another place in his commentary on Genesis, Rashi explains that when the men of the Great Assembly had no trouble figuring out where to build the Second Temple, they did some archaeological digging and discovered the foundation of the First Temple. And when they searched where to put the Temple altar, they discovered a pile of ashes lying on the ground. And they assumed that they must have been the ashes of Isaac.[468]

Rashi's explanation of this tale is clear. God must have assisted them in their time of need, even though, as Rashi has it, "they did not deserve it."[469] In regard to Abraham telling the two servants that "We will return to you," Rashi says that this was a prophecy of Isaac's resurrection. However, Rashi points out that other sages believed Abraham would return with Isaac's ashes.[470] Rashi also held with many of the Rabbinic sages that Isaac was a full-grown man of thirty-seven at the time of the Akedah narrative.[471]

In his commentary on Genesis 22:4, Abraham Ibn Ezra, on the other hand, suggests that at the time of the Akedah narrative, Isaac was only thirteen years old, an age when Abraham could still force his son to be sacrificed against his will. Ibn Ezra does, however, raise a series of questions about the Akedah story—questions that will recur throughout the history of Judaism. Why is Isaac silent in the narrative? Why does he offer no resistance? Where is Isaac in verse nineteen? Why did Abraham not question God? Where is Sarah during the sacrifice, and what were her beliefs about the matter? Why is the Akedah narrative not mentioned directly again in the Hebrew Bible? And, why would an All-Good God require such a command of a follower?[472]

Ibn Ezra also explicitly rejects the Midrash and various other attempts to reconcile the apparent contradictions. He explains:

> And these great scholars requited these interpretations because they said, "It is not possible for God to command something and they say not to do it." But they did not note that the firstborn were replaced by the Levites after a year. Since the text says at the start, "And God tested Abraham." It removes any doubt that God tested him in order for him to receive a great reward.[473]

Here Ibn Ezra endorses the Test View. Ibn Ezra also points out in his Genesis commentary that God sometimes changes His mind. For example, number three states that the firstborn originally had a priestly role because the Levites replaced them. Likewise, God first tells Abraham to sacrifice Isaac and then tells him not to.[474] In his Genesis commentary, Ibn Ezra makes a number of other original and genuine observations about the Abraham and Isaac narrative.

For example, Ibn Ezra treats it as axiomatic that God had no real interest in Abraham actually going through with the sacrifice. In fact, Ibn Ezra suggests that Abraham may have misunderstood the original command on account of the unfamiliarity with the obscure idiom of prophecy. In this regard, Abraham would have mistaken the command *Ha alehu* to mean "Sacrifice him," rather than the more prosaic and harmless meaning, "Take him up" to the top of the mountain.[475] We may also see this view, then, as an example of the Garbled or Miscommunicated Theory, described in the third chapter of this history.

Rabbi Joseph Kara appears to have written contradictory remarks about the Akedah narrative. On the one hand, he says the sacrifice of Isaac is about, "Our obligation to engage in sacrifice in the service of Hashem." On the other hand, he also states that the purpose of the Akedah narrative is to reveal that, "God has contempt for human sacrifice."[476]

Rabbi Samuel ben Meir identifies and connects the Akedah to the act of making the *Berith*, or Covenant, that Abraham made with the Philistines, as recounted at the very end of the previous chapter at Genesis 21:22–32. Rabbi Meir observes:

> God said to Abraham, "You became proud of your son that
> I gave you and you made a covenant with them [the Philis-
> tines]. Now go and make him a burnt offering [*olah*], and let
> us see what will happen with the Covenant."[477]

Abraham Ibn Daud disagrees. He relates in the very last sentence of his *Enumah Ramah* that, "In the Akedah, Abraham does not argue with God but silently obeys him, realizing that there is no common standard by which to compare his insight with Divine Wisdom."[478] Rabbi Daud seems here to be assenting to the Divine Plan Theory in understanding the meaning of the sacrifice of Isaac narrative, as introduced back in Chapter Three of this history of attitudes toward the Akedah story.

At any rate, Rabbi Daud believes that one of the most significant factors in Genesis 22: 1–19 narrative is why Abraham behaves so silently in regard to the command. Some have argued that the primitiveness of the world of ancient sacrifice may have supplied an "excuse" for the silence. And Rabbi Abraham Ibn Daud seems to be solidly against that approach.[479] This brings us to a discussion of the views of Moses Maimonides, in his *Guide to the Perplexed* concerning the Akedah narrative in Genesis 22, the topic of the next section of this sixth chapter.

The Akedah in Moses Maimonides

Of all the medieval Jewish responses and discussions of the Akedah narrative, the one in Moses Maimonides' *Guide for the Perplexed* is the fullest of those approaches. His analysis of the sacrifice of Isaac comes in Book II, section forty-eight of the *Guide*. There Maimonides sets the Akedah in the context of the phenomenon of prophecy:

> Prophecy is...something set forth by the Divine Being through the medium of the Active Intellect in the first instance to have man's rational faculty, and then to his imaginative faculty. And this is the highest degree in his greatest perfection.[480]

Maimonides reveals here his primary philosophical underpinning—the philosophy of Aristotle, with these mentions of "Active" and "Imaginative" intellects, as well as his description of the rational function of the human soul. This reliance on Aristotle also indicates that Maimonides appears to anticipate the views advanced in Judaic philosophy by modern philosophers, such as Baruch Spinoza, for example, in that Maimonides refuses to discuss "symbolic" interpretations of the Akedah in questions like, "Why a ram rather than a lamb?" Maimonides says, "This is an idle inquiry befitting a fool, but not one who is serious-minded."[481]

Maimonides argues that the story of the binding of Isaac contains what he calls, "two great notions."[482] The first of these is "Abraham's willingness to sacrifice Isaac demonstrates the limits of humanity's capability to both love and fear God, at the same time."[483] Maimonides second conclusion about the Akedah is this: Because Abraham acted as a prophet in terms of what God had asked him to do, the story exemplifies how prophetic revelation has the same truth value as the best of philosophical argument, even if the revelation comes in a dream or a vision.[484] Maimonides perhaps hints here at the Suspension of Ethics Model.

For the most part, Moses Maimonides employs what we have labeled the Test Theory back in Chapter Three for explaining the Akedah narrative. For him, the sacrifice came as a "trial or a test of the extreme limits of the love and the fear of God." In describing Maimonides' view, contemporary Jewish scholar Shlomo Riskin says:

> Abraham was asked to do what all subsequent generations
> of Jews would be asked to do. The paradox in Jewish history
> is that, had we not been willing to sacrifice our children for
> God, we would have never survived as a God-inspired and
> God-committed nation.[485]

Riskin suggests Maimonides is assenting to the Isaac as Remnant Theory. In the beginning of part one, chapter 24 of the *Guide for the Perplexed*, Maimonides tells us this about the Test Theory:

> The doctrine of trials is open to great objections. It is, in fact,
> more exposed to objections than any other thing taught in
> Scripture. It is mentioned in Scripture six times, as I will show
> in this Chapter. People have the general notion that the trials
> consist in afflictions and mishaps sent by God to man, not as
> punishment for past sins, but as giving opportunities for great
> reward.[486]

Maimonides goes on to enumerate these six examples of testing. These, Maimonides tells us, can be found at Genesis 22:12; Deuteronomy 13:4, 7:2, and 32:4, as well as Exodus 16:4 and 31:13. In each of these texts, Maimonides tells us that God is "testing" human beings to "test" their moral characters, or to improve those characters—a version of the Moral Qualities View.[487]

In chapter 24 of the *Guide*, Maimonides says that:

> In no case should any wrong be ascribed to God, Who is far
> from it. Nor should one assume that a person is innocent and
> perfect and does not deserve the punishment he has been
> brought.

In another portion of part one, chapter 24 of the *Guide*, Maimonides suggests that the most difficult kind of trials or tests is when the sufferer cannot understand the reason for it. He follows this by indicating that the suffering occasioned by the Akedah narrative is one of these examples of testing.[488] The way that Maimonides puts it is this, "There are those cases when it is difficult to comprehend the object of these trials."[489] Certainly, the prologue of the Book of Job is another example of this kind of testing.[490] The language about the "difficulty to comprehend," of course, is a version of the Garbled or Miscommunicated Theory as outlined in Chapter Three of this history.

Another observation that Moses Maimonides makes about the Akedah narrative is that the story "may have been the product of confusion, rather than of consideration, but the fact that he performed it three days after he had received the commandment, proves that he had the presence of thought, proper consideration, and careful examination of what is due to the Divine Command."[491]

Indeed, when considering the question of "Why a three-day journey?" Maimonides suggests that God chose to give Abraham time for deliberation and introspection and to make sure that Abraham's act of obedience was performed intentionally, and not in a state of shock.[492] In another passage of his analysis of the Akedah narrative, Moses Maimonides tells us that he regarded Abraham as having a higher moral standing than Moses. Maimonides makes this claim in the context of analyzing Genesis 22:12.[493]

In regard to the phrase, "God spoke to Abraham," in Genesis 22:11, Maimonides says, "This may be taken to mean, that 'Abraham felt with all his heart that the sacrifice is what God wanted him to do.'"[494] This thesis is derived from a comment made by Maimonides on verses 11 and 12.[495]

Moses Maimonides also spends considerable time discussing the ideas of "knowing" and "sight" in the Masoretic text. Indeed, the very idea of the Akedah story is to know, *la da'at*, whether Abraham loves God. But this is not a question for God because "the Almighty, All-Knowing God already knows it."[496] Rather, Maimonides notes that "he [Abraham] may prove whether he will walk in God's Law, or not." According to Maimonides, God's mission is "to humble him and to prove that He knows what is in his heart, and whether he will, or will not, keep his commandments."[497] This observation of Maimonides may be construed as an assenting to the Divine Plan Theory as an explanation of the Akedah narrative. God knew beforehand how the drama would play out.

Maimonides also likens the journey to Mount Moriah to the journey of the Jews "trouble and hardships in the wilderness." He comments about the link, "God has first trained you in the hardships of the wilderness, in order to increase your welfare when you entered the Land of Canaan."[498] In that regard, Maimonides indicates that:

> The transition from trouble to ease gives more pleasure than continual ease.[499]

In chapter 24 of part 1 of the *Guide for the Perplexed*, Maimonides also claims that if the Jews "had not undergone the trouble and the hardship of the wilderness, the Israelites would not have been able to conquer the land."[500]

In another section of the *Guide*, Moses Maimonides speaks of Abraham and Isaac and the idea of prophecy and its relationship to Truth. Maimonides puts the matter this way:

> If there are a thousand prophets, all of them of the status of Elijah and Elisha, and all had the same certain interpretation, and one thousand and one rabbis giving the opposite inter-pretation, you shall incline after the majority and the Law after the one thousand and one rabbis, not according to the one thousand venerable Prophets, only from the rabbis, who are men of Logic and Reason.[501]

Maimonides made this pronouncement in the context of a discussion of Prophecy and Visions and the manner of reliability they should be afforded by the Jewish Nation. The comment also came in the context of the weight of Revelation versus that of Reason when it comes to Religious Truth. Maimonides calls the rabbis "men of Logic and Reason," and because of his background in the philosophy of Aristotle, Moses Maimonides seems to take the side of Logic and Reason.[502]

Thus, in our analysis of Moses Maimionides' views in his *Guide for the Perplexed*, we have shown that he endorsed the following theories in regard to the meaning of the sacrifice of Isaac narrative: The Test View, the Isaac as Remnant Theory, possibly the Suspension of Ethics View, The Moral Qualities Theory, the Garbled or Miscommunication View, as well as the position we have called the Divine Plan Theory introduced in Chapter Three of this history.

This brings us to an analysis of the views of Nahmanides and other late medieval philosophers on the Akedah narrative. The topic of the next section of this chapter of the history of views on the Akedah, or the sacrifice of Isaac narrative, at Genesis 22:1–19.

The Views of Nahmanides and Other Late Medieval Jewish Scholars on the Akedah

Rabbi Moses ben Nahman (Nahmanides) (1194–1270), also known by his acronym, Ramban, was born in Spain and died in Palestine. He made his living as a physician. He wrote poetry, dabbled in the *Kabbalah*, and, for our purposes, wrote a lengthy analysis of the Akedah narrative of Genesis 22:1–19.

Nahmanides directly says that sometimes the patriarchs have erred, and he uses Abraham as an example. He tells us that "Abraham, our Father, unintentionally committed a great sin by bringing his righteous wife to a stumbling block of sin, on account of his fear of his life."[503] For the most part, Nahmanides assented to the Test Theory, much like his mentor, Maimonides. Nahmanides also posits an unusual view about Sarah and Ishmael. Nahmanides tells us:

> Sarah saw Ishmael making fun of Isaac, and since he was the son of a servant, Sarah worries about the power imbalance tilting in the direction of Ishmael. So Sarah banishes Ishmael and his mother, Hagar, from the house of Abraham.[504]

Some suggest that Nahmanides may be endorsing the Sibling Rivalry Theory here. Nahmanides was also against the view of Moses Maimonides about the problem of faith and reason, in terms of which of the two has priority when it comes to Religious Truth.[505] In one place of his analysis of the sacrifice of Isaac narrative, Nahmanides says that "Abraham heard God's voice in the wind." This is a view that Nahmanides shares with Benno Jacob (1862–1945), a German-born scholar of Semitic Languages.[506]

According to Rabbi Nahmanides, the implications of the Akedah focus on the difficult problem of reconciling belief in God's foreknowledge with the use of human free will. Nahmanides says God knew how Abraham would behave, but from Abraham's point of view, the test was real since he had to be rewarded not only for his willingness to obey the command but also for actually complying.[507] Nahmanides maybe combining here the Test View with the Divine Plan Theory regarding the mention of God's omniscience.

Rabbi Obadiah ben Jacob Sforno (1475–1550) elaborated on this point of Nahmanides and said this about Genesis 22:1, "Abraham had to transcend his own love of God by converting it from the potential to the actual so that it might more resemble God whose goodness is always actual."[508] Sforno says, "The aim here is to show that any human creation should always imitate the Divine creation."[509]

Nahmanides also makes some interesting comments on verses 12 and 14 of the Akedah narrative. About the former, he says the purpose of the verse is that "God has made known to all men how far humans are obliged to fear God."[510] Nahmanides disagreed with Rabbi Jacob bar Idi in their opinions of what God saw in 22:14. Rabbi Idi was a second-generation Amora sage in the Land of Israel. He thought what God "saw" was "the money of the Atonement," and Nahmanides says he saw the Temple.[511] Nahmanides may also be endorsing the Atonement Theory.

Indeed, Nahmanides thought, "Abraham calling the name of that place, 'The Lord will see,' on the Mount where the Lord was seen" (Genesis 22:14). Nahmanides adds, "Generations later, they will recall the initial revelation on Mount Moriah, as the Angel of the Lord also appeared to David on the very same mountain." Where the Temple would be built.[512]

Another late medieval Jewish interpreter of the Akedah narrative was Rabbi David Kimchi (1160–1235), known by his acronym "Radak." In regard to whether Abraham may have been mistaken about his command, Radak observes:

> But the truth is that this test was in order to show the na-
> tions of the world Abraham's complete love of God. And this

was not done for those generations, but rather for the later generations that believe in the Torah that Moses, peace be upon him, wrote by God's word, and in its stories, so that they would know how far Abraham's love of God extended and would learn from it to love God with their whole hearts and their whole souls.[513]

This idea of loving God with one's "whole heart and soul" is a recurring Biblical theme in both the Old and the New Testaments. We find it, for example, at Deuteronomy 6:5, 11:13, 13:3, 30:6 and First Samuel 12:20 and 24, as well as at the Gospels of Matthew 22:37 and Mark 12:30.

Thus, Rabbi David Kimchi was a member of that camp who believed the primary importance of the Akedah narrative was to understand the patriarch Abraham's love of God, as well as its tension with Abraham's fear of God. Rabbi Kimchi also discusses the Akedah narrative in the context of referring to the Prophet Jeremiah's chapter 7:23. There the Rabbi explains about the patriarchal age, "These sacrifices were never mandatory, though they were voluntary." In regard to God's command to Abraham, He said, *yakribu*, that is, "to offer up." But Kimchi suggests that what God actually said was *Adam ki akrib*, or "if a man shall offer up."[514] Thus, Rabbi Kimchi moves from a declarative to a conditional.

This suggests that Rabbi David Kimchi is in the group of those medieval Jewish rabbis who believed that the command to Abraham was garbled in some way, spoken of in the wind, or misunderstood in some other way. In fact, in the twelfth and thirteenth centuries, this group of rabbis was rather large in Western Europe.

Rabbi Isaac Abravanel (1437–1508) was one of the last medieval Jewish rabbis to analyze the Akedah narrative in Genesis 22:1–19. He completed a commentary on *Bereshith*, or Genesis, where he makes many observations about the sacrifice of Isaac. In one of those, the Spanish rabbi observes:

The Binding of Isaac is forever on our lips and in our prayers. For in it lies the entire strength of Israel and their merit before their Heavenly Father.[515]

Rabbi Abravanel may be assenting here to the Isaac as Remnant Theory. Abravanel also clearly states that there are indeed moral values for which they are worth sacrificing. And one of those—at least for Abravanel—is the sanctity of human life. For Abraham, Abravanel says, "even if that means endangering, or even sacrificing our own children for it."[516] Thus, Rabbi Abravanel appears to be an advocate of the Sanctity of Life Theory introduced back in Chapter Three, or possibly a Deontological Theory of Ethics.

Rabbi Abravanel tells us that Jews should remind God of Abraham's act of loyalty in order to win for ourselves some further merit on account of our ancestors. And Abravanel says, "We remind ourselves of the kind of devotion to moral principles that is requited of observant and committed Jews.[517]

More than any other Jewish, philosophical thinkers in the High Middle Ages—the eleventh to the fifteenth centuries—Rabbi Abravanel's views on the Akedah narrative are as close to a deontological system of ethics than any other medieval Jewish scholar.

Thus, in the late medieval Jewish period, we have seen proponents of the Test Theory, the Message was Garbled Theory, the Sanctity of Life Point of View, the Suspension of Ethics View, the Moral Qualities Approach, the Divine Plan Theory and the Deontological Theory of Ethics.

Another late medieval Jewish commentator on the Akedah narrative is Obadiah ben Jacob Sforno (1475–1555), an Italian Rationalist philosopher. His comments on the sacrifice of Isaac narrative come mostly in his extensive commentary of the Torah. In his commentary on Genesis, Rabbi Sforno makes a number of original observations about the Akedah narrative of Genesis 22. Among these original comments is the view that the Angel of the Lord who halted the sacrifice of Isaac at Genesis 22:11–12 is actually the Angel Michael, the Patron Angel of Israel. Rabbi Sforno also observes that *Malakh* Michael, or "Angel Michael," is also the angel in charge of circumcision.[518]

Additionally, Rabbi Sforno adds some dialogue to the Akedah narrative at verse 16. After Abraham had demonstrated his faith and loyalty to the Lord, God says to the Patriarch, "From now on, these months will be yours to do as you like."[519] Sforno, a sixteenth-century

Italian rabbi, was one of the most creative theological thinkers in the Jewish Middle Ages on the sacrifice of Isaac.

Another late medieval Jewish interpreter of Genesis and the Akedah narrative is Yosef Ibn Caspi (1279–1340). He was an extensive traveler having lived in Spain, France and on the island of Majorca. In a comment on the sacrifice of Isaac, he asked, "How could God ask Abraham to perform such a deplorable act?"[520] Caspi either assents to the Sanctity of Life Theory, or a Deontological View of Ethics, for it breaks the commandment, "Thou shalt not kill."

A final High Middle Ages Jewish treatment of the sacrifice of Isaac comes from Rabbi Ephraim ben Jacob of Bonn (1132–1200), chronicler of the Second Crusade (1147–1149). Ephraim wrote a twenty–six stanza poem on the Akedah. Each stanza is of four lines, with the final line in each stanza being a Biblical verse. AABB is the rhyme scheme employed by Rabbi Ephraim.[521] There are many unique elements in Rabbi Ephraim's poem. The most interesting of these is that Abraham kills Isaac twice. After the first death, Isaac is assumed into Heaven, where the angels worry that he is dead, so the son is allowed to return to Earth, only to have his father kill him again. At this point, God enters Ephraim's poem by halting the sacrifice.[522]

Other features of Rabbi Ephraim's poem, besides the Isaac Redivivus motif, are that Mount Moriah is called Mount Scopus, a 900-meter-tall hill in Israel that later became the site of the first Hebrew University in modern Israel.

Rabbi Ephraim's poem is written in the third person, as though someone was speaking to God and describing what went on in the Akedah narrative. After God halts the sacrifice the second time, He provides the substitute ram in Isaac's stead.

The two sacrificial scenes may seem to be overdone to modern sensibilities. But we must remember that Rabbi Ephraim lived in a time of great suffering and degradation for European Jews. This made him tell the story in a way that seems to make the rabbi feel closer to God and to identify Isaac as just as important a figure as his father, Abraham. In fact, Rabbi Ephraim seems to assent to what we have called the Test View, as well as the Isaac as Remnant Theory.

This brings us to the final section of Chapter Six, the Akedah in the medieval Jewish period. In that section, we shall explore medieval Jewish pieces of art that have depicted the Akedah.

The Akedah in Medieval Jewish Art

French and American archaeologists discovered the oldest depiction of the Akedah narrative in the Jewish tradition in excavations from 1928 until 1932. The site turned out to be a third-century synagogue at a place called Dura Europos, a Roman garrison town in ancient Babylon.[523] The Dura Europos site contained sixteen separate temples, all catering to the needs of a pantheon of Greek, Roman and Persian gods. The site also included a modest Christian chapel.[524]

The synagogue at Dura Europos has paintings covering all four walls of the forty-square-foot room. Several renderings surround the Torah shrine that includes images of Esther, Elijah, Samuel, Moses and the Pharaoh. For our purposes, the most important Biblical rendering at Dura Europos is one of the Akedah. It was found over the opening of the ark in the Torah shrine.[525]

This early piece of Jewish art was primitively made. Abraham, knife in hand, stands resolutely, with his back turned to on-lookers, and a very small bundle on the altar that turns out to be Isaac, also with his back to the on-lookers. Both of the figures have dark hair, and the facial features are difficult to understand. At the synagogue of Dura Europos, the depiction of Isaac is clearly that of a boy, not a grown man. And he does not appear to be bound.[526]

In the distance, a tiny figure can be seen, also with a shock of dark hair. Some interpreters suggest it is one of Abraham's servants, while others say it is Sarah. The figure appears to be wearing the same kind of clothes as Abraham, and therefore, it is unlikely to be Sarah. Another theory suggests it may be Ishmael. If this theory is correct, then the artist could have been an advocate of the Sibling Rivalry Theory, as introduced in Chapter Three.

In the lower foreground of the image, a large ram waits tethered to a tree. The Masoretic text is likely the source of this feature, for the Septuagint version has the ram "behind Abraham."[527] In the Coptic Bibles of the period, however, indicate that the ram "is tied to a tree."[528]

In 1929, two Hebrew University archaeologists named Sukenik and Avigad, discovered the remains of a sixth-century CE synagogue at a place called Bet Alpha, in the eastern Jezreel Valley, not far from Mount Gilboa. All that remained of the building was its foundation that was made of stone and cement. Mosaic tiles could be seen on the floor of the synagogue. The mosaics have a geometric pattern.

Edward Kessler describes the Bet Alpha site this way:

> Another important discovery was made in 1929 during an excavation in the eastern Jezreel Valley, just south of Galilee, which unearthed a mosaic floor of a sixth-century synagogue called Bet Alpha. A sequence of three scenes borders the floor like a carpet.[529]

The three Biblical renderings at Bet Alpha are images of Noah's Ark; a zodiac with the god Helios, one of the Greek titans and son of Hyperion, and his four horsemen; and most importantly for our purposes, a rendering of the sacrifice of Isaac narrative. At the entrance to the site are a lion and a bull accompanied by bilingual inscriptions in Greek and Aramaic. From left to right, the Bet Alpha Akedah shows the ass, the ram, Isaac, the two servants, and, of course, Abraham.[530]

In the Bet Alpha image, Abraham holds a large knife in his right hand, more like a sword than a knife. Isaac is prone on the altar next to the figure of Abraham. The ram is tethered to a tree, and the two servants can be seen off in the distance. Interestingly, the ram is much larger than the tree to which it is tied.[531] Louis Berman writes about the importance of the Bet Alpha Akedah. He relates:

> The Bet Alpha synagogue mosaic again attests to the popularity of the Akedah story in the ancient Palestinian community, for it is the only Biblical story illustrated on the mosaic floor.[532]

A third piece of early Middle Ages Jewish depiction of the Akedah is known as the *Trier Akedah*. The piece is a "Pyxis." or a cylindrical box made of ivory, whose lid contains the Akedah image. The box is owned by the Rheinisches Landesmuseum Trier in Germany and is from the fifth century. In the depiction, the knife is drawn, and Abraham has Isaac by the hair. The Abraham figure appears as a cruel, old man.[533]

Parallel to the Pyxis is the drawing of an Etruscan urn in the National Archaeological Museum in Florence, taken from some scenes of the dramas of Euripides. In fact, the plays of Euripides were among the most popular dramas in the Hellenistic Roman period, as well as for Jewish artistic renderings.[534]

In terms of Jewish artistic renderings in the High Middle Ages, several Jewish Haggadah and other pieces of art on the Akedah are extant. Among these are the following:

1. Akedah at Cathedral of Souillac (twelfth century)

2. Akedah images at the Cathedral of Saint Peter, Jaca, Spain (twelfth century)

3. Akedah image in the *Leipzig Haggadah* (fourteenth century)

4. Akedah in the *Bird's Head Haggadah* (thirteenth century)

5. Akedah scene at Saint Vitus Cathedral in Prague (fourteenth-century stained glass window)

6. Akedah image in the *Second Nurnberg Haggadah* (fifteenth century)

We will close this sixth chapter with an analysis of these four Jewish, late medieval pieces on the sacrifice of Isaac narrative. Between the sixth and the eleventh centuries, very few Jewish artistic renderings of the Akedah are extant. From the twelfth to the fifteenth century, however, there is a proliferation of images of the Akedah.

The twelfth-century Akedah image at the Cathedral of Souillac, for example, shows a young Isaac and an older Abraham wrestling over possession of the knife.[535] Another twelfth-century Spanish cathedral, the Church of Saint Peter in Jaca, Spain, also has a portal that depicts the Akedah narrative. Isaac stands with hands bound behind the back. Abraham prepares the altar for sacrifice. The scene includes the ass, the two servants, and the substitute ram for sacrifice.[536]

What is known as the *Bird's Head Haggadah*, which was discovered in 1946 by an Israeli curator named M. Narkiss, is accompanied by a

Biblical text from Exodus 2:23–24 that says, "Their cries ascended to God from their labors. And God heard our voice, as it is written, 'And God heard their cries and remembered his Covenant with Abraham.'"[537]

Finally, a fifteenth-century Haggadah illumination, from a manuscript known as the *Nurnberg Haggadah*, is now housed at the Schocken Institute for Jewish Research in Jerusalem.

The *Leipzig Mahzor* is one of the most luxurious medieval Hebrew manuscripts that are extant. It comes from the fourteenth century, most likely from southern Germany. Five of the portals represent the five liturgical sequence of the Day of Atonement, including the fifth image that illustrates the faith and obedience of Abraham. The *Mahzor* also includes an image of the ram. The ram's color is blue, perhaps to heighten the Midrashic text that underlies these images.[538]

There is a stained glass window at the Saint Vitus Cathedral in Prague that was constructed the third time, beginning in 1344. The rendering is completed in tones of red and blue glass. The piece contains renderings of Abraham, Isaac, the ram, the ass and the two servants. It most likely dates from the same period as the third restoration of the church.[539]

Finally, a fifteenth-century Haggadah illumination of the Akedah can be seen in a manuscript known as the *Nurnberg Haggadah*. It is now housed at the Schocken Institute for Jewish Research in Jerusalem. This depiction shows the medieval Midrash that Isaac indeed had been sacrificed and then subsequently was resurrected from the dead—what some call the Isaac Redivivus Theory to explain the Akedah narrative, or perhaps it is the Isaac as Remnant View.[540]

This brings us to the major conclusions of Chapter Six. In Chapter Seven of this history of Jewish, Christian, and Islamic perspectives on the sacrifice of Isaac in Genesis 22, we will turn our attention to the phenomenon of how Islam primarily has dealt with the Akedah narrative. It is to Islam, then, to which we turn next.

Conclusions to Chapter Six

We began this chapter with some observations on the Akedah narrative found in the Midrash Tanhuma, a fourth-century CE text. In our analysis, we examined several passages in the Tanhuma, where Abraham and Isaac are discussed. For the most part, the *Tanhuma* repeats many other

Misrashic observations on the Akedah, such as the Isaac Redivivus View, the Test Theory, and the Atonement Point of View.

In the second section of Chapter Six, we introduced and discussed several medieval Jewish thinkers who had written *piyyutim*, or liturgical poems on the sacrifice of Isaac. These poems we have examined came from Jewish poets from the earliest Rabbinic opinions, all the way up to the work of Saadiah Gaon, the great medieval Jewish philosopher, exegete and poet.

This material was followed by the third section of Chapter Six on the views on the Akedah found in the twelfth-century writings of philosopher Moses Maimonides. In this section, we identified and discussed passages on the Akedah in Maimonides' *Guide for the Perplexed,* as well as some of his other works.

Our discussion of Moses Maimonides was followed by an analysis of several late Middle Ages Jewish commentators on the sacrifice of Isaac narrative. These included Nahmanides, David Kimchi, Rabbi Isaac Abravanel, as well as Italian rationalist philosopher, Rabbi Obadiah Sforno, and Rabbi Ephraim ben Jacob of Bonn. Each of these late medieval Jewish thinkers, as we have shown, made original observations about the Akedah narrative.

Finally, in the fourth section of this chapter, we examined several late ancient and medieval works of art that depicted the sacrifice of Isaac. Among the works examined were two early Jewish synagogues, a work of art produced on a Pyxis, an ornamental, marble box, several illustrations contained in medieval Jewish illuminated Haggadah, as well as several features found in medieval churches and cathedrals that were made by medieval Jews.

Altogether, we identified and discussed six pieces of Jewish art that rendered the narrative of Genesis 22:1–19, the sacrifice of Isaac narrative. What we have concluded about these pieces of Jewish art is that, for the most part, they reflect the exegetical materials we identified from the same period. Indeed, in the Jewish High Middle Ages, we examined works of art from the twelfth to the fifteenth centuries.

As indicated earlier, in the seventh chapter of this history, we will examine what the Faith of Islam has had to say and believe about

Ibrahim's sacrifice of his son. Following this chapter, then, we move to the Akedah narrative in the Islamic faith.

Chapter Seven:
The Akedah in the Islamic Faith

One distinctive feature in Moslem depictions of the
Akedah is an angel carrying a ram. Chagall saw this detail
in a Persian miniature, or other Moslem depiction of the
Akedah.

—Louis Berman, *The Akedah*

The Qur'an is not merely inspired by God, it is the word
of God. The Qur'an is not a record of the events of His
people or His interventions among them. It is an exhortation to remember that God is God.

—Carol Delaney, *Abraham on Trial*

We have tried you, as We have tried the owners of the
Garden, when they bowed to gather their fruits in the
morning, but did not add, "If Allah may please."

—The Holy Qur'an, surah 68:17 (Author's translation)

Introduction

The main goal of this seventh chapter is to describe and discuss what
the religion of Islam has had to say about the sacrifice of Ibrahim's
(Abraham's) son. We will begin the chapter with some general remarks
about the figures of Hagar and Ishmael (Hajar and Ismail) in the
Muslim faith. This will be followed by a discussion of the notion of
sacrifice in Islam. These two sections of this chapter will be followed

by an analysis of the places in Al-Qur'an, and then in traditional hadith literature, where Ibrahim's sacrifice of his son is discussed. These sections of Chapter Seven will be followed by an attempt at answering the question, "In Islam, which of Ibrahim's sons is the object of sacrifice, Ishaq (Isaac) or Ismail (Ishmael)? This section is the most central of Chapter Seven. In the final section, we shall explore the places in Islamic art, where the phenomenon of the sacrifice of Ibrahim's son has been depicted. This brings us to some general comments about the figures of Hajar and Ismail in the Judeo-Christian tradition, the topic of the first section of Chapter Seven.

Hajar and Ismail in the Judeo-Christian Tradition

Before turning our attention to the Akedah in the Islamic faith, we first will give a short review of the figures of Hagar and Ishmael (Hajar and Ismail) as they appear in the Hebrew Bible and the history of Islam. The principal reason for this task is that Hajar and her son Ismail became the progenitors of the Islamic faith.

Chapter fifteen of the Book of Genesis closes with a promise of land, "I have given this land to your seed."[541] This is followed by the names of ten people included in the gift to Abraham's seed. Then the opening of chapter sixteen of Genesis tells us this:

> Thus, all of these, viz. the Kenites, the Kenizites, etc. were promised to Abraham's Seed, yet so far, Sarah, Abraham's wife, bore him no children.[542]

The text seems to concentrate on the patriarch Abraham chiding God with what might be called "lifted eyebrows," and the response, "What seed?" After decades of infertility, Sarah decides to submit to the ancient practice of having a servant help her to "build up the seed." The Book of Jubilees identifies Eliezer as a son of Meseq, who was a handmaid, at Genesis 14:2.[543]

Sarah's servant Hagar flaunts her pregnancy in the face of her mistress and yields her pregnancy as a weapon against Sarah. The narrative of Hagar also supplies the origin of the Bedouin tribes near the southern border of Israel in an area known as the "Hagrites," at least according to Psalm 83:7 that tells us, "Gebal and Ammon and Amalek,

Philistia, with the inhabitants of Tyre."[544] Hagar is also the progenitor of rebellious slaves and servants who fled to the desert, mentioned at chapter sixteen of Genesis.[545]

The saving of Hagar's son, Ishmael, like Sarah's son Isaac, is named "God will hear," at Genesis 16:11. The well of Hagar is named "the well of living seeing," and it comes with a promise of great progeny. Like Isaac, Ishmael was a son threatened with death and then saved. And a parent marks the spot of the miracle "God will see."[546]

Both of Abraham's sons, then, take part in an initiation ritual. In his essay, "The Initiation Legend of Isaac," H. C. White points to eight parallels between the fates of Ishmael and Isaac. These are:

1. The possible death of the son (21:5 and 16a and 22:1–6)

2. An appeal from the son (21:16b and 22:7–10)

3. A divine summons (21:7a and 16:8b and 22:11a and b)

4. A human response (16:8b and 22:11b)

5. Divine imperative to save the son (16:9 and 21:17b and 22:12a)

6. The reason for salvation (16:10–12 and 21:18b and 22:12b)

7. Miraculous sight (21:19 and 22:13)

8. Concluding response (16:13–14, 21:20–21, and 22:14 and 15–18)[547]

Professor White also suggests parallels between these initiation rites of Ishmael and Isaac and certain Greek figures in classical mythology, like Athanus and Phrixus.[548] Isaac's initiation, of course, was to fulfill the promise of Jewish Nationhood, perhaps a reference to the Isaac as Remnant Theory. Ishmael's initiation and salvation from death, on the other hand, as to fulfill the promise to be the etiology of the Nation of Islam. Thus, it is important to see that the figures of Ishmael and Hagar, at least for the Moslems, were every bit as important as those of Sarah and Isaac for the Nation of Israel.

This basic presupposition of this seventh chapter always must be kept in mind when discussing Islamic views of sacrifice, as well as the Akedah narrative and which of Abraham's sons is the son for sacrifice. This brings us to an analysis of the idea of sacrifice in the Islamic faith, the topic of the second section of this seventh chapter.

Sacrifice in Islam

There are a variety of words in the classical Arabic language to speak of sacrifice. The most important of these are *Qurban* and *Qurbani*. There are, however, at least six other nouns association with sacrifice, including the nouns *fudaa* and *'adhia* that both mean "sacrifice," and *tadhia* that designates "sacrifice victim." The verb *duhana* means "to victimize," and the noun *dahia* also means "victim of sacrifice." Additionally, the word *udhiya* is sometimes employed in classical Arabic as a synonym for *Qurban* and *Qurbani* that also mean "sacrifice."

There are a variety of passages in the Muslim Holy Book, Al-Qur'an. Most of these simply refer to the idea of making sacrifices in the Islamic faith. At the Holy Book's surah five, 27, for example, tells us this:

> And recite the story of Adam's two sons, in truth, when they both offered a sacrifice to Allah, and it had been accepted from one of them but not from the other.[549]

It is likely that the Muslim Holy Book is referring here to Abraham's two sons, one where the sacrifice is accepted (Ishmael), and the other where it is not (Isaac). Al-Qur'an's 6:162 gives us another representative example:

> Say, "Indeed my prayer, my rites of sacrifice, my living and my dying are all for Allah, Lord of the Worlds."[550]

A variety of other classical Arabic nouns and verbs are also employed in the Islamic faith. Two words, for example, from the THB Semitic root, that is *thabahu* and *thabiha*, are often translated as the verb "to slaughter" that can be found at the Holy Book's 2:67 and

2:71. Another good example of the use of *thabahu* can be seen at surah 22:36, which speaks of a sacrificial animal on its side after it has fallen slaughtered.[551]

The noun, *Bud'na* is a word used to designate the "sacrifice of an animal." And *thabahu* is also employed at surah 108:1–2 of Al-Qur'an. This latter passage in English translation tells us this:

> We have surely given you preeminence in numbers and in following. So, serve your Lord with full dedication and sacrifice.[552]

Many of the passages in the Muslim Holy Book that speaks of sacrifice come in connection to the Feast of *Eid Al-Adha*. Two good examples of this tendency in Al-Qur'an can be found at surah 5:114 and surah 37:100 to 111, particularly ayats, or verses, 105 to 107. The verse in surah 5 uses a word for "sacrifice" to indicate food, which is a sacrificial animal to be eaten. Surah 37:105–107 is a passage we will refer to many times in this chapter. The English translation of this verse tells us this:

> You have fulfilled your dream, and thus do We reward the good. This was indeed a trying test, so we ransomed him for a great sacrifice.[553]

The word for "test" in the passage above, as well as the verb "to try," is the Arabic word *ikhtibar*. It is employed in Al-Qur'an when Allah "tests" the moral characters, or "tries" them, often with evil and suffering. The word *ikhtibar*, and its related terms, is used throughout the Muslim Holy Book, such as at surah 2:155; 3:141; surah 51:14; and surah 68:17, two times. It is also employed at surah 54:27, where it appears as the verb, "to try."

Another classical Arabic term, *imtahan*, is also used many times in the Muslim Holy Book. This word is a noun. It is employed when one takes an examination or a "test." This word is also used many times in Al-Qur'an.

The Semitic tri-consonant root KHTB is the source for a variety of words in classical Arabic that designate terms related to test, try, trial, tempt, as well as the verb "to deceive." This Semitic root is used around fifty times in Al-Qur'an, including the verbal form "to test" at surah 2:249 and 22:53; the verb "to try" at 2:155, as we have indicated earlier, as well as at 3:152; 5:94; surah 51:14, 54:27, and surah 37:106. The same Semitic root is also the source of words related to the noun "trial," such as at surah 1:155, 7:141 and 21:35. A verb designating "to tempt" has as its etiology the same Semitic root that is employed at surah 20:131 and 21:35, for example; and words in Arabic related to "deception" and the verb "to deceive" can be found in the Muslim Holy Book at surah 2:102 and ayat 124.

Other words associated with sacrifice in early Islam include the verb *jaz min* that means "to give up" a *Yajus*, or sacrifice, and the noun *dhabiha* is a word that implies an "offering" in classical Arabic. Another noun that is sometimes employed in the context of sacrifice is the word *khasara* that, in general, designates a "loss." The word *dhabiha* has a synonym in classical Arabic, the term *zubiha*, which often refers to the "sacrificed animal." This word is also employed in discussions of what constitutes *Halah* meat, or that which is acceptable, like the word *Kosher* in Judaism.

The classical Arabic word *dhabiha* comes from the Semitic root DHB. This is the source of many terms in the history of Islam related to testing and tempting, often to evil. In some traditional hadith, the Arabic expression *Al-Dhabihu Ishaq* is employed when speaking of the sacrifice of Prophet Ibrahim's son. It means, "The Sacrificial Son is Isaac." Other more modern Muslim scholars, however, believe that the *Dhabihu* is Ismail (Ishmael).

The word *Khasara* is used a number of times in the Muslim Holy Book, Al'Qur'an, including at surah 108:1–2 that advise us, "We have surely given you your preeminence in number and following, so serve your Lord with full dedication and sacrifice."[554]

Many of these words are related to the Root KHTB, as well as the Arabic word *Ikhtibar*, the most often Arabic term to designate a "test." Indeed, the Test Theory we introduced back in Chapter Three of this history is often the major understanding that is given for the sacrifice of Ibrahim's son in the Islamic faith.

Another word employed in classical Arabic to speak of "testing" is the word *imtahan*. It is used as a noun and as a verb. This is also true of another word, *tajriba*, that designates a "test," but it is more often used as a noun than a verb. The verbal form of *imtahan* is *yamtahin*, which generally means "to test." Another Arabic word, *jedheb*, is used to express the idea of "tempting" often in relation to evil.

Many of these classical Arabic terms are employed throughout Al-Qur'an. We will have several examples in the Muslim Holy Book and the normal English equivalents:

1. surah 2:102 (past tense of "test")

2. 3:141 (test or purify)

3. 8:28 (temptation or testing)

4. 9:126 (tested)

5. 29:3 (tried)

6. 47:31 (to try)

7. 20:85 (trial)

8. 67:2 (to try)

9. 68:17 (tried)

10. 91:8 (to test)

One conclusion we can make about these passages, as well as those related to the sacrifice of Prophet Ibrahim's son, is that one of the major ways followers of Islam have always dealt with the issues of evil and suffering is what we have labeled the Test View back in Chapter Three of this history of attitudes toward the Akedah passage at Genesis 22:1–19.

This brings us to the places in traditional hadith literature, where discussions and traditions on sacrifice can be found, the subject matter of the next section of this seventh chapter.

Sacrifice in Hadith Literature

The Arabic word, *hadith*, as well as its plural form, *ahadith*, are collections of sayings and activities of the Prophet Muhammad. Both

Shiite and Sunni Islam have a number of traditional recorders or collectors of hadith literature that essentially has a similar role in Islam that the ancient Rabbinic opinions had in Judaism or the early church fathers have had in the Christian tradition.

Among the traditional collectors of hadith in Islam in regard to sacrifice, traditions from Abu Bukhari, Sahih Muslim, Sunan Abu Dawud, Al-Albari and Al-Tirmidzi, all have collected sayings and deeds of the Prophet Muhammad that are related to the practice, mostly of animal sacrifice, in the Islamic faith.

In the collection of Abu Bukhari, for example, he refers to the word "sacrifice" 240 times in 153 ahadith. Among these are traditions in book XII, number 818; book III, numbers 67 and 84; book IV, number 140; and book VI, numbers 293 to 313. Among the collection of Sahih Muslim, at book 22, chapter three, the great collector speaks of sacrifice in Islam are numbers 4818, 4819, 4820, 4822, and 4823 to 4845.

At volume VII, book 68, number 454, Bukhari relates the following tradition:

> The Prophet said whoever slaughters the sacrifice before the prayer, then he slaughters it only for himself, and whoever slaughters it after the prayer, he slaughters it at the right time told to the Muslims.

In Abu Bukhari's collection, at volume VII, book 68, number 455, narrated by Muhammad's companion Anas Ibn Malik, relates:

> The Prophet used to distribute among his Companions some animals for sacrifice to be slaughtered on Eid Al-Adha. Uqbi's share was a six-month-old goat. Uqbi said, "Oh Allah's Apostle, I get my share as a six-month-old ram." Then the Prophet said, "Well, slaughtered it as a Sacrifice."

Another tradition of Al-Bukhari, also narrated by Anas Ibn Malik, tells us, "The Prophet used to offer two rams as a sacrifice, and I also used to offer two rams, as well."[555] Anis Ibn Malik was born in Medinah, ten years before the prophet's journey, or *Hegira*, in 622 CE from Mecca to Medinah. Ibn Malik was one of the most renowned imams of the early faith. Another hadith from Sahih Bukhari, at book 68, number 465, the Sunni collector says:

> The Prophet slaughtered two rams, black and white in color.
> As he sacrificed, I saw him put his foot on their sides, and
> mentioning the name of Allah and Tikbar Allahu Akhbar. Then
> he slaughtered the two with his own hands.

In classical Arabic, the expression *Tikbar Allahu Akhbar* means, "God is the greatest." It is employed in a variety of contexts in the Muslim faith, including this mention of *Qurban*, or "sacrifice" in traditional hadith literature.

Many of the ahadith of Al-Bukhari on the issue of sacrifice sketch out the requirements for the practice, and what should and should not be done to fulfill the ritual requirements. For example, in book 22, hadith numbers 4850, 4870, and 4876, we see in the latter passage, "If anyone performs a sacrifice for anyone other than Allah, that person will be cursed by the Prophet Muhammad."

At hadith number 4870 of volume 22, Bukhari tells us, "If you offer sacrifice, don't get your hair or nails clipped beforehand." At book 22, numbers 4838, Bukhari tells us,

> Muhammad gave the gifts of goats to his companions. And
> when they did, this they discovered that one lamb was left
> over. They asked him what to do with it and he replied, 'Sacri-
> fice it yourself.'

Often the purposes that lie behind these judgments of Muhammad about how to conduct sacrifices are not known, like why one should not cut one's hair or nails beforehand, for example.

In the collection of hadith of Sunan Abu Dawud, he refers to sacrifice at book 20, number 27; and book 16, numbers 1 to 5. Al-Tirmidzi discusses *Qurban* throughout his collection, including one hadith that says, "No act is more pleasing to Allah than the act of Sacrifice." In another hadith, at volume XVI, number 1040, Abu Dawud reports that the prophet said about the phenomenon of sacrifice:

When you kill an animal for sacrifice, always use a good method, for one of you should sharpen his knife so the animal feels as little pain as possible.

Many of the ahadith on sacrifice recorded by Abu Dawud speak specifically about what kind of animals should, and should not, be sacrificed. At book XV, number 2784, for example, the collector says, "I saw Ali sacrificing two rams, so I ask him, 'What is this?'" He replied, "The Apostle of Allah has enjoined upon me to sacrifice for his benefit, so that is what I am doing." In the same book, at hadith number 2790, Abu Dawud relates what animals not to sacrifice. He says:

The Prophet said, "Don't sacrifice a one-eyed animal, a sick animal, a lame animal that limps, an animal with a broken leg with no marrow in it. I also detest any animal with defective teeth."

In another hadith from Abu Dawud, narrated by Umm Kirz, relates that "Two resembling sheep are to be sacrificed, and two for a boy and one for a girl, but it does not matter if the animals are male or female." This hadith comes at book 15, hadith number 2828. In another hadith from book 15, number 2795, Abu Dawud also relates that, "You are forbidden to sacrifice an animal with a slit ear, or a broken horn."

Philosopher and collector of hadith, Al-Albari, has a lengthy discussion of the phenomenon of sacrifice in book 68, numbers 453, 454, 462 and 465, among other places in his collection. In addition, other major collectors of hadith, like Abu Hurayra, for example, also discuss the issue of sacrifice in his extensive collection of hadith, that includes 5, 374 ahadith, a dozen or so about sacrifice.

The hadith collection of Sahih Muslim contains several traditions about sacrifice. In volume 22, book VI, numbers 162 and 163, Muslim has the prophet saying, "All of my sacrifices are for nothing more than the greater Glory of Allah." In another work of Sahih Muslim that he called "The book of Hunting, Slaughtering, and What is to be Eaten," he includes a number of traditions about Muhammad and sacrifice, including this one that tells us:

On the day of Eid Al-Adha, before returning, he offered a
prayer when he saw the flesh of the sacrificial animal that had
been slaughtered before the Prophet had finished his prayer.
So he ordered another animal to be sacrificed after he completed the prayer.

Other traditions on sacrifice recoded by Sahih Muslim can be
found at book 22, numbers 4830 and 4834. In the former Muslim says,
"No one should sacrifice an animal unless he has completed his Eid
prayer." In the latter passage, the one at 3834, Sahih Muslim remarks:

When you sacrifice an animal, only a grown animal should be
used for the *Qurban*, or "Sacrifice," unless it is too difficult for
you, in which case you may sacrifice an animal of less than a
year old, but more than six months old.

Many of the earliest ahadith on sacrifice take great care to point out
that the sacrifices performed under the aegis of the Prophet Muhammad
were always performed to the letter of the law. In the tradition from
Sahih Muslim quoted above, Muhammad made sure that he fulfilled
those provisions set out for sacrifice in early Islam.

The *Tafsir* of several commentators of Moslem philosophers and
theologians also contain several traditions about sacrifice in Islam.
One prime example of many is Al-Qummi (603–681), Yemeni scholar
and companion of the Prophet Muhammad. Al-Qummi was among
those who believed the son for sacrifice in Islam was Ismail and not
Ishaq.

On the other hand, the great Iraqi, Muslim scholar Al-Tabari (839–
923), in his two most important works, his *History of the Prophets*, and
in his *Commentary on the Qur'an*, says explicitly that as to the son for
sacrifice in Islam, "It really was Isaac."[556] We will take up this question
of which of Ibrahim's sons was the son for sacrifice in the next section
of this seventh chapter.

For the most part, the three most important topics regarding hadith
on sacrifice almost all speak about the rules of the slaughter and sacrifice
of animals during the Feast of *Eid Al-Adha*, including the weapon to be
used and the manner of the sacrifice, as well as which of Ibrahim's sons
is the one for sacrifice. We must enter this section with the realization

that in hadith literature, there is a good bit of disagreement over who was Ibrahim's son of sacrifice. Al-Baydawi, Athir Kamil, Ahmad Ibn Hanbal, Abu Dawud and Abu Kuraya, all believed the son was Isaac, while Umar Zamakhshari (1074–1143) and many other medieval and modern scholars believed he was Ismail (Ishmael).

Al-Tabari, Ibn Abbas and Ibn Bashar believed the son was Isaac, while many modern scholars, such as Muhammad H. Haykal in his *Life of Muhammad*, is convinced that Ibrahim's son for sacrifice is Ismail.[557] How much weight modern scholars who hold this view put on the fact that Hagar and Ishmael are the progenitors of the Arabs and the Muslim faith is not clear. But this certainly what may be at the heart of arriving at that conclusion. At any rate, we turn now to the issue of the identity of the son for sacrifice in the history of Islam.

Which of Ibrahim's Sons is the Son of Sacrifice?

The account of Genesis 22 and Al-Qur'an surah 37 have both agreements and disparities about the son of Ibrahim for sacrifice. The Torah identifies the son five times as Isaac, while Al-Qur'an leaves the son nameless. Reuven Firestone suggests that thirty-eight early Islamic scholars identify the son as Isaac, and twenty-eight as Ishmael. Firestone also tells us that 131 ahadith, or traditions of Muhammad, name the son as Isaac, while another 133 traditions suggest the identity of the son in question is Ishmael. In one hadith the prophet said,

> Then we ransomed with a tremendous victim, and he said, "He is Isaac." But others say the ransomed one was Ishmael, but the Jews claimed it was Isaac. But the Jews are liars.[558]

We begin this section of Chapter Seven, then, by pointing out that the name of the son for sacrifice is not clear in the Judeo-Islamic tradition.

Perhaps the most controversial question about the phenomenon of sacrifice in early Islam is which of Prophet Ibrahim's sons was the son commanded by God to be sacrificed. In this section of Chapter Seven, we will explore many of the Islamic scholarly views in answering that question. Islamic scholars, however, both early on and modern, disagreed about the son for sacrifice in Islam.

In his 1990 book *Journeys in Holylands: The Evolution of the Abraham-Ishmael Legends in Islamic Exegesis,* scholar Reuven Firestone gives a summary of Muslim scholars on the issue at hand. All tolled, Firestone suggests 131 different scholars who believed Ibrahim's son for sacrifice was Ishaq, or Isaac, and another 133 Islamic views on the matter, who said the son was Ismail (Ishmael).[559]

Among those Islamic thinkers who believed the son was Ishaq, at least according to Firestone, are:

Al-Tabari (839–923)

Ibn Qutaybah (828–884)

Al-Thalbi (950–1035)

Al-Zamakhshari (1075–1144)

Al-Kisa'i (737–804)

Ibn Jarir (839–923)

Ibn Al-Athir (1166–1233)

Ibn Kathir (1300-1373)

Mujit Al-Din (1450–1522)

On the other hand, those Muslim scholars who believe the son of Ibrahim for sacrifice was Ismail, or Ishmael, were:

Abu Al-Ja'far (624–699)

Abdallah Ibn Umar (610–693)

Ahmad Ibn Hanbal (780–855)

Abu Salih (865–915)

Ibn Ishaq (704–767)

Muhammad Ibn Ka'b Al-Qurtubi (1214–1273)

Yusuf Ibn Mihran (680–765)

Al-Kalbi (737–819)

Sa'id Ibn Al-Mussaayyib (642–715)

The most often quoted figure on the Ishaq view is Al-Tabari, who in his *History of the Prophets* tells us this:

As for the above-mentioned proof from Al-Qur'an that it was really Isaac, it is Allah's word that informs us about the prayer of his friend Ibrahim, when he left his people to migrate to Syria with Sarah. Abraham prayed, "I am going to my Lord who will guide me. My Lord, grant me a righteous child." This was before Allah foretold to Ibrahim that he would have a gentile son. Al-Qur'an does not mention any tidings of a male child given to Ibrahim except in the instance where it refers to Isaac, in which Allah said, "And his wife, standing by, laughed when we gave her tidings of Isaac, and after Isaac, Jacob." And then he became fearful of them.[560]

Another early Islamic view regarding which of Ibrahim's sons was the one for sacrifice is the Umayyid Prince and Fifth Caliph, Umar Ibn Abd Al-Aziz, who ruled from 712 to 720 CE. Omar was the son of Umar II and governor of Iraq from 744 to 745. Omar related that he was told by a Jewish scholar who converted to Islam as well as another Jewish convert that:

The Jews were well-informed that Ismail [Ishmael] was the son who was bound for sacrifice, but the Jews concealed this fact out of jealousy.[561]

The other primary source for answering our question about the identity of the son is the text in Al-Qur'an, referred to by Al-Tabari, that comes at surah 37:100–113. This text reveals the following:

100. And he prayed, "Oh Lord grant me a righteous Son."

101. So, we gave him the good news of a clement Son.

102. When he was old enough to go about with him, he said, "Oh my son, I dreamt that I was sacrificing you. What do you think of that?" He replied, "Father, do what you have been commanded. If Allah pleases, you will find me firm."

103. When they submitted to the will of Allah and Ibrahim laid his son down prostrate on the Temple.

104. And we called out, "Oh Ibrahim."

105. You have fulfilled your dream. Thus, do we reward the Good.

106. That was indeed a trying test.

107. So, we ransomed him for a sacrifice.

108. And we left his hallowed memory for posterity.

109. Peace be on Ibrahim.

110. That is how we reward those who do the Good.

111. He is truly among our faithful creatures.

112. So, we gave him the good news of Ishaq, an apostle among the righteous.

113. And we blessed him and Ishaq, among their progeny are many who do the Good, but others who only do wrong things.[562]

Louis Berman sums up the Islamic view of the Akedah in five points:

1. The command to sacrifice his son comes to Ibrahim in a dream.

2. The dream recurs on three successive nights, so it must be from Allah.

3. Ibrahim tells his son about the dream and asks him, "What do you think of that?"

4. The son answers, "You must do what you have been told, Allah willing you will find me patient."

5. Nothing in the Biblical account matches the tenderness,

candor, and devotion of this father-son interchange.[563]

Some Muslim scholars use this narrative from Al-Qur'an to decide which son was the object of the sacrifice. At surah 37:99, Ibrahim asks Allah to grant him a son, and Allah answers his prayer in the next verse when it tells us that Allah says, "So we gave him good tidings of a forbearing boy." Some say this *ayat*, or verse, gives the context of the sacrifice. This episode of the sacrifice is tied to surah 112:3 that tells us, "So we gave him good tidings of Isaac." Indeed Al-Tabari uses this connection as proof that the sacrifice son must be Ishaq because Al-Qur'an only mentions the idea of "glad tidings" when it is to Isaac that the expression is employed.

But if we examine the Arabic text carefully, it is clear that the "glad tidings" at surah 37:102 occurs before the actual sacrifice. Then the sacrifice itself is described, followed by the words, "and we gave him the glad tidings of Ishaq [Isaac], a *Nabi* and one of the righteous." A *Nabi* is the classical Arabic word for "prophet," so Ishaq is given an honorific title and appears to be the son of the sacrifice.[564]

But again, if we examine the Arabic text carefully, we conclude that there are two "glad tidings" mentioned—one prior to the sacrifice and one after. In the first of those, the identity of the son is ambiguous, but the one after the sacrifice, so this view has it, clearly identifies the son as Isaac. Another question that can be raised, however, is why the Muslim Holy Book is redundant on this issue.

In other ways, what is the sense in narrating the glad tidings of Isaac after the sacrifice if it already has been mentioned before the sacrifice? Needless repetition in any writing is never a good thing, for it is extraneous and a mark of poor writing.

Nevertheless, there are many similarities of this narrative in Al-Qur'an and the Masoretic text of Genesis 22:1–19. Among these are the labeling of the event as a "Test," the last-minute halting of the sacrifice, the ransom, the mention of a substitute ram, and the references to the "Seed" or progeny of Abraham-Ibrahim.[565]

But there also are some significant differences between the two narratives. For one thing, rather than on Mount Moriah, the sacrifice takes place in Islam on Mount Mina, near the city of Mecca. Secondly,

Ibrahim "flings" his son down "on his face," or, in some versions, "on his forehead."[566] Thirdly, Al-Qur'an mentions that some of Ibrahim's seed shall be Good, and some not so Good.[567]

Fourthly, the version in Al-Qur'an says nothing of Ibrahim's great faith and fidelity that are certainly central in the Akedah narrative. Fifthly, there is nothing of a dream in the Biblical account where Abraham is given the message to sacrifice his son. Finally, it is presumed that Ismail is the son for sacrifice because elsewhere in Al-Qur'an, the sacrifice is identified with the building of the *Ka'ba* at surah 2:127, for example.[568]

Again, Louis Berman sums up the "significance of the Akedah in the Islamic tradition." Again, they appear, therefore, to be fivefold:

1. To proclaim Islam's continuity with the faith of Ibrahim.

2. To portray Ibrahim as a man of perfect faith.

3. To celebrate Ishmael, and to portray him as obedient to the command of his father and to the will of God.

4. To celebrate the goodness of God, who by accepting Ibrahim's sacrifice, made him a model for all of humanity.

5. To establish animal sacrifice as an important ritual in Islamic religious life.[569]

Louis Berman, in his classic *The Akedah: The Binding of Isaac*, goes on to add, "The Feast that commemorated the Sacrifice is the major, religious holiday in Islam. He speaks here, of course, of the Feast of *Eid Al-Adha*.[570]

For the most part, in more modern Islam, Muslims now believe the son for sacrifice was Ismail. Many Muslim scholars in the contemporary period point out that Ibrahim is told to, "Take your son, your only son, whom you love."[571] Since Ishaq was Ibrahim's second son, there never was a time when he was Ibrahim's "only son." Thus, some modern Muslim scholars conclude the son must have been Ismail/Ishmael.[572]

As we indicated earlier in this seventh chapter, the sacrifice of

Ismail is celebrated in Islam at the Feast of *Eid Al-Adha*. This feast is celebrated on the tenth day of *Dhul Hijja*, a month in the Muslim calendar. The chief purpose of the Feast of *Eid Al-Adha* is to celebrate Ibrahim's willingness to sacrifice his son. This feast of Eid also signals the end of the Hajj, or the Pilgrimage to Mecca.[573]

Contemporary Muslim scholar, Abdus Sattar Ghawri, in an essay entitled, "The Only Son offered for Sacrifice: Isaac or Ishmael," employs a passage from Deuteronomy 21:15–17 that he believes is proof for the Sibling Rivalry View. An English translation of this text looks like this:

> If a man has two wives, one of them loved and the other disliked, and if both the loved and the disliked have given birth to sons, and the first son is born to the disliked wife, then on the day that the husband's will is read, then the man was not to treat the son of the loved wife with a preference to the son of the disliked, who is the firstborn. He must acknowledge as his firstborn who is the son of the one who is disliked, and give him a double portion of all that he owned, since he is the first issue of his virility. Thus, the right of the firstborn son is his.[574]

The parallel here to Abraham and his two sons should be obvious. Another modern Muslim scholar who has weighed in on the question of the son for sacrifice is Hamid al-Din Farahi (1863–1930), an Indian Muslim scholar. In his tome entitled *Al-Ray Al-Sihih fi man huwa al-Dhabih* also suggests several reasons why he believed the son of Ibrahim for sacrifice was Ismail/Ishmael.[575]

In other versions of the dream of Ibrahim about the sacrifice, the patriarch has the dream for three nights in a row in his sleep. Other sources say it is seven consecutive nights with the dream. What to make of these additional narratives, however, is not entirely clear. What is clear is that Ishmael/Ismail, the progenitor of the Arabs and the Muslim faith, receiving a higher status is not surprising. Nor is it surprising that Islam moved the site of the sacrifice from Mount Moriah to an area near Mecca.

Even some Christian traditions advocate the view that Ishmael was the son of sacrifice. *The Oxford Companion to the Bible*, for example, relates that:

> In the Muslim tradition, the Arabs trace their ancestor back to

Abraham through Ishmael because Ishmael was circumcised
[Genesis 17:25], and so are most Muslims. So most Muslims
make Ishmael the Son of Sacrifice in the Islamic faith.[576]

Another way that some thinkers have suggested that the question
about the son of sacrifice might be answered is by asking what Prophet
Muhammad's *Sahaba*, or "Companions," have said about Ibrahim's
sacrifice of his son. Unfortunately, as Rueven Firestone has pointed
out, he identified thirty-eight of the Companions who believed the son
in question was Isaac. But Firestone also identified another twenty-
eight opinions that say that the son is Ismail, or Ishmael.[577]

The major conclusion we may make in regard to this analysis is
that at the beginning of the Islamic faith, scholars were mixed about the
identity of the son of sacrifice, while more modern interpreters, for the
most part, have sided with the figure of Ismail/Ishmael on this issue.
This brings us to another section of this seventh chapter in which the
topic for discussion is the use of sacrifice in the Feast of *Eid Al-Adha*.

Sacrifice in the Feast of Eid Al-Adha

Eid Al-Adha is observed on the tenth day of Dhul-Hijjah, the final month
of the Islamic lunar calendar. Muslims from around the world celebrate
this day, particularly for those Muslims celebrating the performance of
the Hajj, or Pilgrimage to Mecca. Allah had made the Hajj mandatory
during the time of Prophet Muhammad. The Holy Book, Al-Qur'an,
proclaims, "And make a declaration of the Hajj to mankind. They will
come to you on foot and on lean camels from every distant corner of
the Earth."[578]

The Islamic holiday, known in Arabic as *Qurbani Eid* or the
Eid Al-Adha, is known in English as the "Sacrifice Festival." The
Feast of *Eid Al-Adha* is celebrated every year around the world to
commemorate Ibrahim's willingness to sacrifice his son. *Eid Al-Adha*
is the second of two Islamic holidays celebrated worldwide each year,
the other being *Eid Al-Fitr* that celebrates Allah's preventing Ibrahim
from going through with the sacrifice of Ismail (Ishmael) at the very
last moment.

Eid Al-Fitr is usually a three-day festival, while *Eid Al-Adha* lasts a day longer. On the first day, people dress in their finest clothing and pray together in a large gathering of those Moslems who can afford the sacrifice. Usually, the sacrificial animal traditionally has been a sheep, who stands as a symbol of Ibrahim's sacrifice of his son. In Arabic, this sacrifice is called *Qurba*, a classical word that means both "martyr" and "sacrifice."[579]

Historically, the meat from the *Qurba* is distributed among family members and friends, and also to the poor and the destitute. The Feast of *Eid Al-Adha* comes immediately after the Day of Arafat, when Muhammad is said to have pronounced the final seal on the Faith of Islam. On this day, many believers stay in the city of Arafat until after sunset. They chant ritual prayers and spend the remainder of the day glorifying Allah and asking for forgiveness.[580] The Day of Arafat is the culminating event of the annual Islamic Pilgrimage, and the day after it is the first day of the Feast of *Eid Al-Adha*.[581]

The meat from the sacrifice of *Eid Al-Adha* has traditionally mostly been given away to others. One third is eaten by the family, one third is given to friends, and one third is distributed to the poor. This act symbolizes one's willingness to give up things that are of some benefit, or are close to our hearts, to more fully follow the commands that Allah has for us. The classical Arabic term *Eid* only appears one time in the Muslim Holy Book. It comes at surah 2:114. An English rendering of this *ayat*, or verse, goes something like the following:

Said Isa [Jesus] the son of Maryam [Mary], "Of Lord, oh Allah, send down a table well-set with food from the skies, so that this day may be a day of Feast [*Eid.*], for the earlier among us and the latter, and a token from You. And give us our daily bread, for You are the best of all the givers of food."

Although this is the only time the word *Eid* actually appears in the Muslim Holy Book, Al-Qur'an, there is a variety of other passages often associated with the feasts, including surah 2:183–190 and 256; 7:199; 32:11; 49:13; and 59:24. There are also many traditions on *Eid* to be found in traditional hadith literature, such as in the collection of Al-Tirmidzi (824– 887) as well as those of Al-Bukhari (810–870) and Sunan Ibn Majah (824–893).[582]

Among the ahadith of Ibn Majah about *Eid Al-Adha* are numbers

1281, 1315, 1600, 1721 and 1722. The principal hadith of Al-Bukhari on the phenomenon of *Eid Al-Adha* can be found in Book XV, hadith numbers 71, 76, 77, 89, 93 and 98. Among the ahadith of Al-Tirmidzi that speaks of Eid, the most significant come from chapter II, hadith numbers 149 to 158.

One final aspect of the Feast of *Eid Al-Adha* is that traditionally the one who performs the sacrifice recites from the Muslim Holy Book's, Al-Qur'an, surah 6:161–163, that informs us:

> My Lord has guided us into a straight path, a right religion, the faith-community of Abraham who was a *Hanif*, a man of pure faith. He was no idolator... My prayer and my rite of sacrifice, my living and my dying belong to Allah, the Lord of the Worlds. Of His Lordship, there is no partnering. Even so, I was commanded. I am the first among those surrendering to Him.
> [Cragg trans., pp. 215–216.]

In the reenactment of Ibrahim's sacrifice, the one who performs the ritual feels that he, just like Nabi Ibrahim, or "Prophet Abraham," has committed himself completely to the Will of Allah, in the same way that the Nation of Israel eats Matzoh on Passover to reenact the flight from Egypt.[583]

More recently, some contemporary Islamic writers, like Jason Jackson, for example, in an essay he calls, "Ishmael or Isaac? The Koran or the Bible," suggests, among other things that, "Ishmael was thirteen years older than Isaac." Then Jackson adds:

> And Abraham loved God Almighty very much that he wanted to sacrifice his own son to Him. Ishmael's name represents Abraham's gratefulness to God after a long desperate wait to have a son, then it makes perfect sense that Abraham wanted to sacrifice Ishmael to God Almighty by giving Him the most precious thing he ever had.[584]

Mr. Jackson goes on to suggest the real issue that answers the question about the identity of the son for sacrifice is this, "Which text is more reliable, the Bible or Al-Qur'an?" As Mr. Jackson puts the matter this way:

> Which record contains the true historical account? Should we

believe the Bible, which names Isaac, or the claim of Muslim scholars who infer the name of the son from the Koran?[585]

Then, Mr. Jackson goes on to add:

Which book is the revelation of God? Both volumes claim inspiration, but they obviously cannot both be right. The difference of Isaac versus Ishmael is just one of hundreds of discrepancies between the Bible and the Koran. And many of these differences concern crucial themes (i.e., the nature of God, the identity of Christ, and God's plan of Salvation).[586]

Mr. Jackson follows this analysis by invoking a principle that is sometimes called "abrogation." This is a view that certain passages in Al-Qur'an "abrogate" or render invalid like sections of the Bible. Mr. Jackson, whose essay was written for the journal *Christian Courier* in Jackson, Tennessee, concludes that the issue of the identity of the son for sacrifice has been solved by the abrogation of Genesis 22 by Al-Qur'an's surah 37:99–113.[587]

The *Eid Al-Adha* ceremony, then, is related to the fifth pillar of the Islamic faith, the Hajj that is entirely based on Ibrahim's, his son's, and Hagar's story, so in contemporary Islam, few people doubt that the sacrificial son is Ismail. At the Holy Qur'an's surah 37:100, Ibrahim prays to Allah to grant him a son, and Allah answers him in the next *ayat*, or verse 101, he grants Ibrahim a son. But the Holy Book does not indicate which son is mentioned here.

In contemporary Islam, the son is identified as Ismail (Ishmael), while in contemporary Judaism and Christianity, the son of Abraham's for sacrifice is clearly his son Isaac. As we have shown, however, the views of the son in Islam have changed over time, from Ishaq (Isaac) early on to Ismail (Ishmael) in contemporary times.

This brings us to the final section of this seventh chapter in which we will introduce and discuss several depictions in Islamic art of the sacrifice of Ibrahim's son.

Sacrifice of Ibrahim's Son in Islamic Art

In the Islamic tradition, particularly from the twelfth to the fifteenth centuries, there have been many artistic renderings of the sacrifice of Ibrahim's son. In our analysis in this final section of Chapter Seven, we will identify and discuss a half a dozen of these Islamic pieces of art. Scholar Meyer Schapiro published an essay in 1943 entitled "Muslim Art of the Akedah." This work has become the standard text for evaluating Islamic depictions of the sacrifice of Ibrahim's son in the Islamic faith.[588]

Among the unique features of the *Qurban* pointed out by Professor Schapiro, in many of these artistic creations, an angel carries the substitute ram in Islamic renderings of the sacrifice of Ibrahim's son. In fact, in 1973, Marc Chagall observed this feature as a detail in Persian miniatures, so he incorporated it in his own artistic work on the Akedah.[589] Berman asks this question about Chagall's creation: "Did Chagall incorporate this Islamic detail for artistic purposes (portraying a ram carried by a floating angel), or did he do it to foster interfaith dialogue?"[590]

We do not know the answer to this question, but it is clear that Chagall borrowed this feature from Islamic renderings. Marc Chagall (1887–1985) was a Russian-French Jew who grew up in an Orthodox Jewish family. He completed two different images of the Akedah in 1973 and are owned by the Nice Museum. The image that incorporates the Islamic feature of the angel carrying the ram is called the *Message Biblique*.[591] The other rendering of the Akedah is called *The Sacrifice of Isaac*.[592]

One of the pieces of art that employs the feature is entitled *The Sacrifice of Ismail*, which appears in the *Majma Al-Tawarikh* by Hafid i-Abru and is owned by the Baysunghur Library in Iran. In the image, Ismail kneels on the right. Ibrahim stands behind him, holding a sword-like knife in his right hand, while his left pulls back Ismail's head to make his neck available for sacrifice. The image in question is date around 1425 CE.[593] It is also used as an image for the inside cover for the 1997 edition of Shalom Spiegel's *The Last Trial: The Akedah*.[594]

On the left of this image, an angel is carrying the substitute ram for the sacrifice. The angel's large wings are spread behind him. A tether is attached to the ram. The surrounding text is written in Farsi and quotes surah 37 of Al-Qur'an, along with commentary on verses 100 to 113.

A second Islamic rendering is entitled *Ibrahim's Sacrifice* is dated in the early fifteenth century, around 1410 or 1411. It is part of a text known as the *Timurid Anthology*. The work was commissioned by Sultan Iskandar. It consists of two volumes, the first is poetry and the second is prose.[595]

In the miniature in question, Ismail kneels, his father standing behind him. His knife is in his right hand and his left pulls back his son's head, exposing his neck. In an upper register, several angels can be seen in *Jannah*, or Heaven. They look down, inspecting the earthly scene below.[596]

A third Islamic rendering of the sacrifice of Ismail can be seen in a Turkish postcard of the *Qurban*. In the image, Ismail is bound with his hands behind his back on the altar. Ibrahim stands to the left. He is dressed in an Oriental Kaftan. The father holds the knife in both hands above the son's body. The substitute ram is to the far left of the image and his horns are clutched by a flying angel.[597]

A final Islamic rendering of Prophet Ibrahim sacrificing his son can be seen in a Turkish painting that depicts various scenes of the Islamic life of Ibrahim, including one scene on the lower right of the painting that shows Ibrahim standing above the altar on which Ismail is about to be sacrificed. The son lies to the left of his father, his arms akimbo. Other scenes of the life of Ibrahim are also depicted in the same painting.[598]

Other earlier pieces of European art related to Hagar and Ishmael can be seen in several Renaissance paintings. Guercino's *Casting Out Hagar and Ishmael* (1657), Adriaen van der Werff's *Sarah Bringing Hagar to Abraham* (1696), and *Abraham Dismissing Hagar and Ishmael* (1653) by Nicolaes Maes are three examples of this theme.[599]

In our analysis, we may make the following conclusions about artistic representations of Prophet Ibrahim's sacrifice in the Muslim faith. First, in the earliest centuries of Islam, the identity of the son of the sacrifice in Islam tended to be Isaac. Secondly, in more modern and contemporary Muslim thinking, the son of sacrifice has shifted to Ishmael (Ismail), the progenitor of the Arabs and the Islamic faith.

Thirdly, in many of the extant renderings of the sacrifice of Ibrahim's son, the angel who halts the sacrifice is also shown as carrying the substitute ram. And finally, in the Renaissance and Reformation Period, many traditional European painters have rendered Hagar and Ishmael in their works of art. Among these artists, as we have seen, are Guercino, Adriaen van der Werff and Nicholas Maes.

This brings us to the major conclusions we have made in this seventh chapter of this history of Jewish-Christian-Islamic views of the Akedah or sacrifice of Isaac. In Chapter Eight, as we shall see, we will turn to the ways in which Genesis 22:1–19 has been interpreted in the Early Modern Period, from the sixteenth to the eighteenth centuries.

Conclusions of Chapter Seven

The major goal of this seventh chapter has been to explore what the Islamic religion has believed over the centuries about the sacrifice of Prophet Ibrahim's son. We began the chapter with a short review of the figures of Hajar and Ismail (Hagar and Ishmael) as understood by thinkers of the Islamic faith. The most important item of this review was that Hajar and Ismail are believed to be the progenitors of the Arab race, as well as the religion of Islam.

We began the second section of this chapter with a summary of classical Arabic terms related to sacrifice, slaughter, including a discussion of the Semitic root, THB, which is the source of many of these terms, such as *thabahu* and *thabiha*, for example. This was followed by a catalog of a number of places in the Muslim Holy Book, Al-Qur'an, where the phenomenon of sacrifice is discussed, including important passages from surahs two, three, eight, nine, twenty-nine, forty-seven, and sixty-seven, and many more.

This material was followed by the third section of this chapter, where we introduced and discussed many of the places in traditional hadith literature, where the idea of sacrifice in general, or the sacrifice of Ibrahim's son, in particular, were introduced and discussed.

In this section, we introduced ahadith from Abu Bukhari, Sahih Muslim, Anas Ibn Malik, Abu Dawud, Al-Qummi, and Muhammad Al-Albari, among other traditional collectors.

In the fourth and central section of Chapter Seven, we turned our attention to the question, "Which of Prophet Ibrahim's sons was the object of the sacrifice?" As we have shown, Islamic scholars have disagreed about the answer to that question, some siding with Isaac (*Ishaq*), and some siding with *Ismail*, or Ishmael. We also have shown that in modern Islam, for the most part, the son is thought to be Ismail.[600]

In this section of Chapter Seven, we employed a variety of other sources for answering the query about the son of sacrifice in Islam. These included passages in Al-Qur'an from surah six and thirty-seven, traditional ahadith, members of the Prophet Muhammad's *Sabaha*, or Companions, and other sources, as well.

One other conclusion we may make about the identity of the son for sacrifice of Prophet Ibrahim in Islam is that many Moslem scholars suggest that the Bible's Isaac has been "abrogated" by Islam's Ishmael, that is that Isaac has been replaced by the progenitor of the Arabs and Islam, Ismail (Ishmael).

The role of sacrifice in the Feast of *Eid Al-Adha* was the topic of the fifth section of Chapter Seven. In that section we have shown how sacrifice plays a role in the sacrifice, as well as the *Hajj*, or Pilgrimage, and the Day of Arafat. We have shown in this section that the Feast of *Eid Al-Adha*, as well as that of Eid Fitr, tell us a great deal about sacrifice, or *Qurban*, in Islam.[601]

We also provided in this chapter a collection of prescriptions for performing the ritual during the Feast of *Eid Al-Adha* in terms of what can and cannot be done to the animal for sacrifice in the ritual. Among these were that no unnecessary pain was to be induced on the animal, one must employ a sharp blade, and that animals that are whole are preferred to those with blemishes or defects.

This material was followed by a discussion of several Islamic artistic depictions of the sacrifice of Prophet Ibrahim. As we have shown, some of these images were from Persia, while others are Turkish in origin. Indeed, as we have shown, another painting comes from Russian-French artist Marc Chagall, who incorporated the Islamic element of an angel carrying the substitute ram in his composition entitled *Message Biblique*. One conclusion we also have made about the sacrifice of Ibrahim in modern Islamic art is that the son for sacrifice is almost always identified as Ismail, or Ishmael.

The Islamic tradition speculates and gives provisions for the *Qurban* of *Eid Al-Adha*. After the blood is drained from the body, it is ready to be skinned and cut up to be distributed. The limbs, however, should remain intact. And the carcass should not be mutilated in any way. If there is a vow that comes with the sacrifice, the performer of the ritual cannot eat the animal. Indeed, he is to give it away. But if the sacrifice is a free will offering, the performer of the ritual may consume one-third of the offering, donating the remaining two-thirds to those in need.

The classical Arabic term for "Vow" is the word *Adaqah*, usually translated as "charity," in that it is a synonym for the word *Zakat*. But *Aqadah* is also employed with the implication that the act of charity is done freely and with intentions.[602] Thus, the use of the term "Free Will Offering." A variety of other words are also used in classical Arabic to express the idea of a "Vow." Many of these come from the Semitic root, DHR, such as *nedher* and *yindhar*, which are both verbs, and *nidhr*, a noun form from the same root.[603]

This brings us to Chapter Eight. In this next chapter, as we have indicated, we will explore how the Akedah has been used and interpreted in the Early Modern Period, from the fifteenth century to the eighteenth century, beginning with the Reformation Period in the sixteenth century. As we shall see, a variety of other Reformation and Renaissance thinkers also mention Abraham, Isaac, and the Akedah, such as William Shakespeare in three of his plays and John Milton in *Paradise Lost*. We move next, then to views of the Akedah in the fifteenth to the seventeenth centuries.

Chapter Eight:
The Akedah in the Early Modern Period –
Fifteenth to Eighteenth Centuries

The Caravaggio painting focuses on the horror in Isaac's
face. This devout illustration of patriarchal piety is an
example of what Phyllis Trible calls, "a text of terror."
—Jo Milgrom and Joel Duman, "The Binding of Isaac in
Art"

The binding of Isaac is forever on our lips and in our
prayers.
—Rabbi Judah Abravanel, "Commentary of Genesis"

I could not have been an on-looker, much less the performer or slayer. It is an astonishing situation.
—Martin Luther, *Commentary on Genesis*

Introduction

The principal aim in this chapter is to describe and discuss many views
about the Akedah, or sacrifice of Isaac, in the Early Modern Period of
world history, primarily in the Jewish and the Christian traditions. We
will begin the chapter with an analysis of what Late Medieval Jewish
thinkers have observed about the Akedah.

This material will be followed by a discussion of many of the
places in the Protestant Reformation and beyond in the fifteenth to the
seventeenth centuries, where the sacrifice of Isaac is brought to center
stage. This will be followed by three other sections of Chapter Eight.

The first of these will be an analysis of what Islamic philosophy and hadith literature from the fifteenth to the seventeenth centuries has had to say about the sacrifice of Ibrahim's son.

In another section of Chapter Eight, we will explore the phenomenon of the Akedah, or sacrifice of Isaac, in normal, everyday culture in the same period, including observations by Shakespeare, Milton, and others from the period. This material will be followed by a final section of Chapter Eight, where we will explore the image of the sacrifice of Isaac, or the Akedah, in the arts from the same time.

The Akedah in the Late Jewish Medieval Period

Among the Jewish scholars in the Late Medieval Period who have written about the Akedah narrative, the following list is of some help:

1. Hasdai Crescas (1340–1416)

2. Joseph Albo (1380–1444)

3. Isaac Arama (1420–1494)

4. Judah Leon Abravanel (1437–1508)

5. Isaac Karo (1440–1518)

The views on the Akedah narrative from Rabbi Hadai Crescas are important for several reasons. First, during riots in Spain in 1391, his only son was murdered in the riots. Secondly, he criticized Maimonides' comments on Genesis 22. And most importantly, he provided the best criticism of the Christian view of the sacrifice of Isaac that the incident should be seen as a parallel narrative to the death and resurrection of Jesus, or what we have called the Jobus Christi Theory back in Chapter Three.[604]

Rabbi Crescas gained favor in the Court of Aragon and was allowed to operate freely in regard to his scholarship. He became the head rabbi of Saragossa. The comments of Rabbi Crescas on the Akedah narrative can be found in his *Sefer Adonai* and his *Light of the Lord*, published by Oxford University Press in 2018.[605]

Rabbi Joseph Albo, whose principal exegetical work is called *The Principles of Faith*, reduced the entire Jewish religion to three beliefs: revelation, reward and punishment.[606] The Spanish rabbi was a proponent of Natural Law Theory, something he adopted from Thomas Aquinas. In regard to his views of the Akedah narrative, three are most important. First, he maintains that the angel who halts the sacrifice is actually God Himself. Indeed, he likens it to being God speaking to Gideon at Judges 6:12–17, and God communicating with Elijah at First Kings 19:9–10.[607]

A second important point about Rabbi Albo on the Akedah is that he tells us that the narrative is primarily about the shedding of blood, or the lack thereof. In this regard, Albo's major perspective about the sacrifice of Isaac is that it was meant to highlight the Sanctity of Human Life.[608] Albo observes that Genesis 22 is more about what the Jews, as well as Abraham, "did not do" than what they did do.[609] That is, not kill Isaac.

A third conclusion that Joseph Albo makes about the Akedah story is why, after the flood, human beings were allowed to eat meat. He raises this question in the context of a discussion of animal sacrifice in the Hebrew Bible, which Albo was decidedly against. Joseph Albo's comments on the Akedah narrative come mostly in his *Sefer Tuldos Yaakov*, first published by the Jewish Publication Society in 1946 in New York.[610]

For many years Rabbi Isaac Arama, a third Spanish scholar in the fifteenth century, was the head of a Rabbinic academy in the city of Zamora. In his comments on the Akedah, he agrees that the Akedah was the last, and tenth trial, of Abraham. Rabbi Arama criticized the views of both Rabbi Crescas and Joseph Albo on the Akedah narrative. Like many Jewish exegetes before him, he believed that Isaac was thirty-seven years old at the time of the sacrifice.[611]

Rabbi Arama, for the most part, endorses the Sanctity of Human Life Theory. And he finds the Creation narrative to be a key in understanding the meaning of the Book of Genesis 22:1–19.[612] In an earlier chapter of this history, we suggested that Rabbi Judah Abravanel understood that the Akedah narrative was at the heart of what it means to be Jewish. He relates in his Genesis commentary:

> The Binding of Isaac is forever on our lips and in our prayers,
> for in it lies the entire strength of Israel and is merit before
> the Heavenly Father.[613]

Regarding the story of the sacrifice of Isaac, Rabbi Abravanel, who was born in Lisbon, Portugal, was decidedly against the view held by many of his Jewish contemporaries that the Akedah was an expression of *Chinuch*, a term that implies that a father teaches his son important life lessons.[614] In his analysis of the Akedah narrative, Abravanel constructs a collection of twenty-five questions about the story of Genesis 22.[615]

In the end, Abravanel's bottom-line conclusion about the Akedah narrative is that God "would never ask us to sacrifice our innocent children," a version of the Sanctity of Human Life Theory. He also endorsed what we have called the Atonement, or Redemption Model, in that he saw the figure of Abraham to be representing the suffering of the entire Nation of Israel.[616] This is perhaps an example of the Isaac as Remnant Theory.

Finally, Rabbi Isaac Karo was born in the city of Toledo, Spain. In 1492, his family was exiled from Spain and moved successfully to Italy, then to Greece and Turkey, and finally to Palestine/Israel. Rabbi Karo was known for being a great *Posek*, or Preacher, as well as being a physician to make his living in addition to his scholarly work.[617]

For our purposes, Rabbi Karo's most important work was his *Toldot Yitchak*, published in Spain in 1517. In this work, Isaac Karo makes many observations about the Akedah narrative. In many of these, he introduces and discusses many of the theories about the sacrifice we have enumerated in Chapter Three of this history.[618]

Among these theories that Rabbi Karo rehearses is the Influences of Demonic Forces Explanation. He relates that it is entirely possible that the Satan appeared to Sarah in the form of her son Isaac and tried to influence what happened in the narrative.[619] Karo also observes that Satan was ready to move the hand of Abraham if he did not agree to follow up with the command, an example of the Influences of Demonic Forces Theory.[620]

Other theories that Rabbi Isaac Karo evaluates in regard to the Akedah narrative is the view that the Almighty had suspended the rules for the nature of the moral good, a theory he rejects, and that the figure of Isaac stood for all of Israel, another view that Rabbi Karo finds wanting.[621] Karo also turns his attention to the Sibling Rivalry Theory rejecting it with a host of reasons.[622] At other times, he also seems to reject the Isaac as Remnant Theory.

In a more positive vein, Rabbi Isaac Karo falls back on the view that the entire Akedah narrative was nothing more than a test. But he gives a lengthy treatment on whether Abraham and his son, Isaac, passed the test or not. Rabbi Karo also appears to endorse two other theories introduced in Chapter Three.

First, in part two of his *Toldot*, Isaac Karo relates that, because of His omniscience, God knew beforehand that He would bring the sacrifice to a halt at the very last moment, and in the end, the suffering of both father and son will be seen as part of a "larger plan" in which everything will work out for the good. Thus, Rabbi Karo is an advocate of the Divine Plan Perspective regarding the Akedah narrative of Genesis 22.[623]

Not surprisingly, in the final analysis, Rabbi Isaac Karo endorses both the Test Perspective and the Sanctity of Human Life Theory, as many of his Jewish contemporaries like Rabbi Arama and Rabbi Abravanel did, as well.

In summary, then, Rabbi Karo endorses the Test View, the Sanctity of Human Life Theory, as well as Divine Plan Theory, while at the same time, he rejects the Sibling Rivalry Approach, as well as the Suspension of Ethics Theory.

This brings us to the second section of Chapter Eight, in which we shall introduce and explore the views of Christian Reformation thinkers on the sacrifice of Isaac. As we shall see, many Reformers—both major and minor figures, have much to say about the Akedah narrative.

The Akedah Narrative in the Reformation

Among Reformation thinkers and texts that have said something about the sacrifice of Isaac in the Reformation in the sixteenth and seventeenth centuries are the following:

1. Martin Luther (1483–1546)
2. John Calvin (1509–1564)
3. Theodore Beza (1519–1564)

4. Wolfgang Musculus (1497–1563)

5. Jakob Bohme (1575–1624)

6. The Geneva Study Bible (1557)

7. The Formula of Concord (1577)

Each of these seven thinkers or texts have indicated material on the sacrifice of Isaac. We will examine these views one at a time. To make sense of the Protestant understandings of the Akedah narrative in the sixteenth and seventeenth centuries, mostly in Germany and Switzerland during that period.

Perhaps the most extensive treatment of the Akedah in the Early Reformation was Luther's translation and commentary on the Book of Genesis. One of the fundamental principles of Luther's point of view was his notion of *Sola Scriptura*, or "by Scripture alone."[624]

What Luther meant by this idea was that no text outside the Bible could be used to interpret the Bible. In practice, what this meant is that Luther excluded the views of the church fathers and medieval Christian exegesis, as well as views like the Jewish Midrash, in making sense of Scripture. A second theological principle at the heart of Luther's understanding of the Bible is his rejection of the allegorical method of Scripture and his insistence on the historical-literal method. Luther eschews allegory.[625]

Martin Luther's lengthy commentary on the near-sacrifice of Isaac extends for nearly one hundred pages. In these remarks, Luther posits that Abraham is an "exemplar of faith," and he comments extensively on what faith meant to Abraham, and to himself (Luther). Luther believed that the contradiction to Abraham, that his Seed will be a great nation and that he should kill his son, is the essence of Abraham's "Test."

Luther observes:

> I have stated what Abraham's trial was, namely the contradiction of the promise... Human reason would simply conclude either that the promise is a lie, or that the command is not God's, but the Devil's. For there is a plain contradiction. Is Isaac must be killed, the promise is void. It is impossible that this is a command from God.[626]

Ultimately, the way that Luther resolves this contradiction is in terms of his view of resurrection. The German reformer relates:

Even though there is a clear contradiction here—for there is nothing between death and life—Abraham nevertheless does not turn away from the promise but believes that his son will have descendants even if he dies...Thus Abraham relies on the promise and attributes to the Divine Majesty this power, that He will restore his son to life. For just as he saw that Isaac was born from a worn-out womb and a sterile mother, so he also believed that he was to be raised after having been buried and reduced to ashes, in order that he might have descendants, as the Epistle to the Hebrews (11:9) states, "God is able to give life, even to the dead."[627]

One way to interpret this comment from Luther is to suggest that he not only endorses the Test Perspective as described in Chapter Three, but he also is a proponent of the Divine Plan View, for in Luther's understanding, the contradiction, in the long run, works out for the good, because God planned it that way.

In his commentary of the sacrifice of Isaac, Luther also constructs what perhaps might be labeled a "Midrashic Dialogue" about the Akedah narrative. Luther writes:

Now that the altar was built, the knife ready, and the fire kindled, some conversation between the father and the son must have occurred—a conversation in which Isaac was appraised of the will and command of God. The father said, "You are my dearly beloved son, whom God has given me, and has been destined for the burnt offering." Then the son was truly struck by amazement, and in turn, he reminded his father of the promise, "Consider father that I am the offspring to whom descendants, kings, peoples, etc. have been promised. God gave me to my mother Sarah through a great miracle. How then will it be possible for the promise to be fulfilled if I am killed? Nevertheless, let us confer about this matter and talk it over."[628]

Luther goes on to explain this dialogue ought to have been part of Genesis 22. In fact, he says, "I don't know that Moses did not omit it."[629] Luther adds, "But the father's command to the son was extraordinary and I think its main topic was the command of God and the resurrection of the dead."[630] Again, Luther puts words in the mouth of Abraham, "God has given His command, so we must follow it. And since He is Almighty, He can keep His promise even when you are dead and have been reduced to ashes."[631]

Thus, it was the father's address to his son that reconciled these two contradictory claims—that Isaac will be the Seed and the Father of Kings and Peoples, and Isaac will be killed and thus not the Father of Kings and of Peoples. But then Luther goes on to say, "It is impossible for God to contradict Himself—so they cannot really be contradictory." Ultimately, as we have shown above, Luther chose to interpret Genesis 22 in terms of the New Testament, specifically Hebrews 11. In the end, Luther appears to assent to the Test Perspective, as well as Divine Plan Theory, for God could not contradict Himself.

In another place, in his "Lectures on Genesis," Luther again speaks of the Akedah narrative when he observes:

> I could not have been an onlooker, much less the performer and slayer. It is an astounding situation that the dearly beloved father moves his knife close to the throat of the dearly beloved son; and I surely admit that I could not attain to these thoughts and sentiments either by means of words or by reflecting on them. No one else should have expounded this passage than Saint Paul. We are not moved by those sentiments because we did not desire to feel and experience them. The son is obedient, like a sheep for the slaughter, and he does not open his mouth. He thought, "Let the will of the Lord be done," because he was brought up to conduct himself properly and to be obedient to his father. With the exception of Christ, we have no similar of obedience.[632]

It should be clear from this passage that in addition to the Test Theory and the Divine Plan Point of View, Martin Luther is also endorsing the Jobus Christi Model, that is, that Isaac's sacrifice is a precursor to the death and resurrection of Jesus Christ. This brings us to an analysis of John Calvin's *Lectures on Genesis*, the place where he makes his central comments on the sacrifice of Isaac narrative.

In these lectures, Calvin tells us that Genesis 22 "has to do with the greatness of Abraham's faith. He believed that in the first promise, his son would be great."[633] Calvin points out that the original promise to Abraham was before Isaac, and that he calls the Genesis 22 narrative a "labyrinth of temptation."[634] Finally, concerning the contradiction that Abraham faced, Calvin observes, "The only remedy of the contradiction is to leave this event to God."[635] This would seem to be a version of the Divine Plan Theory.

From these comments of John Calvin on the Akedah narrative, we may conclude that:

1. The "leaving the event to God" implies the Divine Plan Theory.

2. The "labyrinth of temptation" remark suggests that Calvin was a proponent of the Test Theory, as well.

Elsewhere, in the *Corpus* of the works of John Calvin, in his commentary on Hebrews 11, for example, Calvin also nods in the direction of what we have called the Jobus Christi Theory in Chapter Three of this history of perspectives on the sacrifice of Isaac narrative. We may add the notion, then, that Calvin saw the Akedah as a parallel to the life and death of Jesus Christ, as another explanation for the Akedah narrative.[636]

In addition, like Luther, Calvin believed that there could be no contradiction in God. Thus, from the perspective of humans, that promise and the command may appear contradictory, while from the perspective of God, these propositions are not at odds with each other.[637] This brings us to Calvin's associate Theodore Beza and the two works he completed on the Akedah, one in 1550 and the other in 1559.

Beza's work completed in 1550 was called *Abraham Sacrifiant*, a kind of drama on the Abraham and Isaac story. The original was written in French. The ardent follower, biographer and successor of John

Calvin devoted many more lines in the drama to the sentimental verses and the self-sacrificing spirits of Abraham and Isaac than he does to the dramatic and tragic content of the drama.[638] In fact, in Beza's drama, even the character of Satan is moved to tears by the tragic dialogue of Abraham and Isaac.[639]

Nine years later, Theodore Beza completed another work on the sacrifice of Isaac narrative. The book was simply called *The Sacrifice of Isaac*. He began writing the book in 1555 and completed it in 1557 and publication in 1559. Leopold Classics published a version of the book in 2015.

For the most part, this drama is a rewrite of his 1550 tragedy, primarily aimed at its critics, many of whom suggested many dramatic flaws in the work. Like his mentor, Calvin, in this rewrite, Beza endorses both the Test View and the Divine Plan Perspective, as introduced in Chapter Three of this history of attitudes on the Akedah narrative.

Many of these critics asked, "Who is the tragic hero, Abraham or Isaac?" What is the tragic flaw? Does the drama begin with Abraham being better than the rest and end with his being worse? In short, many of the critics of this second work of Theodore Beza on the Akedah narrative asked if, indeed, it was a classic tragedy at all.[640]

There are a number of significant differences between the Masoretic version of the Akedah and that in Beza's two dramas. For one thing, it is clear that Sarah knew of the command before the sacrifice. Secondly, a company of shepherds served the function of the chorus in Beza's versions. Thirdly, in the 1559 drama, Sarah, who is called Sara, gives an impassioned speech before her husband and son leave home for Mount Moriah. And finally, Sarah appears more appropriately to play the role of a tragic hero than do either Abraham or his son, Isaac.[641]

Wolfgang Musculus, among other things, adopts the Jobus Christi explanation for the Akedah narrative, but he also makes several other observations about the Abraham and Isaac story in his commentary on Genesis. For example, he tells us that Hagar's acceptance of exile is far more restrained than Christ's on the Cross.[642] Musculus also offers a number of pieces of advice in terms of reading the sacrifice of Isaac narrative. Among these pieces of advice, of which there are many, are these:

1. Don't separate Genesis 22 from Genesis 12 to 21.
2. Don't see Abraham as an example of blind faith.
3. Don't see Abraham's relationship to God to be normative.[643]

In his commentary on Genesis, Wolfgang Musculus says that the tension in the Akedah narrative arises from the contradiction of the promise to the command. Like Luther and Calvin, Musculus resolves the contradiction by suggesting that logic for God is different than that for humans, and thus a nod in the direction of Divine Plan Theory. And that the sacrifice of Isaac narrative should be seen as a precursor to the death and resurrection of Jesus Christ. Thus, Musculus also endorses what we have called the Jobus Christi Model, and perhaps the Isaac as Remnant Theory.[644]

Theologian Jakob Böhme dedicates an entire chapter of his *Magisterium Magnum* to the Akedah narrative of 1623.[645] Böhme relates that it was only in Abraham's trial, the Test View, that the patriarch became face to face with God. Böhme says that Abraham was "forced to demonstrate the rigor of his faith, and to demonstrate it to his son."[646]

Böhme tells us that Isaac is a "symbol of all of humanity."[647] He says, in his trial, Isaac finds the "fire of God." Humanity must mortify its own will in order to be "reborn and regenerated."[648] Ultimately, like many of his reformed contemporaries, Böhme falls back on the Divine Plan Theory that, in the end, everything worked out for the good.[649]

In addition to these perspectives on the Akedah from Reformation theologians and philosophers, a number of Protestant creeds also mention the sacrifice of Isaac narrative. Two good examples of this phenomenon are The Geneva Study Bible, completed in 1557, and the *Formula of Concord* devised in 1577. The former contains many of the comments of Calvin and Beza on the Akedah in the footnotes to Genesis 22.

The *Formula of Concord* is an authoritative Lutheran statement of faith. It was written by a group of Lutheran scholars that included Jakob Andreas (1528–1590, Christoph Korner (1518–1592) and Wolfgang Musculus, among others. The sacrifice of Isaac is discussed in Article VII of the twelve articles. There is also a separate appendix that offers a lengthy discussion on the Akedah.[650]

Much of the material in this appendix was borrowed from insights we have pointed out earlier in this eighth chapter, particularly those comments on the sacrifice of Isaac narrative from Martin Luther and Wolfgang Musculus. This brings us to a discussion of attitudes toward the Akedah narrative from the seventeenth and eighteenth centuries, the topic of the next section of this chapter.

The Akedah Narrative in the Seventeenth and Eighteenth Centuries

In both Judaism and Christianity, the seventeenth and eighteenth centuries also developed many opinions about the nature and meaning of the Akedah narrative. Two figures from Judaism are poet and dramatist Mordecai Zacuto (1625–1697) and philosopher Baruch Spinoza (1632–1677).[651]

In the Christian tradition in the seventeenth and eighteenth centuries, Biblical interpreter Matthew Henry (1662–1714) and English reformer John Wesley (1703–1791) also made lengthy commentaries on the sacrifice of Isaac narrative.[652] Even Konigsberg philosopher Immanuel Kant made some important observations in regard to the ethical status of the narrative in Genesis 22.[653] We will examine these thinkers in reverse order to the way they have been introduced above, beginning with Immanuel Kant.

To fully understand Kant's views on the Akedah, we first must give a short reminder of the German philosopher's moral theory. For an action to be a moral one, at least in Kant's view, the act must follow what Kant referred to as his "Categorical Imperative." In short, this idea of Kant says, "always act in every way as though you could will your action to be a universal maxim, or rule."[654] Kant says that in order for an act to be a morally good one, one must be able to universalize the act. Thus, keeping a promise is a morally good act because one can universalize that behavior in that keeping a promise is always a good thing.[655]

In modern philosophical circles, Kant's moral theory is known as a Deontological Theory. A Deontological Moral Theory is one that believes in universal moral rules that imply universal moral duties, like keep your promises, don't harm innocent people and other sets of moral rules that imply universal moral duties.[656]

Kant also has a second form of the Categorical Imperative that says, "Always treat people as ends, never as a mere means." What he means by this is, "Don't use people." The German philosopher thought you could derive the same set of moral duties from the second form as those from the first form, as well.

The Ten Commandments is another Deontological System of Ethics, for it has ten moral rules that imply a corresponding ten moral duties. The difficulty that arises for Kant's moral theory regarding the Akedah narrative is that what God is commanding Abraham to do goes directly against Kant's Categorical Imperative, as well as the Ten Commandments.

Edward Kessler, in his *Bound by the Bible*, speaks about this problem of the Akedah in Kant's Moral Theory. Kessler observes:

> Kant admitted he was unable to accept that God would command a man to kill his Son—an act that he deemed unethical—and Kant concludes that Abraham should have replied to God as follows, "That I must not kill my good son is quite certain, but that you who appears to me as God, is, in fact, God, I can never be certain."[657]

Kessler adds this editorial comment, "In other words, Abraham should have rejected the command because I was opposed to the moral law."[658] Another way to interpret Kant's fictional account of the Akedah narrative is to ask the question, "How do you know when it actually is God who is commanding you to kill?"

Carol Delaney has also weighed in regarding this view of Kant, his ethics and the Akedah narrative. She observes:

> Kant, in a late and quite obscure little book *The Conflict of the Faculties*, tells us this.[659]

Delaney then goes on to quote directly from *The Conflict of the Faculties*, published in 1798. The quotation in question appears directly to be related to the sacrifice of Isaac narrative. Kant tells us this:

> If God should really speak to man, man could never know

that it was really God speaking. It is quite impossible for man
to comprehend the infinite by his senses, distinguish it from
sensible things, and then to recognize it as such.[660]

Here, Kant clearly indicates the difficulty of knowing when God
is talking to man and when He is not. This is a direct application of
another of Kant's foundational principles, the distinction between what
he calls the "Phenomenal World" and the "Noumenal World." The
former idea is things as they are known to the senses. The latter are
things that cannot be known through the senses, like communications
with God.

In *The Conflict of the Faculties*, Kant goes on to observe:

But in some cases, man can be sure that the voice that he
hears is not God's. For if the voice commands him to do
something contrary to the moral law, then no matter how
majestic the apparition may be, and no matter how it may
seem to surpass the whole of nature, he must consider it an
illusion.[661]

One way to interpret this passage from Kant is to argue that he
is making two points. First, because of the distinction between the
phenomenal and the noumenal spheres, and since God is of the latter
realm, there is no way to "know" if God is really communicating with
man. And secondly, man can never be absolutely sure that God is
communicating with man in a particular instance.

Before she introduced these words from Kant, Delaney spoke
about the role of the Satan figure in the Genesis Rabbah at 56:4. There,
she says, Satan "speaks the words of common-sense morality. He tries
to talk Abraham out of doing this terrible thing." Delaney goes on to
suggest that in the Genesis Rabbah, the Satan says something like,
"What has happened to you, old man? Have you gone crazy? How
could you ever think of doing such a thing? How do you know it is God?
Maybe tomorrow He will change His mind and call you a murderer."[662]

After quoting the passages from *The Conflict of the Faculties*,
Delaney suggests:

Kant's voice, in this case, is not unlike that of Satan's. He is

taking the voice of reason and of human morality. Kant felt
that in these circumstances Abraham should have said a resounding "No."[663]

Delaney seems to conclude two things about Kant in *Faculties.*
First, it is difficult to know when God is, or is not, communicating
with a human. And second, Abraham's moral intuitions should have
told him that the best moral approach, at least in Kantian terms, would
simply have been for Abraham to say, "No!"

At any rate, we may conclude our remarks on Immanuel Kant
by suggesting that the German philosopher appears to endorse both
the Deontological Theory and the Sanctity of Human Life Model, in
his philosophical analysis of the sacrifice of Isaac narrative in Genesis
22:1–19. For Kant, Abraham should have said, "No," because it is
against universal moral duties and because, for him, human life is
sacred.

Although Kant's interpretation of the Akedah takes into account
only two theories about the meaning of the sacrifice, it should be pointed
out that he also left something out in his analysis. The philosopher left
out a third important factor in Genesis 22—that is, God's promise to
Abraham and Sarah to be found at Genesis 17:19. To wit:

God said, "No, but your wife Sarah shall bear you a son, and
you shall name him Isaac. I will establish My covenant with
him as an everlasting Covenant for his offspring after him."[664]

If Abraham had put a permanent end to the life of Isaac, then the
words of God's promise never would have become fulfilled. One might
say that God's command tested Abraham's faith and obedience, but,
at the same time, Abraham's faith and obedience tested God's faith in
Abraham, not to mention Isaac. It might be said that on Mount Moriah,
both God and Abraham demonstrated their fidelity in each other. And
Kant did not appear to believe that this third factor of the Akedah
narrative was an important one.

Another important element of the sacrifice of Isaac narrative that
Immanuel appears not to be cognizant of that after Genesis 22 and the
Akedah narrative, neither Ishmael, the banished son, nor Isaac, the
almost sacrificed son, speaks of their father again. In fact, the next time

that Genesis mentions the father and sons together is at Genesis 25:9, that relates:

> His sons Isaac and Ishmael buried him in the Cave of Mach-
> pelah, in the field of Ephron, son of Zohar, the Hittite, East of
> Mamre.

Thus, the final time when Genesis speaks of Abraham, Ishmael and Isaac together is when the two sons had buried their father, right beside his wife, who apparently died as a result of the near-sacrifice of Isaac. Some Midrashic accounts have both Isaac and Ishmael seeing a "great light" at the funeral and burial of Abraham, perhaps a sign of enlightenment, but whose enlightenment is not clear. Or perhaps it is the enlightenment of both sons.

As indicated earlier in this chapter, other seventeenth- and eighteenth-century Christian thinkers also have commented at some length on the sacrifice of Isaac narrative. We will now turn our attention to two of these religious thinkers—Matthew Henry and John Wesley— and their understandings of the Akedah narrative.

Matthew Henry's (1662–1714) comments on the sacrifice of Isaac come in his *Commentary on Genesis*. Henry was an English Bible commentator. He published his remarks on Genesis in volume I of his six-volume *Commentary on the Whole Bible* in 1706. After his death in 1714, George Burder and John Hughes edited Henry's *Commentary* in an edition published in 1811.[665]

Matthew Henry tells us this about the Akedah narrative:

> It was not God's intention that Isaac should actually be sac-
> rificed, yet nobler blood than that of animals, in due time,
> was to be shed for sin, even the blood of the only Begotten
> Son of God. But in the meanwhile, God would not in any
> case have human sacrifices used. Another sacrifice is provid-
> ed. Reference must be made to the promised Messiah, the
> blessed Seed. Christ was sacrificed in our stead, as this ram
> instead of Isaac.[666]

In this passage, Matthew Henry begins his remarks on the sacrifice of Isaac narrative of Genesis 22 with the employment of a pair of our theories of explanation outlined in Chapter Three of this history. Those views are the Atonement Model and the Jobus Christi Theory. The Atonement Model can be seen in expressions like "nobler blood to be shed for sin," while the Jobus Christi Theory is indicated by the "promised Messiah." It should be clear, then, that Henry sees the sacrifice of Isaac to be an analog to the sacrifice of Jesus Christ.

Henry goes on in his Akedah commentary to say the following:

And observe, that the Temple, the place of sacrifice, was afterwards built upon this same Mount Moriah, and Calvary where Christ was crucified, was near. A new name was given to this place for the encouragement of all believers, to the end of the world, cheerfully to trust in God, and to obey Him Jehovah-jireh, the Lord will provide. This is probably alluding to what Abraham had said, God will provide Himself a lamb. The Lord will always have His eye upon His people, in their straits and distresses, that He may give them seasonable help.[667]

In this passage, Matthew Henry points to many of the parallels between Isaac and Jesus that we introduced in our discussion of Melito of Sardis in an earlier chapter, including the place of sacrifice (Mount Moriah and Calvary); the "God will provide" pronouncement; and the indication that, in Henry's view, the writer of Genesis indicates that human sacrifice should come to an end, even though Christ is like the lamb and the ram is a substitute for Isaac.[668]

John Wesley's remarks on the sacrifice of Isaac narrative come in his *Notes on the First Book of Moses Called Genesis*, a clear indication that Wesley believed that the Torah was written by Moses. In these observations on Genesis 22, Wesley tells us this:

My son, God will provide Himself a lamb—this was the language that either we must offer the lamb which God has appointed now to be offered, thus giving him this general rule of submission to the Divine Will to prepare him for the application of it to himself; or, of his faith, whether he meant it so or not. This proved to be the meaning of it. A sacrifice was provided instead of Isaac.[669]

Wesley goes on in his remarks on Genesis to speak of the Isaac-Jesus parallels. He informs us of them:

> Thus, Christ, the great Sacrifice of Atonement was of God's
> providing. When none in Heaven or on Earth could have
> found a lamb for that burnt-offering, God Himself found the
> ransom. All our sacrifices of acknowledgment are of God's
> providing too. "It is He who prepares the heart, the broken
> and contrite spirit is a sacrifice of God, of His providing..."[670]

In this passage, we get the "representation" between Abraham and God, combined with the Anselmian Atonement Theory. Wesley sees Abraham's sacrifices as a representation of God's sacrifice of Christ on the Cross. This supports the idea that, at least for Wesley, God may bring wrath to human beings, save for Christ's substitution on Calvary. In other words, John Wesley seems primarily to be assenting in these passages to the Atonement Theory, as outlined in Chapter Three.

This brings us to the comments of two seventeenth-century Jewish thinkers on the Akedah narrative, Rabbi Mordecai Zacuto and Dutch-Jewish philosopher Baruch Spinoza. This will be followed by the final section of Chapter Eight in which we explore the phenomena of the Akedah narrative in sixteenth- and seventeenth-century art in the Jewish and Christian traditions.

Baruch Spinoza, perhaps the finest example of seventeenth-century Rationalist Philosophy, received an Orthodox education in his native Holland. He was a precocious student, but by July of 1656, his philosophical ideas were at such odds with the Amsterdam synagogue that he was excommunicated from the Jewish community that had educated him. A decade later, Spinoza was working on his three-part *Ethics*. In this work, the Dutch philosopher criticized a host of traditional Hebraic beliefs, including the existence of angels, the immortality of the soul and the interpretation of Scripture.[671]

It was on this latter issue that Spinoza's observations about the Akedah narrative came about. Another work called *Tractatus Theologico-Philosophicus*, published anonymously in 1670, is another place where the Dutch philosopher speaks about the truth of

Scripture. In the beginning of his publication, Spinoza sketches out his purpose of this work.

He tells us this:

Not only is the liberty to philosophize compatible with devout piety and with peace of the state, but that to take away such liberty is to destroy that public peace and even piety itself.[672]

In the preface to this work, Spinoza says that the biggest mistake people make about Scripture is to try to find philosophical answers in Biblical literature. To take such an approach, Spinoza says, is to abandon all critical faculties, and one of his test cases is the Akedah narrative.

More specifically, Spinoza asks why Abraham appears not to have used his critical faculties when he was first given the command to kill his son. Spinoza asks, "Why did Abraham not say, 'What do you want me to do that for?'"[673] Spinoza does recognize, however, that the story of Genesis 22 is primarily a "test" to judge the faith and obedience of Abraham. And, above all, Spinoza believed that Abraham passed that test.[674]

Baruch Spinoza also raises many philosophical questions—particularly moral ones—that the Akedah narrative calls to mind. Among these are, "How do we know what the nature of the moral good is?" "Are all of the commands of God, by definition since He is All-Good, also morally good commands?" And, "Why did God's command to Abraham not trigger natural understandings of what the morally good is?"[675]

In the *Tractatus*, Spinoza does not offer answers to these questions, but those answers do become clear by many remarks in the work, as well as in his *Ethics*.[676] Along the way, Spinoza more or less invented what is now called the Historical-Critical Method of the Bible, two hundred years before Julius Wellhausen and other thinkers in the nineteenth century.[677] In the *Tractatus,* Spinoza also makes the claim that Moses could not have written the Torah, and that many things happen twice in the Bible, suggesting there may have been more than a single source for the text.

Among these redundancies pointed out by Spinoza are that there are two creation accounts, two versions of the ten commandments, two accounts of the Flood, and many other doublets to be found in the Torah.[678] In the final analysis, Spinoza assents to the Test View, as well as the Sanctity of Human Life Theory, as did Moses Maimonides and many other Jewish thinkers before Spinoza's time.

The other seventeenth-century Jewish account of the Akedah narrative comes from poet, Rabbi, dramatist, and commentator on secular topics, Rabbi Moses ben Mordecai Zacuto (1625–1697). Rabbi Zacuto, like Spinoza, was born into a Portuguese Marrano family. Like Spinoza, Zacuto was a precocious student, and like his Dutch compatriot, he had a tendency to turn to Pantheism, particularly the kind to be found in the *Kabbalah*.[679]

Rabbi Zacuto is important for our purposes because of his unfinished drama, *Yesod Olam*, a play that follows all of Aristotle's classical elements of tragedy, like plot, beginning, middle and end, a tragic hero, and a reversal of fortune. But the drama was almost entirely composed of sonnets, combined with Biblical quotations, as well as Talmudic idioms.[680] The play was not published in Zacuto's lifetime, apparently because it comprised only about a third of the entire drama. It begins with the shattering of idols in Abraham's father's home. It continues to the trial before Nimrod, Abraham's deliverance from the fiery furnace and the death of Haran.[681]

The hero of Rabbi Zacuto's drama, Abraham, is portrayed as an exalted and philosophic personage whose views are remarkably similar to those of Moses Maimonides. There is no trace, however, of Zacuto's Kabbalistic tendencies. In one section of *Yesod Olam*, the rabbi has the Angel of the Lord, who halts the sacrifice, introduce himself this way:

> I am an angel, thou may see blithe,
> That from Heaven to thee is sent.
> Our Lord thanketh thee a hundred times
> For the keeping of His commandments.
>
> He knoweth thy will, and also thy heart
> And that thou dreadest Him above all things;
> And some of thy heaviness for to depart
> A fair ram yonder I did bring.[682]

Rabbi Zacuto continues this speech of the Angel:

He standeth tied lo, among the briars.
Now Abraham amend thy mood
For Isaac the young son that here is
This day shall not shed his blood.

Go make the sacrifice with yon ram.
Now farewell. Blessed Abraham.
For unto Heaven I go now home
The way is full straight.
Take up thy son so free.[683]

Unfortunately, the drama was not finished, but lengthy speeches convey a Rationalistic Philosophy of figures like Spinoza and Rene Descartes. The dramatist, however, did not live to record the actual Akedah narrative in the drama. But it is likely that the work was written before 1640, the year that strains of Rabbi Zacuto's Kabbalah tendencies can first be detected.

This brings us to two other sections of Chapter Eight, the Akedah narrative in popular culture of the sixteenth to eighteenth centuries, and the Akedah in Jewish and Christian art from that period.

The Akedah in Popular Culture: Sixteenth to Eighteenth Centuries

There has been a great variety of pieces of popular culture where the sacrifice of Isaac and the figures of Abraham and Isaac have come to the fore in these centuries. In *Paradise Lost*, for example, John Milton presents the figure of Molech as one of the greatest warriors of the fallen angels. Milton introduces him when he writes, "First Molech, horrid King besmears with blood of human sacrifice and parents' tears."[684]

The dramas of William Shakespeare are full of allusions to Abraham and Isaac, as well as to the scene on Mount Moriah. The Bard mentions the "bosom of Abraham," in *Richard III*. Shakespeare also alludes to the figure of Japheth in two of his dramas. The first comes in *Henry IV*, Part II, and the other in *Hamlet*, at Act II, scene 2.[685]

Recently, Mary Jo Kietzman completed a study of the Bard's uses of the Bible. Her book *The Biblical Covenant in Shakespeare* was published in 2018 by Palgrave Macmillan. For Kietzman, covenant theology, which derives largely from narratives of the Hebrew Bible including, the sacrifice of Isaac, became the foundation of the Protestant Reformation, including the one in Shakespeare's Britain.[686]

After her introduction, Kietzman turns her attention to "a series of Abrahamic plays" between 1593 and 1596, *Titus Andronicus, Richard III* and *King John*. The latter is the best example where John sends Hubert to kill the young pretender to the throne.[687] In his publication *Shakespeare and Abraham*, another contemporary scholar, Ken Jackson, also draws on medieval Abraham and Isaac plays, which we will discuss next in this chapter.[688]

Perhaps the most common use of the Abraham and Isaac story in late medieval drama was in the many uses to be found in English mystery and miracle plays on the Akedah theme. Among these is the Middle English, "Abraham and Isaac," first produced in the late Middle Ages in England.[689] Another play called *Abraham and Isaac* is among the Gloucester Mystery Plays from the first half of the fifteenth century.[690]

Another drama known as the *Brome Play of Abraham* is part of the Chester play series on Abraham.[691] There have been a number of recent productions of this play on contemporary drama in Britain and the United States, as well as in Canada. The play is written in an East Anglian accent and dramatizes the Akedah scene on Mount Moriah. The Poculi Ludique Society in Toronto staged the drama in the 1981 season.[692]

The Akedah scene also appears in the late medieval drama the *Speculum Humaniae Salvitionis*. The drama is written in verse and advocates a version of the Jobus Christi Theory that the sacrifice of Isaac is a precursor to the sacrifice of Jesus Christ. Indeed, the play makes many of the parallels discussed by Melito of Sardis, and others, in a very explicit way. This brings us to the final section of this eighth chapter, in which we will explore the phenomenon of the sacrifice of Isaac as it appears in Jewish and Christian art from the fifteenth to the eighteenth centuries.

The Akedah in Art: Fifteenth to Eighteenth Centuries

Among the many artists and works of art in this period that have used the Akedah as a theme for their depictions are the following:

1. Lorenzo Monaco (1370–1425)
2. Filippo Brunelleschi (1377–1441)
3. Donatello (1386–1466)
4. Lorenzo Ghiberti (1378–1455)
5. Michelangelo (1475–1564)
6. Anthony Van Dyke (1559–1641)
7. Caravaggio (1573–1610)
8. Sixteenth-century tapestry
9. Sixteenth-century carved oak panel
10. Jan Lievens (1607– 1674)
11. Rembrandt (1606–1669)
12. Francesco Guardi (1712–1793)
13. Ibrahim's Sacrifice (1577)

We will examine these thirteen artists and works of art on the sacrifice of Isaac as they are enumerated here, one at a time, beginning with Lorenzo Monaco's painting *Sacrifice of Isaac*. Abraham sits in the center of the painting on a throne. He holds a large knife in his right hand. Isaac kneels on the right. For the painting, Monaco used hues of red, pink and slight hints of green. The work was completed sometime between 1408 and 1410.

Filippo Brunelleschi's version of the Akedah in 1402 is a sculpted piece on a bronze door of the Florence Baptistry. Isaac kneels before his father. Abraham has his knife in his right hand above Isaac's head, which he holds back with his left hand to expose the son's neck. The ram is to the left, his tether caught in a thicket. Above him, also on the left, is the angel who halts the sacrifice by grasping the right hand of Abraham.

Donatello's version of the Akedah in 1418 is a sculpted piece 191 cm. tall. It is made of marble and is owned by the Museo dell'Opera del Duomo in Florence. Isaac kneels before his standing father. The son's hands are bound behind his back. The father's knife is in his right hand and poised above the son. It is among the most evocative pieces of Renaissance sculpture.

Lorenzo Ghiberti's *Sacrifice of Isaac* is a companion piece to Brunelleschi, for it is on the same bronze door and also depicts the scene on Mount Moriah. Abraham is poised to strike a fatal blow. Isaac is nude and kneels on the altar, his hands bound behind his back. Like Brunelleschi's piece, it was completed between 1401 and 1402.

Michelangelo's drawing the *Sacrifice of Isaac* (1530) is a black pencil sketch on the scene by the Florentine artist. It was discovered recently on the back of a painting of the same scene. The sketch is owned by Academia Gallery in Florence.

Anthony Van Dyck completed an oil painting of Abraham and Isaac. Abraham is an old man. His son sits before him. His father's right arm is around Isaac's shoulder. The painting is owned by the National Gallery in Prague.

Caravaggio completed two different paintings he called *The Sacrifice of Isaac*. One is owned by the Piasecka Johnson Collection in Princeton, New Jersey. It is dated 1598. Isaac's hands are bound in front. Abraham holds the knife in his right hand, and Isaac's head is pulled back with the left. A third figure can be seen on the left, most likely one of the lads-servants. The Uffizi Gallery in Florence owns the other Akedah painting by Caravaggio. It was finished in 1603, five years after the other effort of the scene. In the Uffizi version, Isaac's hands are bound behind his back. Again, Abraham holds the knife in his right hand. Another figure on the left is most likely the angel who halts the sacrifice. The figure points to the patriarch, indicating that he should stop the sacrifice.

Louis Berman includes a description of a sixteenth-century tapestry at the Hampton Court Palace in Surrey, England. The tapestry includes seven scenes in the history of the Abraham legend. The tapestry was designed by the Flemish artist Bernard Van Orley (1485–1542). It was woven around the year 1540 by a famous Brussels weaver named Wilhelm Pannemaker.

Berman adds this about the tapestry in question:

The tapestry illustrates three scenes of the Akedah story. In the foreground, Abraham and Isaac walk up the mountain, while the two servants rest on a foothill. In the middle ground, Isaac sits on the altar, Abraham bares his knife and the angel makes his in the nick of time appearance. In the background, both father and son kneel at the altar where the sacrificed sheep is being immolated.[693]

Jan Lievens' 1607 composition of *Abraham and Isaac* is a rendering of Genesis 22:15. Lievens was living in Antwerp at the time of the painting. The father and son embrace. The knife is on the ground to the left of Abraham's legs. To the left of the father is the animal for sacrifice, either a lamb or a ram. The painting is owned by the Herzog Anton Museum in Germany.

Rembrandt completed three separate works on the Akedah theme. One in 1635 called *The Sacrifice of Isaac*. In 1636, he completed a second image that he called *The Sacrifice*, owned by the Munich Museum in Germany. Nine years later, in 1645, Rembrandt produced a small etching of Abraham and Isaac. He sketched them as if they had paused during the journey to Mount Moriah. The father seems to be explaining to the son what was about to occur. Abraham holds his right hand over his heart, and with his other hand, he points to Heaven.

Two eighteenth-century renderings of the sacrifice of Isaac are dated in 1710 and 1752. The first is a copper engraving of the binding of Isaac. It was produced in Amsterdam in 1710, and the artist is unknown. The other eighteenth-century creation on the Akedah narrative is a 1752 painting by Francesco Guardi. The oil on canvas painting is owned by the Cleveland Museum of Art. Abraham is on the left, Isaac on the right, the large knife in father's hand. A third figure, the angel, halts the sacrifice.

Finally, the only Islamic image on our list is a page from the manuscript of the *Qisas Al–Anbiya*, or the "The Lives of the Prophets." The rendering of *Ibrahim's Son and His Sacrifice* is at folio 29v. The son sits on his haunches before his father, who stands with a knife in his right hand. In the upper-right corner of the image, an angel with wide wings carries the substitute ram for sacrifice. The New York City Public Library owns this manuscript.

This brings us to the major conclusions we have made in Chapter Eight. In the ninth chapter of this history of Jewish, Christian and Islamic views on the Akedah, or sacrifice of Isaac, we shall explore what nineteenth-century Danish philosopher Soren Kierkegaard has written about the sacrifice of Isaac narrative. As we already indicated back in Chapter Three of this history, Kierkegaard was an advocate of the Suspension of Ethics Model.

Conclusions of Chapter Eight

We began Chapter Eight with an analysis of several late medieval Jewish thinkers on the Akedah narrative. In this section, we explored the views of Rabbis Hasdai Crescas, Joseph Albo, Isaac Arama, Judah Abravanel and Isaac Karo. What we have seen in this material predominantly was the reiteration of Jewish views on the Akedah from the Midrash and earlier Middle Ages period.

The sacrifice of Isaac among Reformation thinkers was the subject matter of the second section of Chapter Eight. There we have examined the commentaries on Genesis twenty-two of Martin Luther, John Calvin, the drama of Theodore Beza, the Genesis commentary of Wolfgang Musculus, and the work of Reformer Jakob Böhme. In the observations of these thinkers, we have suggested that each of these men had original views about the Akedah narrative— sometimes surprising views.

The views of Jewish and Christian writers in the seventeenth and eighteenth centuries was the material discussed in the third section of Chapter Eight. More specifically, we examined the positions on the Akedah narrative from Rabbi Mordecai Zacuto, as well as those of Matthew Henry, John Wesley, Baruch Spinoza and Immanuel Kant. He developed an extensive discussion of the sacrifice of Isaac in his minor work, *The Conflict of the Faculties*. A work in which Kant speaks of the conflicts between the truth of reason and those of revelation.

In the fourth section of Chapter Eight, we have examined the idea of the sacrifice of Isaac in popular cultures in the sixteenth to the eighteenth centuries. There we primarily discussed the roles of Abraham and Isaac in the dramas of Shakespeare, as well as in the mystery and morality plays of the late Christian medieval period. We also employed the scholarship of Shakespeare and the Bible from two American scholars, Mary Jo Kietzman and Ken Jackson.

Finally, in the eighth chapter, we have examined a dozen or so works of art from the fifteenth to the eighteenth centuries, where the sacrifice of Isaac narrative was the subject matter of these artistic creations. Some of these works of art we have examined were painted or drawn by Renaissance masters like Caravaggio, Michelangelo and Lorenzo Ghiberti. One of these pieces of art was a sixteenth-century tapestry owned by a museum in Surrey, England. A few were pieces of sculpture, like Donatello's *The Sacrifice of Isaac*.

Other pieces of art on the Akedah narrative that we have discussed at the close of Chapter Eight were three creations by Rembrandt, a 1710 copper engraving, a stunning 1752 painting of Franciso Guardi, and two panels for a bronze door made by Ghiberti and Filippo Brunelleschi for the Florence Baptistry. Many of these works of art, as we have seen, are now owned by museums in Italy, Britain and the United States, such as the Cleveland Museum of Art.

Many of these pieces of art discussed at the close of this eighth chapter are among the most evocative and reverent of Western art. In that regard, these works often, above anything else, point to the great faith of those who created them.

At times, these works of art based on the Akedah narrative feature quirky or unusual elements, like Jan Lievens placing Abraham's knife on the ground next to the patriarch, or the various and varied views of how to render the angel who brings the sacrifice to a halt. We also identified and discussed one Persian Islamic image of the sacrifice of Ibrahim's son, Ismail, owned by the New York City Public Library.

In the ninth chapter to follow, we will describe and discuss what is perhaps the most well-known and discussed views on the sacrifice of Isaac narrative of chapter twenty-two of the Book of Genesis. That is the position of the nineteenth-century Danish philosopher Soren Kierkegaard on the Akedah narrative, as expressed in his work *Fear and Trembling*. We will also examine many of the critics and supporters of Kierkegaard's understanding of the sacrifice narrative. We will now move to the work of Soren Kierkegaard.

Chapter Nine:
The Akedah, Kierkegaard and His Critics

Arguably, modern theological interpretation of the Akedah
begins with the writings of one of the most prominent
post-Enlightenment Christian thinkers, Soren Kierkegaard
and his book *Fear and Trembling*.

—Edward Kessler, *Bound by the Bible*

Soren Kierkegaard, the father of modern religious Existentialism, wrote *Fear and Trembling* in the form of a
commentary on the Akedah in which he describes Abraham as a perfect Knight of Faith.

—Louis Berman, *The Akedah*

It is thoughtless to go on calling Abraham the Father of
Faith to speak of it with men who only have interests in
words.

—Soren Kierkegaard, *Fear and Trembling*

Introduction

The purpose of this ninth chapter is to introduce and discuss the
treatment of the sacrifice of Isaac narrative by nineteenth-century
Danish philosopher Soren Kierkegaard (1813–1855). The major place
where the Dane turns his attention to Chapter 22 of Genesis is his book,
Fear and Trembling, published in Denmark in 1843.[694] We will open
this chapter with some preliminary comments on the life and times
of Kierkegaard. This will be followed by an analysis of many central

ideas that are foundational in understanding the views of Kierkegaard on the Akedah narrative.

The central section in this chapter is an exposition of the views on the Genesis twenty-two text by the Danish philosopher, primarily in *Fear and Trembling*. There will then be several commentators on Kierkegaard's views on the sacrifice of Isaac, some who are critical and others who are supportive of his perspectives. This brings us to a discussion of background materials on Kierkegaard and the Akedah.

Background Materials on Kierkegaard and the Akedah

Soren A. Kierkegaard was born in May of 1813 to an upper-class family in Copenhagen, Denmark. He spent nearly his entire life in that city and its environs, save for five different trips when he traveled abroad. Most of his personal time was spent walking about the city and taking jaunts to the surrounding countryside. Kierkegaard was educated at a prestigious boarding school, or *Bergerdyskole* in Danish.

Later, the Dane attended Copenhagen University and received his BA in philosophy in 1832. He continued his studies afterward, receiving the equivalent to a PhD in 1841. Kierkegaard's first major work was called *The Concept of Dread,* published in 1841. From that year until 1855, he is credited with the authorship of forty-two books in those fourteen years. Among the most significant of these are:

1. The Concept of Dread (1841)
2. Either/Or (1843)
3. Repetition (1843)
4. Edifying Discourses (1844)
5. The Point of View for My Work as an Author (1849)
6. The Sickness Unto Death (1849)
7. Training in Christianity (1850)

Soren Kierkegaard died in a Copenhagen hospital on November 11, 1855. He had been sick, most likely from Pott's disease, a form of TB, for more than eight weeks. He is buried, against his will, in a Lutheran cemetery in his hometown. His tombstone simply says, "S. Kierkegaard, That Individual."

Perhaps the most important facts about the background information on Soren Kierkegaard are related to the following things:

1. Existentialism

2. Pseudonyms

3. Stages of Life

Although the word "Existentialism" was not popular in Kierkegaard's lifetime, he is now, in retrospect, usually numbered among the Founding Existentialists. These mostly nineteenth and early twentieth-century thinkers all seemed to have conformed to five necessary conditions for being a proponent of the movement. The first of these is a realization and admission that "Life is Absurd." By this is meant the idea that there is no objective truth for what the meanings in life are. The second aspect of Existentialism is that humans must posit what their lives mean, or in other words, life is *sui generis*, or self-making. The third and fourth characteristics of Existentialism is that the individual is far more important than the collective and that subjectivity is far more important than objectivity.

A final necessary requirement for one calling himself an Existentialist is that, as Kierkegaard puts the matter, "He must be prepared to take a 'leap of faith.'" By this, the Dane means that in the absence of surety in matters of religion, it is proper to take the leap even if there is no evidence that one ought to leap.

The life and writings of Soren Kierkegaard may be seen as conforming to these five conditions for the Existentialists. You see the meeting of these five conditions in Kierkegaard, as well as Friedrich Nietzsche, Martin Heidegger, John Paul Sartre, Albert Camus and many other thinkers in the nineteenth and early twentieth centuries. Some of these are Atheistic Existentialists and some are Theistic Existentialists. Kierkegaard is in the latter category.

A second background aspect of the philosophy of Soren Kierkegaard is that many of his published works are credited to pseudonyms, and not to the Danish philosopher. Interpreters disagree about why Kierkegaard did this with the authorship of his books, but whatever the reason, he did it often. The work in which the Dane discusses the sacrifice of Isaac, *Fear and Trembling*, is attributed to one "Johannes de Silentio," or "John the Silent."[695]

Fear and Trembling was published in 1843 around the same time as Kierkegaard's work called *Repetition*. Both works belong to the group of pseudonymous writings that the Dane later would categorize as "aesthetic works." Kierkegaard used the pseudonyms not to obscure his authorship, for it was common knowledge in Copenhagen that he was the author behind the pseudonyms.

Rather, Kierkegaard communicated indirectly for Socratic and for pedagogical purposes that force the reader to choose between multiple interpretations of events. Thus, the Dane saw truth as existing in the realm of subjectivity. As scholar Jolita Pons tells us about Kierkegaard's method:

> Kierkegaard's pseudonymous texts contain not a description of reality, nor a prescription, but a possibility of reality which can be turned into actuality only by the individual reader himself. The possibility, in its turn, is not presented as a defined idea but as a dialectical horizon, which keeps different movements of reality in tension. The realization of possibility demands not a random surrender to it, but a conscious exercise of freedom.[696]

The final piece of background material on the views of Soren Kierkegaard in regard to Genesis 22 is what he calls the "Stages Upon Life's Way." By this, he means modern Westerners go through three developmental, consecutive stages of life that begin with what Kierkegaard calls the "Aesthetic Stage," followed by the "Ethical Stage" and ending with the "Religious Stage."[697]

In the Aesthetic Stage, according to Kierkegaard, a person lives to gratify his senses. In the Ethical Stage, a person gives up the stage of his youth and replaces it with a moral or ethical stage. This is the point in life, Kierkegaard says, when people begin to settle down. And if the Aesthetic Stage is primarily about the self, the Ethical Stage in life is about the community.[698]

When one gets tired with the Ethical Stage, the person begins to wonder what other transcendent aims that life has, passing to the Religious Stage.[699] But Kierkegaard believed the Religious Stage of life has two separate but distinct types. He calls these Religion A and Religion B. The names he gives these two religious types are the "Knight of Infinite Resignation," and the higher type, what Kierkegaard calls the "Knight of Faith."[700]

The apparent contradiction between the promise and the command to Abraham puts him in a clear position where life seems absurd. The traditional views of right and wrong seem to have gone by the wayside, and in the constancy of his fidelity to God, we see what Abraham has made of himself as a man.[701] Thus it might be said that Abraham was both a Knight of Faith, as well as a Theistic Existentialist. This brings us to the second section of this ninth chapter in which we will more specifically analyze Kierkegaard's views of Abraham and Isaac in his book *Fear and Trembling*.

Kierkegaard, Abraham and *Fear and Trembling*

The text of Kierkegaard's *Fear and Trembling* consists of the following parts:

1. A Preface in which the pseudonym, Johannes de Silentio, speaks of his place as a writer.

2. The Exordium, four different accounts of the story of Abraham and his journey to the ascent of Mount Moriah.

3. Problemata One: "Is there a teleological suspension of the Ethical?"

4. Problemata Two: "Is there an Absolute Duty to God?"

5. Problemata Three: "Was it ethically defensible for Abraham to conceal his undertaking from Sarah, from Eliezer, and from Isaac?"

The Danish philosopher likely arrived at the name for his work on Abraham from the Psalms. At Psalm 2:11, the text informs us to,

"Serve the Lord with fear and trembling."[702] Again, at Psalm 55:5, the text relates, "Fear and trembling come upon me and horror overwhelms me."[703] If these Old Testament texts are not the origin of the title of Kierkegaard's *Fear and Trembling*, then it may be in any of five different passages in the New Testament.

These New Testaments texts may be found at Mark 5:33, First Corinthians 2:3, Second Corinthians 7:15, Ephesians 6:5 and Philippians 2:12. The verse from the Gospel of Mark speaks of a woman who "came in fear and trembling."[704] In both books to the Corinthians, Paul employs the expression, "in weakness and in fear and in much trembling," and "You welcomed him in fear and trembling."[705] In his letter to the Ephesians, Paul gives some advice to slaves that they should "obey their masters with fear and trembling." And finally, at Philippians 2:12, Paul gives early Christians more advice:

> Therefore, my beloved, just as you have always obeyed me, not only in my presence but much more in my absence. Work out your salvation in fear and trembling.[706]

In much of the beginning of *Fear and Trembling*, particularly in the section Johannes Silentio, and by extension Kierkegaard, calls the "Problema I," he relates the figure of Abraham to the Stages Upon Life's Way. After raising his key question at the heading of that section—"Is there a Teleological Suspension of the Ethical?"—he goes on to distinguish the Ethical Stages' universal moral duties to the particularity and individuality of men like Abraham.

Kierkegaard relates:

> The ethical as such is the universal, and as the universal it applies to everyone, which from another angle means it applies for all time. It rests imminent in itself, and has nothing outside itself, that is its *Telos*, or end or purpose.[707]

After giving this description of the Ethical, Kierkegaard goes on to tells us about the individual, particularly people like Abraham. He says:

> As soon as the single individual asserts himself in his singularity, before the universal he sins.[708]

By this, Kierkegaard means, if we judge Abraham's actions and thoughts by the universal and the collective, then the intention to kill Isaac is a sin. "And it is only in acknowledging this that he can be reconciled again with the universal."[709]

Next, Kierkegaard turns his attention to the philosophy of Hegel and his book, *The Philosophy of Right*. He tells us that the German philosopher is both "right" when speaking of conscience, but "wrong" when he comments on "faith."[710] Indeed, Kierkegaard gives his first definition of faith:

> Faith is namely this paradox that the single individual is higher than the universal—Yet, please note, in such a way that the movement repeats itself, so that after having been the universal, he as the single individual isolates himself as being higher than the universal. If this is not faith, then Abraham is lost, and faith has never existed in the world precisely because it had always existed.[711]

Kierkegaard says in situations like those of Abraham's dilemma in Genesis 22, the patriarch had the opportunity to transcend the universal understanding of the Good. As he puts it, "Faith is precisely that paradox that the single individual as the single individual is higher than the universal."[712] Thus, Kierkegaard raises the question, "Are there times when it is permissible to 'teleologically suspend' the universal moral duties?" The Danish philosopher's answer is a resounding, "Yes!"

Kierkegaard tells us this about the answer to his question:

> The story of Abraham contains just such a teleological suspension of the ethical. There is no dearth of keen minds and careful scholars who have found analogies in it. What their wisdom amounts to is the beautiful proposition that everything is the same. If one looks more closely, however, I doubt very much that anyone in the whole wide world will find a single analogy, except for a later one.[713]

Kierkegaard goes on to tell us that Abraham is different from a tragic hero, but "something entirely different." As he puts it, "He is either a murderer or a man of faith." He relates that Abraham does not have that "middle term that saves the tragic hero," and this is why "I understand a tragic hero but cannot understand Abraham." Kierkegaard adds, "Even though in a certain demented sense, I admire him more than all others."[714]

A few paragraphs later, in *Fear and Trembling*, Kierkegaard continues the comparison of Abraham to a tragic hero figure. He relates, "The tragic hero is still within the realm of the Ethical." But Abraham has transcended, or "transgressed" the Ethical altogether and had a "higher *telos* outside of it, in relation to how he suspended it."[715]

Next, the Danish philosopher turns his attention to another question: "Why, then, does Abraham do it?" His answer is an arresting one. Kierkegaard tells us, "He does it for God's sake because God demanded this proof of his faith. And he did it for his own sake, as well, so that he can prove his faith and fidelity." Kierkegaard's conclusion: "The unity of the two together correctly expressed in a word already used to describe the relationship."[716]

The word that Kierkegaard had in mind is "Test," or *Anfaegtelse* in Danish. A test, but what does that mean? "As a rule," Kierkegaard tells us, "what tests a person is something that will hold him back from doing his duty, but here the Test is the Ethical itself, that will hold him back from doing God's will."[717] The Dane goes on to point out that one of the things that makes Abraham's situation unique is that Abraham "cannot be mediated."[718] By this, Kierkegaard means he cannot speak for himself, and there is no one else to speak for him, as well.[719]

A little later on, still in the first part of *Fear and Trembling*, Kierkegaard raises another question. To wit, "How did Abraham exist in his ordeal?" The Dane's answer is this: He had faith. This is a paradox of how he remained at the apex, the paradox that he cannot explain to anyone else, for the paradox is that he is a single individual and as a single individual, he cannot explain to anyone else, for he is a single individual who places himself in an absolute relationship with the Absolute.[720]

Next, Kierkegaard asks, "But is he justified?" His answer? "His justification is the paradox itself." He is justified, "not by virtue," which would be in the Ethical realm, but by "faith," that puts him in the Religious realm.[721] At the very end of Problema I, Kierkegaard offers this final conclusion of his discussion of Abraham up to this point. The Danish philosopher, through Johannes de Silentio, concludes:

> During the time before the event, Abraham was either a murderer every minute, or we stand before a paradox that is higher than all mediations. The story of Abraham, then, contains a Teleological Suspension of the Ethical. As a single individual, he became higher than the universal. This is the paradox, which cannot be mediated. How he entered it is just as inexplicable as how he remains in it. If this is not Abraham's situation, then he is not even a tragic hero but a murderer.[722]

Kierkegaard goes on to further conclude:

> It is thoughtless to go on calling Abraham the father of faith, to speak of it with men who only have an interest in words. A person can become a tragic figure through his own strength— but not the Knight of Faith. When the person walks what is in one sense the hard road of the tragic hero, there are many who can give him advice. But he who walks the narrow road of faith has no one to advise him—for no one understands him. Faith is a marvel, and yet no human being is excluded from it. For that which unites all human beings is passion, and Faith, above all, is a passion.[723]

In the first part of *Fear and Trembling,* then, Danish philosopher Soren Kierkegaard answers the question, "Can there be a teleological suspension of the ethical?" He answers in the positive. In the beginning of Problema II, the second part, Kierkegaard raises another question, "Is there an absolute duty to God?" Ultimately, Kierkegaard answers this question in the affirmative, as well. The principal reason we make this conclusion is that the Danish philosopher, when discussing Problem II, appears to be an advocate of what we have labeled "Deontological Theory" as an explanation for the Akedah narrative back in Chapter Three of this history.

Silentio, or alternately Kierkegaard, seems to consent to a moral theory that has as one of its universal moral duties, "You ought to follow the moral commands of God." Since this is a Deontological view, there can be no exceptions to this duty. If this is the proper view, then it follows that so far, Kierkegaard believed that there could be circumstances where a teleological suspension of the ethical is called for, and secondly, that Abraham should follow the command of God without deviating from it.

In the section on Problem II, Kierkegaard offers up two alternatives. Either Abraham is a Knight of Faith, or he is unable to be socially understood. In order to answer which option Kierkegaard chooses, we first must discuss why the Danish philosopher does not think that Abraham is a tragic hero, nor a Knight of Infinite Resignation. The simple answer to why Abraham is not a tragic hero is that Kierkegaard points out that traditionally the tragic hero offers up something so that in return, we ought to see a clear benefit for the greater good.[724]

For Kierkegaard, in Abraham's case, because of his silence, there is no indication that the patriarch expects back from the sacrifice a consequence that contributes to the greater good. Abraham was not a tragic figure because his decision did not benefit the greater good. In regard to the Knight of Infinite Resignation, Kierkegaard states explicitly many times in the Problem II section that, "The act of resignation does not require faith, for what is gained is eternal consciousness and full awareness of the self in the process.

The act of resignation does not require faith, but to get the least little bit more than the eternal consciousness, the individual must express genuine faith, as Abraham has done. Thus, Abraham can be said not to have been a Knight of Infinite Resignation, as well. But in order to posit faith, one must first find himself or herself in a paradox, again as Abraham's situation exemplifies a paradox.

On the one hand, as early as chapter twelve of Genesis, Abraham had been promised that he would be the father of great nations, even though he had no progeny at the time. On the other hand, Abraham was commanded to kill his son. The promise and the command create a paradox.

The question raised in Problem III is, "Was Abraham ethically defensible in keeping silent about his purpose?" Presumably, this third question is about Sarah, Isaac and the two servants in the Akedah narrative. In other words, did Abraham have a moral obligation to tell these other characters in the drama what was going on? Kierkegaard's simple answer to that question is, "No, he did not have that moral obligation." So the short answer to the query of Problem III, like the very two problems, is "Yes."[725]

Kierkegaard gives a series of arguments for why he believed that Abraham's actions were morally defensible. He says if Sarah was "in the know," earlier, it might have killed her then. He says he did not tell the servants because Abraham was worried that they might try to stop him.[726]

Johannes de Silentio also offers the opinion that the reason Abraham did not tell Isaac earlier than the walk up the mountain is that the father, as well as the Divine Father, were giving the human son the opportunity to become a Knight of Faith, as well.[727] Kierkegaard does recognize, however, that the relationship between father and son is sometimes characterized by paradox and contradiction. Thus, Isaac had one of the more fundamental requirements for a Knight of Faith too.[728]

Since the middle of the nineteenth century, indeed, even as early as his own time, there have been a variety of critics of Soren Kierkegaard's views on the sacrifice of Isaac narrative. In the next section of this ninth chapter, we will turn our attention to an examination of some of those criticisms.

The Akedah, Kierkegaard and His Critics—Nineteenth and Early Twentieth Centuries

In his own time, and in Denmark, Bishop Hans Martensen gave a scathing analysis of Kierkegaard's *Fear and Trembling*. The bishop said the following about the book:

> "Existence," "the individual," "the will," "subjectivity," "unmit-
> igated selfishness," "the paradox," "faith," "scandal," "happy
> and unhappy love," by these and kindred categories of exis-
> tence, Kierkegaard appears intoxicated.[729]

Bishop Martensen not only made fun of Kierkegaard's religious vocabulary, but he is also a critic of the foundations of the Danish philosopher's belief system. The bishop relates:

He declares war against all speculation, and also against such persons as seek to speculate on faith and to strive after the insight into the truths of revelation. For speculation is always a loss of time and leads away from the objective to the realm of the subjective.[730]

At the end of Martensen's review, which was originally published in a Danish journal of theology, he tells us this:

Kierkegaard's deepest passion is not merely the ethical, not merely the ethical-religious but the ethical-religious paradox; it is Christianity itself—such as this exhibits itself to his apprehension.[731]

At first blush, it appears that the "religious paradox" that Martensen had in mind was why God became man. But on further reading of the review of Kierkegaard's book, it becomes clear that the bishop did not understand what the Danish philosopher meant by a "paradox" with respect to the figure of Abraham. Martensen did, however, comprehend for Kierkegaard the importance of the category of passion as being much more "than a mere act of the will."[732]

An anonymous article, published in the 1913 *Hastings Encyclopedia of Religion and Ethics*, relates that, "The message of *Fear and Trembling* is illustrated by the fact that Abraham was commanded to do what was ethically wrong, and yet his faith stayed strong."[733] The anonymous author adds:

Such faith is no common nor easy thing, but it is a relation to the Absolute which defies reason and can be won and held only in an infinite passion.[734]

This positive and very accurate review of Kierkegaard's *Fear and Trembling* was followed by Scandinavian scholar David F. Swenson, who in 1921 gave an equally positive account of the book that begins this way:

Fear and Trembling uses the story of Abraham's sacrifice of his son. Abraham is not a tragic hero, for he cannot claim, like Jephthah or the Roman Consul, a higher ethical justification

for his deed. His intention to sacrifice his son has a purely
personal motivation and one which no social ethic can ac-
knowledge. For the highest ethical obligation that life or the
situation reveals is the father's duty of loving his son.[735]

David Ferdinand Swenson (1876–1940) was born in Sweden
and came to the United States in 1882 at the age of six. He taught at
the University of Minnesota for many years and became the foremost
American scholar on the Danish philosopher Soren Kierkegaard. After
the passage quoted above, Swenson adds this conclusion:

Abraham is, therefore, either a murderer or he is a hero of
Faith.[736]

Professor Swenson's review of *Fear and Trembling* was published
in the journal *Scandinavian Studies and Notes* in August of 1921. A
couple of years later in 1923, in an introduction to an edition of *Fear
and Trembling*, Lee Hollander wrote:

Abraham chooses to be the "exception" and sets aside the
general law, as well as does the aesthetic individual, but not
well "in fear and trembling," and at the express command of
God! He is a Knight of Faith. But because of this direct relation
to the Divinity necessarily can be certain only to Abraham
himself, his action is altogether incomprehensible to others.
Reason recoils before the absolute paradox of the individual
who chooses to rise superior to the general law.[737]

Lee Milton Hollander (1880–1972) taught for many years in the
Department of Germanic Studies at the University of Texas in Austin.
In the above quotation, he correctly identifies Kierkegaard's emphasis
on Abraham's singularity, the fact that he is a "Knight of Faith," and
that he transcends the "general law" because he is an "exception."
Hollander also speaks of Kierkegaard's claim that Abraham's actions
are "incomprehensible to others."[738]

Another early twentieth-century critique of Kierkegaard's *Fear
and Trembling* is from French philosopher Jean-Paul Sartre's (1905–
1980) book *Existentialism is a Humanism*.[739] Sartre calls Kierkegaard
one of the "founders of the Existentialist Movement." He also relates

that Kierkegaard's view of Abraham is an exemplary version of what the French philosopher means by "Existence precedes essence."[740] What he means by this is that one is alive before he decided what his essence shall be. Sartre also relates that in Kierkegaard's version of Abraham, the patriarch's most important question should have been:

Am I really this kind of man who has the right to act in such a manner?[741]

In his *Existentialism is a Humanism,* Sartre asks about Abraham:

In truth, one ought to ask oneself what if everyone did as I am doing? But one indeed also should ask, Was it really an angel, and secondarily, am I really Abraham? Where is the proof that I am the proper person to impose my choice, my conception of man on all of mankind?[742]

In his critique of Soren Kierkegaard's views of Abraham in his *Fear and Trembling,* the French philosopher mostly reduces the figure of Abraham, and the Danish philosopher's understanding of him, to philosophical categories expressed in all of his most important works. Many of these categories were introduced and discussed earlier in this chapter in our attempt to define "Existentialism."[743]

In his 1949 book *Encounters with Nothingness,* German-born philosopher of culture, Helmut Kuhn (1899–1991), who taught for many years at the University of North Carolina and Emory University in Atlanta, suggests in a positive way, that the central point of Kierkegaard's take on Abraham is the category of "choice." "Each little choice of Abraham goes into the making of the identity of the man."[744] For Kuhn, Abraham's choices that he makes along the route of the Akedah narrative were the most important choices of his life. And these choices, Kuhn suggests, make Abraham a Knight of Faith and one who transcends "normal morality" to act entirely as an "individual."[745] Remember that on Soren Kierkegaard's tombstone in Copenhagen it simply says:

Soren Kierkegaard
That individual.

At the end of the first half of the twentieth century, three other scholars who made extensive comments on Soren Kierkegaard's *Fear and Trembling* are Theodor Reik (1946), Rabbi Joseph Gumbiner (1948), and Milton Steinberg. Theodor Reik's comments on the Akedah came in his book *Temptation*. Reik, who takes a psychoanalytic view of Abraham, suggests that Kierkegaard makes an unconscious identification with Isaac, primarily because of Kierkegaard's relationship with his own father.[746]

Rabbi Joseph Gumbiner, in an essay entitled, "Existentialism and Father Abraham," published in an issue of *Commentary* in 1948, admits that *Fear and Trembling* is beautifully written but the book "tells us very little about Abraham," either as a historical figure or as a mythological one.[747]

In his classic book *The Anatomy of Faith*, Milton Steinberg is very critical of Kierkegaard's treatment of the Akedah to the point of calling *Fear and Trembling* an "unmitigated sacrilege," at least as far as Judaism is concerned. Steinberg's dismissal of Kierkegaard's view is to be found in his article, "Kierkegaard and Judaism," published in the *Menorah Journal* in 1949.[748]

Steinberg makes many other criticisms of Soren Kierkegaard's treatment of the Akedah narrative, including his view that Kierkegaard thinks Abraham refuses to take charge of his own life. Steinberg (1903–1950) was an American rabbi, philosopher, theologian and author on cultural subjects. In addition to the 1949 article, Rabbi Steinberg also made extensive comments on the sacrifice of Isaac in his posthumous book, *The Anatomy of Faith*, published in 1960.[749]

In the same essay mentioned above, he reveals another insufficiency in the account of Kierkegaard on Abraham:

> While it was a merit in Abraham to be willing to sacrifice his only son to God, it was God's nature and merit that He would not accept an immoral tribute. And it was His purpose, among other things, to establish the truth.[750]

Rabbi Steinberg seems to indicate here support of the Sanctity of Human Life Theory, and, at the same time, the Deontological point of view—it is always wrong to take a human life. Steinberg supports this view when he suggests that God "never really wished Abraham to kill Isaac in the first place, and that is why the angel, or God, stops him in the end."[751] If this is true, then Steinberg assents here to the position we have called Divine Plan Theory in Chapter Three of this history.

This brings us to an analysis of the critics of Soren Kierkegaard's *Fear and Trembling* in the second half of the twentieth century to the present, the subject matter of the next section of this ninth chapter.

Kierkegaard and His Critics: Second Half of the Twentieth Century to the Present

The second half of the twentieth century saw the development of a host of other views—both Jewish and Christian—about the meaning and the moral and theological significance of the Akedah narrative. Among these thinkers were Eliezer Berkovits and his book *Crisis and Faith* (1962), Princeton philosophy professor Walter Kaufmann and his 1962 treatment of the sacrifice of Isaac narrative, philosopher Bernard Martin and his 1963 comment on the Akedah narrative, and Justin Thompson, another Christian critic of Kierkegaard's views on Abraham and Isaac (1973).

Eliezer Berkovits refers to Kierkegaard in the context of the Holocaust. He says that Abraham does not make a "leap of faith," as Kierkegaard would have it. Rather, Berkovits maintains, "He shows his trust in God and in the continual covenantal relationship between God and Israel." If there is a paradox in the life of Abraham, Berkovits claims, it is the struggle between the promise and the command, as we have seen many other Jewish scholars argue as well.

Berkovits (1908–1992) was a Romanian-born Jew, who received his PhD from the University of Berlin. His most important work is his 1959 book *God, Man, and History,* recently redistributed by Shalem Press in a 2004 edition.[752]

As we have seen in an earlier chapter, since the time of Moses Maimonides in the twelfth century, many exegetes have suggested that the phrase "God spoke to Abraham" has been interpreted to mean that Abraham felt with all his heart that making Isaac a sacrifice is what God wanted him to do. This thesis that Abraham was following the will of God has also been at the center of three early twentieth-century commentaries by Bruce Vauter, Walter Russell Bowie, and Jewish Existentialist philosopher Martin Buber.

Vauter summarizes, as well as rewords Genesis 22:11–12. He says these verses should have said, "The Lord's messenger called him from heaven and told him that no such thing was desired of him from God." Vauter adds, "This means that Abraham had arrived at a new conception of God, and what is pleasing to him, or even if you will, a new conception of God Himself."[753] Vauter may be assenting here to the Sanctity of Human Life Theory or the Deontological View of Ethics or both at the same time.

Walter Russell Bowie, author of the *Interpreter's Bible* commentary of Genesis, agrees with Vauter. Bowie says, "When we read that, 'God spoke to Abraham,' we are told of something that went on in the mind of Abraham, an inward voice, that seemed to press upon his conscience… and he thought it was the voice of God."[754]

In his 1952 article on Kierkegaard published in the French journal *Dieu Vivant*, Martin Buber also wrote about the phrase, "God spoke to Abraham." Buber says the phrase means that Abraham felt with all his heart that the sacrifice is what God wanted him to do. But Buber also raises the question about whether this was indeed God speaking and commanding him to do just that. Buber reminds us that at First Kings 19:12, God speaks in a "still small voice." So, understanding the meaning of the transmission may not have been easy.[755]

Princeton philosopher and Nietzsche scholar Walter Kaufmann, in an introduction to a 1962 edition of Kierkegaard's book *The Present Age*, turns his attention to *Fear and Trembling* and Kierkegaard's views of faith and reason. Professor Kaufmann remarks:

> If it is really axiomatic that God could never contravene our conscience and our reason—if we could be sure that he shares our moral judgments, would not God then become superfluous as far as ethics is concerned? A mere redundancy? If God is really to make a moral difference in our lives, Kierkegaard insists, we must admit that he might go against our reason and our conscience and that he still should be obeyed.

Scholar Bernard Martin, in his book, *The Existentialist Theology of Paul Tillich*, published in 1963, concentrates on the question, "How does Abraham know that it is not the Demonic that is commanding Abraham to kill Isaac?"[756] Martin puts the matter this way:

> Was the revelation to the biblical Abraham of the Divine command to sacrifice his son, we may ask (following Kierkegaard), demonic possession or ecstasy?[757]

Philosopher Bernard Martin continues his analysis:

> And even if it be allowed that the "ethical and logical norms of ordinary reason" clear-cut and easily applicable criteria, how does ecstatic reason in revelation basically differ from ordinary reason, aside from an emotional "shaking," seeing that it merely affirms and elevates the principles of ordinary reason? However, for Kierkegaard, the emotional shaking is an external event, which could signify nothing or everything.[758]

Martin raises a number of questions about how Abraham knows who is commanding him, even to the point of saying it may be the Devil, or it may come as some sort of mystical or "ecstatic" experience. Many interpreters we have seen earlier in this history have asked, "Why did Abraham not believe it was Moloch as the source of the command, the Canaanite god who demanded child sacrifice?"

Finally, in a biography of Soren Kierkegaard published in 1973, Josiah Thompson begins his treatment of the sacrifice of Isaac narrative—the Kierkegaard version—with this paragraph:

> Not merely in the realm of commerce but in the world of ideas, as well, our age is organizing a regular clearance sale, Johannes de Silentio begins in *Fear and Trembling*. A hundred pages later, he ends on a similarly commercial note, "One time in Holland, when the market was rather dull for spices, the merchants had several cargoes dumped into the sea to peg up prices."[759]

Professor Thompson goes on to turn Kierkegaard's *Fear and Trembling* to be understood in a commercial metaphor. He relates:

This frame of commercial metaphors around the book is not
accidental but a device intended to supply essential polarity.
On the one side is the world of commerce and sanity—the
commercial men with their dollars, their calculi, and their
well-ordered state. They have centuries and even millennia
between them and their concussions of existence. On the
other side are those single individuals—Mary, Mother of
Jesus, the Apostles. Above all, Abraham—who in their own
lives have suffered such concussions. These special individuals, their psyches stretched on the rack of ambiguity. Have
become febrile minds, minds flamed with absurdity, their lives
burn with an unearthly glow.[760]

What to make of this commercial metaphor is not entirely clear.
Thompson does, however, catch the flavor of this in the singularity of
the Knights of Faith, whose psyche is "stretched on the rack," that are
"flamed with absurdity." They are so unusual, Thompson points out,
that their lives "burn with an unearthly glow."[761]

British journalist and satirist Malcolm Muggeridge (1903–1990),
in his posthumous book *The Third Testament*, published by Orbis Books
in 2004, calls Kierkegaard the "oddest prophet." He goes on to describe
the Danish philosopher this way:

A melancholic Dane, a kind of uppity clop, ribald Hamlet from
the middle of the last century who peered quizzically into
life, dryly noting, before they occur, such tragic-comic phenomenon of our time, as universal suffrage, mass media, and
affluence abounding.[762]

Muggeridge concludes about the Danish philosopher, as well as
about the patriarch Abraham:

Kierkegaard was insistent that the only way out of the gathering clouds of fantasy was to climb upward to a rocky peak
above them, where God dwells.[763]

This brings us to a discussion of the views on Soren Kierkegaard's
Fear and Trembling in the works of contemporary thinkers and scholars
from the 1990s until the 2000s—the topic of the next section of this

ninth chapter of this history of attitudes toward the Akedah, or the sacrifice of Isaac narrative.

Views of *Fear and Trembling* in the Contemporary Period: 1990 to Present

In this contemporary period, there have been a variety of perspectives on the Akedah narrative in both Jewish and in Christian circles. Among these thinkers and scholars are the following:

1. Mark C. Taylor
2. Dorota Glowacka
3. Emmanuel Levinas
4. Jacques Derrida
5. Claire Katz
6. Carol Delaney
7. Michael R. Michau
8. John J. Parsons
9. And many other thinkers

Mark C. Taylor, who teaches at Fordham University, in his book *Journey to Selfhood*, tells us this about the Akedah narrative:

The Abrahamic God is the all-powerful Lord and Master who demands nothing less than the total obedience of his faithful servants. The transcendent otherness of God creates a possibility of a collision between religious commitment and the individual's personal desire and moral duty. Should such a conflict develop, the faithful self must follow Abraham in forgoing desire and suspending duty, even if this means sacrificing one's own son or forsaking one's beloved. The absolute paradox occasions an absolute decision by posing the absolute Either/Or. Either believe or be offended. From a Christian perspective, the crucial decision is of eternal significance.[764]

Professor Taylor speaks here of the conflict between moral duty and personal desire. He also speaks of the possibility that, at times, some people have to suspend the normal moral duty, like Abraham's teleological suspension of the ethical. In this case, Taylor says, one must forgo one's personal desire."[765] Taylor's view is not so much a criticism, as it is an affirmation of Soren Kierkegaard's view.

Critic Dorota Glowacka, in an essay entitled, "Sacrificing the Text," tells us this about Kierkegaard and Abraham:

> By writing about Abraham, Kierkegaard can perform a panto-
> mime of walking along the patriarch's path, but he will remain
> incapable of the leap of faith that was necessary to accom-
> plish the sacrifice...Abraham believed by virtue of the absurd,
> whereby the impossible will happen and all human calcula-
> tion will be abandoned.[766]

Perhaps the most extensive treatment and criticism of Kierkegaard's *Fear and Trembling* comes from French scholar Emmanuel Levinas, who comments on the sacrifice of Isaac narrative in a number of his works. Levinas begins his analysis by pointing out that:

> Certainly, no religion excludes the ethical. Each one invokes it,
> but tends to place what is specifically religious above it, and
> does not hesitate to liberate the religious from moral obliga-
> tions... Think of Kierkegaard.[767]

Levinas also suggests that we begin to see dimensions of the Divine in human faces. But it has to be a relationship with the Transcendent "free from all captivation by the Transcendent in a new social relation."[768] Levinas does, however, call Kierkegaard's analysis of Abraham into question at certain points. For one, he is troubled with Kierkegaard's treatment of the Ethical.

Levinas observes:

> It is not at all clear that Kierkegaard located the ethical accu-
> rately. As the consciousness of a responsibility towards the
> ethical does not disperse us into generality [or in Silentio's
> terms, 'the universal'] On the contrary, it individualizes treat-
> ing everyone as a unique individual, a Self. Kierkegaard seems

to have been unable to recognize this, because he wanted
to transcend the ethical stage, which he generally identified
["the universal"].[769]

Levinas makes the claim that the key element in the Akedah is not
Abraham's obedience to the first command of God to exact the slaughter
of Isaac. He relates, "The highest point of the whole drama may be the
moment when Abraham pauses and listens to the voice that would lead
him back to the ethical order by commanding him not to commit a human
sacrifice."[770] In Levinas' terms, human subjectivity is always and forever
in a relationship of infinite responsibility to the Other.

In the end, then, Levinas suggests that the Sanctity of Human Life
is the most important aspect of the Akedah narrative. Levinas puts the
matter this way:

It is only here in the ethical than an appeal can be made to
the singularity of the subject, and then life can be endowed
with meaning, in spite of the face of death.[771]

Claire Katz, very much in terms of those like Levinas, asserts that
it was not even the second voice of the angel of God that commanded
Abraham to suspend the sacrifice, "It was the pathetic presence of Isaac
himself, looking to his father, defenseless and afraid." In fact, Levinas
bolsters Katz's argument when he relates, "Infinity presents itself as a face
in the ethical resistance that paralyzes my powers and from the depths of
defenseless eyes rises firm and absolute in its absurdity and destitution."[772]

Again, Katz would agree. She tells us:

The test that Abraham passed was to see the face of Isaac and
then abort the sacrifice. Abraham had to have seen the face
of Isaac before the angel commanded him to stop.[773]

Claire Katz suggests that in the end, the primacy over the ethical,
the teleological suspension of it, brings us to the point of Levinas that,
"The importance of the Akedah is to love the Torah more than God,"
and "This is exactly prevents the act of sacrificing one's son." In other
words, in the same way that God is free to make commands to humans
at will, humans are similarly free not to follow them by refusing an
unethical command.[774]

For both Katz and Levinas, to break the ethical code is to disconnect relations with the Almighty, and, conversely, to act ethically is already to be in contact with God. The moral for Katz and Levinas is not that one's obedience to God wanes in a test of faith, but rather that it increases when Abraham sees the face of Isaac.[775]

Another twenty-first-century commentator on Kierkegaard's *Fear and Trembling* is writer John J. Parsons, who points to the Dane's response to Hegel being central. Parsons writes, "Kierkegaard's point is meant to refute certain philosophers like G. W. Hegel, and liberal theologians who attempt to identify the ethical, or moral duty, with genuine spirituality."[776]

But then Parsons adds, "But if the ethical is all there is to the spiritual life, then Abraham should not be regarded as the 'heroic father of faith,' but rather as a moral monster and as a murderer."[777]

Parsons goes on in his article in a text called *Provocations: Spiritual Writings of Kierkegaard*, edited by Charles E. Moore.[778] Continuing his analysis, Parsons relates:

> Kierkegaard wants to force the issue by creating a dilemma. Faith itself cannot be understood in purely rational terms, since it concerns the individual's personal relationship with God, who is Absolute. And that means that faith can even transcend the universal demands of the moral law.[779]

In the same article, Parsons goes on to conclude the piece this way:

> Indeed, Kierkegaard states that the category of the Ethical can present a temptation to keep us from passionately doing God's will. Ultimately, however, Abraham was justified for his complete obedience to God, which resulted in the heavenly blessing. As he says in the Epilogue, "Faith is the highest passion in the individual." In short, Kierkegaard's view attests to Blaise Pascal's statement that "Faith has its reasons of which reason knows nothing."[780]

Michau's essay "The Ethical and Religious Revelation of the Akedah" advances both the Kantian and the Levinsian views on the sacrifice of Isaac narrative. Along the way, Michau also endorses passages from Claire Katz, Mark Dooley and Milton Steinberg, among others, to arrive at his conclusion that Levinas' account of the Akedah is the fullest analysis available.

In an essay called *Donner la Mort*, or "The Gift of Death," Algerian-born French philosopher and inventor of the philosophical movement known as "Deconstructivism," Jacques Derrida (1930–2004) suggests that the story of the Akedah narrative is principally about the issue of responsibility on the part of Abraham. More specifically, Derrida opines that his "chief responsibility lies in his relationship to the Absolute."[781]

In the essay, the French philosopher goes on to muse over several scenarios in which questions might be raised about Abraham and responsibility. Along the way, he quotes regularly from Immanuel Kant and Emmanuel Levinas on the Akedah. And in the end, Derrida maintains that Abraham was irresponsible for not telling Sarah, Isaac, and the servants what was going on earlier than he did.[782]

Derrida also discusses the sacrifice of Isaac in a 1993 essay he called "Circumfession," which amounts to a new form of personal confession in that the text searches for Derrida's "home." In the process, he eschews Western philosophy, French culture, his Jewishness and any other account of objective truth. Derrida calls the remainder of his life a "second sailing," in which he tries to find his moorings and his place, with no avail, much like Abraham.

Finally, scholar Carol Delaney, in her book *Abraham on Trial*, sketches out her disagreements with Kierkegaard's views on the Akedah in a lengthy footnote. She begins the footnote on p. 274 of her work this way:

> It should be clear that I disagree with Kierkegaard's
> interpretation.[783]

Delaney goes on to tell us that she does not have the time nor space in the book to do in *Abraham on Trial*. This is followed by, "But briefly, I agree with his desire to find the meaning in the existential situation, not in the conclusion. But I do not agree with his eulogy to the individual person, nor with the analogy he makes between what Abraham was going to do and what a mother does in weaning her infant."[784]

Professor Delaney continues her analysis of Kierkegaard:

In one case, the child is to be sacrificed; in the other the
mother is helping the child to make a transition to the food he
will need to grow.[785]

In the same footnote, Delaney goes on to make critical remarks
about Kierkegaard giving of Regine being analogous to what Abraham
was going to do. Kierkegaard could not stand her dependence on him
and decided to set her free. He needed to see what he did, "as sacrificing
his own dear girl." And the methods he chose to wean her was the
acting as a scoundrel. As Delaney puts it, "He saw himself as a heroic
martyr."[786]

This brings us to the conclusions to this ninth chapter of this
history of attitudes toward the Akedah narrative. The subject matter
of Chapter Ten is the Akedah in contemporary life. Including in art,
literature, music, and theology and philosophy.

Conclusions to Chapter Nine:

The principal goal of this chapter has been to describe and to
discuss the views of Danish philosopher Soren Kierkegaard on the
sacrifice of Isaac in his book *Fear and Trembling*. A secondary goal
has been to explore and enumerate the many critics of Kierkegaard's
views as they pertain to the Akedah narrative.

We began the chapter with a very brief summary of the life and
times of Soren Kierkegaard, complete with a discussion of why he is
known as the "Father of Existentialism," as well as an analysis of what
the Danish philosopher referred to as "The Stages of Life's Way."[787]

This material was followed by a series of Kierkegaard's admirers
and critics, beginning in his own time with Bishop Hans Martensen and
extending through the early twentieth century, then the later twentieth
century, and finally in the period from 1990 to the present age.

Along the way, we analyzed the views of Kierkegaard scholar David
Swenson, those of Lee Milton Hollander and French philosopher Jean-
Paul Sartre on the sacrifice of Isaac narrative, as well as those of German
philosopher Helmut Kuhn.[788] Next in Chapter Nine, we introduced and
discussed the views of the Akedah narrative and Kierkegaard's account

of it among Jewish critics Rabb Joseph Gumbiner, Rabbi Milton Steinberg and Theodor Reik. And among these thinkers, we have seen both endorsements of, as well as criticisms of, Soren Kierkegaard's analysis of the Akedah narrative.

Next, our attention in this ninth chapter turned to Kierkegaard's critics in the first half of the twentieth century. Among the views on the Akedah and Kierkegaard we have discussed in this section of Chapter Nine were those of Eliezer Berkovits; Christian exegetes, Bruce Vauter and W. R. Bowie; those of Existentialist Jewish philosopher Martin Buber; Nietzsche scholar, Walter Kaufmann; as well as the perspectives of Bernard Martin and Josiah Thompson.

Again, in this material, we have seen those who admired Kierkegaard and his *Fear and Trembling*, as well as those who were deeply critical of the Danish philosopher and his book on the Akedah. Some far more critical of Kierkegaard than others.

In the final section of Chapter Nine, we examined the perspectives of several contemporary thinkers and scholars on Kierkegaard's view of the sacrifice of Isaac narrative. Among these figures, we have introduced and discussed the positions of Mark C. Taylor, Dorota Glowacka, Emmanuel Levinas, Jacques Derrida, Claire Katz, Michel R. Michau and American philosopher John J. Parsons.

In our analyses of these contemporary thinkers (1990 to the present), Taylor and Parsons are quite positive about Kierkegaard's contributions to the sacrifice of Isaac narrative. Levinas, Derrida, Katz and Michau, on the other hand, have provided a number of telling criticisms. The most lengthy and full treatments of the Akedah narrative come from the Frenchmen Levinas and Derrida.[789]

As we have seen, one of the major criticisms of Kierkegaard by the two French philosophers is that they believe that Abraham, and by extension Kierkegaard, did not fully understand the role of responsibility of the patriarch Abraham in Genesis 22. Indeed, both of these critics suggested that Abraham has a duty to inform Sarah, Isaac and the servants beforehand about the nature of the journey to Mount Moriah.

The critics on Kierkegaard's *Fear and Trembling*, Claire Katz and Michael Michau, mostly were derivative of the analyses of Derrida and

Levinas. John Parsons' observations on the Akedah, however, show a full admiration of Kierkegaard's approach to the sacrifice of Isaac narrative in his 2002 essay.

We have seen figures in this ninth chapter who assent to the Test View, to the Sanctity of Human Life Theory, as well as to the Deontological account of Ethics Position outlined earlier in Chapter Three of this history of attitudes toward the sacrifice of Isaac narrative.

We shall now turn our attention to the tenth chapter in which we will explore the views of Jewish and Christian thinkers on Genesis 22:1–19, or the sacrifice of Isaac narrative, in contemporary life. In this chapter, we will make some observations, among other things, about how the Akedah narrative has been treated in contemporary art, literature and music. We now move to the phenomenon of the Akedah and the Holocaust.

Chapter Ten:
The Akedah and the Holocaust

People concerned about the Holocaust should write about
the Book of Job or the Akedah.

—Emil Fackenheim, *An Epitaph for German Judaism*

It has been customary in writings on the Holocaust to begin by making amends for using the term "the Holocaust."

—Gary Weissman, *Fantasies of Witnessing*

The past has a vote and not a veto.

—Mordecai Kaplan, *Essays on the Tanach*

Introduction

The purpose of this chapter is to make some general observations
about the relationships between the Akedah narrative and what has
come to be called "the Holocaust" in the period from the 1950s until
the present in world history. We will begin by making some general
observations about the Holocaust, including the term's etymology and
the terminology associated with the phenomenon.

This first section will be followed by some reflections on what
roles the Akedah played in the phenomena of the Holocaust from
the late 1930s until the year 1945. We shall call this second section
of Chapter Ten, "The Akedah in the Holocaust." These two sections
will be followed by a third in which we will catalog many of the more
modern responses to the Akedah after the Holocaust.

Along the way, we will also make several observations about thinkers in philosophy, theology and the arts who have spoken of the many roles that the Akedah narrative has played in American, European and Israeli cultures. We move first, then to the etymology and terminology of the Holocaust.

Etymology and Terminology of the Holocaust

Before we discuss the etymology and terminology of the Holocaust, we will first make some very general comments about the nature and the history of the Holocaust that began in 1933 and ended in May of 1945.

The Holocaust was a systematic, state-sponsored persecution and murder of six million Jews by the Nazi regime and its allies and collaborators. It began when the Nazi party came to power in January of 1933. The Germans believed that the Germanic people belonged to a superior race, the Aryans, far superior to any other peoples. The Nazis believed the Jews were an inferior race, as well as a threat to Western civilization.

During the Holocaust, German authorities targeted other groups that they believed were inferior as well. These included the Roma, or Gypsies, people with disabilities, the Slavic Poles, Russians, homosexuals, blacks, Communists, Socialists and Jehovah's Witnesses.

When the Nazis took over in 1933, the population of European Jews stood at about ten million and most lived in countries that the Nazis would later occupy. The Nazis and their allies and collaborators were able to kill more than sixty percent of all the Jews in Europe. After the Nazis came to power, they systematically went to great lengths to exclude Jews from German economic, social and cultural aspects of the German-speaking world and to encourage Jews to emigrate.

World War II provided the Nazi officials the opportunity to pursue a comprehensive "Final Solution" to the Jewish question—the eradication of all Jewish people in Europe. By the end of the war, the Nazis had executed 250,000 of the Roma people, and about 300,000 physically and mentally disabled people. From the beginning, the Nazis also persecuted homosexuals and other people whose lifestyles did not conform to Nazi social norms.

In the final months of the war, SS guards began moving camp and prison inmates by train or on forced marches, in an attempt to prevent the Allied liberation of a large number of prisoners. These Nazi "death marches," as some called them, continued until May 7, 1945, the day that the German armed forces surrendered unconditionally to the Allies. For the British, French and American Allies, the war officially ended the next day in Europe. May 8, 1945, began to be called "VE-Day," or "Victory in Europe Day."

In the aftermath of the Holocaust, more than 250,000 survivors found food and shelter in what were called "displaced persons" camps. Between 1948 and 1951, 140,000 Jewish displaced persons immigrated to Israel, while many others settled in other countries of Europe, as well as in the United States. The final camp of Jewish displaced persons was not closed until 1957. Among the many things lost in the Holocaust were mostly the European Jewish communities, along with the cultures that disappeared with those communities. This is to say nothing of the many Jewish writers, scholars and musicians, who could no longer provide enjoyment for those around them and the rest of the world.

We have no idea how many young Mozarts or Wittgensteins were among the dead. We have no clue what they may have contributed for the good of society, or for that manner, what their progeny may have produced.

Many of the Holocaust survivors, those who were able-bodied when they arrived at the camps, often were spared because they could perform labor that needed to be done there. Most of these workers died from starvation and from disease, or they were killed when they became too weak to work.

The existence of the Holocaust caused many theologians and philosophers to ask why God would allow such a thing to happen. European attitudes toward the Holocaust became very much like those of Europe after the Lisbon Earthquake that killed 40,000 people in three hours of November 1, 1755. We move now to the etymology and terminology of the Holocaust.

In her book, *Abraham on Trial*, scholar Carol Delaney, in a section entitled "Holocaust," the anthropologist tells us this:

> The Akedah also has figured in some Jewish interpretations
> of the Holocaust... It is important to point out that the term

"Holocaust" is the Greek translation rendered into English of
the Hebrew 'olah. The word alludes to "going up in flames,"
and it has traditionally been taken to refer to a type of sacrifice that is a whole burnt offering, the type that Abraham was
asked to make of Isaac. At a later time, it was also a type of
sacrifice performed at the Temple.[790]

In this same section of her book, Dr. Delaney goes on to tells us:

The word Holocaust, in reference to the Nazi extermination
of the Jews, apparently was used for the first time in 1942 in
a British newspaper, but it did not become a common term
until the late 1950s.[791]

Since the late 1950s, particularly in Judaism, the use of the
word "holocaust" has become something of a controversy. Some
Jewish thinkers prefer the Hebrew term *shoah* to describe the Nazi
extermination of the Jews. Dr. David Wilsey, a physician who helped
to liberate the death camps, sent letters home to Spokane, Washington,
in which he employed the word "holocaust" to describe the horrors he
found at Dachau.[792]

When historian Patricia Herber-Rice of the United States Holocaust
Memorial Museum in Washington, DC, first read these letters from
Dr. Wilsey, she wrote, "I immediately wrote down the first time I saw
him using the word."[793] Holocaust historian, Harold Marcuse, at the
University of California at San Diego and author of *Legacies of Dachau*,
remarks about Dr. Wilsey's letters:

The fact that he is using it right then, in that context, makes it a
very interesting historical fact that will contribute to scholarship.[794]

On March 23, 1945, in one of his letters home to his wife written
from his Army unit, the 116th Evacuation Hospital, that moved across
France into Germany at the end of World War II, Dr. Wilsey wrote, "We
were (are) in a nightmarish holocaust…Gosh darling, a guy wonders
just how many times the world is going to ask how these holocaust-
messes will be gone through."

Two days later, Dr. Wilsey wrote another letter to his wife in
which he wrote, "Holocaust after holocaust after holocaust are just

wearing me to a nub." On April 20, 1945, as the 116th was approaching Dachau and rumors circulated about what they would find there, Dr. Wilsey wrote:

We are the only Evacuation Hospital within one hundred miles of this horrible Holocaust.

Four days later, now from Dachau, in another note to his wife, Dr. Wilsey speaks of "another nightmarish holocaust." After this letter, references to "holocaust" and "the Holocaust" taper off until mid-November 1945 when the physician again refers to "this world holocaust." These correspondences from David Wilsey contain the earliest known use of the word "holocaust" when referring to the extermination of the Jews by the Nazi government.

In the years immediately following the Second World War, Yiddish-speaking Jews from Eastern Europe, as well as Holocaust survivors, began referring to the genocide of the Jews using the Hebrew word *churban*, meaning "catastrophe."[795] The word *churban* is the same term to denote the destruction of the First Temple by the Babylonians in 586 BCE. The same word was also employed by the Biblical writers to speak of the destruction of the Second Temple by the Romans in 70 CE.[796]

When Jews speak of the destructions of the First and Second Temples, generally, the Hebrew term *beit mikdash* designates the "Holy Temple" in Jerusalem. The expression *churban ha-byit* literally means "the destruction of the house." In the Book of Leviticus at 26:31, the text uses the word *churban*, when the verse tells us, "I will lay your cities to destruction [*churban*] and will make your sanctuaries desolate, and I will not smell your pleasing odors." The word "desolate" is the Hebrew *shemamah*, another classical Hebrew word that means "destruction."[797]

Most Yiddish speaking victims and survivors of the Nazis refer and referred to the Nazi extermination of the Jews as the *Churban Europa*, or the "European Destruction," or simply as *ha Churban*, "the Destruction." The prophet Zechariah at 8:19 uses the word *churban*, where he suggests that with the rebuilding of the Temple, fast days will become holidays.[798] Other Jews preferred the word *shoah,* a classical Hebrew term that means "catastrophe." For many Jewish scholars, the word has come to mean the killing of the six million Jews in Europe by Nazi Germany between 1933 and 1945. English-speaking countries have preferred to use the word "holocaust."

The modern Hebrew word for the European Jewish genocide is the word *shoah*. The first reference to the use of the word *shoah* to designate the destruction of the Jews is in a Hebrew pamphlet called *Shoat Yehudei Polin*, or the "Destruction of the Polish Jewry," published in Jerusalem in 1940.[799] The word *shoah* is also used to describe the memorial day called the *Yom HaZikaron la-Shoah ve-la-gevurah*, or "The Memorial Day of the Devastation and the Bravery," usually called by its shortened form *Yom ha-Shoah*, or the "Day of Destruction."[800]

The word *shoah* is a much more human-focused term than the Greek "holocaust," which is more God-centered because of its association with ritual in the Torah and the word *olah*. By using the word *shoah*, the writer puts the focus squarely on the tragedy of the annihilation of six million European Jews. In more modern times, the words *shoah* and "holocaust" have been used as synonyms for "genocide." Thus, we find references to the "Rwandan Holocaust," the "Armenian Holocaust" and the actions of the Khmer Rouge, sometimes called the "Cambodian Holocaust."

The word "holocaust" is of Greek origin. The English word comes from the Greek *Holocaustum*. The term is a Greek compound made from *holos*, an adjective that means "completely," and *kaustos*, a verb that means "fire" or "to burn." Thus, etymologically, the word "holocaust" means "to burn completely."

By the early seventeenth century, the editors of the Latin Douay-Rheims Bible of 1609, translated from the Vulgate or Latin Bible of Jerome, renders the word *olah* as "Holocaust." From that time on, we have the English word "holocaust."[801]

John Milton used the word "holocaust" in his 1671 poem *Samson Agonistes*.[802]

Nathaniel Hawthorne wrote a short story entitled "Earth's Holocaust" in 1844. It is a dystopic story in which all the world's art and literature is intentionally burned. This was the same context of the first known use of the word "holocaust" in America, a 1933 *Newsweek* story about the book-burning campaign in Germany.[803]

After the night of *Kristallnacht* in November of 1938, a number of rabbis wrote about a day of memorial to remember the destruction of Jewish homes that were ransacked and whose windows were broken.[804] Even the *New York Times*, in a piece published in 1943, wrote about "hundreds and thousands of European Jews still surviving from the Nazi Holocaust."[805]

The *Oxford English Dictionary* gives the first use of the English word "holocaust," dates from 1833. From that time on, the word gradually began to mean a "massacre."[806] In the late nineteenth century, the word "holocaust" was employed by the *New York Times* to describe the Ottoman Empire's massacre of Armenian Christians.[807] American writer Melville Charter also used the word "holocaust" to describe the genocide of the Arminian Christians in an article written in 1925. This appears to be the first use of the English word in the twentieth century.[808]

It should be clear from the analysis in this first section of Chapter Ten that it is important to make a distinction between the word "holocaust" and "the Holocaust." The former has been used since the early seventeenth century to indicate a conflagration. On the other hand, the latter is a word that has come to be synonymous with the destruction of European Jewry by the Nazi government from 1933 until 1945.

We may see the importance of this distinction in America when, on September 28, 2009, Representative Alan Grayson, a Democrat from Florida, referred to a bill that was before Congress. He suggested, that should it be passed, what would follow "would be an American holocaust."[809] A number of Jewish members of the House of Representatives found Grayson's use of the word to be offensive. Some said Grayson should apologize to those Jewish members.

What followed was an apology from Mr. Grayson in which he said, "I apologize to the dead and their families…"[810] Most of the discussions after the apology were similar to House Majority Adam Hasner, who said, "But there is a big difference between talking about the Holocaust and talking about a generic, lower-case holocaust."[811] Clearly, he was making the distinction we have introduced in the above analysis.

This brings us to the third section of this tenth chapter in which we shall make some observations about the views on the Akedah from the perspectives of those in the camps. We call this section the Akedah in the Holocaust.

The Akedah in the Holocaust

As the heading of this section suggests, in this part of the chapter, we shall explore what survivors of the Holocaust thought of the Akedah narrative while they were in captivity between 1933 and 1945, the years of the Nazi reign in Europe.

The main sources for these views are research and interviews we have conducted over the years of Holocaust survivors about their lives in the camps, as well as interviews with my friend, Dr. Hiltgunt Zassenhaus. In the 1970s and 1980s, we interviewed forty-eight Holocaust survivors about their views on the Nazi camps, their religious beliefs at that time, and their subsequent survival and relationships to religion.

Dr. Hiltgunt Margret Zassenhaus was born in Hamburg, Germany, in 1916. She was the Lutheran daughter of a German school principal. She earned a B.A. at the University of Hamburg in Scandinavian languages and later received her medical degree from the University of Copenhagen in 1952. At that time, she immigrated to the United States, settling in Baltimore, Maryland, where I met her in 1979.[812]

Dr. Zassenhaus was important for our purposes because, in 1941, she was assigned by the Nazi authorities to monitor smuggling and Bible readings of more than 1,200 Scandinavian Jews held in fifty-two prisons and camps. In her travels, Dr. Zassenhaus compiled what she called the "card file," a systemized list of the activities and beliefs of the Scandinavian prisoners.[813] Over the course of our friendship, which lasted from 1979 until her death in 2004, we had many conversations and interviews about her work for the Nazis, as well as her "counter-Fascist" activities against Hitler and his followers.

Rather than translating letters for the Nazis, she mostly smuggled food, bibles and other materials into the prisons and camps. The Gestapo rarely questioned anything she did with the Scandinavian Jewish prisons. Indeed, in that regard, she was permitted to act freely, ostensibly as a "double agent."

From these interviews with Holocaust survivors and with Dr. Zassenhaus, several conclusions may be made about the phenomenon of the Akedah, or the sacrifice of Isaac, in the Nazi prisons and camps. First, the two most popular biblical passages read and discussed were the Akedah narrative in Genesis 22 and the Book of Job. Of the forty-eight Holocaust survivors interviewed between 1976 and 1988, fourteen listed Genesis 22 and the Book of Job as the two biblical texts most often read and discussed in their times of captivity. Secondly, when asked why this was true, all fourteen survivors gave the same response—because these texts are about innocent suffering.[814]

In my interviews and conversations with Dr. Zassenhaus, as well, she told me that smuggling the entire bible into the camps was extremely difficult, but bringing portions of the Hebrew text was considerably easier. When asked what portions of the Hebrew Bible she most often smuggled into the Nazi prisons and camps, she told me in a 1981 interview over lunch at a French restaurant in Baltimore, "Is it not obvious? Number one is the Book of Job, and number two was the Sacrifice of Isaac narrative."[815]

In our interviews with the four-dozen Holocaust survivors, another ten people listed the Books of Ruth and Jonah as favorites. Again, it should be clear that both of these texts are primarily about Jewish heroes and how they responded to hardship and suffering, the same themes we see in the Akedah narrative and the Book of Job.[816]

What is striking about this material is how familiar the survivors were with these biblical narratives. One man told us, "I heard the reading of the Akedah story more than a hundred times in my time at Dachau."[817] Another man related, "Job was more like our lives in the camp than any other figure in the Bible. Like us, he lost everything."[818] A woman interviewed in Italy in 1983 told us, "The story of Ruth is one of the few female heroes in all of the Bible. I often thought of her while in prison in Poland."[819]

From these many interviews, it should be clear that the Akedah narrative of Genesis 22 had a central place in the lives of prisoners in the Nazi prisons and camps. In 1979, in a panel discussion at Center Stage in Baltimore, after a performance of Lillian Hellman's *Watch on the Rhine*, Dr. Zassenhaus was asked what the Scandinavian prisoners most valued in their time in the prison camps. Her response was riveting, "The scraps of the bible they were able to read in the prisons."[820]

When asked specifically about which scraps, she related, "Particularly the Sacrifice of Isaac and the Book of Job."[821] When she was asked in a follow-up question about why these texts, the German-born physician and linguist answered, "Is it not obvious? Those stories are about the causes of innocent suffering."[822]

Thus, it should now be clear that the Akedah narrative, or the sacrifice of Isaac story, appears to have been alive and well in the years of the Nazi concentration and death camps. The story was smuggled in, read aloud and discussed, often within the context of the question of why the innocent suffer. This brings us to the third section of Chapter Ten, in which we explore the Akedah after the Holocaust.

The Akedah after the Holocaust

Since the close of World War II, there have been countless philosophical, ethical, theological and psychoanalytic responses linking the Akedah to the phenomenon of the Holocaust. In this third section of Chapter Ten, we will explore eight of these responses. We will list them here and then discuss each one in turn over the next several pages of this history. These eight theories, and some of the thinkers who have been identified with them, are the following:

1. The Enduring Love Theory or Ambivalent Gnosticism (Marco Roth)

2. The Incomprehensibility Theory/The 614 Commandment (Emil Fackenheim)

3. The Israel *Redivivus* Theory (Jacob Neusner)

4. The Martyrdom Approach (Aharon Agus)

5. The Anti-Martyrdom Theory (Elie Wiesel)

6. The Psychoanalytical Approach

7. The Rejection of Psychoanalytic View (Silvano Arieti)

8. The Testing of Sarah Approach (Eleanor Wilner)

A variety of other views on the Akedah in the contemporary world will also be explored in the following chapter, that is, Chapter

Eleven. We now turn to the Enduring Love Approach as outlined by writer Marco Roth in an essay from July 19, 2007, published in *Tablet* magazine.[823] Mr. Roth is a New York-born Jewish writer who now lives in Philadelphia. Mr. Roth begins his essay by telling us, "There is an argument that Abraham should have refused to sacrifice Isaac." Roth adds:

> Just as Abraham pled with God to spare the handful of good men in Sodom, so should he have pled with Him to withdraw the impossible command. In failing to do so, he failed the test of his own autonomy. Although God spared Isaac, the result was a broken bond of trust between father and child. Afterwards, Isaac went his own way in the world.[824]

Next in his essay, Mr. Roth turns to a discussion of his own Jewish father, who "since his bar mitzvah in 1952, must have experienced something like this rejection of God." Roth says, "He lost his trust in God, rather than his faith in God's existence."[825] Roth adds about his father:

> Although he could talk the talk of scientific atheism, he probably felt something closer to betrayal than liberation.[826]

Later, in the same essay, Roth suggests that his father's view of God turned to rage, rather than betrayal. Again, Roth says of his father:

> There seemed a peculiar, personal quality to my father's outrage when he spoke not just about the rottenness of the Germans and Austrians, the weakness of the French, the stunned complicity of the *Judenrat*, the painful theodicy of the *Hasidim* but also the whole idea of civilization.[827]

Toward the end of his essay, Mr. Roth sums up his and his father's approach to God after the Holocaust. He says, "Pressed to come up with a one-word theological description for the oddly negative relationship to Judaism that comes if you approach the religion through the Holocaust, I would settle for "Gnostic." Roth adds:

> My father's God was either good but terminally weak, or a malevolent, tyrannical usurper of some other, better deity.[828]

Our first response to the Akedah post-Holocaust, then, as outlined by Marco Roth, is simply to call it the "Ambivalent Gnostic View." In the time since 1945, this theological approach seems to have been taken by many secular Jews. They often lit candles on Friday evenings and celebrated Passover, but never too seriously or with too much zeal. But beneath these practices is often a lack of belief in foundational religious principles that may serve as support for those practices.

A second post-Holocaust view of the Akedah narrative is what we will call the "Incomprehensibility Theory," exemplified by Jewish philosopher Emil Fackenheim, particularly as expressed in his 1987 book, *What is Judaism?*[829] In that work, the philosopher writes several times about the Akedah narrative, "We must somehow confront its ultimate inexplicability."[830] In the same book, Professor Fackenheim observes:

> Our subject resists the usual capacities of mind. We may read the Holocaust as a central event of this century, we may register the pain of its unhealed wounds, but finally, we must acknowledge that it leaves us intellectually disarmed, staring helplessly at the reality, or, if you prefer, the mystery of mass extermination.[831]

In addition to this notion that the Holocaust is incomprehensible, the German-born Fackenheim is best known for a single phrase that complements this idea. This idea is a new commandment that said, "In addition to the 613 *mitzvahs* of commandments in the Hebrew Bible, the Jews should also observe a 614 commandment: "Do not grant Hitler a posthumous victory."[832]

Dr. Fackenheim says,

> We are commanded first to survive as Jews, lest the Jewish people perish. Second, to remember our very guts and bones the martyrs of the Holocaust and that their memory may not perish. Third, to deny or despair of God lest the memory of him will perish. Finally, we must not deny the possibility that the world is a place where the Kingdom of God might flourish, lest we help to make it a meaningless place in which God is dead or irrelevant, and where everything is permitted.[833]

The Israel *Redivivus* Theory, our third view listed earlier, is exemplified by the work of philosopher Jacob Neusner. He begins his analysis of the Akedah narrative after the Holocaust by observing:

> No passage of Scripture so demands a reading in light of the Holocaust as does the Akedah. For Abraham had to be ready to give one, but mothers and fathers in our own time gave all. And Abraham was commanded by God, but Israel in our own time is compelled by Satan.[834]

After quoting directly from Genesis 22, Dr. Neusner relates, "In this rebirth of the Jewish state we see…the resurrection of Israel, the ever-dying people out of the gas chambers of Europe…The biding of Isaac today stands for the renewal of Israel."[835] Thus, we see the name "Israel *Redivivus*," or "Israel Reborn." Indeed, for Neusner, the word martyrdom is the one word that describes the Holocaust. His description of the Holocaust tends both to sanctify the Jews and to demonize the Germans and their allies.

Professor Neusner relates:

> The Germans sent their mothers and the children from the freight car to the gas chamber, and the mother had to choose which of her children she would hold in her arms, as she and the child suffocate in the gas…No wonder, then, that after the war we found scraps of paper, prayers to God, "Abraham chose one and was ready to offer him but didn't. And I chose them all and they all died."[836]

Dr. Neusner's view seems to rest on the thesis that the Akedah narrative provides the key to understanding the Holocaust by putting emphasizing the theme of martyrdom. There is a good bit of disagreement, however, among post-Holocaust thinkers, like Elie Wiesel, for example, who argues that the Akedah narrative has nothing to do with martyrdom. We will say more about Wiesel's views later in this chapter. It is enough now to say he was against the Neusner thesis that the Akedah is about martyrdom or reviving the State of Israel.

Another thinker who did hold the Martyrdom Theory of the Akedah post-Holocaust is Israeli Aharon Agus (1943–2004). Louis

Berman says of Agus in *The Akedah*, "Perhaps no other Jewish writer of our time has so glorified martyrdom as a religious experience as Aharon Agus."[837] Berman continues about Agus:

> He sees the Akedah as a martyrdom story. Isaac, bearing a heavy load of wood, is a symbol of Jewish suffering. Likewise, the ram that Abraham sacrifices in place of Isaac represents the future Martyrdom of Israel. Unlike Isaac, the ram is not spared from death, because Martyrdom is the real Akedah, and the actual Holocaust.[838]

Berman goes on to quote Agus directly on martyrdom:

> Martyrdom is not always a result of the cruelty of history alone—something deep within the nature of religious man that drives toward the heroic, the final, and the complete. Martyrdom is the Akedah...the Law can be at once redemptive and oppressive. The beauty of the message imbedded in our texts is that Israel will find its true deliverance in precariously hesitating between the absolute embrace of the Law and the daring yet freeing heroism of martyrdom.[839]

In the end, then, Aharon Agus' view of the Akedah is quite like that of philosopher Jacob Neusner in that both see the word martyrdom as the most important category for understanding the Akedah in the post-Holocaust era.

The Psychoanalytic Approach to the Akedah narrative in the post-Holocaust period began in the 1950s with scholars like George Devereux and Erich Wellisch and his 1954 work *Isaac and Oedipus*.[840] Devereux views on Abraham and Isaac can be found in his 1953 article, "Why Oedipus Killed Laius."[841] Other thinkers, like Leon Kass, for example, in his 2003 book, *The Beginning of Wisdom*, also discusses the Akedah narrative from a psychoanalytic point of view.[842] In this book, Dr. Kass tells us this about the sacrifice of Isaac narrative:

> No story in Genesis is as terrible, as powerful, as mysterious, as elusive, as this one. It defies easy and confident interpretations, and despite all that I shall have to say about it, it continues to baffle me. Indeed, my approach seems even to

me to be too shallow, precisely because I am attempting to be reasonable about this awesome and shocking story.[843]

For the most part, psychoanalytic interpretations of Genesis 22 tend to emphasize the psycho-pathology of Abraham and Isaac. Classical psychoanalytic interpretations of the narrative have focused on the resemblance to the Oedipus Complex, concentrating on the murderous drives operating in the father and son. In his 2002 book, *Biblical Commentary as a Psychoanalytic Defense*, M. H. Sherman suggests that Isaac actually was sacrificed on Mount Moriah, as an expression of Abraham's murderous unconscious wishes about his son.[844]

Sherman suggests that these elements of the tale have been "edited out" over time in order to adapt the narrative to the social mores of the time. He also believes that Isaac was actually slain on the altar and then resurrected afterward. Thus, in his work, we see the combining of the Psychoanalytic Approach with the Israel *Redivivus* View.[845]

A second psychoanalytic approach to the Akedah in the post-Holocaust era can be seen in the view of Erich Wellisch mentioned earlier.[846] Wellisch begins his *Isaac and Oedipus* with an observation that seems to ratify with Sigmund Freud's formulation: Psychology is based on the relationships of parents to children and children to their parents. All other human relationships are modifications or extensions of the basic experiences within the family.[847]

Wellisch goes on in his work to suggest that the parent-child relationship goes through a development of three stages from primitive to intermediate to a "morally advanced" level. At the most primitive level, parents understand their children as their own property, and they feel free to use these children in any way they wish.[848] Wellisch finds the Oedipus Complex as the intermediate stage. At the stage, a sense of guilt prevents the parent from expressing their most aggressive desires toward the son.[849]

Dr. Wellisch argues that the final stage of development, the morally-higher stage, is expressed in Genesis 22:12, when God says, "Do not raise your hand against the boy, or do anything to him."[850] Wellisch says this about the third stage:

It calls for the abandonment of possessive, aggressive, and

especially infanticidal tendencies and their replacement by a covenant of love and affection between parent and child.[851]

If M. H. Sherman and Erich Wellisch are representatives of the Psychoanalytic View, then Silvano Arieti and Theodor Reik are proponents of what we will call the Anti-Psychoanalytic Approach. The latter's remarks about the Akedah narrative may be found in his book, *The Temptation*.[852] The former's views in chapter four of his 1981 work, *Abraham and the Contemporary Mind*.[853]

Theodor Reik objects to Wellisch's thesis in *Isaac and Oedipus*, as well as that of Soren Kierkegaard in his *Fear and Trembling*. About the former text, Reik points out:

It is unimaginable that with the interruption of Isaac's sacrifice— the Akedah experience—a new and entirely different attitude in the relationship between father and son suddenly entered the world, as this psychoanalyst asserts. All historical and psycho- logical indications contradict such a venturesome assumption. Emotions of such a deep kind do not occur abruptly. The ambiv- alent attitude of father to son and son to father is a fateful and lasting one and can never be entirely obliterated.[854]

In *Abraham and the Contemporary Mind*, Silvano Arieti devotes six pages to the psychoanalytic views on the Akedah narrative of Erich Wellisch. In those six pages, Arieti mostly concentrates on the claim made by Wellisch that the Akedah was written as a condemnation of child sacrifice among the ancient Jews. Arieti remarks:

Child sacrifice, after all, has been outlawed for a very long time, and yet the Abraham-Isaac maintains its great spiritual value even today.[855]

Arieti goes on to say that if the sacrifice of Isaac still has that spiritual value in the modern world, the Akedah should tell us something about the Holocaust in the middle of the twentieth century and beyond. Arieti raises the question, "Did God command the Akedah to give Abraham a foretaste of the terrible tasks that Abraham's descendants will have to sustain through the centuries?" Arieti answers this question in the affirmative.[856]

A few pages later, in the same work, Arieti gives these observations about the meaning of the Akedah narrative:

> Isaac symbolizes the many aspects of love: family love for Isaac is his son; love for one's neighbors, or the other, for Isaac is a fellow human being; self-love, for Isaac is his only son and one of the most meaningful parts of Abraham's life, not only because Isaac is a human being but also the progenitor of a great people, chosen to give to the world Abraham's revelation of the One True God, the God of Love who cannot be seen but is everywhere.[857]

For Silvano Arieti, as Louis Berman says, "The Akedah served as a message to Abraham of the perils that await a Holy People, and also served to demonstrate once more God's love of Abraham and Isaac."[858] Berman concludes his evaluation of Arieti's view of the sacrifice of Isaac this way:

> Arieti's main use of the Akedah was not to demonstrate the power of the psycho-analytic method, but to probe the problem of evil, to raise questions that cannot be answered and cannot go away, the meaning of the Holocaust.[859]

Finally, in the Testing of Sarah Theory, our eighth model for understanding the Akedah narrative in the post-Holocaust era, for the most part, concentrates on what modern feminists in the last fifty years have said and written about the sacrifice of Isaac narrative. The sources for these opinions are many. In his classical text, *The Akedah: The Binding of Isaac*, Louis Berman catalogs some of these feminists views. Carol Delaney, as well, in her *Abraham on Trial*, also makes many remarks representative of these feminist perspectives.[860]

Many of the feminist thinkers mentioned by Berman are Christians, like Trevor Dennis, who is the former Vice-Dean of the Chester Cathedral. In his 1994 book, *Sarah Laughed, Women's Voices in the Old Testament*, Dennis denigrates the role of Abraham, while raising the status of Sarah to a great degree. About the pair, Dennis relates:

> Abraham was turned into a saint by the Jewish theologians of the period between the Old and New Testaments...In Genesis

itself, both Abraham and Sarah are fully rounded characters, subtly drawn, with their strengths matched—one is almost tempted to say *more* than matched by their weaknesses.[861]

Dennis goes on to say that by Abraham saying that Sarah is his sister and permitting his son to be taken into the household of the Pharaoh, "puts Abraham on a high pedestal of obedience and faith." Dennis adds, "But it knocks him to the floor and puts the Pharaoh's boot on his back for good measure."[862]

Dennis makes this conclusion about Abraham and Sarah:

There is something of a rags to riches story about this, and there is also a somewhat coarse and very male humor at work. Look at what this simple nomad has gotten from the Pharaoh... We have been taught over the years not to expect humor in the Bible. In fact, there is plenty of it, at least in the Old Testament, and I am sure it is intended here. And yet, if we persist in looking at this story from Sarah's angle, it is not funny at all.[863]

Louis Berman, in criticizing the views of Dennis on Abraham and his wife, points out that we know what is coming when the cleric gives this as the opening line of Genesis 22, "God has now commanded Abraham to take the child who is her son and also to slit his throat."[864] The view of Dennis is not the only male feminist who has written about the Akedah. Another perspective can be seen in W. Lee Humphreys' "Where's Sarah: Echoes of a Silent Voice in the Akedah." Dr. Humphreys begins his essay simply by saying, "Sarah is silent and silenced."[865]

Humphreys goes on in his essay to make the point that because of ancient-world chauvinism, Sarah is silent and silenced by her husband. Another male feminist that speaks of Sarah from a feminist point of view is Rabbi Paul Kipnes, who co-authored an essay with Michelle November that they called, "Where Was Sarah During the Akedah (the Binding of Isaac?"[866]

The essay is in the form of a Midrash in which they imagine Sarah at the end of her life, recounting the most difficult experiences from earlier in her life, particularly the Akedah narrative and the roles of

Hagar and Ishmael in their lives. Kipnes and November portray Sarah as much more open with Hagar than the Torah suggests.[867]

Colleen Ivey Hartsoe, in her "Christian Midrash on the Akedah," shows Sarah reacting with horror, screaming, and weeping, when Abraham tells her of God's command that he offer up Isaac. In Hartsoe's account, Abraham returns home to tell Sarah of the command before returning to Mount Moriah.[868]

Berman also speaks of the work of Jewish feminist Alicia Suskin Ostriker, who also finds the absence of Sarah in the Akedah narrative to be "extremely significant."[869] In her 1993 book, *Feminist Revisions and the Bible*, Ostriker notes that Sarah emerges as "aggressive, willful, and protective of her perogatives, a lively and formidable personality." In Ostriker's view, the main argument of the Akedah narrative is that Abraham could do exactly what he wants with Isaac, regardless of what Sarah might have said about the matter.[870]

Alicia Ostriker's views on Sarah and the Akedah narrative also can be seen in a poem she calls, "The Story of Abraham." In the poem, she begins by describing what happened at the scene on Mount Moriah in the first twenty lines of the poem, and then she as Abraham say this:

> Hold on, I'd interrupted. I would like to check some of this out
> with my wife.

Another feminist poet, Eleanor Wilner, in a poem called "Sarah's Choice," has Sarah say to the voice of an angel telling Abraham and Sarah to sacrifice their son, has Sarah respond to the command this way:

> "No," said Sarah to the voice. "I will not be chosen. Nor shall
> my son—if I can help it. You have promised Abraham through
> this boy, a great nation."[871]

We will say more about Ostriker and Wilner in Chapter Eleven to follow, when we speak of the phenomenon of the Akedah narrative in contemporary culture, as well as the views of Sarah of a number of other feminist thinkers in the late twentieth and early twenty-first centuries. Not all of these views, however, are about the perspective of Sarah. Contemporary Syrian-American poet, novelist, and professor

Mohja Kahf, for example, in an essay she entitled, "Reconciling the Descendants of Sarah and Hagar," she has Hagar communicating with Sarah in the form of a poem. The letter begins:

Dear Sarah:

Life made us enemies
But it doesn't have to be that way.
What if we both ditched the old man?
He could have visitation rights with the boys
alternate weekends and holidays,
especially the Feast of the Sacrifice
that it began with me abandoned in the desert
watching my baby dehydrate for days—
I dared God to let us die.

Anyway, you and I,
we'd set up house,
raise the kids,
start a catering business, maybe.
You have brains,
so do I.
We could travel.
There are places to see
Besides Ur and this nowheresville desert
With its tribes of hooligans.[872]

Dr. Kahf goes on for several stanzas then concludes with:

Oh Sarah, you need years of therapy
Can't you admit that what he did to me was cruel?
It won't make you hate me forever
just long enough to know that the world will not fall apart
long enough to pity him, yourself, me.
Laugh, Sarah, laugh
Imagine
God, the Possibility.

Sincerely (Love),
Hagar.[873]

In her poem, Dr. Kahf presents the story of the family of Abraham (Ibrahim, in Arabic) from the perspective of Hagar (Hajah). She concentrates on the suffering of Hagar and her son, Ishmael (Ismail). This is a very different view than that of contemporary feminist Judeo-Christian views.

Rabbi Amy Eilberg points out that Genesis 16 describes Hagar's marriage to Abraham, her pregnancy and her ill-treatment by Sarah, "to be a glimpse of things to come in the relations between Jews and Muslims, and Israelis and Palestinians." Rabbi Eilberg goes on to say:

Hagar rightly chafes as being seen merely as her mistress' possession. When Hagar becomes pregnant, she responds with understandable, if unfortunate, human emotion, gloating over her own ability to conceive. Hagar's resentful reaction, in turn, angers Sarah, leading to the banishment of the pregnant Hagar to the wilderness. The rest, as they say, is history.[874]

The female rabbi goes on to make this observation:

Reading the text through a feminist lens, we are pained by the way in which the two women, both of degraded status in their society because of their gender, turn to one another.[875]

But then Rabbi Eilberg raises this question, "What if the two women had joined hands, pooled their gifts, and collaborated (or at least commiserated to defeat the oppressive, patriarchal system?"[876] Eilberg ends her essay by speaking of how precarious is the security of both Jews and Palestinians in the contemporary Middle East. Speaking of Palestinian women, Rabbi Eilberg remarks:

Like our foremother Sarah, they are keenly aware of the security they lack, and so are quick to react the vulnerable in their midst. Nonetheless, we must imagine, work and pray our way to a different reality, when the privileged and the under-privileged will join hands for the sake of love and the society of peace and justice they hope to build together.[877]

This brings us to the major conclusions we have made in this tenth chapter on perspectives on the Akedah in the post-Holocaust era of history. We will now turn our attention to views of the Akedah, or the sacrifice of Isaac in contemporary life.

Conclusions to Chapter Ten

In this tenth chapter, our major goal has been to speak of the relationships of views about the Akedah in relation to the Holocaust. We have divided the chapter into three parts. In the first of these, we have made some preliminary remarks about the Holocaust, as well as the etymology and the terminology of words related to the Holocaust, including words like holocaust, *churban* and *shoah*.

In the second section of Chapter Ten, we made some remarks about what roles the Akedah, or the sacrifice of Isaac, may have had in the Holocaust prisons and camps of the Nazi government. The major sources for this section was a collection of interviews with Holocaust survivors conducted in the 1970s and 1980s. As indicated, the number of individuals interviewed was forty-eight.

A second source of the second section of Chapter Ten was a series of interviews and discussions over the years from 1979 until 2004 with physician and linguist Hiltgunt Zassenhaus, who operated as a double-agent from 1941 until 1945. We have shown that during that time, Zassenhaus worked as a translator of Scandinavian Jewish prisoners. In the Nazi camps, while clandestinely, she also smuggled in food, pencils and portions of the Bible into those camps.

In the second section of Chapter Ten, we have shown that the following conclusions may be made about the phenomenon of the Akedah, or the sacrifice of Isaac, in the Nazi prisons and camps. The first of those conclusions was that the two most popular biblical passages read and discussed in the camps were chapter 22 of Genesis, the Akedah narrative, and the Book of Job.

We also have shown in the second section that Dr. Zassenhaus told us of the difficulty of smuggling the entire Bible into the camps. So instead, she brought entire books like Job or Ruth, or several successful chapters like the Book of Genesis or the Major Prophets.

This second section also suggestsed that what most struck us about these smuggled texts is how familiar the Jewish prisoners already were of these Hebrew texts. In the same section, we also have shown several answers that survivors gave us when asked about their lives in the camps, particularly as it related to the Biblical text.

In the third section of this tenth chapter, we have written and discussed eight separate theories or modes of inquiry by which many scholars in the West have understood the Akedah narrative in the post-Holocaust period of history. These eight theories are: The Enduring Love View, or Ambivalent Gnosticism; the Incomprehensibility Theory; the Israel *Redivivus* View; the Martyrdom Theory; the Anti-Martyrdom Approach; the Psychoanalytic View of the Akedah; the Rejection of the Psychoanalytic View; and the Testing of Sarah or the Feminist Perspective of the Akedah narrative.

In each of these eight theories or modes of inquiry about the Akedah in post-Holocaust times, we have shown which scholars and writers should be identified with each of these theories. The Enduring Love or Ambivalent Gnosticism View has been identified with New York-born Jewish writer Marco Roth. The Incomprehensibility Theory, or the 614 Commandment Perspective, is associated with the writings of Jewish philosopher Emil Fackenheim.

The third approach, the Israel *Redivivus* Theory, has been championed by philosopher Jacob Neusner. The theory we have labeled the Martyrdom Approach is most often identified with Israeli thinker Aharon Agus, and the Anti-Martyrdom Approach with many of the writings of noble Prize winner Elie Wiesel.

We have shown in the third section of Chapter Ten that a number of thinkers and scholars have been associated with a psychoanalytic reading of the Akedah narrative. Among these is Erich Wellisch in his *Isaac and Oedipus*, as well as Leon Kass, George Devereaux, and M. H. Sherman and his *Biblical Commentary as a Psychoanalytic Defense*, published in 2002.

In this portion of the third section of Chapter Ten, we have shown that each of these thinkers, in their own way, have used the idea of the Oedipus Complex as the starting point of their inquiries, although these four thinkers go in many different directions after that starting point. The Anti-Psychoanalytic View of the Akedah, as we have shown, may be identified with Theodor Reik and Italian psychoanalyst Silvano Arieti. For the most part, these two thinkers criticized the views of Erich Wellisch regarding the Akedah narrative in post-Holocaust times.

The final theory of views of the Akedah after the Holocaust is what we have called the Testing of Sarah or the Feminist Approach to the sacrifice of Isaac in post-Holocaust times. In this portion of Chapter Ten, we examined both male and female feminists in their views of the Akedah. Among the male feminists cited are Trevor Dennis, W. Lee Humphreys and Rabbi Paul Kipnes.

Among the female feminists identified and discussed in Chapter Ten were Michelle November, Colleen Ivey Hartsoe, Alicia Suskin Ostriker, Eleanor Wilner, Dr. Mohja Kahf and Rabbi Amy Eilberg. Each of these women, in their own way, has made valuable contributions to the understanding of the Akedah narrative, or the sacrifice of Isaac story, in post-Holocaust times.

This brings us to Chapter Eleven, in which we will discuss the phenomenon of the Akedah narrative, or the sacrifice of Isaac, in the contemporary world. That is, the Akedah in culture, art, music and in contemporary literature from the 1960s until the present.

Chapter Eleven:
The Akedah in Contemporary Life

The command of God is that Isaac be killed. It follows that there will be no descendants, no future, simply barrenness. The entire pilgrimage from 11:30 has been for naught. Abraham had trusted the promise fully. Our promise is to be abrogated. Can the same God who promised life also command death?

—Walter Brueggemann, *A Bible Commentary for Teaching and Preaching*

Jewish orthodoxy based its claims to superiority over other religions from its beginning on its superior rationality. Far from invoking the teleological suspension of the ethical, Judaism has traditionally dealt with the apparent clashes between divine commands and morality by re-interpreting the divine commands in a way that takes into account moral concerns.

—Leo Strauss, *Spinoza's Critique of Religion*

Two basic attitudes can be discerned in relation to the Akedah. Whereas the first view the Akedah as the deepest symbol of modern Israel…the second rejects both the myth and its implications,

—Anonymous article on the Akedah in *Encyclopedia Judaica*

Introduction

The purpose of this eleventh and final chapter is to explore the many places in contemporary life that the Akedah narrative of Genesis 22 has played a role in cultural, religious, artistic, literary, philosophical and musical ways. We will begin with a section in this chapter on the role of the sacrifice of Isaac narrative in Israeli and American cultures. The material will be followed by a discussion of the Akedah in art in the contemporary period. Similar sections of this chapter on literature, music and philosophy will follow the one on literature. We begin, then, with the places in contemporary Jewish and American cultures where the Akedah narrative has found a place.

The Akedah in Contemporary Culture

The first place to look for the presence of the Akedah in contemporary culture is the use of the sacrifice of Isaac narrative that is read on the second day of *Rosh Hashanah*. Each year in the Jewish calendar, those of the faith collectively struggle with the psychological impact and personal ethics of the narrative. How could a father do such a thing? What was Isaac's feelings, as well as those of his mother, Sarah?

In the Akedah reading on *Rosh Hashanah*, God tries to "test" Abraham. We have no reason why He would do such a thing, but we have some hints, as well as a lot of questions. What does Abraham tell Sarah? What did Abraham say to Isaac? Does Abraham talk to God ever again after this life-changing event? What else is this man prepared to do to placate his God? We do not know the answers to any of these questions. But as Rabbi Walter Rothschild puts the matter:

> The gaps tell us much as or even more than the words in this troubling text. We learn too that God can change His mind. Perhaps too this is also a message for *Rosh Hashanah* that on the day of Judgment we can still hope for a change of destiny at the very last moment. We also learn that, confusing for some, that blind obedience to God's commands is not what is demanded of us.[878]

Many sermons on the Akedah narrative in Judaism are designed to speak of how we are to deal with the phenomenon of evil and suffering when it impinges on our daily lives. In other words, what are we to do when we get "tested." Again, as Rabbi Rothschild tells us:

> We have to respond by arguing, not by obeying. And sometimes we have to listen to the silence inside us, and not just the words.[879]

Rabbi David R. Blumenthal, in an essay entitled "The Akedah and *Rosh Hashanah*" states that:

> Invoking the Original Oath God Was Forced to Make," suggests that the best way to understand the Akedah reading on *Rosh Hashanah*, is to remember that the two are connected in ritual, because of the Shofar, and in the liturgy on the second day. Abraham sacrificed a ram in Isaac's stead, and so a ram's horn becomes the Shofar, that is sounded every year on the Day of Judgment.[880]

Rabbi Blumenthal ties the reading of the Akedah narrative on *Rosh Hashanah* to the taking of an Oath, such as at Genesis 24:7, 26:2–3 and 50:24. It was also an oath, of course, with which God begins his journey with Abraham at Genesis 12:1–3 and 7. The three-fold blessing given at Genesis 22:15–18 is repeated later at Genesis 48:3–6 when Jacob blessed his children before his death with a three-fold blessing.

At any rate, the first mention of the Akedah narrative read during the second day of *Rosh Hashanah*, and its meaning, is our first way that the narrative can be seen in contemporary culture. Another way is the reference to the Akedah in Orthodox Jewish daily prayers. Of the three required times of prayer, the Akedah narrative is mentioned in the morning service, seven days a week, twelve months a year.

One of the epigrams for this chapter indicates that Israeli society, after the establishment of modern Israel, saw the formation of two separate views of the Akedah narrative. In the first view of the sacrifice of Isaac narrative, the text is seen as a symbol of modern Israeli existence that epitomizes the Zionist Revolution and the sacrifices it endured to regain the Land.[881]

In the other modern view of the Akedah, the myth, symbols and rituals related to it are completely rejected. The former view can be seen in Abraham Shlonsky's comment when he observed, "Father, take off your *tallit* and *tefillin* today, and take your son to a distant land to Mount Moriah." The "distant land," of course, is the modern state of Israel.[882] Hiam Gouri, another representative figure in the first view described above, tells us that, "Isaac's descendants were born with a knife in their chests."[883]

In 1967, the Six-Day War was seen as the first time that the founders were now too old to fight. And the dedication of the next generation was recorded in works such as *The Seventh Day*, in which soldiers speak of their participation in the Six-Day War. The book records one father of a soldier who said:

> We do knowingly bring up our boys to volunteer for combat units. These are moments when a man is given greater insight into Isaac's sacrifice.[884]

Our second modern, cultural view of the Akedah—the one that rejects traditional Jewish myth, symbol and ritual about the Akedah narrative, began almost immediately after Independence Day in Israel. A representative example of this view is S. Yizhar, who in 1958 in his *Days of Ziklag* (vol. II, p. 804) relates:

> There is no evading the Akedah…I hate our father Abraham, who binds Isaac. What right does he have over Isaac. Let him bind himself. I hate the God who sent him and closed all paths, leaving only that of the Akedah. I hate the fact that Isaac serves merely as a Test between Abraham and his God.[885]

Protests against the Akedah myth also surfaced after the Lebanon War in 1982. Yehudah Amihai, for example, in his "The True Hero of the Sacrifice" suggests that the true hero of the Akedah was the ram. Indeed, Amihai gives life and lines to the ram, while rejecting traditional Jewish views of the Akedah narrative.[886]

Poet Yitzhak Laor is another representative example of the Rejection of the Akedah Myth View. In a poem called "This Fool, Isaac," Laor writes:

> To pity the offering / To trust a father like that,
> Let him kill him first. Let him slam his father

His only father, Abraham
In Jail, in the poorhouse just so
He will not slay
Remember what your father did to you brother Ishmael.[887]

One way to see the role of the sacrifice of Isaac in American culture, besides in the *Rosh Hashanah* service, is in American literature going back to the nineteenth century and Melville's novella, *Billy Budd*, that involves the execution of a young sailor at the hands of his captain, a father figure for the sailor. The captain, a man named Vere, is worried about his British ship because there had been a 1797 great mutiny on another British ship.[888]

In his 1969 novel *Portnoy's Complaint*, Philip Roth borrows on similar themes to the Akedah narrative of child sacrifice with some fascinating role reversals, without ever mentioning the Biblical text. At one point, the narrator, a young boy, says:

So my mother sits down in a chair beside me with a long bread knife in her hand. It is made of stainless steel and has little saw-like teeth. Which do I want to be, weak or strong, a man or a mouse?[889]

Roth follows this with a later description of the young boy to his psychiatrist:

Doctor, why oh why, of why, of why oh why, does a mother pull out a knife on her own son. I am only a young boy, how do I know she won't use it? What am I supposed to do for Christ's sake? I believe there is an intention lurking somewhere to draw my blood. Only why? What can she possibly be thinking in her brain...because I will not eat some string beans and a baked potato, point a bread knife at my heart?[890]

Bernard Malamud's 1982 novel *God's Grace* imagines an apocalyptic world in which the only human survivor, a man named Calvin Cohn, struggles vainly to teach a group of apes to live in harmony with his Jewish beliefs and customs. As his frantic struggle fails, his adopted son, one of the apes, captures Cohn and takes him to a mountain top. When the son is ready to sacrifice his father, Calvin Cohn yells, "But where is the ram in the thicket, or am I to be the burnt offering?"[891]

A piece of literature in the period between Melville and Malamud is Wilfred Owen, a World War I British poet who was killed in combat on November 4, 1918, in France. Before his death, he had penned a poem entitled the "Parable of the Old Man and the Young," that begins:

> So Abram rose, and clave the wood, and went,
> And took the fire with him, and a knife.
> And as they sojourned both of them together
> Isaac the firstborn spoke and said, "My father,
> Behold the preparations, fire and iron
> But where is the lamb for the burnt offering?[892]

Mr. Owen continues the narrative poem:

> Then Abram bound the youth with belts and straps,
> And built parapets and trenches there.
> And stretched forth the knife to slay his son.
> When lo, An Angel called him out of Heaven, saying
> Lay not your hand upon the lad, neither do anything
> To him, thy son.
>
> Behold! Caught in the thicket by its horns,
> A ram. Offer the ram of pride instead.
> But the old man would not so, but slew his son
> And half the seed of Europe, one by one.[893]

The works of writer Franz Kafka, which have been very popular in contemporary literature in the 1970s to the present, makes a number of parallels to the Akedah scene. At the end of his novel, *The Trial*, for example, the hero, one Josef K., is spread-eagle on a rock with the executioner poised above him with a knife in his hand.[894] There is another unmistakable parallel to the Akedah in Kafka's short story "The Penal Colony."[895] But as critic Hillel Barzel points out, "There is no rescuing Angel."[896]

Another way in American culture where the shadows of the Akedah narrative can be seen is in the work of many feminist thinkers in contemporary times, where the figure of Sarah becomes central to the narrative. Hilene Flanzbaum of Butler University in Indiana has collected various feminist writers' views on the Akedah in her "Introduction to Feminists Literary Interpretations of the Akedah."[897]

Among these feminist writers are Eleanor Wilner and Alicia Ostriker, among many others. Wilner entitled one of her poems, "Sarah's Choice," in which Isaac's mother speaks directly about her family's situation. She writes:

> The voice of the prophet grows shrill
> He will read even defeat as a sign
> of distinction until pain itself
> becomes holy. In that day how shall we tell
> the victims from the saints?[898]

Alicia Ostriker, another Jewish feminist poet, in her work "The Nakedness of the Fathers," retells many of the narratives of the Torah, including Sarah's point of view about the Akedah narrative. In Ostriker's version of Genesis 22, she has Abraham say "No!" to the command, but she admits that Sarah would have been "powerless to do so."[899] Both Ostriker and Wilner are representative examples of feminists writers who make sure that Sarah finally gets her due.

This brings us to a discussion of the Akedah in contemporary art, the subject matter of the next section of this history of Jewish, Christian and Islamic attitudes toward the sacrifice of Isaac.

The Akedah in Contemporary Art

Discussion of renderings of the sacrifice of Isaac in contemporary art begins with the work of Marc Chagall, whose 1966 painting *The Sacrifice of Isaac* is a depiction of the Akedah that connects the Akedah, as many early Christian artists did, to the Crucifixion of Jesus Christ.

Chagall, a man raised in an Orthodox Jewish home in Eastern Europe, saw the connection between the word "thicket" at Genesis 22:13, with the "crown of thorns" in the Gospels at Matthew 27:29. The connection is further made by the Semitic root SBCH, which is the origin of the word for "thicket" and for "thorns," or *sebak* and *sobek*.[900]

The painting of Chagall's of the Akedah was worked on from 1960 until 1966. Abraham stands above his son, prone on the altar. The father holds the knife in his right hand. An angel hovers above the pair; his left arm extended toward Abraham. Sarah is to the left, observing the scene. She is adjacent to a tree to which the substitute ram is tethered. In the upper right corner of the painting, an image of the Crucifixion is playing out. Jesus carries his cross, while several other figures, including a woman holding an infant, observe the scene.[901]

Seven years later, in 1973, Chagall began a project to design a set of stained glass windows as part of the restoration of the thirteenth-century Saint Stephen's church in Mainz, Germany. The project consisted of four sections of Akedah windows, completed in a luminous royal blue background, with the foreground figures in black with white sparkles.[902]

Louis Berman suggests there are two unique features in the Saint Stephen's windows. First, two angels, not one, hover above Abraham, who stands at the altar holding a knife. At the upper right is the angel who brings the message not to touch the lad. On the upper left is the angel carrying a ram. Here a Jewish artist designed an Akedah for a Christian church.[903]

Since that time, a variety of other Jewish and Christian painters and sculptors have depicted the sacrifice of Isaac motif, including the following artists:

1. Richard McBee (1947–) (1980, 1982, and 1987)

2. Menashe Kadishman (1932–2015) (1982–1985)

3. Frederick Terna (1923–) (1989–1990)

4. Robert Kirschbaum (2011)

5. Albert Winn (1998, 2015)

Richard McBee completed a series of paintings on the Akedah in the 1980s. His 1982 *Akedah* is an oil on canvas, 70 by 90 inches. It shows a tall and old, bearded Abraham, dressed in white linen vestment with a modern black jacket. Abraham's right hand grasps the knife, which is down by his side. His left hand is either grasping his son Isaac, or the substitute ram. Critic Matthew Baigell observes about the painting:

> It is based on the understanding of the human mind before it became aware of itself, before self-consciousness, subjectivity, and free will be-came common.[904]

A second painting in the series of McBee's, indeed, the first in the series, is also an oil on canvas from 1980. The painting is 68 by 68 inches and is entitled *Abraham and Isaac*. It shows Isaac kneeling on the altar in the center. His enormous father stands behind him, dressed in a dark cloak with a hood. A sword-like knife is in the father's right grasp. In front of the altar and around the right are bones and skulls. To the left are three females standing. Two of them hold their arms above their heads toward Heaven, while the third figure, perhaps Sarah, examines a pit of bones and skulls. The painting is very dark, as well as evocative and suggestive about the Biblical scene.[905]

The third piece of McBee's series on the Akedah is a "Sculptamold" of Abraham completing the building of the altar and was completed in 1987. Abraham is prone on an altar built of enormous square blocks. Abraham is erect behind the son, a large knife in his right hand. The hand of God enters the scene from the upper left. The substitute ram is on the lower right attached to the thicket.[906]

In a 2004 interview, McBee was asked about his thinking in the making of the Akedah series. He responded this way:

> I simply did not understand Abraham or God Him-self. But I thought that we had to come to terms with both of them. Isaac's passivity was plausible, but ultimately, troubling. And Sarah, Sarah we mourn. After working with the subject for close to thirty years, I still don't understand; but now

I don't understand in a deeper more troubling way.[907]

In the same interview, McBee observed about his Biblical works:

Our encounters with the Divine are precious moments of personal religiosity. We believe that when we pray we are speaking directly to God and at that moment we are in the Divine presence. And yet, we are seldom conscious of the awe and the fear we also fear.[908]

Israeli painter and sculptor Menashe Kadishman (1932–2015) completed *Binding of Isaac* between 1982 and 1985. It is an iron sculpture owned by Tel Aviv University, Israel. The image looks like a large sheep, or perhaps a ram. It has an oval face. Its forelegs are spread wide; its hind legs are two metal posts stuck in the ground.[909] The sculpture invokes Genesis 22:13, the substitute animal for the sacrifice. Kadishman included this sculpture in several public shows, including two in 1985—one at the Hebrew Home at Riverdale in The Bronx, and the other at the Fred Jones Jr. Museum of Art in Norman, Oklahoma.

Another image of the Akedah narrative by Kadishman, a crayon drawing of the sacrifice, was part of a November 1987 exhibit at the Israel Museum of Art, which displayed 253 separate items. What is unusual about this rendering of the sacrifice of Isaac scene is that there is no Abraham and no intervening angel. There is a prostrate Isaac, with a ram hovering over the son. Another peculiar thing about the Kadishman crayon work is that next to Isaac is a wolf. One wonders if it still can be called an Akedah if there is no Abraham and if the wolf has been added to the composition of the piece.

Born in 1923, Frederick Terna is a Holocaust survivor who now resides in Brooklyn, New York. Terna was born in Vienna, lived in Prague as a child and spent nearly four years in Auschwitz and Dachau. In 1946, he moved to Paris and then to the United States in 1952. He completed a painting entitled *An Offering Set Aside* in 1987. In the image, we see the ram as an egg in the womb of what is perhaps an angel. Joanne Tucker, in an article on Terna, says this about the painting:

Drawn to the piercing questions of the Akedah, Frederick Terna has wrestled with this text for many years. As a Holocaust survivor he has found in this story one vehicle to deal with his own life experiences and to express deep-seated emotions in a most creative way.

An Offering Set Aside reminds us that from the very outset of creation, the ram, the Salvivic vehicle and through its horns, the symbol of the Messianic, is waiting. Programed into human existence from its inception is the potential for redemption.[910]

In 2011, Robert Kirschbaum completed a series of abstract paintings known as the "Akedah Series." These paintings are sequentially numbered with gaps in the numbering, perhaps representing other images not chosen for exhibits. Akedah number 39 begins the series. It shows three ovals floating above a central space as a rectangle emerges from the bottom center of the piece. This image represents the beginning of the construction of the altar in the Akedah narrative. The painting features a series of dark marks that come together, suggesting Isaac standing on the altar. The next painting is number 40. The altar is now fully formed, with a broad base and square top, behind which can be seen a dark, brooding sky. The altar's image is so realistic, it casts a shadow.[911]

The next two paintings continue the sequence of the altar at the center, the place where God, Abraham and Isaac were to meet—the *Axis Mundi*, if you will. In the fifth painting, however, there is a radical shift to ten squares appearing in a vaguely familiar pattern. Each of these large squares is constructed of nine smaller squares, three by three. According to Mr. Kirschbaum, "These represent the typical division of the sacred from the profane."

Not accidentally, the entire design of these floating squares "depict the ten *Sefirot* of the Kaballah." The standard chart of the Ten Sefirot are representations of ten Divine essences, starting from the top at the Crown that expresses the ineffable, and then moving downward until it connects with the mundane world, the Divine Presence, or the *Shekinah*. Kirschbaum relates that this painting is a representation of the Divine meeting Abraham and Isaac "at the moment of the aborting of the sacrifice."

The next three paintings are not easy to interpret. It seems the relationship now has transitioned to the chaotic. The experience of the Divine had been overwhelming. Now, in number 48, we see the appearance of another small rectangle, rising over half of the height of the paper. Finally, in the last painting, the rectangle now becomes a portal of an archetypical doorway. Floating ovals have reappeared in the painting. "Through the door," Kirschbaum relates, "we must find new encounters with the Divine."

In 1995, writer and photographer Albert Joseph Winn (1947–2014) completed a series of photographs he called "The Akedah." The most important of these is the image that shows the photographer's torso and arm, with a bandage and *tefillin* of Jewish observance attached. These photographs now are owned by the Library of Congress, Division of Prints and Photographs, in Washington, DC. These photographs have appeared in a number of exhibitions since 1995, including the "Art Aids America," at the Tacoma Art Museum in Tacoma, Washington, in October of 2015.[912]

One of the most provocative pieces of contemporary Akedah art is George Segal's *Sacrifice of Art*, unveiled at the Mann Auditorium in Tel Aviv in May of 1973. Segal explained that he was deeply affected by reading Kierkegaard's *Fear and Trembling*, and he created a very modern sculpture of the scene. Segal's Abraham is middle-aged and a bit flabby. He wears a pair of jeans.[913]

Controversy arose over the piece. Eventually, it was installed on the campus of Princeton University in New Jersey. In the Segal scene, Isaac is a beautiful youth lying on a barren rock, but he does not appear to be frightened. He also seems not to want to flee. He could very easily come to his feet, perhaps to embrace his father.

Finally, what is certainly the smallest piece of Akedah art in the contemporary period is a 1978 postal stamp of the Israeli government that depicts the Sacrifice of Isaac. The stamp, which was designed by Moya Smith, was made available to the Israeli public in January of 1978.[914]

Although there are many other artistic pieces that render the sacrifice of Isaac narrative in contemporary art, we will move instead to an analysis of the Akedah in contemporary music, the subject matter of the next section of this eleventh chapter, in this history of perspectives on the Akedah in Judaism, Christianity and Islam.

The Akedah in Contemporary Music

Discussions in contemporary music of the sacrifice of Isaac narrative begin with Russian composer Igor Stravinsky's (1882–1972) work entitled *Akedah Yizhak*, or the "Binding of Isaac," produced in 1962 to 1964. It was called a sacred ballad for baritone and chamber orchestra. It was first performed in Jerusalem in 1964. Stravinsky was perhaps the most well-known composer in the contemporary period.

Stravinsky wrote a number of pieces of sacred music, many with Biblical themes, including his best-known work, *Le Sacre du Printemps*, or "The Rites of Spring," that was a spasmodic rhythm with dissonant harmonies depicting a fertility sacrifice in ancient, pagan Russia. Later, the Russian composer, who became an American citizen, wrote his *Symphony of Psalms*, a grand, choral symphony. It was written in 1930 and was commissioned by the Boston Symphony.

In the symphony's three movements, Stravinsky sets the work with the background of Psalms 38, 39, and 40, respectively, using the edition of the Vulgate. Stravinsky also used Gregorian chant, polyphony of Bach, and Russian rhythms, in the symphony, as well as the Impressionist harmonies of Debussy, combining them all through a brilliant Art Deco Modernism.

Stravinsky wrote another religious music piece in 1944, a short cantata called *Babel*. It was written for a narrator, a male chorus and a full orchestra. By this time, Stravinsky had settled in Hollywood, California. *Babel* was commissioned as part of his larger *Genesis Suite*, in which the spoken words of the Bible are combined with orchestra and choral music. The music of *Babel* is much more descriptive than is usual for the Russian composer. In a lot of ways, the piece is like a film.

Around the same time as *Babel*, Stravinsky worked on his one and only Mass, completed in 1948 and called "A Mass for Choir and Wind Instruments." Stravinsky said it was written for "spiritual necessity."

In his later years, Stravinsky wrote a *Cantata* in 1953, based on an Old English text; a *Canticum Sacrum*, in 1958, a sacred cantata first performed in Saint Marl's Basilica in Venice in 1958. The word is loosely based on the lamentations of the Prophet Jeremiah.

Stravinsky also completed the following religious pieces of music from 1958 until 1966:

1. *A Sermon, a Narrative, and a Prayer*, 1961. A Biblical cantata.

2. *The Flood*, 1962. A musical play for television the Biblical Flood narrative and Medieval Mystery plays.

3. *Abraham and Isaac*, 1962–1964. A sacred ballad in Hebrew.

4. *The Requiem Canticles*, 1966. Selected verses from the Requiem Mass in the Vulgate Bible.[915]

A second piece of contemporary music that mentions the Akedah is Bob Dylan's 1965 ballad, "Highway 61." The song begins provocatively with a partial retelling of the Abraham and Isaac narrative. The first stanza of the song reads as follows:

Oh God said to Abraham, "Kill me a son." Abe says, "Man, you must be puttin' me on." God says, "No." Abe say, "What." God say, "You can do what you want, Abe, but the next time you see me comin' you better run." "Well," Abe says, "Where do you want this killin' done?" God says, "Out on highway 61."

A few years after the Dylan song, Leonard Cohen released his own version of the Akedah narrative called "The Story of Isaac."[916] A good part of the motivation for the work was a message of protest against the sending of young American men to the war in Vietnam. In Cohen's lyrics, he relates:

You who build these altars now, to sacrifice their children, you must not do it anymore. A scheme is not a vision, and you have never been tempted by a Demon or a God. You who stand above them now, your hatchets blunt and bloody, you were not there before. When I lay upon a mountain and my father's hand was trembling with the beauty of the world.

In 1972, Judith Kaplan Eisenstein (1909–1996) composed her sacrifice of Isaac, "A Liturgical Drama," that was first performed in Jerusalem. Louis Berman describes Eisenstein's drama this way: "She uses the old poem, 'Et Sha-arey Ratzon,' interspersed with several penitential poems to produce a musical drama in the tradition of the Jews of medieval Spain and southern France."[917] The *Et Sha-aray Ratzon* is a Jewish prayer book in a four-column format, complete with English transliteration for those who do not know Hebrew. It also provides a commentary on the text and answers questions about it like, "What is the spiritual meaning of this passage?" And, "How is this related to this part of the service?" Although the *Et Sha-aray* has a traditional text, it is not simply a conventional prayer book. The pages provide both information and inspiration.

Eisenstein was an author, composer and musicologist. She also was the subject of the first Bat Mitzvah performed in the United States on March 18, 1922. Many of Eisenstein's books were about Jewish music, including *The Gateway to Jewish Song* (1939), *Songs of Childhood* (1981), *The Song of Dawn* (1974), as well as the 1972 *Sacrifice of Isaac*.

In 1992, folk singer Joan Baez wrote and performed a song entitled, "Isaac and Abraham," the order in the title suggesting that the son is the more important character. The lyrics for the song include the following:

Play me backwards, Isaac and Abraham
Hard times, hard times in Canaan land
Trouble in the mind of a man
A voice came whispering softly to him;
Go offer, offer up the land.

The second stanza of the Baez song tells us this:

Abraham took his only son
High up on a hill
His test of faith had finally come
As the wind, the wind began to chill.

This is followed by stanza three:

Cold steel, cold steel in the father's hand.
Tears falling from the sky
The angels, the angels did not understand
Why the righteous, the righteous boy had to die.

The song of Baez contains another two stanzas, ending in this one:

Oh Isaac
The light of all your days
Will shine upon this mountain high
And never, never fade away,
And never fade away.

It should be clear that Ms. Baez has a fundamental understanding of the Akedah narrative. She sees God's original call to Abraham to be a "soft voice," like the Bible's First Kings 19:12. Baez alludes to the Test Theory in the second stanza, and she describes well the existential situation of Isaac and its repercussions in the closing stanza of "Isaac and Abraham."

Singer and musician Cat Stevens, now called Sufijan Stevens, wrote and performed two separate songs on the sacrifice of Isaac narrative. One was in 2002 and simply entitled "Abraham." The second song was five years later and called "My Shiny." The former is the better song. Stevens employs the Test Theory and the Sanctity of Human Life Theory in the lyrics of "Abraham."

American songwriter and performer, Madonna included a song called "Isaac" in her 2005 album *Confessions on a Dance Floor*, as well as the world tour in support of the record. Two things, however, make Madonna's uses of the Akedah narrative different from other songwriters. First, she employed a popular Yemenite Jewish song as a chorus for the song. The song is called *Im nin'alu daltei nadivim*, which is based on a medieval Jewish mystical song written by famed Yemenite Kabbalist, Rabbi Shalom Shabazi, in which he alternates between Hebrew and Arabic verses.

Rabbi Shabazi (1619–1720) was a Jewish poet and lyricist. In

Jewish circles, he is still known today as the "Poet of Yemen." The song of Shabazi also was recorded by Israeli singer Ofra Haza in 1978. That lovely performance has been viewed millions of times since the turn to the new millennium.[918]

The second reason that Madonna's "Isaac" is unusual is that she acquired the reputation of someone interested in mysticism and the Kaballah, and so her song might be seen as a mystical commentary on the Akedah narrative. Madonna's Isaac begins with a Yemeni singer named Yitzhak Sinwani, blowing the shofar, and then singing part of the opening verse. The lyrics and the dramatic sequence of the song go like this:

> Sound of the Shofar blowing
> If the Gates of Heaven are locked
> Then the Gates of Heaven are not locked.
>
> Sound of the Shofar blowing
> If the Gates of Heaven are locked and they are not locked
> Then living God, exalted above the cherubim—
> They all rise with his Spirit.
>
> Figure in a blue cape dancing in a cage, with sand dunes,
>   Madonna appears
> Staring up into the Heavens
> In this Hell that binds your hands
> Will you sacrifice your comfort
> Make your way in a foreign land?

Madonna's "Isaac" goes on for another seven stanzas ending with these words:

> Wrestle with your darkness.
> Angels call your name
> Can you hear what they are saying?
> Will you ever be the same?

Critic David Blumenthal gives this summation of the Madonna song and performance from 2005:

Madonna's interpretation thus interweaves the themes of liberation and of life as a Test together with Shabazi's mystical poem. But it is a wedding poem and not an Akedah poem, though it is a loose and a very modern interpretation of the Akedah, not unlike other secular interpretations; redemptive without direct allusions to the story of Genesis 22. It is an amazing palimpsest of texts.[919]

Blumenthal's critique is a fair and honest one. The Gates of Heaven being open and closed at the same time in the second stanza is an indication of Rabbi Shabazi's, and perhaps Madonna's mysticism. Lyrics like "Staring into the Heavens" and "Will you ever be the same?" are indications of Madonna's understanding the dread and the angst that comes with understanding the Akedah narrative.[920]

Another Jewish source of music on the Akedah narrative is the tradition of what is known as the *Niggun Akedah*, a traditional melody concerning the binding of Isaac. It is an Ashkenazi Jewish tradition set to penitential poems about the sacrifice of Isaac. This source, above all else, shows that in addition to the vast literary and artistic Jewish sources of the Akedah narrative, there is also a vast musical tradition on the theme of the sacrifice of Isaac in Judaism.[921]

There have been a countless number of Jewish musicians and performers who have written or performed the *Niggun Akedah*, including Abraham Zvi Idelsohn's 1932 in the key of F, with no fixed meter. And more recently, Michel Heymann's 2017 composition in the key of C, with multiple meter, but mostly in triple time. Michael Heymann is a Cantor who was born in Germany in 1952.

Finally, Elie Wiesel, in a1974 cantata, he called *Ani Maamin*, presents Isaac as the remnant and the embodiment of the Nation of Israel in the cantata, three patriarchs travel to Heaven with complaints about what is happening to their descendants, in spite of the ancient promise that the Nation of Israel will survive. Now, in the death camps of the Holocaust, at one point, Isaac intones in addressing God:

Do you recall the Akedah/over there om Moriah/
Among all the men on earth/it was me, you claimed...
In Holocaust.../you made me climb and then descend/
Mount Moriah/crushed and silent/
I did not know. My Lord, I did not know/
It was to see my children/ old and young/
Arrive in Majdanek.
And still no rescuing Angel.[922]

This brings us to the final section of this eleventh chapter on the Akedah narrative in contemporary life—the many roles and appearances of the sacrifice of Isaac narrative in contemporary literature.

The Akedah in Contemporary Literature

In his essay, "The Meaning of the Akedah in Israeli Culture and Jewish Tradition," published in *Israel Studies*, Israeli scholar Avi Sagi speaks of the contrast of the Biblical descriptions of the Akedah narrative and uses the Genesis 22 passage in modern and contemporary Jewish literature. Sagi mentions three differences "worth noting." First, Sagi tells us, "Contrary to the passive figure of the Biblical story, the Isaac of modern literature is an active hero, who usually initiates the Akedah scene."

Secondly, Avi Sagi informs us:

Modern literature lays greater emphasis than the Biblical text on intergenerational cooperation, as if no rift divided the father's offering of the sacrifice is disconnected from the son.

Third, rather than a single, lonely hero, Isaac is the moral exemplar of the Zionist pioneer. Sagi says the first two points, which, as noted, are missing from the Biblical narrative, but they are fully developed in the Midrash literature. In modern Israeli literature, the Zionist Isaac tells the story of an entire generation. Rather than being a passive victim, the Zionist Isaac assumes responsibility for their destiny and is willing to sacrifice himself on the altar of the national renaissance.[923]

From the 1970s until the present time, there have been a vast number of employments of the Akedah narrative in contemporary literature, both Jewish and Christian. In this final section of this history, we will list a short variety of those uses of Abraham and Isaac, and then, in turn, discuss that variety individually.

1. David Baaumgardt, "Man's Morals and God's Will" (*Commentary*, March 1950)

2. Shapira Kalonymus, *Es Kodesh Jerusalem* (1960)

3. Amos Oz, "The Way of the Wind" (poem, 1990)

4. The film, *Fail-Safe*

5. Nancy Jay, *Throughout Their Generations Forever*

6. Nahum Sarna, *Commentary on Genesis* (1989)

7. Elinor Wilner, "Sarah's Choice"

8. *An Anthology of Akedah Stories in Japanese* (2012)

9. M. Tyler Sasser, "The Binding of Isaac: Appropriations of the Akedah in Contemporary Picture Books in Children's Literature," vol. 45, 2017, pp. 138–163

10. Eli Wiesel, *Night* and other works

These works of literature on the Akedah narrative cover a period from 1950 to the present age. We will analyze them one at a time, in sequence. David Baumgardt wrote his piece for *Commentary* magazine in March of 1950. In this essay, Baumgardt pulls together sources as divergent as Fourth Maccabees, the *Bereshith* Rabbah, Reformation thinker Jakob Böhme, Kierkegaard's *Fear and Trembling*, Rabbi Abraham Ibn Daud, and contemporary Rabbi Gumbiner. But rather than giving a definitive meaning of the Akedah narrative, Mr. Baumgardt mostly asks questions about it.[924]

Rabbi Shapira Kalonymus (1889–1943), whose *Es Kodesh Jerusalem* was published posthumously in 1960, suggests that the primary importance of the Akedah narrative is that the Divine command itself determines morality—a version of Divine Command Theory with respect to Ethics. The rabbi relates:

> The nations of the world, even the best of them, think that
> the truth is a thing in itself, and that God commanded the
> truth because the truth is intrinsically true. Not so, Israel, who

say, "You God are truth and we have no truth besides Him."
And all the truth found in the world is only there because God
wished it and commanded it. Stealing is wrong because God
commanded it. Stealing is forbidden because the God of truth
has commanded it. When God ordered Abraham to sacrifice
his son Isaac, it was true to sacrifice him, and, had God not
said later that "neither do anything to him," it would have
been true to slaughter him.[925]

Israeli novelist Amos Oz, in his story "The Way of the Wind,"
presents a father who intentionally deceives his wife—the boy's
mother—and signs a paper that permits the son to join the Air Force.
The son desperately wants to escape from the father, but he cannot
because of the father's desire that the son must prove himself as a man
and a worthy son.[926]

In her book *Throughout Your Generations Forever*, Nancy Jay
suggests that the best way to approach the Akedah narrative is by
contrasting various theories about the nature and the uses of sacrifice.
Jay asks, "Why not develop a theory of sacrifice through the story
rather than interpreting the story through the theory of sacrifice?"[927]

The 1964 novel *Fail-Safe* by Eugene Burdick and the film
directed by Sidney Lumet and starring Henry Fonda, Walter Matthau
and Fritz Weaver, in the final chapter of the novel and at the end of
the film, the President of the United States makes the decision to drop
four nuclear bombs on New York City, thereby sacrificing millions
of his own countrymen, including his wife and children, in order to
honor a promise he made with another Father of State—the Russian
Premier.

Needless to say, the analogs to the Akedah narrative are many
and profound. Biblical scholar Nahum Sarna, in his 1989 book, tells
us that Abraham would be willing to sacrifice himself in order to save
his son. But the Bible scholar points out that there is little evidence for
this view in the Biblical text. Sarna points out, "Even is that theory is
true, then why does Abraham do nothing to try and save his son. Why
does he not argue with God, as he did when trying to save Ishmael from
banishment and Sodom from destruction?"[928]

We have discussed Elinor Wilner's "Sarah's Choice" earlier in this history in terms of seeing the Akedah from the perspective of Sarah, so we will not comment further on it here. A work called *An Anthology of Akedah Stories in Japanese*, published in 2012, contains a number of Japanese Christian stories on the Akedah theme by Japanese Christian writers. The volume includes stories by:

1. Inazo Nitobe, "The Soul of Japan"

2. Kanzo Uchimura, "The Sacrifice of Isaac"

3. Kitaro Nishida, "Ethics of Place and Religious World View"

4. Hissao Miyamoto, "The Suffering of Abraham"

5. Seizo Sekine, "Philosophical Interpretations of the Sacrifice of Isaac"[929]

These Japanese works tell us something of the wide-ranging influence of the sacrifice of Isaac narrative in the modern world. The foundations from which these Japanese writers begin are not all that different than what we have seen in Western literature.

M. Tyler Sasser, in his essay for the journal *Children's Literature*, catalogs many contemporary books for children that employ and exhibit renderings of the Akedah narrative, including more than two dozen examples.[930]

Finally, in his novel *Night* as well as in several of his other works, Jewish writer Eli Wiesel incorporates the Akedah narrative in both his fiction and his non-fiction. In his novel, *Night*, the narrator of the work, Eliezer, frequently mentions religious observances and ceremonies. He mentions the Talmud, the Sabbath and the Jewish holidays. But Eliezer does not mention the *Kaddish*, the mourning ritual upon the death of an observant Jew.

Around the time of the death of Eliezer's father, the younger man begins to lose his faith. He specifically begins to avoid religious language, and it ceased to be a part of his life. Although religious language vanishes from his life, it still becomes a metaphor for the structure of the rest of the novel. Indeed, Wiesel often makes references to Biblical passages and holidays, particularly texts like the Akedah and the Book of Job, as well as holidays like Yom Kippur.[931]

Elie Wiesel also refers to the Akedah in his 1976 book, *Messengers of God: Biblical Portraits and Legends*.[932] In this work, the Jewish writer sees the Akedah as a double-edge test. God starts it, but Abraham understands the true opportunity, "As tough Abraham said, 'I defy you, and I shall not submit to your will, but let us see if You shall go to the end. Whether You shall remain passive and remain silent when the life of my son—who is also Your son—is at stake.'"[933]

Wiesel then goes on in the book to speaking of "three victories" that Abraham achieves. First, Abraham forces God to change His mind. Second, Abraham forces God to cancel the order Himself. It was not enough to simply have the angel speak to the patriarch. Third, Abraham forces God to agree that whenever the children of Israel would be sinful, they need only to retell the story of the Akedah to learn something about the mercy of God.[934]

Since the fourteenth century, there has been a variety of Judeo-Christian works that have turned the Akedah narrative into a drama. The fifteenth-century mystery play called the *Brome Abraham and Isaac*, so-called because it was discovered in the library of the Brome Manor, is a one-act play written in verse. The drama concentrates on the moral characteristics of Abraham and his son, Isaac.[935]

In the seventeenth century, Rabbi Moses ben Mordecai Zacuto also wrote an Akedah drama. Zacuto's drama was rendered into English by Joseph Quincy Adams and published in Boston in 1924.[936] In the Adams' version, an angel tells Abraham:

Go make thy sacrifice with your ram,
Now farewell, blessed Abraham.
For unto heaven I go now home
The way is full straight
Take up thy son so free.[937]

The subject of the Akedah also has appeared in the contemporary Israeli theatre, beginning with the 1940 drama *Ha Adamah hazot* by Aharon Aschman. In this drama, a father who settles in modern Israel loses his son to an outbreak of malaria. The father cries at the end of the drama:

> Abraham, our father, burnt the ram and I have burnt my son,
> my only Son... I dragged you to the Akedah against your will.[938]

In his novel-drama entitled *Be-tihilat kayitz*, or "Early in the Summer," Yehoshua resurrects the idea of the Jewish medieval Midrash that Isaac was, in fact, killed and then resurrected from the dead. Although this work is not technically a play, it is, nevertheless, quite evocative in its treatment of the sacrifice of Isaac narrative.[939]

Another contemporary Israeli drama called the *Milkat Ha Ambatyah*, or "The Queen of the Bath," by Hanach Levin, was staged at the Habinah Theatre in May of 1970. The drama had a very short run with only five performances. Levin follows the chronology of the Akedah narrative very closely, but she also concentrates on the moral characteristics of the two central characters. She also raises the question of what Sarah was thinking as the story developed.[940]

This brings us to the major conclusions made in this chapter on the Akedah in contemporary literature. This will be followed by an Afterword, in which we will make some final thoughts on the sacrifice of Isaac in Judaism, Christianity and Islam.

Conclusions to Chapter Eleven

The central goal of this eleventh chapter has been to analyze and discuss how the sacrifice of Isaac narrative of Genesis 22 has been used and understood in the world of contemporary culture, art, music and literature. We began Chapter Eleven with an analysis of several aspects of contemporary culture where we might find the Akedah narrative or its many parallels.

Among the aspects of contemporary culture where the sacrifice of Isaac can be seen are in Jewish liturgical services connected to *Rosh Hashanah*; in two fundamentally different interpretations of the Akedah narrative in contemporary Israel. We have labeled these the Isaac as Zionist View, and the Rejection of the myth, symbol, and ritual associated with the scene, or the Rejection of Myth Perspective.

In the culture section of this eleventh chapter, we also explored the role of the Akedah in several pieces of American literature, beginning with Melville's *Billy Budd*, and continuing to the novels of Bernard Malamud and Philip Roth.

We showed that another aspect of looking for places in contemporary Western culture where the Akedah narrative can be seen is in several twentieth- and twenty-first-century feminists, who primarily, as we have shown, are interested in giving Abraham's wife, Sarah, her due. Among these feminist thinkers were Alicia Ostriker and Eleanor Wilner.

In the second section of this eleventh chapter, we introduced and discussed several pieces of contemporary art, where the theme of the Akedah has been employed. Among the paintings of the Akedah narrative, we identified in this section were paintings by Richard McBee, M. Kadishman, Frederick Terna, Robert Kirschbaum, and photographer Albert J. Winn.

This material was followed by the third section of Chapter Eleven, in which we explored many of the places in contemporary music, where the Akedah narrative was employed. In this section, we examined work by classical composers, such as Igor Stravinsky, as well as popular musicians and performers, including Bob Dylan, Leonard Cohen, Joan Baez, Cat Stevens and Madonna.

We introduced and discussed many musical compositions on the Akedah narrative related to the *Niggun Akedah*, such as Cantor Michel Heyman. We also analyzed and discussed a musical piece by Elie Wiesel in a 1972 cantata called *Ani Maamin*.

The fourth and final section of this chapter has been an attempt to distill the many pieces of contemporary music with uses of, or parallels to, the sacrifice of Isaac narrative. But since there are so many pieces in this genre about the Akedah narrative, we have chosen to discuss ten representative literary examples to give a flavor of what is available in the literary genre.

Among these ten representatives, we introduced and discussed one film/novel, the 1964 *Fail-Safe*; one collection of Japanese short stories on the sacrifice of Isaac; one children's book writer; one Biblical scholar; an Israeli novelist; a few poets; and the contribution of a journalist who wrote an essay for *Commentary* magazine on the Akedah narrative in 1950.

We will now turn our attention to an Afterword, in which we have two primary goals. The first is to give a summary of the major conclusions of these eleven chapters. The second goal of the Afterword is to make some final comments about the author's take on the sacrifice of Isaac narrative.

An Afterword:
Conclusions and Final Thoughts

The Akedah influenced both Christian and Islamic thought. In early Christian doctrine, the sacrifice of Isaac is used as a type for the sacrifice of Jesus.

—Anonymous, "Akedah," *Encyclopedia Judaica*

Abraham as a Knight of Faith differs from the ethical man because the moral law is universal, and it has a categorical claim to greatness.

—Soren Kierkegaard, *Fear and Trembling*

And do not say that you have brought a sacrifice because I was the one who brought the sacrifice. Dear father, when you stand on my grave, Old and weary and very lonesome, And when you see how they lay my body to rest, Ask for my forgiveness, father.

—Hanoc Levin, "What Does it Matter to the Bird?"

Introduction

In this Afterword, we have two major goals. First, to record and discuss the major conclusions we have made about the phenomena of the Akedah or sacrifice of Isaac narrative to be found in the Book of Genesis 22:1–19. Our second goal in this Afterword is this: to make some final observations and add some final comments about our take on the sacrifice of Isaac narrative.

Major Conclusions of this History of Views on the Akedah

We began this history of attitudes and perspectives on the sacrifice of Isaac by making a number of comments about the practice of human sacrifice in the ancient world. We began our analysis with a discussion of ancient Egyptian beliefs on the afterlife, followed by the second section of Chapter One on the practice of human sacrifice in ancient Egypt. In that section, we have seen that there is evidence for the practice of human sacrifice in Egypt, even in the .

In subsequent material in Chapter One, we have analyzed and discussed the evidence that human sacrifice went on in the ancient world in several other places, including China, Mesopotamia, among the Ammonites and Canaanites, the Greeks, and the Carthaginians. Indeed, we have shown that the latter practiced human sacrifice in a variety of its colonies, including Carthage, places on Sicily, and other locales.

We brought the first chapter to a close with an analysis of evidence that human sacrifice was practiced in pre-modern Europe in a variety of locales. This evidence is related to places of Viking culture, an archaeological dig near Saint Louis called "Mound 72," an archaeological dig in Germany called the "German Stonehedge," as well as archaeological material found near Bristol, England, among Celtic culture.

The major goal of Chapter Two in this Akedah history was to describe and to discuss the many places in the Hebrew Bible/Old Testament, besides the sacrifice of Isaac narrative, where the idea of child sacrifice in mentioned or discussed. We began Chapter Two by carefully looking at what we have called "Background Material on Old Testament Child Sacrifice," which included a discussion of archaeological finds of the Canaanite Ras Shamra site, evidence from the Moabite culture of the Ancient Near East, as well as archaeological finds in ancient Israel itself.

In another section of Chapter Two, we cataloged the evidence in the Biblical materials both for and against the practice of child sacrifice in the Hebrew Bible/Old Testament. There we have seen that in addition to Genesis 22, there is also evidence from Leviticus 27:28–29, at Numbers 31:25–40, and at Second Samuel 21:1 and 21:8–14, and First Kings 13:1–2, that the ancient Jews did indeed practice human sacrifice.

Counter to these passages, however, are a series of places in the Biblical text where the practice of human sacrifice is explicitly forbidden. Among these passages are verses from Deuteronomy 12:21, Jeremiah 19:4–5, and Psalm 106:38, among many other places. In the third section of Chapter Two, we explored the places in the major Prophets where human sacrifice is discussed. Jeremiah 7:31–321 and 32:34–35 speak of human sacrifices to both the god Baal and to Molech. At Ezekiel 20:31, it is clear that the prophet takes a grim view of child sacrifice, as he does a few verses later, at 25 and 26.

We also have seen in Chapter Two that the Prophet Isaiah also condemns the Canaanite practices of human sacrifice at 57:4–6. We also have seen negative responses to the idea of human sacrifice in minor prophets such as Hosea, Amos, Micah and Jonah.

In another section of Chapter Two, we explored the phenomenon of human sacrifice in the books of the *Kethuvim*, or the "Writings," the third portion of the Hebrew text. There we have seen more passages from the Psalms, from Proverbs, and a few in the Book of Daniel.

In another lengthy section of Chapter Two, we explored the idea of child sacrifice in "Non-Canonical Literature," including the Books of Maccabees, the Book of Jubilees, the Wisdom of Solomon, as well as the Books of Enoch, and the ancient work known as "Pseudo-Jonathan." And in this material, for the most part, we have seen a condemnation of the practice of human sacrifice.

There were two major goals for the materials developed in the third chapter of this history. First, we cataloged and discussed thirteen separate theories or explanations in regard to the most fundamental meaning of the sacrifice of Isaac narrative. These thirteen theories subsequently have been employed throughout the remainder of this history. The other goal of Chapter Three of this work has been to give a close reading of Genesis 22:1–19. We began this task by dividing the chapter into five parts: The Command to Abraham, Father and Son, the Sacrificial Altar, Abraham's Reward, and the Return of Father and Son. In the third chapter, we then went on to explore a section on each of the five parts. Before we moved to that analysis, however, we gave a short history on the lives of Abraham and Sarah before the time of the sacrifice.

The principal subject matter of Chapter Four of this history has been the roles that the Akedah has played in early Judaism, including the Talmud, the Genesis Rabbah, the *Mishnah*, in the views of Philo, *Pseudo-Philo*, and Josephus, and the Dead Sea Scrolls. In each of these thinkers and works, early Judaism developed a variety of interpretations of the Akedah narrative.

"The Sacrifice of Isaac in Early Christianity" was the focus of Chapter Five. We began the chapter with the places in the New Testament where Abraham's command has been discussed. This was followed by a catalog of early Christian thinkers, between the first and fifth centuries, who have written about or spoken of, the importance of the sacrifice of Isaac in early Christianity. Among these thinkers were Tertullian, Origin, Clement, Cyril of Alexandria and many others. As we have seen, the predominant theme of these works was the parallel of the sacrifice of Isaac to the death and resurrection of Jesus Christ.

As we have shown, this same theme continued among major Christian thinkers between the fifth and tenth centuries, such as Augustine of Hippo and Pope Gregory the Great of Rome, as well as Saint John the Great and the Byzantine hymnist, Romanos. For the most part, this material also continued the parallel of the Akedah to the passion of Christ.

In an additional section of Chapter Five, we examined and discussed a number of pieces of art in the Christian tradition, related to the sacrifice of Isaac, that have depicted the scene on Mount Moriah in Christian art, from the fifth to the eleventh centuries. Some of these paintings were constructed by major painters and sculptors in that era, and some by lesser-known figures.

The chief subject matter of Chapter Six of this history has been Jewish points of view on the Akedah in the medieval period. We began the chapter with an analysis of the Midrash Tanhuma and what it has to say about the Akedah narrative. This was followed in Chapter Six with a discussion of the many *piyyutim*, or sacred poems about the Akedah. These sections of Chapter Six were followed by the views of many

Jewish philosophers and theologians, who have made fundamental observations about the narrative, including Saadiah Gaon, Moses Maimonides, Rashi, and Nahmanides. This section was followed in Chapter Six by an analysis of Jewish pieces of art, where the Akedah was the subject matter.

The Akedah in Islam was the focus of Chapter Seven of this history. We began that chapter with a review of the history of the figures of Hagar and Ismail in the Muslim tradition. This was followed by an introduction to the idea of sacrifice in the Islamic faith. The central question of Chapter Seven has been, "Which of Abraham's sons was the one for sacrifice?" As we have shown, in early Islam, the answer to that question was Isaac. But in more modern times, the answer has shifted in Islam to suggest it was Ishmael.

At the close of Chapter Seven, we explored a number of pieces of Islamic art where the Abraham son of sacrifice is depicted. As we have shown, for the most part, these pieces of art are from the modern period, from the fifteenth to the eighteenth centuries, and most of those indicate that the son for sacrifice was Ishmael, or Ismail, in Arabic.

The focus of Chapter Eight of this history has been an exploration of the Akedah, or sacrifice of Isaac narrative, in the early modern period of history, from the fifteenth to the eighteenth centuries. We began the chapter with a description of late medieval and early modern Jewish views of the Akedah story. This material was followed by several figures from the sixteenth and seventeenth centuries, the Reformation period, where the sacrifice has been discussed or written about. These figures included Martin Luther, John Calvin, Theodore Beza, and many others.

This material was followed in Chapter Eight by the exploration of Christian thinkers in the seventeenth and eighteenth centuries, who made important observations about the sacrifice of Isaac narrative. Among the thinkers in this section, we examined the views of Baruch Spinoza, Immanuel Kant, Matthew Henry, and many other Jewish and Christian thinkers and writers. We brought Chapter Eight to a close with a discussion of the Akedah, or the sacrifice of Isaac, in fifteenth- to seventeenth-century art. As we have seen, among the artists who depicted the Mount Moriah scene are Caravaggio, Michelangelo, and many other major painters from the Renaissance period.

The principal subject matter of Chapter Nine of this history of views on the Akedah has been the work of Danish philosopher Soren Kierkegaard and his work, *Fear and Trembling*. We began the chapter with some very general background materials on the life and times of Kierkegaard. This was followed by a close reading of *Fear and Trembling*. In the remainder of Chapter Nine, we examined a series of criticisms of *Fear and Trembling*, beginning with a section on Kierkegaard's critics from the nineteenth and early twentieth centuries. This was followed by a separate section where we explored the Kierkegaard book from the standpoint of the late twentieth century.

The subject matter of Chapter Ten of this history has been the relationships between the Akedah and the Holocaust from the mid-twentieth century to the present. We began the chapter with some very general remarks on the nature and extent of the phenomenon known as the Holocaust. This was followed by a section on the etymological sources and the terminology of words in English related to the Holocaust, *shoah*, and *churban*.

Next, in Chapter Ten, we explored what prisoners of the Nazi prisons and camps believed about the Akedah narrative while they were prisoners. We garnered these views by interviewing forty-eight separate Holocaust survivors in the 1970s and 1980s, as well as from interviews with German-born physician and linguist Dr. Hilgunt Zassenhaus about her work as a double-agent in the 1940s in the Nazi camps. We have labeled this section, "The Akedah in the Holocaust."

This material was followed by a lengthy section about the "Akedah After the Holocaust," in which we have cataloged various views of the many relationships of the Akedah **After** the Holocaust. In that section, we have explored the contributions of poets, writers, philosophers, theologians, and an anthropologist or two.

Finally, the central purpose of Chapter Eleven has been an exploration and discussion of the many facets of attitudes toward the Akedah or sacrifice of Isaac in contemporary life. More specifically, in Chapter Eleven, we devoted sections to contemporary culture, art, music and literature, where the story of Abraham and his two sons are in focus. This brings us to some final comments on the history of the Akedah, or sacrifice of Isaac narrative, in human history.

Some Final Thoughts

I have spent my entire forty-five-year academic career on a few philosophical and theological questions. These are mostly related to the Problem of Evil and the Biblical Book of Job. What these two issues have in common, of course, is what may be called "The Problem of Innocent Suffering." My senior thesis at the University of Maryland, my work for both of my Master's degrees at Yale and Oxford, and my PhD thesis at Saint Andrews in Fife, Scotland, have all been about this issue.

I have spent my life writing and thinking about evil and suffering. It seems only appropriate that I would still be devoted to these issues at the end of my academic career. Over the years, dealing with these issues has only made my personal faith stronger. I have no doubts about the existence of God, nor that He has a reason for all the suffering that occurs in the world. This seems an appropriate way to end this book.

As I sit and write these final thoughts, the deadly virus COVID-19 has quickly moved from where it began in mainland China to places all over the world. It will likely continue for many months to come. It is probable that my mother, Myra Vicchio, was a victim of the virus. She died on April 17, 2020, on her ninety-first birthday, no less.

In His infinite wisdom and power, I can only hope that God can find a place in this current crisis where He finds a special kind of grace for those who have, and will, suffer from repercussions related to this pandemic. In J. R. Tolkien's novel, *The Hobbit*, Frodo and Gandalf have the following conversation in a time of pandemic:

> "I wish it had not happened in my time," said Frodo. "So do I," said Gandalf, "and so does everyone else who lives in such times, but that is not for them to decide. All we have to do is to decide what to do with the time that has been given us."

This dialogue reminds me of the Stoic philosophers—you may not control all the events that happen to you, but you can decide not to be reduced by them. Amen to that.

Appendix A:
Classical Hebrew Words and Phrases

Adam ki akrib	a man shall offer up
Ahab	to love
Ababah	love
Ahabab	love
Akod	to bind
Ashar	medieval family of rabbis
At'sah	to fashion
Ayin	am
Beit mikdash	destruction of the Temple
Bereshith	Genesis
Chas'ah	sacrifice
Chim'ual	life's vision
Churban	destruction
Churban ha-Byit	destruction of the temple
Debar(im)	word *and* words
Emorim	animals for sacrifice
Ets	wood
Gha'bab	test
Heneni	here I am
Hereq	sacrifice

hokmah	wisdom
Kethuvim	writings
La do'at	to know
lekh lekha	go forth
Machlezeh	vision
Maat Kheruin	true voice
Mahalaph	knife
Mekelith	knife
Mesh'iac	Messiah
Mezlezeh	vision
Modein	sacred altar or town in Israel
Na'ar	lid
Nabim	prophets
Naphtali	medieval family of rabbis
Nissah	to test
Nissoth	test
Olah	sacrifice offering
Piyyut(im)	poem / poetry
Ra'ah	to see
Racham	love
Ral'am	test
Saraph	offering
Satan	the Devil
Sederim	offerings
Selilah	forgiveness
Shac'ats	knife
Shac'cah	to worship
Sheva	oath
Shekinah	the presence of God

Sebak	thorn
Sobek	thorn
Shoah	the Holocaust
Subek	thorn
Tallit	prayer shawl
Tefillin	prayer shawls
Thabilu	an ancient scribe
Thibiha	ancient scribes
Tophet	place of sacrifice
Uz	Job's home
Ya'ar	to take *or* kill *or* to thicken
Yahweh	God
Yahweh yireh	God will provide
Yellinnedenu	make the sages teach

Appendix B:
Greek and Latin Words and Phrases

Apocryphon	apocryphal (Greek)
Cur deus homo	Why did God become man? (Latin)
Glossa ordinaria	glosses on the Bible (Latin)
redivivus	back to life (Latin)
Jobus Christi	Christ-figure (Latin)
Mastema	name of the Demonic (Greek)
Mysterium magnum	the large mystery (Latin)
Sophia	wisdom (Greek)
sui generis	self-making (Latin)
ver sacrum	sacred stream (Latin)

Appendix C:
Other Foreign Words and Phrases

'adhih	sacrifice (Arabic)
akh	soul (Egyptian)
Anfgegtelsels	test (Danish)
ayat	verse (Arabic)
ba	soul (Egyptian)
Baeven	trembling (Danish)
Bergerdiskole	boarding school (Danish)
Chemosh	Moabite god
Dahia	victim of sacrifice (Arabic)
Din'iah	victim (Arabic)
Duhami	to victimize (Arabic)
Edniyah	sacrifice (Arabic)
Eid al adha	feast of sacrifice (Arabic)
Eid al-fitr	three-day festival in Islam (Arabic)
Fristede	temptation (Danish)
Frygt	fear (Danish)
Fudaa	sacrifice (Arabic)
Iktibar	to test (Arabic)
Imtihan	test (Arabic)
Jedheb	test (Arabic)

Jiz min	to go up (Arabic)
ka	another word for soul (Egyptian)
Ka'bah	sacred cube in Mecca (Arabic)
Klisara	loss (Arabic)
Malakh	angel (Arabic)
Marwa	hill in Mecca (Arabic)
Milcom	(Canaanite god)
Og	or (Danish)
Qurba	sacrifice (Arabic)
Qurban	sacrifice (Arabic)
Renji	god of sacrifice (Chinese)
Safa	hill in Mecca (Arabic)
Sahabah	companions of Muhammad (Arabic)
Shabti	funeral figurine (Egyptian)
Tidhat	sacrifice victim (Arabic)
Udhiya	sacrifice (Arabic)
Yawtihin	test (Arabic)
Yijus	sacrifice (Arabic)
Zubi'ha	sin, sacrifice (Arabic)

Endnotes

1   Walter Budge, *The Book of the Dead* (New York: Create Space, 2013). For more on the *Book of the Dead*, see:Ogden Guelet and Raymond Faulkner et al, *The Egyptian Book of the Dead* (London:Chronicle Books, 2015).

2   Daniel Soliman, *The Identity Marks at Deir El-Medina* (The Hague: De Gruyter, 2020), 19.

3   Muata Ashby, *The War of Heru and Set:The Struggle of Good and Evil for Control of the World and the Human Soul* (London:Sema Institute, 2005), 34–35.

4   Ibid., 35.

5   The expression *maat kheruin* in ancient Egyptian meant the "true voice." It referred in the Egyptian afterlife to one receiving his proper place in the great beyond.

6   In Egyptian mythology, Herkate was the goddess of magic, witchcraft, the night, the moon, necromancy and ghosts. She was the only child of titans Perses and Asteria from whom she received her power from Heaven.

7   Meskhanet was the Egyptian goddess of childbirth. She also was responsible for transferring the Ka of a dead person to the body of a newborn.

8   Jacques Kinnaer, "Human Sacrifice," quoted in Caroline Seawright, "Human Sacrifice in ancient Egypt," https://bit.ly/3hoeeb3.

9   Ibid.

10 Bridget McDermott, *Death in Ancient Egypt* (London: Sutton Publications, 2006), 187.

11 Ibid.

12 Ibid., 188.

13 Ibid.

14 Ibid.

15 Ibid., 189.

16 Ibid.

17 Ibid.

18   Ibid., 190.

19   Nancy Lovell, quoted in the *Oxford History of Ancient Egypt*, eds. K. H. Bard and I. Shaw (Oxford:Oxford University Press, 2004), 71.

20   Ibid., 72.

21   Herbert Winlock, *Excavations at Deir El-Bahri* (London:Macmillan, 1942), 117.

22   Daniel Fouquet and S. Mathey, "Unknown Man E," *French Institute of Oriental Archeology* (1889.0, pp. 526–528). For more on Unknown Man E, see Bob Brier, "The Mystery of Unknown Man E," *Archeology*, 59, no. 2, March–April 2006, https://bit.ly/37BwpFA.

23   Ibid.

24   Anonymous, "5,000 Year Old Tomb Excavated in Turkey," *Archeology*, June 29, 2018, https://bit.ly/3deJGVX.

25   Miles Russell, "Did Ancient Brits Built Stonehenge as a Temple of Sacrifice?" *The Daily Mail*, September 7, 2015.

26   V. Gordon Childe, *New Light on the Most Ancient East* (Oxford: Routledge, 2014), 222–229.

27   Ibid.

28   Anonymous, *Ancient China* (Beijing: Independent Publications, 2019), 11–14.

29   Ibid., 11–12.

30   Ibid., 12.

31   Ibid., 13–14.

32   John Basil Hennessy, *The Foreign Relations of Palestine During the Early Bronze Age* (Canberra:Quaritch, 1967), 25.

33   Ibid.

34   Hershel Shanks, "First Person:Human Sacrifice to an Ammonite God?" *Biblical Archeology Review*, September/October 2014, https://bit.ly/2N5TkiJ.

35   Ibid.

36   Ibid.

37   Ibid.

38   Ibid.

39   Ibid.

40   J. Snodgrass, *Romancing the Minotaur: Sex and Sacrifice and Some Greek Mythology* (New York:Create Space, 2017), 39.

41   Ibid.

42   Ibid., 40.

43   Ibid.

44   Peter Warren, "Circular Platforms at Minoan Knossos," *British School at Athens* 79 (1984): 307–323. For more on the dig at Knossos, see *World Archeology* 51 (January 5, 2012).

45   Ibid., 311.

46   Ibid.

47   Ibid., 313–314.

48   Jan Bremmer, quoted in an anonymous article entitled, "Skeleton Remains Confirm Ancient Greeks Practiced Human Sacrifice," *The Guardian*, August 10, 2016.

49   This account appears in the *Mahabharata*, and is discussed in *Scribner's Monthly*, 1874, vol. 4, p. 169.

50   Geoffrey W. Bromily, "Tell Soukas," *International Standard Bible Encyclopedia* (1995) vol. 4, p. 232.

51   Warren, p. 317.

52   Ibid.

53   Ibid., 318.

54   Plato, *The Republic* (New York: Hackett Classics, 1992), section 337a.

55   Samuel Wolff and Lawrence Stager, "Child Sacrifice at Carthage," *Archeology Review* 10, no. 1 (1984): 30–51.

56   The word *Tophet* appears a number of times in the Hebrew Bible, including Jeremiah 7:31, 19:2 and 19:11; Second Kings 23:10; and Isaiah 30:33. In Jeremiah, it is called a "place of burning." More will be said about *Tophet* in the second chapter of this study.

57   Stephen Langdon, "The History and Significance of Carthaginian Sacrifice," *Journal of Biblical Literature* 23, no. 1 (1904): 79–93.

58   Ibid., 83.

59   Snodgrass, 45.

60   Langdon, 87.

61   Jason Daley, "Germany's Stonehenge Reveals Evidence of Human Sacrifice," *The Smithsonian*, June 29, 2018. Dr. Daley estimates that the site is 4,300 years old. It was discovered in 1999 in the forest near the bank of the Elbe River.

62   Ibid.

63   Ibid.

64   Ibid.

65   Ibid.

66   Ibid.

67   Ibid.

68 Tia Ghose, "Viking Graves Yield Grisly Find: Sacrificed Slaves," *LiveScience*, October 30, 2013, https://bit.ly/37UeeuJ.

69 Ibid.

70 Elise Naumann quoted in, Lasse Biørnstad, "Vikings Abused and Beheaded Slaves," *ScienceNordic*, July 18, 2011, https://bit.ly/3epel4d.

71 Cat Jarman, "Data Reveals Mass Grave in Bristol Dates from the Viking Period," *EurekAlert*, Feb. 2, 2018, https://bit.ly/3el8eOd.

72 Ahmad Ibn Fadlan, *The Risala: By the River Volga 922: Viking Ship Burial*, J. Willard Marriott Library, University of Utah, May 21, 2015, https://bit.ly/3fFUb6a. The Arabic term *risala* means "account" or "journal." For more on Ibn Fadlan, see Judith Gabriel, "The Remarkable Account of Ibn Fadlan," *Aramco World* 50, no. 6 (December 1999), https://bit.ly/2Z1BlKn. Fadlan wrote his account in classical Arabic. His account is most notable for providing a detailed description of the Volga Vikings, including a ritual sacrifice and the eyewitness account of a ship burial.

73 Jayne Carroll, *The Vikings in Britain and Ireland* (London: British Museum Publications, 2014), 19–21.

74 Ibid., 20.

75 Ibid.

76 Ibid., 20–21.

77 Jarman.

78 Carroll, 22.

79 Ibid.

80 For more on the Celts in Turkey, see: Peter Selinsky, "Celtic Ritual Activity at Gordion," *International Journal of Osteoarcheology*, September 28, 2012, https://bit.ly/2YnmMqY. Also see: Mary Voight, "Celts at Gordion," *The Penn Museum* 45, no. 1 (2003), https://bit.ly/3drnHuX.

81 Ibid.

82 The Holy Qur'an 6:137 (author's translation).

83 The Latin expression *ver sacrum* means "sacred spring." For more on the ritual, see: Karin Tithanen, "On the Building of a Narrative: The *Ver Sacrum* Ritual," *Mnemosyne* 70, no. 6 (2016) 958–976.

84 For more on the Pittsburgh study, see K. J. H. Swartz et al., "Skeletal Remains from Punic Carthage do not Support Systematic Sacrificing of Infants," *PLOSOne* (February 17, 2010), https://bit.ly/3137QA9. The study makes a compelling argument that the Carthage tophet is a giant cemetery of fetuses and neonates.

85 Elon Gilad, "When the Jews Believed in Other Gods," https://bit.ly/2ATlDyH.

86   Akan Takruri, *Who Were the Hebrew Israelites?* (Cairo: Lulu Press, 2017) 41. Adrammelech was a West Semitic god worshipped by the Assyrians during the time of King Sargon.

87   As indicated in Chapters One and Two, Molech, or Moloch, was a Canaanite deity associated with Biblical sources, such as Leviticus 18:21, and Second Kings 16:3 and 21:6. King Josiah destroyed the places of sacrifices to Molech, or so Second King 23:10 suggests.

88   Chemosh was the national god of the Moabites and the Ammonites. He was also the god of child sacrifice. See: A. H. Sayce, "Polytheism in Primitive Judaism," *Jewish Quarterly Review* 2, no. 1, October 1889, 25–36.

89   These Phoenician sites in the Western Mediterranean were located in present-day Mogadon, Morocco, Carthage, on Sardinia, and in sites like Tharros, for example, on Sicily. Other cities where child sacrifice was conducted include: Nora, Bythia, Sulcis, and at Motya, on the west coast of Sicily.

90   For more on the Megiddo site, see: P. L. O. Guy and M. Engberg, *Megiddo Tombs* (Chicago: University of Chicago Press, 1936) and R. S. Lamon and W. Clayton, *Megiddo* (Oriental Institute Publications: 1932).

91   Hugh Pope, "The Excavations at Gezer," *Dublin Review* 141 (1906).

92   Ernst Sellin, *The Old Testament and Archeology* (New York: Peter Lang, 1971).

93   Leviticus 20:2 (Author's translation).

94   Deuteronomy 12:31–32 (Author's translation).

95   Second Kings 16:3 (Revised Standard Version).

96   Second Kings 17:31 (RSV).

97   Second Kings 23:10 (RSV).

98   Ezekiel 16:20–21 (RSV).

99   Judges 11:29–30.

100 Exodus 22:29 (Author's translation).

101 Leviticus 27:28–29 (RSV).

102 The heave offering, at places like Numbers 15:20–21 and 6:20 and Leviticus 7:34, was an offering that was raised and lowered by the priest during sacrifices. The heave offering later was to be consumed by the priest and no one else.

103 Second Samuel 21:1–14 (RSV).

104 First Kings 13:1–2 (Author's translation).

105 Second Kings 23:20 (Author's translation).

106 Second Chronicles 34:1–5 (RSV).

107 Deuteronomy 18:9–12 (RSV).

108 Deuteronomy 12:31 (RSV).

109 Psalm 106:38 (Author's translation).

110   Exodus 13:1–2 (Author's translation).
111   Exodus 22:29–30 (RSV).
112   Exodus 34:19–20 (RSV).
113   Second Kings 21:5–6 (RSV).
114   Second Kings 21:4–5 (RSV).
115   Deuteronomy 18:10 (Author's translation).
116   Deuteronomy 12:29–30 (RSV).
117   Leviticus 18:21 (Author's translation).
118   Jeremiah 7:31–32 (RSV).
119   Jeremiah 19:4–6 (RSV).
120   Jeremiah 32:34–35 (RSV).
121   Ezekiel 20:31 (Author's translation).
122   Ezekiel 20:25–26 (RSV).
123   Ezekiel 23:37 (RSV).
124   Isaiah 1:15 (Author's translation).
125   Isaiah 57:4–6 (RSV).
126   Hosea 13:1–2 (Author's translation).
127   Amos 1:13.
128   Jonah 2:8–9 (RSV).
129   Micah 6:7 (Author's translation).
130   Psalm 5:3–6 (RSV).
131   Psalm 105:34–35 (RSV).
132   Psalm 105:36 (RSV).
133   Psalm 105:37–38 (RSV).
134   Psalm 106:36–38 (RSV).
135   Proverbs 6:16–17 (Author's translation).
136   Proverbs 21:3 (Author's translation).
137   Daniel 9:27, 11:31 and 12:11 (RSV).
138   Among those who believe that the "abomination of desolation" refers to the destruction of the Temple in Jerusalem are John Wesley, Joseph Smith, Roman historian Cassius Dio, and the Babylonian Talmud. Jesus uses the term in the Gospel of Matthew 24:15. Saint Augustine and others believe the phrase refers to the Crucifixion.
139   Second Maccabees 2:23–28. See also Daniel J. Harrington, S. J., *First and Second Maccabees* (Collegeville: Liturgical Press, 2013).
140   Ibid. For more on the town of Modein, see G. A. Buttrick, "Modein," in *Interpreter's Dictionary of the Bible* (Nashville: Abingdon, 1962) vol. 3, p. 421.

141   First Maccabees 7:17 (Author' translation).

142   Second Maccabees 12:39–45 (Harrington translation).

143   Fourth Maccabees 5:4ff and 8:3ff (Harrington translation).

144   Book of Jubilees 17:1–14. R. H. Charles, translator, *The Book of Jubilees* (New York: Create Space, 2017). Also see: Ken Johnson, *The Ancient Book of Jubilees* (New York: Create Space, 2013) and Derek Schalp, *Enoch, Jubilees, and Jasher* (New York: Create Space, 2013). Mastema is the name of an angel in the Book of Jubilees. His name means "Persecuted One." In the book, Mastema carries out punishments meted out by God in order to test their faithfulness. Mastema is to be numbered among the bad angels.

145   *The Biblical Antiquities of Pseudo-Philo* (Oxford: Oxford University Press, 1993), 109.

146   Targum Pseudo-Jonathan, ed. Jonathan ben Uzziel (New York: Create Space, 2016), 53.

147   Ibid.

148   *Book of Tobit*, ed. Adolf Neubauer (Eugene: Wipf and Stock, 2005), 11:16.

149   *The Wisdom of Solomon* 3:5–7 (Osterley translation). See *The Wisdom of Solomon*, trans. W. O. E. Osterley (London: Forgotten Books, 2011) and Henry Morris, *The Wisdom of Solomon* (London: Master Books of Remembrance, 2001).

150   *The Wisdom of Solomon* 14:2–3 (Osterley translation).

151   Second Enoch 59 (Hammond translation). See Edward Hammond, *The Books of Enoch* (New York: Create Space, 2009). Also see Joseph Lumpkin, *Second Enoch* (Washington: The Fifth Estate, 2009). Achuzan was the name of a hill where the Temple in Jerusalem was located. Enoch was thought to have ascended to Heaven from that spot.

152   R. H. Charles, *First Book of Enoch* (New York: Digireads, 2018), chapter 8:1–3 (Charles' translation).

153   The expression "Tophet on high places" is an Old Testament expression used to refer to the places in Palestine and surrounding areas where child sacrifices were conducted. See Jeremiah 7:31–32, 19:6 and 11–14; and Isaiah 30:32–33.

154   Second Enoch (Lumpkin translation).

155   *Testament of Job*, ed. Maria Haralambakis (Edinburgh: T&T Clark, 2012).

156   *The Testament of Levi*, Rutherford Platt (London: Kessinger, 2010), 1–16.

157   Ibid.

158   Ibid.

159   Ibid.

160 *The Apocalypse of Moses*, ed. C. C. Fred (London: Isa Books, 2013). Also see ed. Charles F. Horne, *The Apocalypse of Moses* (London: Kessinger Books, 2010). We have used both translations in this chapter. Targum Pseudo-Jonathan, p. 54.

161 Targum Pseudo-Jonathan, p. 55.

162 Ibid.

163 Ibid., 56.

164 Ibid.

165 Ibid.

166 Ezekiel 39:17–20. A host of other Old Testament passages may be cited to confirm the many parallels about sacrifices in the Testament of Levi.

167 Noah Ginsburger, Targum Pseudo-Jonathan, quoted in Uzziel and Rose, pp. 4–5.

168 Targum Pseudo-Jonathan on Genesis 22:1. Genesis 22:20 (NRSV).

169 Targum of Pseudo-Jonathan on Genesis 22:18.

170 Genesis 22:18 (NRSV).

171 Targum Pseudo-Jonathan on Genesis 22:14.

172 Deuteronomy 12:29–31; Leviticus 18:21 and 27:28–29.

173 The Ashar and Naphtali families were two families of rabbis responsible for producing the Masoretic texts of the Hebrew Bible. For more on them, see Stephen Vicchio, *The Book of Job in the Ancient World* (Eugene: Wipf and Stock, 2006) 52–71.

174 For more on these theories, see Stephen Vicchio, *The Voice From the Whirlwind: The Problem of Evil and the Modern World* (Westminster: Christian Classics, 1989), particularly chapter three.

175 For more on the Divine Plan Theory, see ibid., pp. 129–153.

176 Among the early Church fathers who commented on the Akedah include Origen, Tertullian, Melito of Sardis, and many others. More will be said about these figures in Chapter Five.

177 For more on the Divine Command Theory, see Yoel Benhabib, *Divine Command Theory* (New York: Amazon Digital Services, 2017).

178 See Exodus 20:13 and Deuteronomy 5:17.

179 Soren Kierkegaard, *Fear and Trembling and Repetition* (Princeton: Princeton University Press, 1983).

180 The Talmud, *Sanhedrin,* tractate 89b.

181 For more on the Moral Qualities Approach, see Vicchio, *Voice From the Whirlwind*, 129–134.

182 Ibid., 1–44.

183   Micah 6:7 (RSV).

184   Genesis 18:19–20 (RSV).

185   Mary Douglas, *Purity and Danger* (New York: Routledge, 2002), 2–3.

186   Genesis 22:1–3 (KJV).

187   Septuagint version of Genesis 22:3.

188   Flavius Josephus, *The Jewish War* (Princeton: Princeton University Press, 2019), 43.

189   Mount Girizim is one of the two mountains near the West Bank city of Niblus, the Biblical city of Shechem. It has an elevation of nearly 3,000 feet above sea level.

190   *The Peshitta*, ed. David Bauscher (New York: Lulu Press, 2019). Also see the translation edition by George Lamsa (San Francisco: Harpers, 1989).

191   Targum Pseudo-Jonathan, ed. Michael Maher (New York: Michael Glazier, 1992).

192   Babylonian Talmud Ta'anit, tractate 16a.

193   The Holy Qur'an, Surah 2:158 (Author's translation).

194   Psalm 78:18 (RSV).

195   Numbers 14:22 (RSV).

196   Psalm 78:56 (RSV).

197   Exodus 15:25 (RSV).

198   Exodus 16:4 (RSV).

199   Deuteronomy 8:2–4 (RSV).

200   Deuteronomy 13:2–4 (RSV).

201   "Sacrifice," *Eerdmans Bible Dictionary* (Grand Rapids: Eerdmans, 1987), 899.

202   A variety of other classical Hebrew nouns are used to designate a sacrifice, for example, *saraph*.

203   Genesis 15:5 (RSV).

204   Genesis 12:1–3 (RSV).

205   Genesis 22:5 (RSV).

206   Ibid.

207   We will see this phenomenon of identifying Mount Moriah with Mount Sinai in Chapter Four of this work.

208   Genesis 22:13 (RSV).

209   Exodus 20:20 (RSV).

210   Genesis 22:8 (RSV).

211   Genesis 22:9 (RSV). Also see Genesis 12:7–8 and 14:14.

212   Ibid. Also see Numbers 19:3 and Leviticus 14:13 (RSV).

213 Joshua 5:2. Also see Proverbs 23:2 and 30:14, Jeremiah 36:23, and Leviticus 19:27 and 21:5, for example.

214 Joshua 17:15 and 18 (RSV).

215 Exodus 22:6 (RSV).

216 Exodus 3:2 (RSV).

217 Jeremiah 5:14 (RSV).

218 Genesis 15:5 (RSV).

219 Genesis 15:1 (RSV).

220 Genesis 22:13 (RSV).

221 See Genesis 31:53, 42:18 and 46:1–7, for example.

222 Genesis 22:17. Also see Exodus 29:15 and 17–18.

223 This will be discussed more fully in chapter four.

224 For the word *Moshiac*, see First Kings 19:16 and Psalm 133:2.

225 This view will be explored more in Chapter Five of this study.

226 See Note 179.

227 Outline for Genesis 22:1–19.

228 We have made extensive comments on the classical Hebrew terms: *achar*, *yirat, machezeh, ra'ah, ets, esh*, and many other words, as well.

229 Schottenstein Daf Yomi edition of the Talmud (New York: Art Scroll, 2002), 431.

230 Ibid., 499.

231 Ibid., 517.

232 Ibid., 434.

233 Ibid.

234 Ibid.

235 Ibid., 438.

236 Ibid., 455.

237 Deuteronomy 21:15–21 (RSV).

238 Schottenstein, 519.

239 Ibid.

240 Saadiah Gaon, *The Book of Theodicy* (New Haven: Yale University Press, 1988), 121.

241 Schottenstein, 444.

242 Ibid., 439.

243 Ibid., 445.

244 Ibid., 441.

245 Ibid., 435.

246 Schottenstein, 444.

247 Ibid., 388.

248 Ibid.

249 Ibid., 389.

250 Ibid.

251 Ibid., 507.

252 Ibid.

253 Ibid., 454.

254 Ibid., 518.

255 Ibid., 519.

256 Ibid., 518.

257 Ibid.

258 Ibid., 222.

259 The classical Hebrew word *Shekinah* appears more than twenty-five times in the Hebrew Bible/Old Testament, such as at Exodus 13:21–22, 24:16–18, 40:34–38, Psalm 18:7–15, and Numbers 10:11–36. The Greek version of the same term can also be seen at Colossians 2:9, Luke 1:35 and 2:9, and Second Peter 1:17.

260 Schottenstein, 225.

261 Ibid., 256.

262 Ibid., 119.

263 Ibid.

264 Ibid.

265 Ibid.

266 Ibid.

267 Ibid.

268 Ibid., 453.

269 Soren Kierkegaard, *Fear and Trembling* (New York: Penguin Classics, 1986).

270 Jo Milgrom, *The Binding of Isaac* (Oakland: Bibal Press, 1988), 107.

271 Ibid., 158–159.

272 Ibid., 149.

273 Ibid.

274 Ibid., 144.

275 Ibid.

276 Ibid.

277 Ibid., 155.

278 Ibid.

279 Schottenstein, 152.

280 Milgrom, 156.

281 Ibid.

282 Ibid.

283 Ibid., 157.

284 Ibid., 159.

285 Ibid., 152.

286 Psalm 134:14 (Author's translation).

287 Milgrom, 154.

288 Ibid.

289 Herbert Danby, *The Mishnah* (Grand Rapids: Hendrickson, 2012), 17–18.

290 Edward Kessler, *Bound by the Bible* (New York: Cambridge University Press, 2004), 26.

291 Ibid.

292 Ibid.

293 Rabbi Eli Kaunfer, quoted in Hannah Weiss, "Reflections on Redemption in Nisan," https://bit.ly/3fpBpiL.

294 Ibid.

295 Schottenstein, 191.

296 Ibid.

297 Ibid., 192.

298 Ibid., 195.

299 Danby, 154.

300 Ibid. For more on Josephus' *History of the Jews*, see the edition edited by Miriam Maranzenboim (New York: Jet Launch, 2018).

301 Ibid., 156.

302 Ibid., 194.

303 Schottenstein, 196.

304 Danby, 195.

305 First Peter 1:19–20 (RSV).

306 Danby, 196.

307 Ibid.

308 Ibid., 197.

309 Kessler, 37–38.

310 Josephus, quoted in Kessler, 40.

311 Milgrom, 73.

312 Ibid.

313 Ibid.

314 Ibid., 74.

315 Ibid.

316   Ibid.
317   Ibid., 75–76.
318   Ibid., 76.
319   Ibid.
320   Ibid., 79.
321   Ibid., 76.
322   Ibid.
323   Ibid.
324   Ibid.
325   Ibid., 77–78.
326   Ibid., 78.
327   Ibid.
328   J. Randall Price, ed., *The Dead Sea Scrolls* (New York: Rose Publishing, 2005).
329   Ibid., 10–11.
330   4Q255 in Price.
331   Ibid.
332   Ibid. The *Pirkei de Rabbi Eliezer* is a Haggadic Midrash on the Torah containing the retelling of various Biblica narratives including the Akedah passage. According to Jewish tradition, it was composed in Italy shortly after 830. Nearly all Jewish scholars agree that it is an eighth- or ninth-century work.
333   Ibid.
334   Ibid. For more on the Akedah at Qumran, see E. J. C. Tigchelaar and F. Garcia Martinez, "The Sacrifice of Isaac in 4Q225," in *Qumranica Minora* II (January, 2007), 131–144. Also see Joseph A. Fitzmyer, "The Sacrifice of Isaac in Qumran Literature," in *Biblical Studies on the Web*, vol. 83 (2002), 211–220. For more on the figure of Mastema, who some say is a fallen angel and others that he is the angel of disaster, see the Book of Jubilees, chapters 10, 11, 17 and 48. The attack at Jubilees 48:1–3 is very much like Exodus 4:24. Mastema does, however, need permission from God before tempting people, much like in the prologue of the Book of Job.
335   Matthew 1:1 (RSV).
336   Matthew 5:17 (RSV).
337   Hebrews 11:17–19.
338   Epistle of James 2:21 (RSV).
339   Romans 8:32, John 3:16, and Genesis 22:12 (RSV).
340   Genesis 22:12.
341   The Epistle of Barnabus 7:3.
342   Acts of the Apostles 20:28.

343 Second Corinthians 6:16–18.

344 Luke 1:31.

345 Philippians 2:7.

346 Edward Kessler, *Bound by the Bible* (New York: Cambridge University Press, 2004).

347 Romans 5:12.

348 First Corinthians 15:45–49.

349 Romans 6:2–11.

350 *Epistle of Barnabus 7:3.*

351 S. G. Hall, ed., *Melito of Sardis* (Oxford: Clarendon, 1979), 43.

352 Ibid.

353 Ibid., 44.

354 Ibid.

355 Ibid., 71.

356 Ibid.

357 Ibid., 92.

358 Ibid., 17.

359 Epistle of Diognetus, https://bit.ly/2ZhzsPq.

360 Hippolytus, *Commentary on Song of Songs* 2:15 (London: Gorgias Press, 2015), 62.

361 Irenaeus, *Against Heresies*, trans. John Keble (New York: Create Space, 2015), book IV, chapter five, 118.

362 Origen, *Homilies on Genesis* (Washington: Catholic University Press, 2002), 291.

363 Ibid.

364 Origen, commentary on Psalm 110:4.

365 Ibid.

366 Ibid.

367 Origen, 293.

368 Clement of Alexandria, *Homilies on Genesis* (London: Franklin Classics, 1018), 227.

369 Ibid.

370 Ibid., 229.

371 Ibid.

372 Cyril of Alexandria, *Exegesis on the Gospels* (New York: Create Space, 2014), 66.

373 Carol Delaney, *Abraham on Trial* (Princeton: Princeton University Press, 1998), 148.

374   Ibid.

375   *Exegesis on the Gospels*, 70–99.

376   Ibid., 83.

377   Athanasius, *Paschal Letters: On the Incarnation* (New York: Create Space, 2016), 49–69.

378   Ibid., 56.

379   Gregory of Nyssa, quoted in Kessler, 49.

380   Ibid.

381   Ibid., 95.

382   Ibid.

383   Ibid., 107.

384   Ibid., 131–132.

385   Ibid., 132.

386   Ibid., 144.

387   Ibid., 71.

388   Ibid., 74.

389   Ibid., 126.

390   Ibid., 74.

391   Ibid.

392   Ibid.

393   Ibid., 133.

394   Augustine, *City of God*, ed. David Clarke (New York: Create Space, 2017), book IV, chapters 3–5. *The Confessions*, ed. Maria Boulding (New York: City Press, 2017), book III, chapter 9.

395   Ibid.

396   Romanos, quoted in Kessler, 77.

397   Ibid.

398   Ibid.

399   Delaney, 151.

400   Saint John the Great, *The Little Catechism of the Cure of Ars* (London: Tan Books, 1994), 141.

401   *Glossa Ordinaria of Genesis: Isaac on Jewish and Christian Altars* (New York: Fordham University Press, 2012), 100.

402   Ibid.

403   Ishodad of Merv, *Commentaries on the Bible* (London: Forgotten Books, 2012), 91.

404   Ibid.

405   Targum Pseudo-Jonathan quoted in Jo Milgrom, *The Akedah* (Berkeley: Bibal Press, 1988.), 91.

406   *Glossa Ordinaria of Genesis*, 111.

407   Ibid.

408   Ibid.,112.

409   Anselm, *Cur Deus Homo: Why the God-Man?* (New York: Create Space, 2016), 11–13.

410   Paba De Andrado, *The Akedah Servant Complex* (Leuven: Peeters, 2013), 139–140.

411   Peter Abelard, *Commentary on Romans* (Washington: Catholic University Press, 2011).

412   Thomas Aquinas, *Summa Theologica* (Casper: Coyote Wyoming Press, 2010), part two, question 85.

413   Ibid., 441–449.

414   Ibid., 443.

415   Andrado, 1.

416   Ibid.

417   The mosaics and frescoes at Saint Sophia's Cathedral in Kiev, which was bult by Taoslav the Wise in 1037, contains a number of features of biblical subjects, including Abraham meeting the three strangers, Abraham entertaining the angels, Abraham and the three youths of the Fiery Furnace, and, most importantly for our purposes the sacrifice of Isaac.

418   *Sacrifice of Isaac*, fresco. Via Latina Catacomb, fourth century. In an upper register, the image shows the altar with fire on the left. Abraham stands above a bound Isaac who kneels. A large knife in the father's right hand is above his head. In a lower register over of Abraham's servants and the ass on which he rode is depicted.

419   *Sacrifice of Isaac*, Conde Museum, Chantilly, France. See p. 298 of Milgrom.

420   Ibid.

421   *Life of Saint Remy,* binding scenes. *The Sacrifice of Isaac* scene is an ivory plaque, probably from a book cover made in the ninth century. The sacrifice is displayed along with the *Life of Saint Remy*, and the *Baptism of Clovis*.

422   Ibid.

423   *Sacrifice of Isaac*, St. Vitale, Ravenna, Italy, sixth century.

424   *Sacrifice of Isaac*, Necropolis at El-Bagawat.

425   Ibid.

426   Milgrom, 298.

427   Ibid., 296. *The Cloisters Cross*, ca. 1150–60. The Metropolitan Museum of Art, The Cloisters Collection, 1963.

428   Ibid., 298.

429   *Vita Christi*, Getty Museum, ms. 101, fol. 11.r.

430   Ibid.

431   *Sacrifice of Isaac*, twelfth century, Victoria and Albert Museum.

432   *Life of Isaac* cycle, twelfth century, Fitzwilliam Museum, Cambridge University.

433   *Sacrifice of Isaac*, Saint Petronius Basilica in Bologna, Italy.

434   Milgrom, 304.

435   Martin Buber and John Townsend, eds., *Midrash Tanhuma* (Tel Aviv: Ktav Pub. 1989).

436   Ibid., 20.

437   Ibid., 27.

438   Ibid., 29.

439   Ibid.

440   Ibid., 30.

441   Ibid.

442   Ibid., 32.

443   Ibid.

444   Ibid.

445   Ibid., 35.

446   Ibid.

447   Ibid.

448   Ibid., 36.

449   Ibid.

450   Ibid., 38.

451   Ibid.

452   Saadiah Gaon, quoted in *Comparative Semitic Philology: From Saadiah to Ibn Brun*, ed. Aharon Memon. (Leiden: Brill, 2002), 73.

453   Rabbi Yose ben Yose Hannai was a rabbi during the Maccabean Revolt. He was perhaps a disciple of Antingonus of Soko.

454   Rabbi Eleazer Bar Kallir (570–640) was a Palestinian rabbi in what in Christianity is called the Dark Ages. He wrote a number of commentaries, including one on Genesis.

455   Eleazer Bar Kallir, quoted in *Studies in Medieval Piyyut*, ed. Jacob Josef Petrouchsky (Oxford: Routledge, 1977), 49.

456   *Comparative Semitic Philology*, 74.

457 Ibid.
458 Edward Kessler, *Bound by the Bible* (New York: Cambridge University Press, 2004), 147.
459 *Comparative Semitic Philology*, 75.
460 Eliezer Toledano, ed., *Orot Sephardic Selihot* (Tel Aviv: Orot Press, 1999), 53.
461 Louis Berman, *The Akedah* (Jerusalem: Jason Aaronson, 1997), 207.
462 Ibid., 208.
463 Saadiah, quoted in *Comparative Semitic Philology*, 75.
464 Ibid.
465 Ibid., 76.
466 *Pentateuch and Rashi's Commentary* (New York: S. S. and R. Publishing, 1950), 59.
467 Ibid.
468 Ibid., 60.
469 Ibid.
470 Ibid.
471 Ibid., 61.
472 Norman Strickland, ed., *Ibn Ezra's Commentary on the Pentateuch: Genesis* (New York: Menorah Pub., 1988), 44.
473 Ibid.
474 Ibid., 45.
475 Ibid.
476 Joseph Kara, *Commentary on Genesis* (Tel Aviv: Moznaim Press, 1991), 202.
477 Samuel ben Meir, *Commentary on Genesis* (New York: Edwin Mellen Press, 1989), 62.
478 Abraham Ibn Daud, *Sefer ha Qabbala*, ed. Gershon D. Cohen (Lincoln: University of Nebraska Press, 2010), 99.
479 Ibid.
480 Moses Maimonides, *Guide for the Perplexed*, ed. Julius Guttman (New York: Hackett Books, 2018).
481 Ibid., 108.
482 Ibid.
483 Ibid.
484 Ibid., 109.
485 Schlomo Riskin, quoted in Chaim Trachtman, "The Maimonidean Akedah," https://bit.ly/3gaBp7g.
486 Maimonides, *Guide*.
487 Ibid.

488   Ibid.
489   Ibid., 44.
490   Ibid.
491   Ibid.
492   Ibid., 45.
493   Ibid.
494   Ibid.
495   Ibid., 46.
496   Ibid.
497   Ibid.
498   Ibid., 47.
499   Ibid.
500   Ibid.
501   Ibid., 48.
502   Ibid.
503   Nahmanides, *Commentary on Genesis*, ed. Michelle J. Levine (New York: Society of Biblical Literature, 2009), 91.
504   Ibid.
505   Ibid.
506   Ibid., 92.
507   Ibid.
508   Ibid.
509   Ibid., 93.
510   Ibid.
511   Ibid.
512   Ibid.
513   David Kimchi, *Kommentar zur Genesis* (London: Wentworth Press, 2019), 70.
514   Ibid.
515   Hans Von Mutious, ed., *Isaac Abravnel on Genesis* (Berlin: Olms, 1978), 107.
516   Ibid.
517   Ibid., 109.
518   Ephraim ben Jacob of Bonn, "Akedah," in *The Last Trial*, Shalom Spiegel (New York: Jewish Lights Press, 2007), 143–152.
519   Ibid.
520   Joseph Ibn Caspi, quoted in Chaim Trachtman, "The Maimonidean Akedah," https://bit.ly/3gaBp7g.
521   Ephraim ben Jacob.
522   Ibid.

523 Dura Europos synagogue image, see Jo Milgrom, *The Akedah* (Berkeley: Bibal Press, 1988), 297. Also see p. 163 of Kessler and pp. 217–220 of Berman.

524 Ibid.

525 Ibid.

526 Ibid.

527 Ibid.

528 Ibid.

529 Milgrom, 297. Also see Berman, pp. 220–221.

530 Kessler, 169.

531 Berman, 220–221.

532 Ibid.

533 Milgrom, 298.

534 Ibid.

535 Milgrom, 298.

536 The image of the Akedah in the Romanesque cathedral at Jaca, Spain, is on one of the capitals. The church was one of the first medieval cathedrals in the High Middle Ages. The capital shows Isaac standing, hands tied behind his back. Abraham stands to his left, knife in right hand. His left hand pulls back the son's head, revealing his neck. To the right is the altar with a fire beneath it. To the right of the altar is the angel with the ram on a tether. The servants/lads are behind the scene in the distance.

537 "The Bird's Head Haggadah," see Milgrom, 299. This is the oldest surviving illuminated Ashkenazi Passover Haggadah. It was produced in the Upper Rhine region around 1300. For more on this Haggadah, see Marc Michael Epstein's webpage at Vassar College.

538 Leipzig Mahzur, see Milgrom, 299 and Richard McBee, "Leipzig Machzor: A Vision of the Past," https://bit.ly/2VyNLOC and https://www.facebook.com/McBeeJewishArt/. The illuminated manuscript is a large-scale text that includes a number of scenes in the life of Abraham, including Abraham and Nimrod, Abraham being thrown into the fiery furnace, and the Akedah narrative.

539 *The Sacrifice of Isaac* stained glass window, Saint Vitus Cathedral, Prague. Saint Vitus is the largest and most important church in the Czech Republic. The coronations of kings were held there until 1836. It is one of the best examples of Gothic architecture, and the building of the church started in 1172. The Saint Agnes Chapel contains two scenes in the life of Isaac. On the right, we see Hagar, the mother of Ishmael, when they were banished to the wilderness, but rescued by God. The scene on the left illustrates God asking Abraham to kill Isaac. But seeing a ram, Abraham sacrificed it instead.

540   Akedah scene, *Nuremberg Haggadah*, also called the *Second Nuremberg Haggadah*. It comes from mid-fifteenth-century Germany. In 1957, the illuminated manuscript was acquired by the Schocken Collection in Jerusalem. This manuscript contains beautiful renderings related to Genesis and Exodus, including one of the Akedah narrative.

541   Genesis 15:18 (NRSV).

542   Genesis 16:1 (NRSV).

543   Genesis 14:2 (NRSV).

544   Psalm 83:7 (NRSV).

545   Genesis 16:1–10 (NRSV).

546   Genesis 16:11 (NRSV).

547   H. C. White, "The Initiation Legend of Isaac," in *Zeitschrift fur die Alttestamenatica wissenschaft* 91, no.1 (January 1, 1979).

548   Ibid.

549   The Holy Qur'an, Surah 5:27 (Author's translation). Unless otherwise stated, all the Arabic to English translations are those of the author.

550   Ibid., 6:162.

551   Ibid., 22:36.

552   Ibid., 108:1–2.

553   Ibid., Surah 37:105–107 (Ahmed Ali translation). The Holy Qur'an (Princeton: Princeton University Press, 1993).

554   Ibid., 108:1–2.

555   Buhari, vol. 7, book 68, no. 465.

556   *The History of Al-Tabari*, trans. Franz Rosenthal (Albany: SUNY Press, 1989), vol. 1, 111.

557   Muhammad H. Haykal, *The Life of Muhammad* (Washington: American Trust, 2005), 75.

558   Reuven Firestone, *Journeys in the Holylands* (Albany: SUNY Press, 1990), 125–143.

559   Ibid., 127–129.

560   Tabari, 112.

561   Omar Ibn Azizi, quoted in *Omar Ibn Azizi*, ed. Younas Hamida (New York: Amazon Services, 2019), 23.

562   The Holy Qur'an, Surah 37:100—113 (Author's translation).

563   Louis Berman, *The Akedah* (Jerusalem: Jason Aaronson, 1997), 100.

564   Tabari, 113.

565   The Holy Qur'an, Surah 37:102.

566   Genesis 15:6 (NRSV). See also: Romans 9:6–7 and Galatians 3:2, 9, and 14.

567 The Holy Qur'an, Surah 37:99–113.

568 Ibid., Surah 2:127.

569 Berman, 190.

570 Ibid.

571 *Eid Al-Adha Sacrifice*, ed. Hasan Rizzi (New York: Amazon, 2017), 1–16.

572 Ibid., 9.

573 Ibid.

574 Abdus Sattar Ghawri, "The Only Son offered for Sacrifice: Isaac or Ishamel," in *Renaissance* (Islamabad: Al-Mawrdi, 2013), 10–11.

575 Hamid Al-Din Farahi, "The Son for Sacrifice," in *Reading the Bible in the Islamic Context* (Oxford: Routledge, 2017), 124–156.

576 "Akedah," in *Oxford Companion to the Bible*, ed. John Walton (Grand Rapids: Zondrevan, 2006).

577 Reuven Firestone, "The Binding of Isaac," https://bit.ly/325pHGY. Also see: *Journeys in Holy Lands* (Albany: SUNY Press, 1990).

578 The Holy Qur'an, Surah 22:27.

579 Ibid.

580 John Van Ess, *The Spoken Arabic of Iraq* (Oxford: Oxford University Press, 1961), 175 and 215.

581 The Day of Arafat is celebrated on the ninth day of Dhul-Hijjah. This day is the culminating event of the Islamic Pilgrimage to Mecca, the Holy City in Islam. At dawn on this day, two million or more pilgrims make their way from the town of Mina to a hillside nearby called Mount Arafat, which is twelve and a half miles from Mecca. Traditional Islam holds that the Prophet Muhammad gave his "Farewell Address" on this spot.

582 *Sunan Al-Majah*, "Chapters on Sacrifices," https://sunnah.com/ibnmajah/26.

583 Surah 37:99–113.

584 Jason Jackson, "Ishmael or Isaac?" https://bit.ly/31ZFreO.

585 Ibid.

586 Ibid.

587 The Holy Qur'an 37:99–113 (Ahmad Ali Translation).

588 Meyer Shapiro quoted in Berman, 221.

589 Marc Chagall, see: Milgrom, 301–303. Also Berman, 225–226 and Kessler, 187.

590 Berman, 225.

591 Milgrom, 303.

592 Ibid.

593 Ibid.

594 Shalom Spiegel, *The Last Trial: The Akedah* (New York: Jewish Lights, 1997), opposite title page.

595 *Timurid Anthology*, ed. Charles Melville (Islamabad: I. B. Tauris, 2020), 33.

596 Ibid.

597 Carol Delany, *Abraham on Trial* (Princeton: Princeton University Press, 1998), 161.

598 Ibid.

599 *Casting Out Hagar and Ishmael* (1657), Giovanni Barbieri, known as Guernico (1591–1666); *Sarah Bringing Hagar to Abraham* (1696), Willem Van der Werf (1665–1722); *Abraham Dismissing Hagar and Ishmael* (1653), Nicholas Maes (1634–1693).

600 See Jackson and Rizzi.

601 For more on Eid Al-Adha, see: Robert Walker, *Eid Al-Adha* (New York: Crabtree Press, 2010); *Eid Al-Adha: Muslim Celebration of Abraham's Sacrifice* (no pub., no date); and *Eid Al-Adha Sacrifice*, ed. Hasan Rizzi (New York: Amazon, 2017).

602 Van Ess, 131.

603 Van Ess, 250.

604 Moses Maimonides, *Guide for the Perplexed*, ed. Julius Guttman (New York: Hackett Books, 2018), 194.

605 Rabbi Hasdai Crescas, *Sefer Adonai* (Tel Aviv: Isla books, 2013).

606 Joseph Albo, *Principles of Faith*, ed. Isaac Hussik (New York: Jewish Publication Society, 1946), 100–121.

607 Judges 6:12–17 and First Kings 19:9–10 (NRSV).

608 Albo, 101.

609 Ibid.

610 Ibid., 102–103.

611 Isaac Arama, *Sefer Urim Ve-Tamim* (London: Nabu Books, 2013), 55–56.

612 Ibid., 56.

613 Judah Abravanel, *Dialoghi d'Amore* (New York: Amazon, 2012), 92–95.

614 Ibid., 93.

615 Ibid.

616 Ibid., 94–95.

617 Isaac Karo, *Derashot Rabbi Yitchak Karo* (Tel Aviv: University of Ilan Press, 1995).

618 Ibid., 71.

619 Ibid.

620 Ibid., 72–73.

621 Ibid., 73.

622 Ibid.

623 Ibid., 74.

624 Joseph Karo, *Tolodot* (New York: Jewish Publication Society, 1977).

625 Martin Luther, *Commentary on Genesis*, ed. Taylor Anderson (New York: Create Space, 2018).

626 Ibid., 62.

627 Ibid.

628 Ibid., 63–64.

629 Ibid., 64.

630 Ibid., 65.

631 Ibid.

632 Ibid., 66.

633 Ibid.

634 John Calvin, *Commentary on Genesis*, two volumes (Grand Rapids: Christian Classics, 2009).

635 Ibid., vol. 1, 253.

636 Ibid.

637 Ibid., 254.

638 Theodore Beza, *Abraham Sacrifiant* (New York: Leopold Classics, 2015).

639 Ibid.

640 Theodore Beza, *The Sacrifice of Isaac* (New York: Andesite Press, 2015).

641 Ibid.

642 Wolfgang Musculus, *On Righteousness, Oaths, and Usury* (Berlin: CLP Press, 2013), 71.

643 Ibid.

644 Ibid., 72.

645 Jakob Boehme, *Magisterium Magnum* (New York: Hermetica Press, 2007), 113–126.

646 Ibid., 113–115.

647 Ibid., 115.

648 Ibid., 116.

649 Ibid., 117.

650 *Formula of Concord* (Chicago: Concordia Press, 2005).

651 Mordecai Zacuto, *Yesod 'Olam* (Los Angeles: University of California Library, 1874).

652 John Wesley, *Commentary on the Whole Bible* (New York: Grace Works, 2011), 55.

653 Immanuel Kant, *Kant on Ethics* (New York: Hackett, 1980), 249–253.

654 Ibid., 249–250.

655 Ibid., 250.

656 Ibid., 252–253.

657 Edward Kessler, *Bound by the Bible* (Cambridge: Cambridge University Press, 2004), 184.

658 Ibid.

659 Carol Delaney, *Abraham on Trial* (Princeton: Princeton University Press, 1998), 123.

660 Ibid., Kant quoted by Delaney.

661 Ibid.

662 Ibid.

663 Ibid.

664 Genesis 17:19 (NRSV).

665 Matthew Henry, *Commentary on the Whole Bible* (San Francisco: Harper Collins, 1964).

666 Ibid., 91.

667 Ibid.

668 Ibid., 92.

669 Wesley, 58.

670 Ibid.

671 Baruch Spinoza, *Theological-Political Treatise* (Cambridge: Cambridge University Press, 2007), 97–117.

672 Ibid., 97–98.

673 Ibid., 98–99.

674 Ibid., 99–100.

675 Ibid., 100.

676 Ibid., 101–102.

677 Ibid., 105.

678 Ibid., 111.

679 Zacuto, 95.

680 Ibid.

681 Ibid., 96–97.

682 Ibid., 97.

683 Ibid.

684 John Milton, *Paradise Lost* (New York: Penguin Classics, 2003).

685 William Shakespeare, *Collected Plays* (London: Canterbury Classics, 2014).

686 Mary Jo Kietzman, *The Biblical Covenant in Shakespeare* (New York: Macmillan, 2018).

687 Ibid., 43.

688 Ken Jackson, *Shakespeare and Abraham* (South Bend: University of Notre Dame Press, 2015).

689 *Abraham and Isaac*, ed. Vincent Harper (New York: Barrons, 1962).

690 *Abraham and Isaac*, Mystery Series Gloucester, England.

691 *Brome Play of Abraham*, ed. C. A. Harper (London: Paulala Press, 2016).

692 Ibid.

693 Louis Berman, *The Akedah*, 222.

694 Soren Kierkegaard, *Fear and Trembling* and *Repetition*, ed. and trans. by Howard V. Hong (Princeton: Princeton University Press, 1983).

695 Kierkegaard, xl.

696 Jolita Pons, *Stealing a Gift* (New York: Fordham University Press, 2004), 69.

697 Kierkegaard, 112–115.

698 Ibid., 228.

699 Ibid.

700 Ibid., 38–39.

701 Ibid., 274–275.

702 Psalm 2:11 (RSV).

703 Psalm 55:5 (RSV).

704 Mark 5:33 (RSV).

705 First Corinthians 2:3 and Second Corinthians 7:15 (RSV).

706 Philippians 2:12 (RSV).

707 Kierkegaard, 54–56.

708 Ibid., 33.

709 Ibid., 76–77.

710 Ibid., 17–19.

711 Ibid., 30–31.

712 Ibid., 57.

713 Ibid., 66.

714 Ibid.

715 Ibid., 67.

716 Ibid.

717 Ibid., 76–77.

718 Ibid., 59.

719 Ibid., 57.

720 Ibid., 341.

721   Ibid.

722   Ibid.

723   Ibid., 72.

724   Ibid., 59.

725   Ibid., 78–79.

726   Ibid., 117–118.

727   Ibid., 80–81.

728   Ibid., 86–99.

729   Hans Martensen, quoted in Elizabeth Palmer, *Faith in a Hidden God* (Minneapolis: Fortress Press, 2017), 164.

730   Ibid.

731   Ibid.

732   Ibid.

733   Anonymous, "Fear and Trembling," in James Hastings, *The Encyclopedia of Religion and Ethics* (New York: 1913).

734   Ibid.

735   David F. Swenson, review of *Fear and Trembling*, in *Scandinavian Studies and Notes* 6, no. 7 (1921): 21.

736   Ibid.

737   Lee M. Hollander, *The Writings of Kierkegaard* (Austin: *University of Texas Bulletin*, 1923), 119–124.

738   Ibid., 125–127.

739   Jean-Paul Sartre, *Existentialism is a Humanism* (New Haven: Yale University Press, 2007), 25–26.

740   Ibid., 26.

741   Ibid.

742   Ibid.

743   Ibid., 76.

744   Helmut Kuhn, *Encounters with Nothingness* (London: Routledge, 1951. Reissued 2019), 47.

745   Ibid.

746   Theodor Reik, *Temptation* (New York: George Braziller, 1961), 43.

747   Joseph Gumbinder, "Existentialism and Father Abraham," *Commentary* (February 1948).

748   Milton Steinberg, "Kierkegaard and Judaism," *Menorah Journal* 37, no. 21 (1949): 163–180.

749   Milton Steinberg, *The Anatomy of Faith* (New York: Harcourt Brace, 1960), 101.

750 Steinberg, "Kierkegaard and Judaism," p. 171.

751 Eliezer Berkovits, "On Kierkegaard and Abraham," *Crisis and Faith* (New York: Sanhedrin, 1979), 119.

752 Eliezer Berkovits, *God, Man, and History* (New York: Shalem Press, 2004).

753 Bruce Vawter, *Kierkegaard and the Self Before God* (New York: Paulist Press, 1983), 57.

754 Walter Russel Bowie, *Interpreter's Bible on Genesis* (Nashville: Thomas Nelson Press, 1957), ii–ix.

755 Martin Buber, "On Kierkegaard," *Dieu Vivant* (Spring, 1952).

756 Bernard Martin, *The Existentialist Theology of Paul Tillich* (New York: Bookman Books, 1963), 42–43.

757 Ibid., 43.

758 Ibid.

759 Josiah Thompson, *Kierkegaard* (New York: Random House, 1973), 106.

760 Ibid.

761 Ibid., 107.

762 Malcolm Muggeridge, *The Third Testament* (New York: Orbis Books, 2004), 70–94.

763 Ibid., 93–94.

764 Mark C. Taylor, *Journey to Selfhood* (Los Angeles: University of California Press, 1981), 172–152.

765 Ibid., 174.

766 Dorota Glowacka, "Sacrificing the Text," *Animus* (1997), 35–45.

767 Emmanuel Levinas, *Totality and Infinity* (Pittsburgh: Duquesne University Press, 1969), 119.

768 Ibid.

769 Ibid., 120.

770 Ibid.

771 Ibid., 121.

772 Claire E. Katz, *Levinas and the Crisis of Humanism* (Bloomington: Indiana University Press, 2012), 143.

773 Ibid.

774 Ibid., 144.

775 Ibid.

776 John J. Parsons, *Zola's Introduction to Hebrew* (Dallas: Zola Levitt Ministries, 2002), 49.

777 Ibid.

778 John J. Parsons, "Mystery and Humility," https://bit.ly/2WyMk3d.

779   Ibid.

780   Ibid.

781   Jacques Derrida, *The Gift of Death* (Chicago: University of Chicago Press, 1995), 130–143.

782   Ibid., 140.

783   Carol Delaney, *Abraham on Trial* (Princeton: Princeton University Press, 1998), 274.

784   Ibid.

785   Ibid.

786   Ibid.

787   *Fear and Trembling*, 112–115.

788   See Notes 738 and 739.

789   Levinas, *Totality and Infinity*, see also, Derrida, *The Gift of Death*.

790   Delaney, 129.

791   Ibid.

792   Jim Camden, "Dispatches from Dachau," *The Spokesman Review*, June 3, 2020, https://bit.ly/3fO3fpR.

793   Ibid., quote by Patricia Herber-Rice.

794   Ibid., quote by Harold Marcuse.

795   First Samuel 7:9.

796   Leviticus 26:31.

797   Deuteronomy 33:24.

798   Zechariah 8:19.

799   Ibid.

800   The classical Hebrew word *Shoah* appears in the Hebrew Bible fourteen times, including Isaiah 54:8–9.

801   The Douay-Rheims Bible (1609), Genesis 22:6.

802   John Milton, *Samson Agonistes* (1671) I, 80, line 15.

803   Nathaniel Hawthorne, *Earth's Holocaust* (Amazon Digital Services, 2014).

804   Martin Gilbert, *Kristallnacht* (San Francisco: Harpers, 2007), 131.

805   Unknown author, "Nazi Holocaust," *New York Times*, January 21, 1943.

806   "Holocaust" *The Oxford-English Dictionary* (1899 edition).

807   Unknown author, "Armenian Holocaust," *New York Times*, June 17, 1897.

808   Melville Charter, quoted in John Kifner, "Armenian Genocide," *New York Times*, May 30, 1925.

809   Jonathan Allen, "Grayson Likens Health Crisis to Holocaust," *Politico*, September 30, 2009.

810   Ibid.

811   Ibid.

812   Dr. Hiltgunt Margret Zassenhaus, *Walls* (Boston: Beacon Press, 1993), 17–18.

813   Ibid., 101.

814   Notes from personal research of the author.

815   Interview with Hiltgunt Zassenhaus, April 14, 1981, Baltimore.

816   Ibid.

817   Author interview with Holocaust survivor, February 18, 1983, Baltimore.

818   Author interview with Holocaust survivor, March 19, 1982.

819   Author interview with Holocaust survivor, June 15, 1983.

820   Panel discussion of *Watch on the Rhine*, January 27, 1979, Baltimore.

821   Ibid.

822   Ibid.

823   Marco Roth, "Enduring love," *Tablet*, July 19, 2007.

824   Ibid.

825   Ibid.

826   Ibid.

827   Ibid.

828   Ibid.

829   Emil Fackenheim, *What is Judaism?* (New York: Summit Books, 1987).

830   Ibid., 233.

831   Ibid., 121.

832   Ibid.

833   Ibid., 122.

834   Jacob Neusner, "Take Your Son, Your Favored Son," *The Bible and Us* (New York: Warner Books, 1990), 103–115.

835   Ibid., 109–110.

836   Ibid., 110.

837   Aharon Agus, *The Binding of Isaac and Messiah* (New York: SUNY Press, 1988), 101.

838   Louis Berman, *The Akedah* (Jerusalem: Jason Aronson, 1997), 39, 102.

839   Agus, 61. Berman, 102.

840   Erich Wellisch, *Isaac and Oedipus* (London: Routledge & Kegan Paul, 1954).

841   George Devereaux, "Why Oedipus Killed Laius," see: pp. 212–213 of Delaney.

842   Leon Kass, *The Beginning of Wisdom: Reading Genesis* (Chicago: University of Chicago Press, 2006).

843   Ibid., 333.

844   M. H. Sherman, "Biblical Commentary as a Psychoanalytic Defense," in *Modern Psychoanalysis* 32, no. 2, pp. 295–313.

845 Ibid.
846 Wellisch, *Isaac and Oedipus*.
847 Ibid., 3.
848 Ibid., 48–52.
849 Ibid., 52.
850 Ibid., 30–38.
851 Ibid., p. 4.
852 Theodor Reik, *The Temptation* (New York: George Braziller, 1961), 225–226.
853 Silvano Arieti, *Abraham and the Contemporary Mind* (New York: Basic Books, 1981), 135.
854 Reik, 225.
855 Arieti, 136.
856 Ibid., 148.
857 Ibid., 79.
858 Berman, 167.
859 Ibid., 169–170.
860 Berman, 65–84. Delaney, 158–160.
861 Trevor Dennis, *Sarah Laughed, Women's Voices in the Old Testament* (1994).
862 Ibid., 35.
863 Ibid., 39.
864 Berman, 60–61.
865 W. Lee Humphreys, "Where's Sarah: Echoes of a Silent Voice," *Soundings: An Interdisciplinary Journal* 81, nos. 3 and 4 (1988): 491–512.
866 Rabbi Paul Kipnes and Michelle November, "Where Was Sarah During the Akedah?" https://bit.ly/30BeXxE.
867 Ibid.
868 Colleen Ivey Hartsoe, "Christian Midrash on the Akedah," quoted in Berman, 70–71.
869 Ostriker, quoted in Berman, 132–133.
870 Alicia Ostriker, *Feminist Revisions of the Bible* (Oxford: Oxford University Press, 1993), 40–41.
871 Elenora Wilner, quoted in Delaney, 133–135.
872 Mohja Kahf, "Reconciling the Descendants of Sarah and Hagar," https://bit.ly/3eJVobz.
873 Ibid.
874 Rabbi Amy Eilberg, "An Inner Altar of Holiness Exists Inside Every Human," *Jewish News of Northern California*, March 17, 2000, https://bit.ly/2E6C0ZT.
875 Ibid.

876   Ibid.

877   Ibid.

878   Rabbi Walter Rothschild, "Rosh Hashanah Morning: Akedah," *Polish Jews Reviving*, September 28, 2019, https://bit.ly/2WKzm2t.

879   Ibid.

880   Rabbi David Blumenthal, "The Akedah and Rosh Hashanah," *The Torah*, October 3, 2019.

881   Anonymous, "The Akedah," in *Encyclopedia Judaica* (New York: Macmillan, 1972), vol. 1.

882   Abraham Shlonsky, quoted in Avi Sagi, "The Meaning of the 'Akedah' in Israeli Culture and Jewish Tradition," *Israel Studies* (1998), 45–60.

883   Hiam Gouri, "Heritage," quoted in Robin Bates, "Born With a Knife in the Heart," https://bit.ly/30yceFp.

884   Yu Hua, *The Seventh Day* (New York: Random House, 2015), 92.

885   S. Yizhar, quoted in Louis Berman, *The Akedah: The Binding of Isaac* (Jerusalem: Jason Aronson, 1997), 212.

886   Amihai, quoted in Berman, 208.

887   Yitzhak Laor, "This Fool, Isaac," quoted in Iain Provan, *Discovering Genesis* (Grand Rapids: Eerdmans, 2015), 149. Laor (born in 1948) is an Israeli poet and writer.

888   Herman Melville, *Billy Budd* (New York: Dover Thrift Editions, 2017). Melville (1819–1892) was an American poet, novelist and short story writer. Also see Berman, 201–202.

889   Philip Roth, *Portnoy's Complaint* (New York: Random House, 1967), 151. Roth (1933–2018) was an American novelist and short-story writer.

890   Ibid.

891   Bernard Malamud, *God's Grace* (New York: Farrar, Straus, and Giroux, 2005). Malamud (1914–1986) was a Brooklyn-born novelist and short story writer. Also see Berman 205–206.

892   Wilfred Owen, "Parable of the Old Man and the Young," in *Collected Poems* (London: Chitton and Windus, 1963), 166. Owen died of a gunshot wound in World War I. Also see Berman, 206.

893   Ibid.

894   Franz Kafka, *The Trial* (New York: Dover Editions, 2009). Kafka (1883–1924) was a Bohemian novelist and short story writer.

895   Franz Kafka, *In the Penal Colony* (New York: Penguin Books, 1996).

896   Hillel Barzil, quoted in Anne Golomb Hoffman, *Between Exile and Return: S. Y. Agnon and the Drama of Writing* (New York: SUNY Press, 1991), 119.

897 Hilene Flanzbaum, "Introduction to Feminist Literary Interpretations of the Akedah," in *The Americanization of the Holocaust* (Baltimore: Johns Hopkins University Press, 1995), 18–32.

898 Elinor Wilner, "Sarah's Choice," March 28, 2017, http://www.crookedshore. com/.

899 Alicia Ostriker, *The Nakedness of the Fathers* (New Brunswick: Rutgers University Press, 1997), 67–72.

900 Marc Chagall, *The Sacrifice of Isaac*, 1966. Saint-Paul-de-Vence, France. Chagall (1887–1985) was a Russian-French painter.

901 Ibid.

902 Chagall windows, https://bit.ly/2WOPaRQ.

903 Berman, 225–226.

904 Matthew Baigell, *Jewish Art in America* (New York: Rowan Littlefield, 2007), 158.

905 Richard McBee, https://bit.ly/3fTioGr.

906 Ibid.

907 Matthew Baigell, interview with Richard McBee, *Shofar* 31, no. 1 (Spring, 2011), 1–24.

908 Ibid.

909 Menashe Kadishman, *The Binding of Isaac*, 1985, sculpture, https://bit. ly/3joRHvH.

910 Joanne Tucker, "The Beginning of a New Piece Based on the Akedah and Terna's Paintings," April 5, 2019, https://bit.ly/2OMoqNh.

911 Robert Kirschbaum, "Akedah Series," 2011, https://bit.ly/2WLl55w.

912 Albert Joseph Winn, "The Akedah," 1995. Winn (1947–2014) was a printer as well as a painter.

913 George Segal, "Sacrifice of Art," 1973. Segal (1924–2000) was an American painter and sculptor.

914 Akedah postage stamp, Israel, 1978, https://bit.ly/3gaBp7g.

915 Robert Craft, *Conversations with Stravinsky* (New York: Faber and Faber, 2011), 22–23. Craft (1923–2015) was an American conductor.

916 Leonard Cohen, "The Story of Isaac," 1968. Cohen (1934–2016) was an American writer, composer and songwriter.

917 Berman, 197.

918 Rabbi Shalom Shabazi, "Song in the Akedah," in Arabic and Hebrew, 1978.

919 David Blumenthal, "Madonna's 'Isaac'/Madonna's *Akedah*," the *Immanent Frame*, May 14, 2015, https://bit.ly/30Gs4xX.

920 Ibid.

921   Berman, 195.
922   Elie Wiesel, *Ani Mamin: A Song lost and Found Again* (New York: Random House, 1974).
923   Avi Sagi, "The Meaning of the Akedah," *Israel Studies* 3, no. 1 (1998): 45–60.
924   David Baumgardt, "Man's Morals and God's Will," *Commentary*, March 1950, https://bit.ly/3hlwy3w. Baumgardt (1890–1973) was a writer and philosopher in Israel, the U.S. and Europe.
925   Rabbi Shapira Kalonymous, *The Holy Fire* (New York: Aronson, 1960), 111.
926   Amos Oz, "The Way of the Wind," *The Amos Oz Reader* (New York: Mariner Books, 2001), 25–46. Oz (1939–2018) was an Israeli writer and journalist for many years.
927   Nancy Jay, *Throughout Your Generations Forever* (Chicago: University of Chicago Press, 1990), 17–30.
928   Nahum Sarna, *Understanding Genesis* (New York: Jewish Theological Seminary of America, 2014), 153–165.
929   Anonymous, *An Anthology of Stories on the Akedah in Japanese* (Tokyo: N.P., 2012).
930   M. Tyler Sasser, "The Akedah in Children's Literature," *Journal of Children's Literature* 45 (2017): 138–163.
931   Elie Wiesel, *Night* (New York: Hill and Wang, 2006).
932   Elie Wiesel, *Messengers of God: Portraits and Legends* (New York Simon and Schuster, 1985), 69–97.
933   Ibid.
934   Ibid.
935   Berman, 198.
936   Berman, 199.
937   Ibid.
938   Berman, 209.
939   Berman, 209–212.
940   Hanoch Levin, *Milkat Ha Ambatyah*, or "Queen of the Bath," Habinah Theatre, May 1970. Levin (1943–1999) was an Israeli composer, conductor and musician.

Index

About the Author

Before his retirement in 2016, Stephen Vicchio taught for more than forty years at the University of Maryland, Johns Hopkins, St. Mary's Seminary in Baltimore, and other universities in Britain and the United States. He has authored over two dozen books, as well as essays and plays, mostly about the Bible, philosophy and theology. Among his books since 2000 is his interpretation of the Book of Job, *The Antichrist: A History*; *Biblical Figures in the Islamic Faith*, and books about the religions of American presidents George Washington, Thomas Jefferson and Abraham Lincoln, including *Ronald Reagan's Religious Beliefs* out now with CrossLink Publishing.

Made in the USA
Las Vegas, NV
19 March 2024

87449468R00208